Frontier Doctor

D0072414

Missouri Biography Series
William E. Foley, Editor

Frontier Doctor

WILLIAM BEAUMONT, AMERICA'S FIRST GREAT MEDICAL SCIENTIST

Reginald Horsman

University of Missouri Press
Columbia and London

Library of Congress Cataloging-in-Publication Data

Horsman, Reginald.

   Frontier doctor : William Beaumont, America's first great medical scientist / Reginald Horsman.

     p. cm.

   Includes bibliographical references and index.

   ISBN 0-8262-1052-X (alk. paper)

   1. Beaumont, William, 1785-1853. 2. Surgeons–United States–Biography. 3. Physiologists–United States–Biography. I. Title.

   [DNLM: 1. Beaumont, William, 1785-1853. 2. Physicians–biography. WZ 100 B379H 1996]

RD27.35.B42H67   1996

610'.92–dc20

[B]

DNLM/DLC

for Library of Congress   95-49849

CIP

Designer: Stephanie Foley

Typesetter: BOOKCOMP

Printer and binder: Thomson-Shore, Inc.

Typeface: Walbaum

For Allison, Benjamin, Erin, and Landon

CONTENTS

ACKNOWLEDGMENTS

I WISH TO THANK the College of Letters and Science of the University of Wisconsin–Milwaukee for helping to support the research that led to this book, and the numerous librarians and archivists who were generous with their time and knowledge. I received particular help from Paul G. Anderson, Ph.D., of the School of Medicine Library, Washington University, St. Louis; Ferenc Gyorgyey of the Medical Library, Yale University, New Haven; Martha Clevenger of the Missouri Historical Society in St. Louis; Rebecca Jabbour of the Bancroft Library, University of California–Berkeley; Gordon R. Garrett of the St. Louis Metropolitan Medical Society; Dr. Keith Widder of the Mackinac Island State Park Commission; Di L. Adams of the Neville Public Museum, Green Bay; Mary Freymiller of the University of Wisconsin–Platteville Library; and a number of most helpful librarians and archivists at the Joseph Regenstein Library at the University of Chicago; the National Archives in Washington, D.C.; the State Historical Society of Wisconsin; the Health Science Library in Madison; and the Golda Meir Library at the University of Wisconsin–Milwaukee. I would also like to thank Ronald L. Numbers, William Coleman Professor of History of Science and Medicine at the University of Wisconsin, Madison, for his perceptive reading of the manuscript.

ABBREVIATIONS

BC, UC   William Beaumont Collection, Joseph Regenstein Library, Chicago, Illinois.

BC, WU   William Beaumont Manuscript Collection, School of Medicine Library, Washington University, St. Louis, Missouri

BP, YU   William Beaumont Papers, Beaumont Medical Club, Medical Library, Yale University, New Haven, Connecticut.

MHS   Missouri Historical Society, St. Louis, Missouri.

SHSW   State Historical Society of Wisconsin, Madison, Wisconsin.

WD, AG, IMOF   War Department, RG 94, Office of the Adjutant General, Individual Medical Officers Folders, National Archives, Washington, D.C.

WD, AG, LR   War Department, RG 94, Office of the Adjutant General, Letters Received, National Archives.

WD, IG, Reports   War Department, RG 159, Office of the Inspector General, Inspection Reports, 1814–1842, National Archives.

WD, QG   War Department, RG 92, Office of the Quartermaster General, National Archives.

WD, SG, LR   War Department, RG 112, Office of the Surgeon General, Letters Received, National Archives.

Frontier Doctor

INTRODUCTION

IN THE EARLY FALL of 1902, William Osler lectured to the members of the St. Louis Medical Society on the subject of their famous predecessor, Dr. William Beaumont. Beaumont, who had served for more than twenty years as an army surgeon, had in the last part of his life established a successful practice in St. Louis. By 1902, Beaumont had been dead for almost fifty years, but his reputation as a research scientist was undiminished. Osler's conclusion was that "Beaumont is the pioneer physiologist of this country, the first to make an important and enduring contribution to this science. His work remains a model of patient, persevering investigation, experiment, and research."[1]

Beaumont's chance for permanent scientific fame had come in a most unlikely fashion on June 6, 1822, on beautiful, lonely Mackinac Island. On that day, Beaumont had been called to treat the Canadian voyageur Alexis St. Martin, who had been accidentally shot in the stomach at close range. The wound appeared fatal, but to Beaumont's surprise St. Martin recovered. He recovered, however, with a permanent hole into his stomach; a hole through which food or other items could be inserted, and through which some of the actions of the stomach could be observed. There had been previous cases of individuals living with a permanent gastric fistula, but never before had an attending physician taken such advantage of the situation to reach important conclusions about the process of human digestion.

Before Beaumont there was still considerable controversy as to the nature of human digestion, but his research established beyond question that digestion was a chemical process. His observations on the action of gastric juice, both inside and outside of the stomach, revealed a great deal about digestion in the stomach that had never before been observed in a human subject. In the United States he brought a new understanding of digestion and

1. William Osler, "A Backwood Physiologist," 185.

1

dietetics; in Europe he immediately influenced the course of physiological research.[2]

Beaumont had become a physician without attending a medical school and with little more than a year of formal apprenticeship, but within two years after the accident he came to realize that he had been presented with an ideal opportunity for scientific research. With no previous experience as a researcher, and while continuing as an army surgeon at isolated frontier posts, Beaumont conducted a series of experiments from which he was able to make a major contribution to the knowledge of human digestion, and which made him the first American to gain an international reputation for physiological research.

The basic importance of Beaumont's work has continued to be recognized both by researchers on human digestion and by historians of science. As late as the 1940s, two researchers were able to state that while others had observed patients with holes in their stomachs in the more than one hundred years that had elapsed since Beaumont had published his work, "there has been only one investigation which has compared in scope with Beaumont's work."[3] Medical historian Ronald Numbers, writing on Beaumont and medical ethics in 1979, commented that "William Beaumont long ago won a secure place in the history of science for his physiological experiments on Alexis St. Martin."[4]

St. Martin provided Beaumont's opportunity for fame, enabled him to win the close friendship and support of the army surgeon general, Joseph Lovell, and for a brief time brought him into contact with the political and medical elite along the eastern seaboard, but St. Martin was also a source of great frustration. To keep St. Martin available for experiments involved money, and Beaumont was very careful with his money. Relations between the two men were often strained as Beaumont wanted St. Martin available for research, but wanted him without his family. When he was with Beaumont, St. Martin missed his home in Canada, at times was lonely for his family, and was naturally irritated by the daily routine of experiments. Moreover, Beaumont himself was often very busy with his military duties. The result was that

2. See Ronald L. Numbers and William J. Orr Jr., "William Beaumont's Reception at Home and Abroad," 590–612.

3. Stewart Wolf and Harold G. Wolff, *Human Gastric Function: An Experimental Study of Man and His Stomach,* 3.

4. Ronald L. Numbers, "William Beaumont and the Ethics of Human Experimentation," 113.

Beaumont's research was much interrupted, and it was nearly ten years after beginning his experiments before Beaumont was able to publish the full results.

If Beaumont had never seen St. Martin, his life would still be of interest for the light it throws on the life and practice of an army surgeon and private physician in the first half of the nineteenth century. In moving to the northern frontier of New York, deciding to improve his lot by becoming a physician, serving in the War of 1812, making a career in the medical department of the army, building a successful private practice in St. Louis, and speculating in land, Beaumont followed a general path that was available, in different ways, to many who left New England farms in the early nineteenth century.

But the chance of St. Martin's accident, and the way in which the wound healed, gave Beaumont an exceptional opportunity that he was able to grasp. He overcame his complete lack of training in research and showed a dogged determination in carrying out his experiments, even while in the old, decrepit military log hospital in the tiny frontier outpost of Prairie du Chien. His ability to understand what questions needed answering took him out of the host of upwardly mobile, westward-moving New Englanders, and out of the array of run-of-the-mill nineteenth-century medical practitioners, into a permanent place in the history of science.

O N E

Apprentice Years

IN THE HALF CENTURY after the American Revolution, many of the younger sons of southern New England farmers sought their fortunes somewhere on the sweeping arc of frontier that stretched from Maine westward to the Ohio Valley. Even when population had been sparse, New Englanders had often looked for ways to supplement the living they could wring from their rocky soil, but population growth in the late eighteenth century meant that there was a shortage of land for profitable farming. In the years after the Revolution, there were strains and even tears appearing in the stable fabric of New England society. The young were less willing to accept the traditional religious and political leadership, and were demonstrating a desire to break out of the measured ways of the past to share more fully in the material rewards of a burgeoning society. New Englanders had always been ready to turn to the sea to make the money that was hard to extract from their soil; they were now showing an increasing enthusiasm to share in the new opportunities that were opening on a rapidly expanding frontier.

On the eve of the Revolution, the family that was to produce William Beaumont was farming in Lebanon, Connecticut. The Beaumonts had Connecticut roots stretching back to the early years of New England settlement, and Beaumont's paternal grandfather had settled in Lebanon in the middle of the eighteenth century. Lebanon was a prosperous farming town, recognized in the state as the residence of the politically prominent Trumbulls, and known even beyond its bounds for the quality of Nathan Tisdale's famous school.

For more than thirty years, into the late 1780s, Tisdale ran a school that was regarded as one of the best, if not *the* best, in New England.[1]

William Beaumont was born in Lebanon on November 21, 1785. He was one of four brothers and five sisters. The Revolution had brought personal disruption to the immediate Beaumont family and to their many relatives in the region. William's father, Samuel, along with his brothers, had served in the army. Samuel was a strong-minded, independent man. Eventually, he became an ardent Jeffersonian in an area well known for its devoted Federalists. William's mother, Lucretia, is a shadowy figure, seemingly unassertive; later, after the death of his father, her son felt no qualms in lecturing her on how to deal with his brothers and sisters.[2]

There are no details available about the first twenty years or so of Beaumont's life. Like the vast majority of young men or women of his generation, he was brought up on a farm. He received a sound, basic education, and a respect for learning, almost certainly in the school made famous by Tisdale, but fading in reputation since Tisdale's death. It is possible that he was taught there by Silas Fuller, whose career in some ways paralleled that of Beaumont. As a young man, Fuller taught school in Lebanon, received medical training there as an apprentice to a Lebanon physician, and practiced in the town until the War of 1812, when he entered the army medical service. Fuller's example may have stirred ideas in Beaumont.[3]

Whatever Fuller might have done to shape Beaumont's future, there is no doubt of the impact of his uncles and of his older brother Samuel. Beaumont's uncles, William and Daniel, had left Connecticut to move to the northern New York frontier. They were among the early settlers in the Champlain region, north of Plattsburgh within two or three miles of the Canadian border. The village of Champlain had been founded in the new Clinton County in the late

1. On the Beaumont family, see Jesse S. Myer, *Life and Letters of Dr. William Beaumont*, 1–8; Rodney B. Nelson, *Beaumont: America's First Physiologist*, 11–15; Phoebe A. Cassidy and Roberta S. Sokol, comps., *Index to the Wm. Beaumont, M.D. (1785–1853) Manuscript Collection*, 14–15. On Lebanon, see Robert G. Armstrong, *Historic Lebanon: Highlights of an Historic Town*, 6–40; Jedidiah Morse, *The American Gazetteer*, entry for Lebanon; George McLean Milne, *Lebanon: Three Centuries in a Connecticut Hilltop Town*, 8–12, 22.

2. Account of the life of William Beaumont by his son, Israel Beaumont, and Beaumont to Lucretia Beaumont, August 16, 1814, William Beaumont Manuscript Collection, School of Medicine Library, Washington University, St. Louis. Hereafter cited as BC, WU; Myer, *Beaumont*, 10–11.

3. Archibald Welch, "A Biographical Sketch of Silas Fuller, M.D.," 109–15; Genevieve Miller, ed., *Wm. Beaumont's Formative Years: Two Early Notebooks, 1811–1821*, 80n90.

1780s. Uncle William held various local appointments, including the position of town supervisor of Champlain. The two Beaumonts were in a good position to help the children of their brother Samuel in Lebanon, and by the spring of 1804 young Samuel, Beaumont's brother, was settled in Champlain as the local schoolteacher. By 1806 he was serving as town clerk.[4]

Much later in the nineteenth century, the story that had survived in Beaumont's family had young William setting off from Lebanon with no particular destination in mind, and finishing up near the Canadian border friendless and alone. In reality, he followed the time-honored frontier settlement practice of building on the foundation laid by his relatives. They were ready to welcome him in Clinton County, and in the winter of 1807, when snow made traveling easier, young William set out by sled to make his fortune in northern New York. Family tradition (the same one that had him wandering off with no particular location in mind) said that he had a horse, a cutter, a barrel of cider, and one hundred dollars.[5]

Samuel had given up schoolmastering to open a store, and William succeeded him in the Champlain school. He showed every sign of being happy to leave home. Neither then nor later did he demonstrate the slightest nostalgia for Lebanon and his family there. He was very happy to be earning money, and after two quarters of teaching and a three-month summer break spent working in his brother's store, he told his father that he was "well satisfied with this place, my employment, and encouragements."[6] Throughout his life, Beaumont made the best of any new situation he found himself in. He wanted to get on, was prepared to work, and was willing to advance steadily rather than dramatically.

Beaumont arrived on the Canadian border at a tense time. British-American relations were in a state of crisis. Restrictive British maritime policies had culminated in June 1807 in the *Chesapeake* affair. An American frigate had been fired into off the American coast, boarded, and suspected British deserters were removed. In the United States, there was much excitement, and talk of war. Even among the opposition Federalists, many were ready to fight. But in northern New York there were mixed feelings. Most of the

4. *History of Clinton and Franklin Counties, New York,* 118–19, 258–64; Nelson, *Beaumont,* 12–13, 18–19; Samuel Beaumont to Lucretia Beaumont, May 5, 1804, William Beaumont Papers, Beaumont Medical Club, Medical Library, Yale University, New Haven, Conn. Hereafter cited as BP, YU.

5. Account of the life of William Beaumont by his son, Israel Beaumont, BC, WU.

6. Beaumont to Samuel Beaumont Sr., August 23, 1807, BP, YU (I used the typed copy in the BC, WU).

region's trade was with Canada, and war would ruin it. Moreover, in the event of war northern New York was likely to be directly in the path of any British invasion. The line of attack from Montreal into the United States ran along the western shore of Lake Champlain, through Champlain and Plattsburgh.

Beaumont did not have the doubts and worries so typical in Champlain and its vicinity. He was not in business, and he had his father's patriotism and Jeffersonian convictions. He reported proudly to his father that "a spirit of patriotism prevails in this vicinity." His storekeeper brother Samuel had more fears for the future. Samuel no doubt pleased his father by writing of the need to defend America's liberties, but he also pointed out that in the event of war he stood to lose a substantial amount in outstanding debts; people would scatter in the event of a British invasion.[7]

In spite of the air of crisis, William Beaumont continued to be well satisfied with his life and prospects in Champlain. For the time being he continued to teach school, served as secretary of the local debating society, and confidently told his father that he did not expect to lack for profitable employment while he stayed in northern New York. Beaumont was never a fearful man, and the prospect of war caused him little concern. He said he saw no reason to fear danger until he had more reason than "the mere suspense of timid people." With an avowed trust in divine help that perhaps partially reflected what he knew his parents would like to hear, he asserted that when danger came he would take the proper means to defend himself "with the assistance of a higher power."

Beaumont was far more concerned about his future prospects than he was about any possible danger on the exposed border with Canada, and after telling his parents that he would trust in God if danger came, he went to the heart of his interests when he said that "he that steereth the most regular diligent and faithful course will by the Blessing of *God* come nighest the prize." He wrote that a young man who was born and who went out into the world with "little or no fortune" needed to take every advantage of adverse happenings to pursue his goals.[8]

Although later in life Beaumont was not a publicly religious man, he came from a family and an environment deeply steeped in religious belief. In writing to his parents he reflected values that had been inculcated into him from an early age. The family were Congregationalists, but William, like

7. Ibid., also Samuel Beaumont to Samuel Beaumont Sr., July 26, 1807, BP, YU.
8. Beaumont to Samuel Beaumont Sr., September 13, 1807, BP, YU.

many New Englanders of his generation, drifted away from overt religious observance, and showed little interest in formal religious rites until near his death. More typical of the later Beaumont in these early statements of values and aims was his determination to make his way in the world; a belief that he needed to pursue every advantage if he were to compensate successfully for the lack of a silver spoon. In his early twenties, Beaumont was already a very determined young man.

That Beaumont was not particularly concerned about the border situation was demonstrated when his brother suddenly decided to get married. William knew that his brother was paying attention to a young widow, the sister of his business partner, but only learned that the pair were to be married when the partner approached him to go to Montreal to pick up a suit for Sam to be married in. He left immediately for Montreal, returned with the suit, and the marriage took place two days later. A few days after the wedding, William wrote a cheerful account of the ensuing festivities to his parents. On the day after the wedding, the partners' store had been festooned with hangings, an American flag placed over the door, tables erected, a clarinet and violin provided, and a dinner held for all who wished to attend. The occasion was rounded off by the firing of guns, toasts, and general cheering. William commented that his brother and bride "appear to be on the summit of *Love*."[9]

In pursuing a career, William often demonstrated little patience in dealing with the outside world and was quick to quarrel, yet he was warm and supportive to those close to him. Later in life, the face he showed to his family and intimate friends was very different from the one he showed to outsiders. On this occasion, he seemed quite unperturbed that, in the little village of Champlain, he had first heard of his brother's wedding from his brother's business partner. He told his parents, without any apparent pique, that Samuel had not consulted him, "but I freely give my consent and think myself honored."[10]

Beaumont was not easily rattled. Only weeks after the happiness of his brother's wedding, he took in his stride the news that his uncle William, who had been at the festivities, had killed himself. Writing home at the end of December, he apologized for not having written about the event sooner, but explained that he understood his brother had written and that

9. Ibid.
10. Ibid.

his schoolteaching had been keeping him extremely busy; he had more than sixty pupils.[11]

The Beaumonts in Lebanon frequently complained that the two boys in Champlain did not visit them in Connecticut; Sam had not been home since leaving for Champlain four years earlier, and William was also showing a reluctance to go home. When William sensed in his letters from home that his parents would have perhaps liked him to return permanently to Lebanon, he quickly found reasons to deflect them from this idea. He said that he would do it if it was not a bad move for him, but that prospects were better in northern New York than in Connecticut. There was little conviction in his statement that, if they wanted him to return to try something else, he would consider it "his duty to comply" whenever they made such a request. He wrote that he was planning to come back to see them a year from the time that he had left "if I can without material disadvantage and inconvenience."[12]

A few months later he acknowledged that the time had passed when he had given his parents hope of a return visit, but he hoped they understood, for "without frugality faithfulness and a strict application to business a young man of my circumstances cannot expect to attain a very respectable situation in life." Again, Beaumont told his parents that he was better off in Champlain than he would be elsewhere, and that he had been given no advantages in life. He said that his school salary for the past year amounted to "a very handsome compensation" for his first attempt "with no more assistance than I have." A young man who believed that schoolteaching in Champlain provided "a very handsome compensation" was not beset by any delusions of grandeur. He stressed that he intended to stick to his present job for the present, because he did not want "to exchange a certainty for an uncertainty."

To salve his conscience in regard to his parents, Beaumont repeatedly emphasized his sense of duty toward his Champlain pupils. What was keeping him away, he said, was his duty to his employers and to his pupils—"the tender buds of mankind." He would have returned before now, "but *reason–conscience–humanity* forbid it." To come would mean material injury to himself and to the community. "The object of Money," he wrote, "does not deter me from coming." He did not want his pupils "to wander into the boundless field of Idleness and folly."[13] All this must have seemed a little strained, even to devoted parents.

11. Beaumont to his parents, December 29, 1807, BP, YU.
12. Ibid.
13. Beaumont to his parents, March 8, 1808, BP, YU.

While both William and Samuel had come to Champlain imbued with their father's ardent Jeffersonianism, Sam was wavering, and William was finding that his stance was becoming increasingly unpopular. Rumors of war, though less active than a few months earlier, were still hurting business, but a more immediate problem was the Jeffersonian embargo passed in December 1807. This had cut off exports to Canada. Many on the northern borders were now infuriated at President Jefferson and his Democratic-Republican policies, and the Beaumonts there were not in agreement. Uncle Dan was "a *Fanatick*" on the other side, railed against Jefferson and his administration, and called William "the imp" of his father. This had considerable truth in it. Beaumont's political interests were at their height in this period just after he left home, when he was still strongly shaped by his father's political beliefs and when his natural combativeness was stirred by the bitter political arguments aroused by Jeffersonian policies in this vulnerable area of New York state. Later in life, Beaumont was to show no strong political interests, though in the 1830s, when a second American party system took shape, he supported the Democrats.[14]

In the summer of 1808, William had a chance to recharge his political batteries when, at last, he went home for a visit. He bought a horse for the journey, and he arrived back in Champlain early in October after a return trip of ten days. With his usual care and success in financial matters, he later disposed of the horse "without loss." He had less success in making a profit on items made of silk that his sisters had asked him to sell in Champlain; business was still bad, and competition among the local merchants was severe.[15]

Beaumont took up his teaching immediately on his return, commenting that this was with the "expressive joy & satisfaction of the people." Dispassionate indications of how Beaumont actually fared as a teacher are slight. He was hired with regularity as long as he wanted the job, but in this frontier community it was obviously not a position with a long list of applicants. After three years of teaching, Beaumont told his brother Abel that although he believed he had given satisfaction to his employers, he had always felt a deficiency in his qualifications. Much later in the nineteenth century, when William Beaumont was dead and his name was known, a resident of Wisconsin reminisced about the summer of 1808 when he boarded in Champlain and attended the school. He said that under Beaumont's tuition he "greatly

14. Ibid. (quotations), also Beaumont to his parents, December 29, 1807, Samuel Beaumont to his parents, July 30, 1808, BP, YU.
15. Beaumont to his parents, October 2, December 11 (quotation), 1808, BP, YU.

improved himself in grammar, geography, &c, but at that early day I never saw a school atlas." Along with grammar and geography, Beaumont taught reading, writing, and arithmetic.[16]

The old Wisconsin resident apparently had no bad memories of his summer of 1808 in Champlain, but in the following winter Beaumont responded vigorously to serious charges. A prominent local resident, Pliny Moore, repeated a story that Beaumont had excessively beaten a child. In an age when corporal punishment was expected, the singling out of such an occasion was a reason for concern. Beaumont reacted under attack as he was to act throughout his life—he went on the offensive. He wrote to Moore and asked for an investigation of the subject, commenting on the injury that he had suffered "by such an atrocious, ungrateful & inhuman idea, as that of abusing & beating a child to such an unmerciful degree as has been asserted." Beaumont emphasized that he was keen to have his conduct in general, and this case in particular, "thoroughly inspected & critically investigated." If he was guilty of such an act, he said that he deserved to be banished from the school and from society.

Beaumont apparently suspected that Moore had got the story from his own child, and said that if such a story was carried by a child old enough to know the difference between right and wrong he should not escape with impunity. He also lectured Moore on the duty of the parent to correct and reform a child who dealt in such falsehoods. He clearly felt on strong ground, and that the normal run of early-nineteenth-century corporal punishment had been exaggerated in some child's report. Later in life, he was to write impassioned protests to far more important men than Pliny Moore. There seem to be no existing records of any investigation, but presumably Beaumont's version of the event was accepted. He continued to teach in the school, and was rehired at a later date. It is quite possible that the whole incident involved Beaumont overreacting to some general comment about his conduct. He was always quick to anger, never dodged a quarrel, and was quick to protest when he believed that his conduct or integrity was being questioned in any way.[17]

A strong hint of Beaumont's likely pedagogical style is present in what seems, in a different age, a very pompous letter to his younger brother Abel.

16. Beaumont to his parents, October 2, 1808, Beaumont to Abel Beaumont, in letter to his parents, September 12, 1810, BP, YU; James H. Lockwood, "Early Times and Events in Wisconsin," 99.
17. Beaumont to Pliny Moore, February 5, 1809, in Gertrude L. Annan, ed., "Early Letters of William Beaumont Never Before Published," 657–58.

To Abel, it may well have seemed that in 1809. It seems quite possible that
Beaumont's parents had asked him to try to instill a little of his own will to
succeed in his younger brother. Whatever the origins, Beaumont's injunctions
to his brother give a good idea of what he was trying to instill in his pupils,
and also give a good idea of how Beaumont himself hoped to rise from what
he perceived as his disadvantaged beginnings.

Beaumont warned his brother that he was at the age when error and
impropriety would beset him from every side. The strongest barrier against
these insidious influences was to cultivate his mind and to "procure a stock of
familiar Ideas & useful information." Abel was told to take his mind away from
dancing, and think how he could be of use to himself and to society. He should
not neglect any opportunity to qualify himself for "public use." To achieve this,
he needed to obtain all the scholastic information his circumstances would
allow—"reflection" was to "go before passion—reason before judgement." If
Abel would qualify himself as far as possible in all the branches "of a common
and useful Education," then he would find vacancies opening up for him.

After telling Abel he should be judicious in his choice of friends and pursuits, William ended his admonitions with a carefully composed peroration—
"let *virtue, truth, & honor*" be your "planetary guides—*temperance, justice, fortitude*, & *prudence* your cardinal points—*faith, hope*, & *charity* your horizon—
Philanthropy, *benevolence, friendship*, & *Philosophy* your *atmosphere*, & the
elements of life will be *smooth, transparent*, & *pleasant*." Beaumont obviously
spent a great deal of time composing this letter to his brother, and after
finishing the part of the letter that had obviously become a set piece, he
let himself slip into a more informal, brotherly style, commenting about a
friend's wife who, despite the embargo, had managed to give birth to twins.[18]

In the winter of 1808–1809, the embargo was one of the main topics
of conversation in Champlain. Smuggling was rampant. In August 1808,
the efforts of the government to stop smuggling on Lake Champlain had
produced a serious clash. Smugglers were captured, and, in an attempt to
free them, their friends attacked a government revenue cutter. In the attack,
one of the crew was killed. All the smugglers and their friends were later
taken, and in November one of them was hanged at Burlington, Vermont.
The commander of the original smugglers was sentenced to stand in the
pillory, receive fifty lashes, and serve ten years of hard labor.[19]

18. Beaumont to Abel Beaumont, February 16, 1809, BP, YU.
19. *History of Clinton and Franklin Counties*, 48.

The reactions of the two Beaumont brothers to these events were quite different. Samuel, the merchant, feared for his business and his future. He complained bitterly to his father that the government had stopped Americans from selling produce to Canada, and said the next orders will be "Fight or Die." He was also worried that Congress was now debating a nonintercourse act that would also ban any purchases of Canadian goods. In anticipation of this situation, he and his partner bought a large quantity of Canadian salt in the hope of turning a large profit if the nonintercourse act was passed. William's reaction must have been much more pleasing to his father. He poured scorn on those who opposed the embargo, praised the wisdom of Jefferson's administration, and wrote of the *"Iron rod* of *British Tyranny"* from which the United States had so recently escaped. His view was that the smugglers were "criminals." Of Samuel, he commented that though the possibility of a complete cutting off of trade with Canada clouded his prospects, he should *"remember* that the wheel of Fortune is ever revolving."[20]

The problems besetting Champlain's merchants had not lessened attendance at the local school, and Beaumont had nearly seventy pupils in the winter of 1808–1809. When Beaumont expressed satisfaction with this in a letter to his father, it produced an effect he neither expected nor welcomed. His father asked the brothers if they could advance him money. Throughout his life, Beaumont was tight with money for everyone except his wife, children, and intimate friends. From his earliest years away from home, he adopted the attitude that he had been thrust into the world with few resources, and that only his own efforts, scrupulous care, and financial caution would give him the money and position he desired.

The brothers sent their replies together, and both said that they could not help. As a teacher in Champlain, William billed and received payments from the individual parents rather than receiving a salary. He said that though he had three hundred dollars due to him for his teaching, economic conditions made it very difficult for him to collect. There was some truth in this. The nonintercourse act of March 1809 had gone further than the embargo in cutting off all official trade with Canada, and was disastrous for the trade of northern New York. Yet it seems almost certain from previous comments, and from future events, that Beaumont had been saving money. He simply did not believe that filial devotion meant sending money home. His comment

20. Beaumont to Samuel Beaumont Sr., December 11, 1808, Samuel Beaumont to Samuel Beaumont Sr., December 17, 1808 (this letter includes notes from William, dated December 17, 1808, and January 18, 1809), BP, YU.

that he was daily dunning his debtors to collect money "to assist a grateful & tender Father" rang hollow, particularly when he added that though he would let his parents have what money he could raise, "no certainty" could be assured.

No money at all was to be forthcoming from Champlain because Samuel wrote that the business situation made it impossible for him to send anything, but that if he was fortunate in collecting his debts he would do all in his power to assist. Samuel, the businessman, in view of the depressed state of trade, and with a wife and two stepchildren to support, was in fact probably more truthful about his inability to send any money than his brother. Samuel's business was so bad that in the summer of 1809 he decided to suspend business operations, work his farm, try to collect his debts, and plan his next move.[21]

It seems likely that at the time Beaumont told his father that he could not send any money, he was saving all he could with the intention of embarking on a different career. In the following year, presumably somewhat embarrassed by his inability or unwillingness to send money to his father, Beaumont was not in regular touch with his family. When he wrote to them in April 1810, he announced that he had resigned as a teacher and was in the hopes of engaging in other pursuits; what these would be they would be "informed in time."[22]

Beaumont was proceeding with his usual caution, but he had already decided that he would, if possible, seek a career in medicine. Since the spring of 1809, Beaumont had been engaged in a course of medical reading under the direction of Dr. Benjamin Moore of Champlain. In the first decade of the nineteenth century, the possibilities for medical training were extremely limited. Many practiced medicine with no formal training at all, and the great majority of physicians who did have some formal training obtained it by apprenticing themselves to a practicing physician. There were still few American medical schools, and only a small minority of students could afford to travel to Europe to seek medical education in Edinburgh, London, or Paris.[23]

21. Beaumont to Samuel Beaumont Sr., January 18, 1809, Samuel Beaumont to Samuel Beaumont Sr., December 17, 1808, Beaumont to Samuel Beaumont Sr., May 10, 1809, Samuel Beaumont to Samuel Beaumont Sr., May 10, 1809, to his parents, October 10, 1809, BP, YU.

22. Beaumont to his parents, April 3, 1810, BP, YU.

23. Beaumont to his parents, April 23, 1811, BP, YU (I used the typed copy in the BC, WU); Martin Kaufman, "American Medical Education," 7–11; William G. Rothstein, *American Medical Schools and the Practice of Medicine: A History*, 25–26; also Martin Kaufman, *American Medical Education: The Formative Years, 1796–1811.*

Beaumont's arrangement with Dr. Moore appears to have been informal; he probably believed that he needed to expand his general knowledge of science and medicine before entering on a formal apprenticeship with any physician. Apprenticeships varied, but students might work with their preceptor for as long as three years and pay as much as one hundred dollars a year. Both the time and payment could vary. The period of training involved reading on basic medical subjects and acting as general helper in the doctor's practice, including perhaps mixing drugs. Clinical experience involved accompanying the doctor on his calls, and helping there and in his office, if he had one, by performing the simpler procedures. Opportunities for dissection were, of course, extremely limited, if not nonexistent.[24] The best chances for dissection were usually in the cities.

Beaumont gave only minimal information about his new studies to his family, but his vocabulary occasionally began to reflect his reading. Writing in August 1810, after more than a year of study, he commented that he was in good health, except for a slight touch of "Erysipelas." Presumably, he had a rash. At this time, he also mentioned a new project that was deflecting him from his reading, and was to continue to do so into the spring of 1811. Apparently believing that there was a market for medicines in Champlain, Dr. Seth Pomeroy of Champlain had proposed that the two of them open an apothecary shop in the vacant store previously occupied by Samuel Beaumont and his partner. The arrangement between William Beaumont and Pomeroy was that William would take care of the store while pursuing his studies, and that they would share profit and loss. They sent to New York for drugs and medicines.

In pursuing the study of medicine, Beaumont had decided that he could no longer afford to devote any time to political concerns; he had to pursue medical knowledge with no distractions. *"Philosophy* more than *Politics* be my study," he told his father, "the latter I conceive to be the basis of Contention & discord–the former that of Peace–Morality & useful improvement." When Beaumont wrote, "Philosophy" encompassed the scientific studies he was pursuing. He did, however, remember enough of his political roots to mention that Republicanism was flourishing in northern New York despite "the torrent of *Federal calumny* & tempest of Toryism" that had spread across the region for the past two years.[25]

---

24. William G. Rothstein, *American Physicians in the Nineteenth Century: From Sect to Science,* 85–87.
25. Beaumont to Samuel Beaumont Sr., August 5, 1810, BP, YU.

With the ultimate hope of becoming a physician and the immediate plan of prospering with his apothecary store, Beaumont felt that he was on the upward path he so much desired. He was determined "to pursue the Study of Physic [medicine] under every possible advantage that my circumstances & situation will afford." With his training to pay for, Beaumont continued to dodge any obligations in Lebanon. When his sister Lucy expressed an interest in coming to Champlain, he suggested the two brothers might be able to help with the travel expenses, but also put her off by mentioning that Samuel's family was out of town, Sam was with him in a boarding house, and that to take care of her would be extremely difficult until Sam's family returned. He vacillated between wanting to please a sister he liked and not particularly wanting the inconvenience, and possible cost, of having her in Champlain.

His suggestion to his brother Abel was that he might follow in the footsteps of his two brothers and become the Champlain schoolmaster. Beaumont told Abel that if he thought he was qualified to teach school, the job in Champlain was open and Beaumont would recommend him for it; adding the somewhat odd comment that he could not recommend him unless Abel's qualifications were better than his own had been when he began the job. Beaumont also urged his young brother John to use his youth for improvement, even waxing into verse: *"Philosophy* be your soul-delighting theme / And may her radient [*sic*] brightness on you beam."[26]

The apothecary business died before it really began. Pomeroy and Beaumont opened, discovered there was not enough business, and immediately closed.[27] There appear to be no surviving records of the financial arrangements between Dr. Pomeroy and Beaumont, but it seems likely that much of Beaumont's contribution was to be his work in the store and that Pomeroy put up the money for most of the stock. Beaumont had saved money from his school teaching in the previous years, but undoubtedly not enough to stock an apothecary's store, particularly as he was putting money aside in preparation for more formal training as a physician.

To raise money in the winter of 1810–1811, Beaumont again became Champlain's schoolteacher. He told his parents that this was at the urgent request of the district; this probably meant that there was no one else. By the spring, he was prepared to take the decisive step that would shape his future. Late in April, he told his parents that he would soon leave Champlain,

26. Ibid., Beaumont to his parents, September 12, 1810.
27. Beaumont to his parents, April 23, 1811, BC, YU (I used the typed copy in the BC, WU).

cross Lake Champlain to St. Albans, Vermont, and study "Physic" with Drs.
Benjamin Chandler and Truman Powell. He undoubtedly received advice
from Powell of Burlington, Vermont–Powell gave him a reference when he
left St. Albans–but the actual preceptor who directed his apprenticeship was
Chandler, with whom he lived. Beaumont admitted at this time that although
he had begun reading medicine two years before, he had advanced very
little in theory during the past year because of his preoccupation with other
matters.[28]

While William Beaumont's prospects continued their steady improvement,
his brother Samuel, who was in considerable financial trouble, again paved
the way for his brother. Even before William left for St. Albans, Samuel
had taken his family a short distance south to the more important center
of Plattsburgh. His business was bankrupt, all his property had been given
up for the benefit of his creditors, but he hoped to be out of debt by October.
To get started again, he had returned to his career as a schoolteacher. Samuel
was again to have mixed fortunes in Plattsburgh, but the town was to play an
important part in his brother's life.[29]

Beaumont's formal period of medical apprenticeship was to last little
longer than a year, although he had also read while under the direction of Dr.
Moore. It is unlikely that Beaumont had access to any rich store of medical
literature either in the frontier community of Champlain, or in the somewhat
more established St. Albans, but, like other apprentices, he undoubtedly read
what medical books his preceptor owned.

In the early nineteenth century, even those who undertook a medical
apprenticeship received a wide variety of training dependent upon the skill
and care of their particular preceptor. In a major urban center, with a well-
known physician, the training could be quite ambitious. In 1813, when Dr.
David Hosack of New York issued the details of the training he provided to
private pupils, he made it clear that his expectations, or at least his hopes,
of the amount of work he expected were very high. He announced a three-
year course of study encompassing anatomy, physiology, chemistry, botany,
materia medica, the practice of physic and surgery, mineralogy, midwifery,
and the diseases of women and children. He also suggested more than one
hundred works and more than thirty periodicals that might be read.[30]

28. Ibid.
29. Samuel Beaumont to Samuel Beaumont Sr., August 4, 1811, and Beaumont to
his parents, August 10, 1811, BP, YU.
30. Christine C. Robbins, *David Hosack: Citizen of New York*, 102–4.

Such expectations were obviously at the high end of the possible range of apprenticeships, and Beaumont in his directed reading in Champlain, and his apprenticeship in St. Albans, could hardly hope to approach this range of subjects, or to have access to the same variety of sources as in studying with a major figure in New York City. Fifteen years later, when Beaumont advised his brother Abel on the best way to obtain a medical education with limited means, he told him to get the best terms he could from a skillful practitioner. This would involve giving the professional services that were within his ability in partial payment for the expenses of board and tuition. When he had completed his studies, he should continue to practice with his preceptor until the debt was canceled, or he should take some more advantageous offer and pay off the debt as soon as he was able. "This is the way I got my profession," wrote Beaumont, "& that too, to the entire satisfaction, good will & esteem of my patron & preceptor."[31]

It is typical of Beaumont that this advice to his brother consisted entirely of how to make the financial arrangements for his future career. Beaumont respected learning, but he was no believer in art for art's sake. In these years, he demonstrated in his comments on his own status, and his advice to his brothers, that he believed a Connecticut farm boy should use education, like all other opportunities, to advance himself.

Under the direction of Benjamin Chandler, Beaumont took little time to become a practicing physician. Little is known of Chandler, or of his training, though it was later said of him that he was "most skillful in his medical practice and notably in surgery." In politics he differed entirely from Beaumont, who called him the hottest Federalist he ever knew. Chandler's political reputation was such that word was carried back to Lebanon that Beaumont had become a Federalist. Writing home, he ardently denied this. He assured his father of his undying allegiance to true Republican principles, and said he was under daily threat of being turned out of doors because of them. Notwithstanding all this, Beaumont appeared to admire Chandler as a physician. There are also some indications that Beaumont had his eyes on Chandler's daughter, Mary, but if there was any attachment it never developed into a permanent relationship.[32]

31. Beaumont to Abel Beaumont, March 6, 1826, BP, YU (I used the typed copy in BC, WU).

32. Myer, *Beaumont*, 18–20 (quotation regarding Chandler, 19); Henry K. Adams, *A Centennial History of St. Albans, Vermont*, 54; Beaumont to his parents, November 24, 1811, BP, YU (I used the typed copy in the BC, WU).

At this key moment in his life, Beaumont began to keep both a medical and a general notebook. His notes are quite brief, and he did not keep them particularly systematically, but at this time of his medical training they make it possible to learn something of his reading and interests. At different times of his life, Beaumont kept journals, both medical and general. They are often quite disorganized. In a notebook of cases in the 1820s, a recording of experiments on the stomach is followed by a recipe for tomato catsup, a pickle for beef, and a treatment for gonorrhea.[33]

It would appear that Dr. Chandler was much taken by the theories of the Scotsman John Brown. Later, after he had qualified and was in the army medical service, Beaumont commented in a letter to Chandler, "No peculiar treatment is needed to save the men; the old Brunonian practice, a little varied and changed into the Chandlerian, succeeds almost to a miracle." It is clear from Beaumont's early medical journal that Chandler had introduced him to Brown's work, and that he had paid careful attention to his therapeutic suggestions. Brown's basic work, *Elementa Medicinae,* first published in 1780, had also appeared in the United States.[34]

At the time when Beaumont began his studies with Dr. Chandler, monistic theories, by which attempts were made to find a single cause for all diseases, were enjoying a revival. Not all rejected the nosological approach, by which an attempt was made to classify diseases by their symptoms, but the monistic theorists had considerable vogue in the first years of the nineteenth century. Of particular force were the theories of two men—Brown and the American Benjamin Rush—both of whom had studied at Edinburgh with the famous Scottish teacher, William Cullen. Cullen himself had stressed that the nervous system was the source of all disease, but the theories of Brown and of Rush were better known in the United States.

In his *Elementa Medicinae,* Brown argued that the body had to maintain an even balance of excitability. This excitability was achieved by stimuli, but illness would result if the stimuli were too little or too much. For Brown, there were two basic forms of disease—"sthenic," which resulted from an excess of excitability, and "asthenic," which stemmed from insufficient excitability. Brown believed in active and powerful intervention by the physician. "Sthenic" conditions, according to Brown, required debilitation, including

33. The various notebooks are in the BC, WU.
34. Beaumont to Benjamin Chandler, April 13, 1813, in Myer, *Beaumont,* 36 (quotation). For the Brunonian influence in this first medical notebook, see Miller, ed., *Beaumont's Formative Years,* xi and n, 21–24, 35n, 37–39.

purging, moderate bleeding, and a vegetarian diet. "Asthenic" conditions needed stimulants. For these, Brown advocated opium, as well as musk, camphor, and ether. At the end of the eighteenth century, the Brunonian approach achieved some popularity in Italy and in Germany, and his ideas also influenced American practice.[35]

As a practicing physician, Beaumont was attracted to the "heroic medicine," which called for aggressive intervention on the part of the physician. In the United States, "heroic medicine" became particularly associated with the name of Benjamin Rush, although other physicians both in the United States and Europe had long practiced aggressive therapy. Rush had adopted his more extreme views late in life. He was much influenced in his thinking by the nature of the Philadelphia yellow fever epidemic of 1793 and the supposed success of the therapies he adopted at that time. Rush saw all disease emanating from convulsive action in the walls of the blood vessels, and was a great advocate of massive bleeding and purging to relieve tension. His therapeutic approach was often used even by those who did not accept his monistic theory.

In the Philadelphia yellow fever epidemic, Rush had reached the conclusion that it was beneficial to draw seventy to eighty ounces of blood from his patients in five days; sometimes he took more. He also devised his own mixture for effective purging: a powder comprised of fifteen grains of jalap (a dried root) and ten grains of calomel (mercurous chloride) to be taken three or four times a day. Although calomel was in constant use in the first half of the nineteenth century, it had injurious effects, particularly in the mouth, where it often produced bleeding gums and loss of teeth.[36]

35. Karl E. Rothschuh, *History of Physiology*, trans. and ed. Guenter D. Risse, 131; Joseph F. Kett, *The Formation of the American Medical Profession: The Role of Institutions, 1780–1860;* Günter B. Risse, "The Brownian System of Medicine: Its Theoretical and Practical Implications," 45–51; Guenter B. Risse, "The Quest for Certainty in Medicine: John Brown's System of Medicine in France," 11–12. For the actual practice of medicine in the United States, and the extent to which Brown and other theorists had an impact in the early nineteenth century, see John Harley Warner, *The Therapeutic Perspective: Medical Practice, Knowledge, and Identity in America, 1820–1885.*

36. In "Sanguine Practices: A Historical and Historiographic Reconsideration of Heroic Therapy in the Age of Rush," 211–33, Robert B. Sullivan argues that the practices usually associated with "heroic therapy" long preceded Rush. See also Richard H. Shryock, *Medicine in America: Historical Essays*, 233–51; Nathan G. Goodman, *Benjamin Rush: Physician and Citizen, 1746–1813*, 231–35; John Duffy, *From Humors to Medical Science: A History of American Medicine*, 62–68; Carl Binger, *Revolutionary Doctor: Benjamin Rush, 1764–1813*, 88; James H. Cassedy, *Medicine and American Growth, 1800–1860*, 81.

Brown's ideas and aggressive intervention of the type practiced by Rush are reflected in Beaumont's notebooks, but appropriately for a man who was to gain himself a permanent name in the history of physiology, the first entries in his medical notebook are from Albrecht von Haller's *First Lines of Physiology.* Beaumont copied the definitions of "attention," "judgement," and "genius." Among the other standard works from which Beaumont copied brief extracts into his medical or general notebook were Rush's edition of *The Works of Thomas Sydenham,* Joseph Townsend's *Elements of Therapeutics,* John Huxham's *Essay on Fevers,* Van Swieten's *Commentaries,* John Armstrong's *The Art of Preserving Health,* and William Saunders's *A Treatise on . . . Diseases of the Liver.* He also wrote out William Cullen's definition of fevers, and descriptions of various diseases—intermittent, acute, and spotted fevers, and pleurisy—and a number of prescriptions.

Beaumont did not always distinguish between his medical and his general notebook. "Finery is the affectation of dress," he wrote on the very first page of his medical notebook, "and covers a great deal of dirt." Later, he copied an extract attacking the reading of novels as seeking enjoyment "beneath the level of a rational being," and a number of passages of inferior, semi-humorous poetry, but even in his general commonplace book his extracts reflect his medical reading. Several passages are taken from Robert John Thornton's *Philosophy of Medicine.*[37] Beaumont was a very dedicated, even driven young man, anxious to make his way in the world.

Reading was only part of Beaumont's apprenticeship. After half a year with Chandler, he told his parents that he was in the habit of riding with his preceptor, and that when Dr. Chandler was making his rounds he had charge of many of his patients. He may have been exaggerating a little regarding the extent of his responsibilities, but in this little community Beaumont clearly had ample opportunity to observe and participate in the actual practice of medicine. He was even able to observe, and possibly take part in, dissection.[38]

The very first case that is written up in his medical notebook concerned a young woman who died after suffering eight days with "the common autumnal fever." This was very early in his apprenticeship, and he was still enough of a young man to comment on "the groans & lamentations of her sympathetic companions, & congenial friends & associates deluged in tears of grief, for the loss, so amiable a *daughter, Sister,* friend & companion," but

37. Miller, ed., *Beaumont's Formative Years,* xi, 3–25, 34–35, 38–43, 75.
38. Beaumont to his parents, November 24, 1811, BP, YU (I used the typed copy in the BC, WU).

he also noted that "the body was immediately open'd" and he commented on the abnormal state of the abdomen and ovaries.[39]

Beaumont also described the case of Mary-Maria, who in the spring of 1812 was "violently attacked with a Pulmonic Inflamation." She had been "very much out of health" for many months. Following the initial attack, she had fever, nausea, and vomiting for about ten days, when she had what was described as a fit, in which she complained of "great heat & pain in the head." She was put into a cold bath, but soon died. Beaumont commented in his notebook that the symptoms of "hydrocephalus Internus" were so obvious, that they thought it would be useful for future knowledge to open the head. They obtained permission, and found the blood vessels all distended with thick black blood, and strong evidence of "an inflamation of the membranes of the brain."[40] Dr. Chandler apparently had more scientific interest than many of his contemporaries, and also was able to persuade families to allow him to conduct a postmortem. This gave Beaumont experience he might not have obtained with another preceptor.

Chandler also gave Beaumont some training in surgery. Writing to his parents in November 1811, Beaumont mentioned that Dr. Chandler had left to travel twenty or thirty miles to perform an amputation. Much of American surgery in the first years of the nineteenth century was concerned with a variety of injuries, common in a rural society. Physicians frequently resorted to amputation. Other surgery was extremely limited in scope, although physicians were willing to cut out abscesses and very accessible cancers. In amputation, the mortality rate was extremely high. The lack of anesthesia meant that speed was the prime attribute of any surgeon. Even if the patient, drugged with opium or whiskey, survived the shock of the operation, there was a high probability of developing infection, and physicians were often helpless to either prevent it or to cure it.[41] When he became a practicing physician, Beaumont, like most early nineteenth century doctors, had no hesitation in ranging across the whole area of medicine, including surgery.

Some indication of the general state of medical education in the early nineteenth century is given by the fact that just half a year after beginning his formal apprenticeship, Beaumont felt it necessary to explain to his parents his "slowness" in becoming a doctor. Apparently, it had been mentioned

39. Miller, ed., *Beaumont's Formative Years*, 6.
40. Ibid., 7–8.
41. Rothstein, *American Physicians*, 249–56; Duffy, *From Humors to Medical Science*, 130.

that someone in Lebanon had become a doctor within two years of beginning his training. Beaumont explained that while they might train faster in Connecticut, in his area it required at least five or six years to become an expert theorist, and even longer to perfect the art. Excepting quacks, he wrote, physicians in the cold climate of Vermont did not come to majority as quickly as the "geniuses" of Lebanon. He assured his parents, however, that unless some extraordinary events intervened, he would be able to meet the costs of his education without any difficulty, although his explanation for not answering his brother Abel's letter was that he had deferred it because of the expense of postage.[42]

Beaumont hardly needed to apologize for his slower pace. Although he had begun reading medicine two years before starting his formal apprenticeship, he had admitted that other concerns had often kept him from his studies for the second of those two years. He began his formal apprenticeship in the spring of 1811; he was qualified by June 1812. In an age when there were few medical schools, many "physicians" simply hung out their shingles and began to practice medicine, but those who had undertaken a formal apprenticeship with a practicing physician usually obtained a certificate from a medical society testifying that they were qualified.[43] In Beaumont's case, he applied to the Third Medical Society of Vermont. In June 1812, the medical society certified that Beaumont had presented himself for examination on the anatomy of the human body, and on the theory and practice of "Physic and Surgery," and had been approved.[44]

For a few months after he was licensed, Beaumont remained with his preceptor, Dr. Chandler. From his later comments to his brother Abel, it seems likely that he was still paying off the costs of his apprenticeship. Some indication of his modes of treatment at this time can be gained from a case that he was obviously proud of, and which was one of the few cases he wrote up in his early medical notebook. In the middle of August 1812 he was called to treat a young woman who had been seized with "a Synocha or inflamatory fever." She had been ill and in pain for several days before the attack, but had continued her regular household duties while taking heavy doses of laudanum to relieve her pain. Beaumont was called when she was seized "with violent pains in her head, Side, back, loins, muscles & limbs,

---

42. Beaumont to his parents, November 24, 1811, BP, YU.
43. Kett, *The Formation of the American Medical Profession,* 181; Rothstein, *American Physicians,* 101–8.
44. Certificate from the Third Medical Society of Vermont, June 1812, BC, WU.

cold chills, rigors, universal lassitude, and nausia–face red as scarlet, eyes, inflamed, & great soreness on motion–tongue thick coated & very black, skin dry & hot, & puls, strong, full & hard."

Having decided that the basic problem was an inflammatory fever, Beaumont pursued vigorous depletive or antiphlogistic therapy. On his arrival, he immediately took about fourteen ounces of blood and gave her an emetic and a cathartic. The latter two worked, and she also lost about another twelve ounces of blood by "spontaneous emission" from the incision in her arm. All this reduced "the high arterial action" and the other symptoms. Beaumont now gave a saline draught to help induce perspiration, and through the night continued the saline draught together with Dover's Powder (a mixture of ipecac and opium).

On the following afternoon, Beaumont again used a cathartic, which left her "considerably exhausted," although he said he attempted to alleviate the exhaustion by the free use of the Dover's Powders and Serpentaria (Virginia Snakeroot). He also gave "Pill. Alterans," which contained derivatives of both antimony and mercury. For several days, he continued to freely administer "Bark, Wine, Serpturia, & Brunan. Pill." The last pill was Brown's suggestion for Sthenic conditions, and, among other ingredients, contained opium and mercury. The patient had a setback, which Beaumont attributed to the shock given her by a bell tolling for the death of a child, but he was obviously delighted when after a few days she recovered. His last entry was that she was "so far recovered as to ride in Waggon to Cambridge, 20 miles in a day, got married, & enjoyed–good health, &c &c–."[45]

Beaumont was ready to leave his preceptor and strike out on his own. He saw his opportunity in the war that since June 1812 had been waged between the United States and Great Britain. Early in September, he recrossed Lake Champlain to Plattsburgh, one of the places at which an American army was slowly gathering to prepare for the invasion of Canada. Before he left St. Albans, Beaumont obtained letters of reference for future use. Chandler recommended him as "a safe and judicious practitioner," who had attentively studied physic and surgery and had progressed well not only in theory but also in the practice of physic and surgery. Beaumont also obtained character references. One of these was from the Champlain chapter of the Royal Arch Masons. Beaumont's preceptor, Dr. Chandler, signed this in his capacity as High Priest.[46]

---

45. Miller, ed., *Beaumont's Formative Years*, 8–9, 34. See also Warner, *Therapeutic Perspective*, 91–95.
46. The letters of reference, September 1812, are in the BC, WU.

Since moving north to Champlain in 1807, Beaumont had done much to achieve his ambition of rising in the world. As a physician who had served his apprenticeship in a small Vermont town, he could not hope to compete immediately with those who had taken a university degree, apprenticed in New York or Philadelphia, and perhaps spent a year or two in Edinburgh or Paris, but he was a step up from the "irregulars" who had no apprenticeship and no recognition by a medical society. As medical schools grew in the first decades of the nineteenth century, and as the distinctions between physicians became more important, Beaumont could at least take his rank with the "regulars." He was proud of this, and he had little patience with the many irregulars who proliferated for the rest of his life.

In 1812, it would have been very difficult to believe that William Beaumont stood any chance at all of becoming a physiologist of permanent, international renown, but he was well on his way to achieving his personal goal of rising above his origins as a Connecticut farm boy.

T W O

_____

Surgeon at War

ON JUNE 18, 1812, The United States had declared war on Great Britain, and
for those in northern New York and northern Vermont this event had more
immediate significance than for most Americans. As William Beaumont had
been made well aware through the business fortunes of his brother Samuel,
the trade of this northern American frontier gravitated far more strongly
toward the St. Lawrence River and Montreal than to any American region.
On the northern borders, illegal trade was to be a fact of life in war as well
as in peace, and there were many on the northern frontiers who thought
it was madness to declare war on England. William, who had retained his
father's Jeffersonianism and patriotism, was not one of them. For Beaumont,
the war was a just struggle that also offered a chance for professional ad-
vancement. While an elegant Philadelphia- or European-trained physician
might well have scoffed at the lowly position of surgeon's mate in the United
States Army, Beaumont conceived of it as another opportunity to advance
his future prospects while satisfying his patriotic zeal. Even the rate of pay–
thirty dollars a month–which was a paltry amount to a well-established city
physician, appeared quite attractive to young Beaumont, who so recently had
been happy with his pay as a Champlain schoolteacher.[1]

On September 8, 1812, Beaumont left Dr. Chandler's home, crossed Lake
Champlain, and on the thirteenth enlisted, with the brevet rank of surgeon's

1. Mary C. Gillett, *The Army Medical Department, 1775–1818,* 150; Charles W. Ayars,
"Some Notes on the Medical Service of the Army, 1812–1839," 506.

mate. He was assigned to the Sixth Regiment of the United States infantry. The modern historian of the army medical department has argued that the period from 1788 to 1812 was a low point in its history. As late as December 1807, there had been only two surgeons in the army, with only one of them on duty, and thirty-one surgeon's mates, with twenty-seven on duty. Since 1802, the surgeons and mates had been assigned to garrisons rather than to individual regiments. When the army was increased in 1808, five surgeons and fifteen surgeon's mates were authorized for hospital service, but most of the positions existed on paper rather than in reality. Not until six months before the war began was it arranged for surgeons and mates to be assigned to specific regiments. At that time, it was decided that each regiment was to be assigned one surgeon and two mates, and that there were to be hospital surgeons and mates where necessary.[2]

In the fall of 1812, Plattsburgh should have been the very center of activity of the American war effort, but reality was very different. Although the basic strategy of the War of 1812 was to invade Canada to force a change in British policies, the United States was ill-prepared for war on land. The general plan of attack called for an invasion of Canada on three fronts: in the west at Detroit, in the center on the Niagara frontier, and in the east along the west shore of Lake Champlain north from Plattsburgh to the Richelieu River and Montreal. Ideally, these attacks should have been launched simultaneously, with the greatest force on the Plattsburgh front, for the capture of Montreal would have severed British communications on the St. Lawrence and prevented them from supplying the fronts farther west. This did not occur. The greatest enthusiasm for the war was in the West and South, the greatest opposition in New England. The invasions depended on raising more regulars and volunteers, and the enlistment of state militias. In the first months of the war it proved extremely difficult to assemble enough forces on the Lake Champlain front.[3]

When Beaumont arrived in Plattsburgh and enlisted in the army, General Henry Dearborn was still attempting to raise an army to invade Canada along Lake Champlain. During the summer, he had set up his headquarters at Greenbush, on the east bank of the Hudson River, directly opposite Albany, New York. Troops slowly began to assemble there and at Plattsburgh.

2. Miller, ed., *Beaumont's Formative Years*, 10, 26, 43; Gillett, *Army Medical Department, 1775–1818*, 129–33; James D. Edgar, "The Army Medical Department in the War of 1812," 303–13; Ayars, "Some Notes on the Medical Service," 505–6.
3. See Reginald Horsman, *The War of 1812*, 32–34.

The medical director of the northern army, James Mann, reported that the most common diseases they encountered that summer were dysentery and diarrhea. Treatment often followed patterns that Beaumont had learned in St. Albans. Depletive (antiphlogistic) therapy to reduce the body's excitement, and to remove anything that might harm its function, was in frequent use for a variety of fevers, but there was no consistency. Different physicians tried different therapies that they thought effective, and individual physicians made use of a variety of medications.[4]

In September, when Beaumont assumed his duties at Plattsburgh, he found that the main diseases were intermittent fevers, typhus, dysenteries, and rheumatism. He began his treatment of intermittents with emetics and cathartics, followed by sudorifics, "chiefly Antimonials, & Alkalis," together with a free use of bark (cinchona). When patients did not respond, and for typhus, he gave bark wine, opium, Virginia Snakeroot, and Brown's Sthenic pill ("the Brunonian pill") in which mercury and opium were basic ingredients. He commented that with this treatment he did not lose more than one out of fifty, but he came to the conclusion that the best treatment was small and repeated doses of ipecac or tartar emetic with opium. In cases of dysentery and diarrhea, Beaumont said he had good success using opium and ipecac, with a simple solution of Sal Natron (sodium carbonate). Rheumatism was difficult to cure, for there were no barracks for the men at Plattsburgh until the end of the year. Beaumont used opium, Guaiac (a wood resin), and Spirits Terebinth (turpentine) to relieve the pain.[5]

There was particular difficulty in raising troops for the attack north from Plattsburgh because the New England states were reluctant to send their militia into federal service. That, combined with General Dearborn's chronic caution, was to prolong the waiting period and increase the medical problems for the waiting troops. Mann reported that with the first frosts in early October also came "acute and chronic rheumatism." In the early fall there were also the first signs of pneumonia, which was to become a major problem in the

4. James Mann, *Medical Sketches of the Campaigns of 1812, 13, 14*, 12–14, 179; Gillett, *Army Medical Department, 1775–1818*, 192–93. For Mann, see James M. Phalen, "Surgeon James Mann's Observations on Battlefield Amputations," 463–64. See also Warner, *Therapeutic Perspective*, 3–5, 91–92. For a discussion of the problems experienced in the early nineteenth century in defining fevers in relation to specific diseases, see Dale C. Smith, "The Rise and Fall of Typhomalarial Fever: I. Origins."

5. Miller, ed., *Beaumont's Formative Years*, 10–11, 34; Allan S. Everest, *The War of 1812 in the Champlain Valley*, 57.

coming winter. Life for the troops at Greenbush and Plattsburgh in this first fall of the war was also complicated by an epidemic of measles; nearly one-third of the troops came down with it.[6]

Any dreams Beaumont had of dramatic, patriotic service and striking victories over the British must have seemed distant after weeks of coping with the diseases of the ill-housed troops in Plattsburgh. By November, Plattsburgh had become the main assembly point, and General Dearborn arrived there to take command. But it was getting very late in the season for a major campaign into Canada, and Dearborn had no stomach for it. In mid-November, he reluctantly moved his army of some six thousand men north from Plattsburgh to Beaumont's old residence of Champlain close to the Canadian border. Beaumont commented that the men had no tents and were destitute of covering, except a blanket or two. There was skirmishing across the Canadian border, but Dearborn, with some of his militia reluctant to cross into Canada, had no real desire to attempt an attack on Montreal. Within a week, he took his army back to Plattsburgh. Most of the militia went home, and the regulars tried to prepare for winter in Plattsburgh or across the lake in Burlington, Vermont.

Beaumont's regiment remained in Plattsburgh, where he was appalled by the inept planning for the men under his care. In wet and windy conditions, the men were encamped in the woods without shelter. After two nights in the open, they moved a short distance into camp on the Saranac River. They were still in the open, among the trees, "lying upon the cold wet ground, with only a fire before their tents."[7]

The building of the huts was painfully slow. It was nearly the end of the year before they were ready to be occupied. Beaumont deplored the "wretched & deplorable" condition of the men, who were "seized with *Dysentary*, Intermittants, Pleurisy, Peripneumony, Cynanchy [sore throat], & Rheumatism, which made the very woods ring with coughing & groanings." Beaumont's treatments followed a pattern he had already established: opium and ipecac for dysentery; opium and tartar emetic for intermittents (a grain of the latter every three or four hours); copious bleeding for pleurisy and pneumonia, followed by opium, antimony, and digitalis. Blistering, by which irritants

6. Mann, *Medical Sketches*, 15–19; John S. Haller, *American Medicine in Transition, 1840–1910*, 68–77; Gillett, *Army Medical Department, 1775–1818*, 157–59.

7. Horsman, *War of 1812*, 50; Everest, *War of 1812 in the Champlain Valley*, 90–92; Miller, ed., *Beaumont's Formative Years*, 11.

were applied to produce counterirritation, was used in obstinate cases. He proudly noted that out of more than two hundred cases he had in his care not one man had died.

In the first two weeks of December, Beaumont was constantly occupied in treating the sick. He also noted in his journal his complete disagreement with the treatments being used by Surgeon Samuel Gilliland of the Sixteenth Regiment. He commented that in the camp disease that was now prevailing Gilliland was giving from one to three emetics and many cathartics, and then gave tonics. The result, wrote Beaumont, was that in two weeks twenty-six men had died out of four hundred: "Behold the *gasping* Mortals how they die!–from, two to five in a day!" Gilliland was totally wrong, concluded Beaumont, "depletion by blood-letting & antimonial sudorifics & diaphoretics, & an entire disuse of all tonic medicines is the proper plan of cure." Beaumont's approach was approved by Medical Director James Mann, who later wrote that the greatest mortality was in December 1812 when stimulants were employed. The mortality nearly ceased in the following month, he claimed, when emetics, cathartics, and antiphlogistic practice was the preferred treatment.[8]

When Beaumont had arrived in Plattsburgh in September, the troops who were gathering were under the command of Brigadier General Joseph Bloomfield. It was Bloomfield who gave Beaumont his brevet appointment in the Sixth Regiment, and when in November a vacancy arose because of a resignation in the Sixteenth Regiment, Van Bloomfield recommended Beaumont for a regular appointment. In mid-December, Beaumont was notified of his appointment as surgeon's mate in the Sixteenth Regiment, but it was not what he wanted. He had set his heart on continuing with the Sixth Regiment, and he had privately reached the conclusion that Gilliland was incompetent. Beaumont wrote to the adjutant general, stating that as it was his particular wish to be attached to the Sixth Regiment he wondered if a mistake had been made. He said that he would defer acceptance of an appointment until the matter was straightened out, and in the meantime would continue his duties with the Sixth Regiment.[9]

Disturbed by the military failures, the inaction, and the prospect of leaving

---

8. Miller, ed., *Beaumont's Formative Years,* 11–14; Everest, *War of 1812 in the Champlain Valley,* 57; Mann, *Medical Sketches,* 45.

9. Beaumont to T. H. Cushing, December 19, 1812, War Department, RG 94, Office of the Adjutant General, Letters Received, National Archives, Washington, D.C. Hereafter cited as WD, AG, LR; Everest, *War of 1812 in the Champlain Valley,* 63.

the regiment on which he had set his heart, Beaumont contemplated returning to private practice. His comment in his notebook was that "I suspended
duty on account of the unfavorable prospects of the Army at that time." On
January 11, 1813, he advertised in the *Plattsburgh Republican* his intention
of beginning the practice of physic and surgery, and asked for the patronage
of the residents of the town and its vicinity.[10]

Quickly, Beaumont's plans changed again. On February 13 he received
word that he had been transferred from the Sixteenth Regiment to the Sixth
Regiment, and he immediately accepted an appointment as surgeon's mate
in the Sixth. When he told his parents of this appointment, he said the opportunity for practical knowledge was superior than in any private situation he
could obtain, that the pay was "handsome," and the payments prompt.[11] The
common view in the early nineteenth century was that both schoolteachers
and surgeon's mates were poorly paid, but Beaumont expressed considerable
satisfaction with his pay in both situations. Beaumont was ambitious, but he
was able to enjoy each rise in status and income, and make the best of what
he had while he looked for his next opportunity.

Beaumont told his old preceptor, Dr. Benjamin Chandler, that one cause
of giving up the plans for private practice and returning to the army was
his gratitude to the officers of the Sixth Regiment for securing him his
appointment, and their desire for him to continue with them. But he also said
that given his financial position, he was swayed by the prospect of receiving
prompt payment for his services, and that military service would present him
with the prospect "of an immediate and more extensive practice in surgery."
Beaumont commented that Chandler (an ardent and presumably antiwar
Federalist) would probably say that he was returning "like a dog to his vomit."

It also seems possible that Beaumont's decision to return to the army and
abandon plans for private practice stemmed from more private reasons. A
tradition persisted to the beginning of the twentieth century that when Beaumont lived with the Chandlers he had been attracted to Chandler's daughter
Mary. In writing to Chandler of his decision to return to the army, Beaumont referred to "unpleasant reflections" and "melancholy impressions"
that could only be suggested with "impropriety." He added that if he should
ever return to the friendly house in St. Albans to enjoy "the pleasures of

10. Miller, ed., *Beaumont's Formative Years*, 43; *Plattsburgh Republican*, January 11,
1813 (facsimile in Myer, *Beaumont*, 39).
11. Beaumont to T. H. Cushing, February 13, 1813, WD, AG, LR; Beaumont to his
parents, February 26, 1813, BP, YU (I used the typed copy in the BC, WU).

domestic friendship and mutual esteem," Chandler would know his "most secret impressions and be satisfied as to the real motive of my heart."[12] It seems quite possible that Beaumont had envisioned opening a practice in Plattsburgh with Dr. Chandler's daughter by his side.

For more than a month after returning to the Sixth Regiment, Beaumont was kept extremely busy caring for the regulars at Camp Saranac, four miles from Plattsburgh on the Saranac River. There were about two thousand men there, with that number increasing daily as recruits came in. It had become apparent by this time that the troops in the northeastern region of the country, along with the other citizens of the region, had been afflicted with a severe and unusual epidemic of pneumonia, which differed from the type known previously in the region. This was later usually referred to as the winter epidemic, but physicians at the time gave it a variety of names— pneumonia, peripneumony; bilious epidemic fever; typhus fever; putrid or malignant pleurisy; typhoid peripneumony; pneumonia notha, and bilious pneumonia were all used to describe it. Symptoms varied, and at times physicians were undoubtedly describing different diseases, but typically patients experienced severe pains in the side or chest, difficult breathing, coughs, and chills.[13]

The disease made great inroads among the troops exposed to the bitter weather in northern New York, but even in the Third Military District, which covered New Jersey and the southern part of New York, the most prevalent disease was pneumonia, and about one-fifth of those who became ill died. James Mann stated that the epidemic of measles in the fall had made the troops in the Plattsburgh area particularly susceptible to the disease, and that in February 1813 pneumonia, "with a catarrhal affection," was universal among the men.[14]

Beaumont had encountered the disease in the previous fall, and when he rejoined his regiment in February 1813 he noted that "Peripneumonics" was "prevailing" in the camp. He was convinced that the proper treatment for the disease was "depletion"—with purges, emetics, and bleeding—and was certain that tonics had to be avoided. Beaumont's strong opinions were typical of

12. Beaumont to Chandler, March 10 and April 13, 1813, in Myer, *Beaumont,* 34–37.

13. *Medical Repository,* n.s., 1 (1813), 247, 252, 261, 264, 336; Mann, *Medical Sketches,* ix.

14. *Medical Repository,* n.s., 1 (1813), 412–14; Mann, *Medical Sketches,* 255–56, 412–14, 256 (quotation).

the arguments raging among physicians as to the proper treatment for this "winter epidemic."[15]

The basic argument was between those physicians who viewed it as a *"typhoid pneumonia,"* requiring only stimulants, and those who believed that bleeding and "antiphlogistic" remedies were needed. The *Medical Repository* devoted many pages to the epidemic, and a variety of treatments were suggested. One physician who was quoted in the magazine argued that the time was not far distant when experience (with few exceptions) would reduce the whole materia medica to two simple articles—emetics and cathartics. He believed that they would be "exclusively and successfully employed in *fevers of every grade under every condition of the system."*[16] The physicians argued, but the soldiers suffered.

Mann maintained that it was necessary to distinguish between two types of the disease—when there was a hard pulse he advocated cautious bleeding, but in the case of a weak pulse he believed that bleeding could be injurious. In general, however, he agreed with Beaumont in advocating cathartics, emetics, and blistering; like Beaumont he had faith in calomel, jalop, antimony, and Dover's Powder. Dr. James Tilton, a Revolutionary veteran who became surgeon general of the army in 1813, was a great believer in calomel, and thought that army surgeons should mainly use calomel and opium, along with blistering.[17]

An obvious reason for the arguments about treatment was that physicians had great difficulty in defining the diseases they were trying to treat, and in understanding the causes. Many believed that there was an intimate connection between the state of the weather, the atmosphere, and disease, and tried to identify relevant miasmas. An article in the *New England Journal of Medicine and Surgery* argued that the cause which led to the "winter epidemic" existed in the atmosphere, and that the *"exciting causes"* were "exposure to cold, and moisture, and fatigue." In one article in the *Medical Repository,* it was said that the disease appeared to depend "on some peculiar state of the atmosphere, as a remote cause; and an exposure to wet, cold and

15. Miller, ed., *Beaumont's Formative Years,* 14.

16. Archibald Welch, "A Biographical Sketch of Silas Fuller, M.D.," 111; *Medical Repository,* n.s., 1 (1813), 338–40.

17. *Medical Repository,* n.s., 1 (1813), 257–59 (James Mann); Cassedy, *Medicine and American Growth,* 20–21; Erskine Hume, "The Foundation of American Meteorology by the United States Army Medical Department," 202.

fatigue, or some imprudent irregularity, as an exciting cause." Mann wrote that it could be viewed as an epidemic "produced by some latent, remote cause; an unknown state of the atmosphere." He also thought that there was greater susceptibility among those who drank hard liquor excessively, had too much animal food, or were exposed to cold and fatigue.[18]

Beaumont was convinced that "depletion" was the only answer. When one sergeant was "taken violently with all the alarming symptoms" of the winter epidemic, Beaumont immediately bled and blistered him, and gave him preparations containing calomel, antimony, and opium. Only on the fourth day, after he had improved, did he attempt to moderate this with wine and "mucilage of barley," but he also gave Seneca Root and Virginia Snakeroot. In another case, in which bleeding had already been used by another physician, Beaumont thought it had probably not been of much use, but he blistered, and gave preparations that contained opium, calomel, and antimony. When the patient was on the mend, Beaumont gave him wine, barley water, and the Brunonian pill. He commented that "Sundry cases of Peripneumony" all yielded to his treatment.[19]

While many of the contemporary physicians wrote fearfully of the symptoms and the mortality of the winter epidemic, Beaumont, even in his private journal, wrote with confidence of the therapies he used, and only occasionally mentioned the death of a patient. Writing home, he was even more upbeat about the medical state of those under his care. Late in February, he said that though the sickness among the troops in the first part of the winter had been "very mortal," it had now subsided, and the men were "very healthy." Yet he almost immediately contradicted himself when he added in a postscript that he was unable to write to his brothers and sisters because he was constantly employed in prescribing for the sick.[20]

There was extensive sickness among the troops at Plattsburgh in the winter of 1812–1813, but Beaumont was a young and enthusiastic doctor who was happy to be serving in the United States Army. He had received only limited medical education, and he had only limited experience. Like

18. *New England Journal of Medicine and Surgery* 2 (1813), 246; *Medical Repository*, n.s., 1 (1813), 259–60, 330–31. For a discussion of the history of the belief in the intimate links between climate and disease, see Frederick Sargent II, *Hippocratic Heritage: A History of Ideas about Weather and Human Health.*

19. Miller, ed., *Beaumont's Formative Years*, 14–15.

20. Beaumont to his parents, February 26, 1813, BP, YU (I used the typed copy in BC, WU).

most physicians, he had great faith in his treatments, and he placed more stress on those who recovered than on those who remained sick or died.

In the winter of 1813, the United States was planning attacks that would at last enable Beaumont to see the action he sought. In February, General Dearborn was ordered to assemble some four thousand men at Sackett's Harbor on Lake Ontario to attack Kingston and York (the modern Toronto). He was then to join some three thousand men at Buffalo to launch an attack against the British forts on the Niagara River. Two brigades were to be transferred from the Lake Champlain front to make these attacks possible. The cautious Dearborn decided that Kingston presented too many difficulties, but he prepared to attack York.[21]

On March 19, the Sixth Regiment marched from Plattsburgh for Sackett's Harbor, more than 180 miles away. Not all the men actually marched–some were in sleighs–but the move was a difficult one. The spring thaw was on, the weather varying from warmth to snow, and at night the men lay on the ground or in barns. It took eight days to reach Sackett's Harbor. As usual at this time of his life, Beaumont relished his new experiences. He said no sick had been left behind on the march, and was impressed by the "delightful country & many beautiful Villages & Settlements" through which they passed.[22]

At Sackett's Harbor, Beaumont was dealing mostly with *"Intermittents* in many cases complicated with Pneumony." The symptoms were general pain, cold chills, and nausea, sometimes with acute pain in the side and a cough. He treated pneumonia by bleeding, blistering, and dosing with antimonials. When the symptoms were primarily those of intermittent fever, he said the best treatment was to give the *"Pillule Chandler,"* which consisted of tartar emetic and calomel, "so as to puke & purge smartly." He followed this up with the Brunonian pill and more of the tartar emetic and calomel. Beaumont's regiment was encamped in mud and water, in open huts, with nothing but blankets as a cover. They even lacked straw. But with his usual rosy view of the state of health of the men under his care, Beaumont told his old preceptor Dr. Chandler that the troops were very healthy, and that he had but three or four sick in his regiment.[23]

Beaumont was still in debt to Chandler, but was showing his usual reluctance to part with his cash. Just before the army had marched from

21. Horsman, *War of 1812*, 90–91.
22. Miller, ed., *Beaumont's Formative Years*, 15, 43–44 (quotation).
23. Ibid., 15; Beaumont to Chandler, April 13, 1813, in Myer, *Beaumont*, 35–37.

Plattsburgh, he had received a message from Chandler requesting money (Beaumont presumably still owed him for his preceptorship), and he now apologized that he had been unable to send him any. He said that he had used his pay to settle debts and to defray necessary expenses, and that he had not ten dollars left for the long march to Sackett's Harbor.[24]

With action in prospect, Beaumont's strong streak of patriotism came to the fore. He told his father that patriotism and the prospects of a battle had brought him back to the colors. If he survived the war, he intended to visit his old Connecticut home "with quickened pace," but he thought that duty should come before pleasure, and the defense of the nation's rights and liberty before love, friendship, or affection. This was what his Jeffersonian father wanted to hear, but it also reflected Beaumont's own patriotism.[25]

On April 22, Beaumont, with three companies of the Sixth Regiment, embarked at Sackett's Harbor on board the schooner *Julia*. In all, some fourteen vessels with some seventeen hundred men took part in the attack on York. It was a slow voyage. The fleet did not weigh anchor and sail until the next day, and even then adverse weather forced them to return to the harbor. No one was allowed to disembark, and on the twenty-fourth they sailed again. Beaumont, along with everyone else on his schooner, thought they were going to attack Kingston, but he quickly realized they were about to attack York, the capital of Upper Canada. It was five days after they embarked before the troops were again on land, and during that time they were either crowded below, or sitting or lying on deck. They reached York on the evening of the twenty-sixth, but lay off the harbor until the following morning.[26]

York had fewer than one thousand defenders and weak fortifications, but the battle turned out to be a costly operation. On the morning of April 27 the American troops landed in boats under the protective fire of the fleet. They met stiff resistance, but landed successfully and fought throughout most of the morning. To this point casualties had been light, and when a small magazine in one of the British batteries blew up the Americans seemed to be carrying the day without heavy casualties. But as the British retreated, they blew up the main magazine. Beaumont told his parents that stones fell like drops of rain in a thunderstorm. Some two hundred Americans were wounded and about forty were killed, including the American commander, Brigadier General Zebulon Pike, who died of the wounds inflicted by a large

24. Myer, *Beaumont*, 36–37.
25. Beaumont to Samuel Beaumont Sr., April 1813, BP, YU.
26. Miller, ed., *Beaumont's Formative Years*, 16, 44–45.

stone from the magazine. The Americans occupied the town and caused much controversy by burning the Parliament building and the house of the lieutenant governor.[27]

Beaumont's Sixth Regiment was leading the American charge, and was within a quarter of a mile of the explosion when the main magazine blew up. They suffered heavy casualties. "A most shocking scene ensued," wrote Beaumont, "the stones falling thick as hail in all directions, cut bruis'd & mangled the men most shockingly." His estimate of total losses was a little high–60 killed and 250 wounded–but he pointed out that more than 100 of these casualties were suffered by his own regiment. "Their wounds," he said, "were of the worst kind, compd fractures of *legs, thighs & arms & fractures* of *Sculls.*" That night and the following two days, the surgeons were constantly amputating, and dressing the wounds of those most severely wounded. Beaumont himself performed four amputations, and he trephined three skulls. The latter operation involved using a cylindrical saw to remove bone in an attempt to relieve pressure on the brain. Beaumont was at last getting the surgical experience that he said had been one of his reasons for remaining in the army, and for the rest of his life he prided himself on his surgery.[28]

Beaumont's first action had been a particularly bloody one, with unusual problems for the surgeons, and it deeply impressed him. He used his general notebook as well as his medical journal to record his impressions. His account was very similar in both, but in his general notebook he moved away from any medical detachment to write of the agony of the troops, of the "most distressing scene" in the hospital, where "nothing but the Groans, of the wounded & agonies of the Dying" were to be heard. The surgeons, he wrote, were "wading in blood, cutting of [*sic*] arms, legs, & trepanning heads to rescue their fellow creatures from untimely deaths–to hear the poor creatures, crying–Oh, Dear! Oh Dear! Oh my God! my God! Do, Doctor, Doctor! Do cut of my leg! my arm! my head! to relieve me from misery! I cant live! I cant live! would have rent the heart of Steel, & shocked the insensibility of the most harden'd assassin & the cruelest savage!" No one, he thought, could have beheld all this without agonizing sympathy. He said he "cut & slashed" for forty-eight hours without food or sleep.[29]

27. Ibid., 16, 45–46; Beaumont to his parents, May 11, 1813, BP, YU; Mann, *Medical Sketches,* 58–59; Horsman, *War of 1812,* 91–93.

28. Miller, ed., *Beaumont's Formative Years,* 16.

29. Ibid., 46.

On the days following the action, Beaumont continued to work constantly, dressing wounds and operating. His patients had wounds ranging from simple contusions to the worst compound fractures. One of his amputees, who had a very badly fractured and contused thigh, died twelve hours after the operation. The magazine explosion had produced particularly severe injuries. Five months later, when a military surgeon was directed to take wounded men to Greenbush, New York, he found that many of them "had been distressingly mutilated by the fall of stones at the explosion of the York magazine." Some still required surgical dressings.[30]

In the early nineteenth century, the death rate following amputation was extremely high, and the rate was even worse under battlefield conditions. But given the problems of dealing with fractures, bullet wounds, and infection, amputation was resorted to with great frequency. The immediate problem was the lack of any anesthetic; surgeons tried to dull the patient's response with opium, whiskey, or the like, and carried out the procedure with great speed, but amputations were a horrifying ordeal for the patient.[31]

One of the biggest arguments about amputation among military surgeons was whether to perform the operation immediately after the wound was sustained, or whether to wait, observe, and act only if it became absolutely necessary. James Mann generally endorsed the position that amputations should be immediate when the damage was severe, but was prepared to modify this in more doubtful cases. One surgeon who in 1814 worked in a military hospital in Buffalo, New York, later wrote that "when the large cylindrical bones were broken, our resort was, for the most part, amputation." He went on to comment that in summer large amputations "were very unsuccessful, so much so, as almost to discourage us from performing them; many of the recent stumps mortified; in others that did not, the patient gradually sank into the arms of death." In general, he commented that "mortification of the extremities" from wounds was common, and that wounds that had much discharge "were frequently infested with maggots," in spite of the efforts of the attendants to prevent it.[32]

Whether amputation was immediate or delayed, the constant problem was infection, and there had long been an argument about whether any large wound was better left open or closed. Simple wounds were closed, and healing by "first intention" was planned for, hopefully with only minor

30. Ibid., 46–48; *Medical Examiner*, n.s., 96 (1852), 757.
31. See Rothstein, *American Physicians*, 249–50.
32. Mann, *Medical Sketches*, 206–33; Phalen, "Surgeon Mann's Observations," 463–66; *Medical Examiner*, n.s., 97 (1853), 2–4.

suppuration. Severe wounds generally were treated in a different manner. Premature closing of severe wounds usually led to infection, and surgeons kept such wounds open, hoping to produce what was termed "laudable pus" in the course of healing. In the cases of amputation, whatever the methods used, the mortality rate was often high.[33] Beaumont had difficulty retaining his usual optimism about rates of recovery when engaging in the crudities of military surgery.

On April 29 the surgeons at York were ordered to embark the sick and wounded for transportation to Sackett's Harbor, but after putting them on the ships they had to take them off again, "very much to the injury of the patients." On May 1 Beaumont amputated an arm, but had to suspend other operations when they were again ordered to put the sick on board. This was done, but the winds being unfavorable and a storm arising, they did not weigh anchor for a week. All this time the wounded were scattered throughout the ships of the fleet with the other troops. The surgeons, who remained on shore for much of this time, often could not reach vessels to dress the wounded. By May 7, Beaumont commented that men were complaining of diarrhea and dysentery, but that the wounded were doing "far better than could be expected, in such a miserable condition."[34]

The fleet finally sailed from York on May 8, bound for the Niagara River to carry out the attack that had been ordered on the British forts. They arrived at the mouth of the river on that night, but it was no surprise that the men were in poor condition when they disembarked. Beaumont commented that in the course of the day one of the men crowded in the hold of his ship died; he thought it must have been of suffocation, because he had only a slight wound on his back caused by a stone. General Dearborn decided that the men had to be given some time to recuperate, and the fleet sailed to Sackett's Harbor to bring reinforcements, carrying with it some of the sick and wounded. The main force that had returned from York remained in tents some four miles from Fort Niagara.[35]

While Beaumont had some cases he diagnosed as typhus and a few cases of intermittent fever, his main duty in the days after arriving at Niagara was dressing the wounds of those injured in the magazine explosion; those

33. Rothstein, *American Physicians,* 253; Owen H. Wangensteen, Jacqueline Smith, and Sarah D. Wangensteen, "Some Highlights in the History of Amputation Reflecting Lessons in Wound Healing," 98–112; Gillett, *Army Medical Department, 1775–1818,* 16–18.
34. Miller, ed., *Beaumont's Formative Years,* 47–48.
35. Ibid., 48, 76.

with compound fractures and the amputees had been sent to the hospital. A soldier who had received a severe contusion at the time of the explosion came to Beaumont with "a soft, fluctuating tumor on the point of the buttock." Beaumont simply treated this with poultices until he thought it was time to lance it. This brought a slow discharge of blood and suppuration. He applied another poultice (of black alder bark and flour), and the patient recovered.[36]

As the severely wounded had been removed to the hospital, Beaumont even had time to act the tourist along the Niagara River. On May 11 he attended the auction of the effects of Major General Roger Sheaffe, the British commander at York. In the British flight Sheaffe's baggage had been lost. Sheaffe's "most superb Scarlet coast," which Beaumont said "was the most elegant thing I ever saw, . . . most elegantly embroydered in *Gold*," brought fifty-five dollars. His other items, said Beaumont, were also of good quality, and brought high prices as they were much desired by the American officers. Beaumont attended, very much admired the items on sale, but bought nothing.[37]

A week later, Beaumont visited that "Great Natural Curiosity," Niagara Falls, which he said "at one view impresses the mind of evry [sic] sensible beholder with sublime & reverential, Ideas." Contemplating such a magnificent work of creation, with its gushing waters, spectacular descent, mountains of foam, clouds of fog, and all the colors of the rainbow, he wrote, "would force the incredulity of an Atheist, to acknowledge the existance of a God!" Returning from the falls, he visited an Indian village, and expressed great pleasure at what he saw—industriously cultivated farms, and lands well tilled.[38]

In this part of his life, Beaumont relished his freedom from farm life in Lebanon, and even the action at York had not dimmed his usual optimism. He was proud of being a surgeon's mate, was satisfied with his pay, and enjoyed the excitements of an army life in time of war. Even though he had conjured up the cries of the wounded after the battle of York, he never was overwhelmed by the horrors of war.

Late in May, Beaumont again went into action with his regiment. This time the object of the attack was Fort George, just across the Niagara River below the American post of Niagara. After a bombardment by the American fleet, several thousand American troops were taken across the Niagara River to land about two miles from the British fort. Beaumont was with the vanguard

36. Ibid., 16–17.
37. Ibid., 49.
38. Ibid., 49–50.

of the American force, and he told his brother that he was in one of the first boats to land, with bullets flying like hail around his head. The Americans lost a total of about 150 killed and wounded, but Beaumont escaped unscathed. When the British realized that they were considerably outnumbered, they abandoned the fort and retreated westward. The Americans took possession of Fort George and the town of Newark.[39]

In the aftermath of the battle, Beaumont was attached to the American military hospital that was set up in Newark. This gave him the opportunity to work with Dr. Joseph Lovell, a physician who became of great importance to him later in his life. As the army's surgeon general, he was to be Beaumont's generous patron in his research on digestion. Lovell's background was very different from that of Beaumont. A Bostonian, Lovell had graduated from Harvard Medical School before joining the army medical service. He had become surgeon of the Ninth Regiment, and he had won praise for the work he accomplished when in charge of the military hospital at Burlington, Vermont. Mann thought that Lovell had "an accurate and discriminating mind," and that "as an operative surgeon," was "inferior to none."[40]

Conditions in military hospitals varied considerably in the War of 1812. In general hospitals, such as the one at Burlington, which could hold as many as seven or eight hundred patients in its forty wards, high standards of cleanliness were maintained, and there were usually sufficient hospital surgeons, but conditions in the field, or after battles, were often far more chaotic. Hospitals were set up in tents, barns, or requisitioned buildings, regimental surgeons were frequently hard-pressed in treating the wounded, and infectious diseases flourished in insanitary conditions.[41]

The case in which Beaumont had the opportunity to observe Lovell at work was that of a soldier wounded in the head in the attack on Fort George. Beaumont described the musket ball as depressing a large section of the occipital bone, over the lateral sinus, and lodging under the integuments. The patient had walked about and shown few symptoms, except sporadic nausea and vertigo, during eight or ten days after he received the wound. In describing the case in his journal, Beaumont perhaps enhanced his role in relation to Lovell and the hospital surgeon, Dr. John Moncure Daniel. He wrote that the three of them decided that it was advisable to carry out

39. Ibid., 50–51; Samuel Beaumont to Samuel Beaumont Sr., July 7, 1813, BP, YU.
40. Mann, *Medical Sketches,* 43, 256 (quotation); Estelle Brodman, "Scientific and Editorial Relationships between Joseph Lovell and William Beaumont," 127–32.
41. See Gillett, *Army Medical Department, 1775–1818,* 167–70, 172–75, 177.

the procedure of trephining the skull, to remove the part of the bone that had been damaged by the ball. Beaumont commented that the operation was carried out by Dr. Lovell "in a most adroit & masterly manner." At one point in the operation, when blood gushed from the lateral sinus, Dr. Lovell compressed the sinus with his finger until the fractured pieces could be taken out, and then by compressing it with lint stopped the bleeding. After Lovell put on dressings, "the patient got up and walked about as before, apparently."[42] There is no record of the fate of the patient, but in an age before anesthetics, this was a formidable operation.

On June 21, the hospital staff moved some two hundred wounded a short distance from Newark to the military hospital in Lewiston, New York, where Beaumont assumed duties as assistant hospital surgeon. He was pleased with his hospital assignment, because "the emoluments & advantages are greater than that of a Regimental Mate."[43]

Beaumont had regained his optimism in discussing the troops and their ailments. "The troops are healthy, as usual," he wrote to his father, "& in good spirits—anxious to meet their foe, confident of power to give them a flaying." This was written in spite of his acknowledgment that there were about four hundred sick and wounded at his post.[44]

In reality, the summer was bringing with it great sickness for the American troops. By August 1 there were between six hundred and seven hundred patients, accommodated in barns and tents, which Mann considered comfortable accommodation. During the month of August more than a third of the troops in the area were on sick report. Diarrheas and dysentery were the most prevalent diseases, the troops also suffered from intermittent fevers, and physicians often diagnosed typhus. The patients were generally treated with purges and emetics, followed by opiates and astringents. Later, in writing about the Lewiston hospital, Mann attacked those who had made excessive use of calomel and tartar emetic. There had been 59 deaths out of the 950 to 1,000 patients admitted to the hospital at Lewiston in the last six months of 1813, and nearly half, wrote Mann, were in a ward where tartar emetic was administered injudiciously. He described patients who died with their faces and jaws "dreadfully mutilated" from their medications.[45]

---

42. Miller, ed., *Beaumont's Formative Years,* 17–18.
43. Ibid., 51; Mann, *Medical Sketches,* 62–63; Beaumont to Samuel Beaumont Sr., July 18, 1813, BP, YU.
44. Beaumont to Samuel Beaumont Sr., July 18, 1813, BP, YU.
45. Mann, *Medical Sketches,* 63–89.

The general sickness at Lewiston also severely affected the medical corps; half of the surgeons and mates attached to the regiments were off duty, and of the seven mates on hospital duty, one died, three were given leaves of absence, and the other three were sick for a short time. Beaumont was among the sick. From the middle of August he was unable to perform his duties, and on August 22 he was suspended from active duty and ordered to go to Fort George.[46]

Beaumont remained in military service for the rest of the war, but there is no extant journal depicting his detailed activities. In the fall of 1813 Beaumont apparently accompanied General James Wilkinson from Sackett's Harbor on his abortive attempt to sail down the St. Lawrence, link up with General Wade Hampton, and attack Montreal. The whole attempt was a complete failure. Hampton, who was advancing from Lake Champlain to the Chateaugay River, turned back before reaching the St. Lawrence, and in November, after meeting stiff resistance and hearing of Hampton's withdrawal, Wilkinson abandoned the invasion and went into winter quarters at French Mills on the Salmon River, just across the American border in northern New York.

Beaumont, who was still recovering from his sickness of the previous summer, now spent some very uncomfortable weeks with the rest of the American army in the harshness of a northern winter. Mann commented that until the beginning of January, even the sick had no shelter except tents, and that the mortality rate was high. The medical and hospital supplies had been lost or destroyed in coming down the St. Lawrence. In February the Americans abandoned their position; many of the troops went to Sackett's Harbor, the rest to Plattsburgh.[47] For Beaumont, the sufferings of the northern army only compounded his personal problems. The winter of 1813–1814 also brought sickness and death to the Beaumont family.

William's brother Samuel had remained in Plattsburgh during the war, and was again running a store. From the time of the embargo, Sam had carried out his business endeavors under difficult circumstances, and his latest venture was no exception. Plattsburgh was a vulnerable town, and in late July 1813 the British landed a force that burnt the barracks and the public stores, and also damaged private property. Sam temporarily sent his family some eight miles south of the town for safety, but he was so worried that

---

46. Ibid., 63–67; Miller, ed., *Beaumont's Formative Years,* 51; William S. Miller, "William Beaumont, M.D. (1785–1853)," 31–32.

47. Horsman, *War of 1812,* 123–31; Nelson, *Beaumont,* 40–42; Mann, *Medical Sketches,* 112–24.

he sent his family to Lebanon. He remained in Plattsburgh to look after his business and his property.[48]

Sam's family never saw him again. On December 10 he died of "pleurisy," after a short, severe illness of five days. An express was sent to French Mills to inform his brother, and a family friend who informed Sam's father of his death told him that William was expected to arrive in the very near future.[49] The army was cooperative about granting leave, and Beaumont went to Plattsburgh to help settle his brother's estate. There, in January, he was temporarily reunited with his brother Abel and his sister Lucretia, who came up from Lebanon. The family situation in Plattsburgh and in Connecticut was a little tense, as the Beaumonts were bickering with their brother's widow. Her children were still living in Lebanon, and William thought it would be best if his father became their guardian. Sam's widow would not accept this, made arrangements to keep the guardianship herself, and in May Abel informed his father that Sam's widow expected him to have the children ready when she called for them. Abel commented on her "ingratitude" and on her "constant clamour."[50] This was the sort of dispute that William had been able to escape when he had separated himself from his family, but in the following months he was in the middle of a family squabble and family business. It helped convince him to do everything possible to avoid such complications in the future.

From the time that Beaumont left Lebanon in 1807 it was quite apparent that he was happy to have given up farm life and the responsibilities of living within a large family. He had not the slightest intention of returning permanently to Lebanon, and he was quite reluctant even to visit. His brother Abel also hoped to leave the family farm. Instead of returning home from Plattsburgh, he found temporary work in stores there and in Burlington, and explained to his father that William had encouraged him to stay, with the suggestion that Abel was poorly constituted for the hardships of farm life. Abel decided to study Latin to prepare himself for some future pursuit. Like William he was able to support himself, but unlike William he showed a willingness to send money home; he left fifty dollars for William to send to

48. Peter S. Palmer, *History of Plattsburgh, N.Y.*, 54; John K. Mahon, *The War of 1812*, 136; Samuel Beaumont to Samuel Beaumont Sr., August 8 and September 27, 1813, BP, YU.

49. John J. Freligh to Samuel Beaumont Sr., December 10, 1813, BP, YU.

50. Beaumont to his parents, January 26, 1814, Abel Beaumont to Samuel Beaumont Sr., May 6, 1814, BP, YU.

his sisters. In the spring of 1814, the whole family in Lebanon was sick, and the father, Samuel, died.[51]

William traveled to Lebanon on leave, and late in May requested a further leave of absence because of the continued sickness of his mother, sister, and brother. In July, on returning to duty, he took with him his brother's widow and her two children to escort them to their home in Plattsburgh. Beaumont was to enjoy a good relationship with his own children, and the strained family relationships with his sister-in-law did not prevent him from taking pleasure in the company of his young nephew Carlisle. In Albany, he took him to the museum, and wrote approvingly of his "laughable" questions.

For Abel, the death of his father had shattered his hopes of leaving home. He was now back in Lebanon—the oldest male at home—and Beaumont, as so often in the future, was ready to offer advice rather than practical help. He said he had been much moved when he left the family on this occasion, but that his feelings had been "painfully suppressed by a manly resolution not to suffer a *womanish weakness* to overcome me." Abel was told to be firm and steadfast, and that "perseverance is the parent of success." To "beguile the lonesome hours that will otherwise occur," Beaumont advised him to join the girls "in seeking diversions and amusements in cheerfulness & sociability among yourselves." He was obviously hoping to leave the responsibilities in Lebanon to Abel, and was no longer telling him that he was unfit for farm life.[52]

A month later, after returning to duty, Beaumont sent his mother a formal and carefully thought-out letter of consolation, beginning with "My Mother, My Aged & tender Mother." After citing his father's "excellent precepts & worthy examples," Beaumont suggested to his mother that their grief should be moderated "by reason & common prudence, for, to mourn without measure, is a weakness of nature, a crime & an injury to health and happiness."

On the more practical matters relating to his father's death, Beaumont made it clear that he was leaning on Abel. He suggested that his brother, with some advice from others, would be able to manage the settlement of his father's estate, but that if Abel fell ill, Beaumont himself would attend to it "whatever the sacrifice." He even expressed a willingness to send money if it were needed (though he did not actually enclose any). Beaumont's relief

51. Abel Beaumont to Samuel Beaumont Sr., n.d. [1814], May 6, 1814, BP, YU.
52. Beaumont to the adjutant general, May 28, 1814, WD, AG, LR; Beaumont to Abel Beaumont, July 16, 1814, BP, YU.

at being away from the cheerless scene in Lebanon had been evident in the letter he had written on arriving in Albany a month earlier. He hoped that with Abel back in Lebanon he would be left to pursue his own ambitions in a wider world.

Yet for all his emphasis on perseverance and daily effort as a means to achieve success, Beaumont demonstrated a toleration toward the young and their vagaries that was often missing in the nineteenth century. He felt it necessary to advise his mother that children had a natural propensity "to partake of the customary amusements of juvenile society," and that she should be indulgent with them. "In youth," he wrote, "the mind is naturally prone to volatility & mirth & ought to be freely indulged, otherwise it cramps the rising genius—contracts the boundaries of the soul, suppresses thoughts and chains down the mind to a narrow and limited sphere of action." Beaumont did not confuse hard work and dedication with denial of pleasure.[53]

Beaumont returned to duty at a time of great crisis on the northern frontier, and at a decisive moment in the war. When the war began, many in the United States Congress had been confident that the United States could force changes in British policies by successfully invading Canada. In 1812 and 1813, the attempts at invasion had failed. In 1814 the United States itself was imperiled. In Europe, Napoleon was losing his war. England was now able to transfer large-scale reinforcements to the New World, and to contemplate total victory by invading and crushing the United States. The most important invasion route was by way of Lake Champlain, and Plattsburgh lay directly in the path of the British advance.

When Beaumont rejoined the Sixth Regiment, it was encamped at Cumberland Head, just north of Plattsburgh. In August, the regiment moved north to hold positions near the Canadian border, but Beaumont remained at Cumberland Head with the sick. The men had generally been healthy in the early summer, with the exception of mild intermittent fevers, but in mid-August diarrhea and dysentery occurred with increasing frequency; some men were so sick that they were transferred to the general hospital in Burlington, Vermont. As usual, the treatment was frequent bleeding, purging, and blistering.[54]

53. Beaumont to Lucretia Beaumont, August 16, 1814, BP, YU.

54. Henry Huntt, "An Abstract Account of the Diseases which Prevailed among the Soldiers, Received into the General Hospital, at Burlington, Vermont, during the Summer and Autumn of 1814," 176–79.

The inept planning and deficient execution that had characterized American military actions in so many of the engagements along the Canadian border reached a climax in late August 1814 when American Secretary of War John Armstrong ordered the commander on the Lake Champlain front, Major General George Izard, together with a large part of his force, to march west to Sackett's Harbor. This left fewer than two thousand effective troops to meet a British invasion force of more than ten thousand, most of them veterans of the British campaigns against the French.[55]

On August 31 and September 1, the British invasion force crossed the Canadian border into American territory. Beaumont was now stationed at Fort Moreau, one of the three main defensive positions built to protect Plattsburgh. He remained unperturbed, but told his brother Abel of the panic that had seized the inhabitants of the area. Plattsburgh was "hourly" threatened with attack, and the residents were moving with anything they could carry. Beaumont said many of them loved and upheld the British, blamed the American government for their predicament, and would not take up arms to protect themselves.

Even with the British approaching, Beaumont continued to offer his usual brotherly advice on life and the pursuit of a career. He repeated his message that industry and perseverance were the parents of success, and suggested that Abel should try to get a job in the village school and use part of his wages to hire help for the farm. In seeking the school position, Beaumont's suggestion was to secure the interest of some influential person. The key was to "maneuver right." Beaumont was no longer encouraging Abel to leave Lebanon; he needed him there. Again, he offered financial help if it were needed, though again he did not actually send any money. He said he was waiting for his pay.[56]

Beaumont ended his letter to Abel as he was called to duty. The British had reached Plattsburgh. Beaumont had been given a temporary appointment as "Acting Surgeon" to an artillery company, and on September 6, when the British reached the American fortifications, and in the following days, Beaumont saw considerable action. The British retreated on the eleventh, after the defeat of their fleet in the battle of Plattsburgh Bay, but in the meantime the outnumbered American land forces put up a stiff resistance. The surgeons were in the middle of the action. "During the investment of

55. Everest, *War of 1812 in the Champlain Valley,* 141–59; Horsman, *War of 1812,* 185–87.
56. Beaumont to Abel Beaumont, September 1, 1814, BP, YU.

Plattsburgh by the enemy," James Mann later wrote, "the surgeons were constantly passing from fort to fort, or block-houses, to dress the wounded, exposed to a cross fire of round and grape shot; while the greater part of the army were covered by fortifications." In his letter to Surgeon General James Tilton, Mann specifically mentioned Beaumont, as well as two other surgeon's mates and two surgeons.[57]

Many years later, Plattsburgh residents were asked to give their reminiscences of the battle of Plattsburgh. One or two of them had faint recollections of Beaumont's role in that battle. One woman remembered surgeons borrowing her pair of straight surgeon's scissors to use in dressing three wounded who had sheltered in her house; she thought it was Dr. Beaumont who made use of them. Another remembered hearing his father say that Dr. Beaumont did a good deal of dissecting on the dead soldiers. This story was probably apocryphal, because he also referred to his father being in Beaumont's office afterwards, and Beaumont did not have an office in Plattsburgh until the following year. One later account that was accurate was that when the Americans destroyed a number of Plattsburgh buildings to prevent them providing cover for the British troops, the buildings included the house and store that had been owned by William's brother Samuel, and were now owned by his widow.[58] Samuel had always seemed to be the less fortunate of the two brothers who had left Lebanon for northern New York.

In the weeks following the battle, Beaumont tried to take steps to keep the position of surgeon to which he had been temporarily assigned. On several occasions he had already sought promotion, and he now tried to enlist influential support for his request. To the surgeon general, he pointed out that there were several vacancies for surgeon, both in infantry regiments and the corps of artillery, and that since entering the army in 1812 he had seen almost continuous service.[59]

Along with his letter of request, Beaumont sent supporting documents signed by officers of the corps of artillery and by a variety of other officers at Plattsburgh, including Dr. Thomas Lawson, the surgeon of the Sixth Infantry. Many years later Beaumont was to view Lawson as one of his main enemies. To make sure that his request would not slip by unnoticed, Beaumont

57. Mann to James Tilton, November 1814, in Mann, *Medical Sketches*, 271. For the British attack, see Everest, *War of 1812 in the Champlain Valley*, 161–92; Horsman, *War of 1812*, 188–93.

58. David S. Kellogg, *Recollections of Clinton County and the Battle of Plattsburgh, 1800–1840*, 39, 54.

59. Beaumont to James Tilton, October 10, 1814, WD, AG, LR.

also sent the same request, along with recommendations, to James Monroe, who had replaced Armstrong as secretary of war. Beaumont was also ready with follow-up support. Less than a week later James Mann recommended Beaumont's promotion to the surgeon general, pointing out that it was disappointing to surgeon's mates long in service to see themselves passed by while civilians were appointed directly to the position of surgeon.[60] Beaumont, of course, like many surgeon's mates, had very limited medical credentials, and civilian applicants with better training and wider medical experience, as well as influential connections, were likely to gain precedence.

Beaumont had advised his brother Abel to obtain influential support in seeking a schoolteaching position in Lebanon, and he followed his own advice in seeking promotion. The next letter to reach Tilton came from Colonel Melancton Smith, who had been influential in the Plattsburgh area before the war and who had commanded the fort to which Beaumont had been attached at the beginning of the battle of Plattsburgh. Smith recommended Beaumont's promotion, said he had known him since the beginning of the war, and that his industry "and particular care" that he took of the sick under his charge had been noticed by every officer under whom he had served.[61]

While Beaumont waited anxiously for the result of his application, the war came to an end. In the fall of 1814 there was still fear in Plattsburgh that the British would return in force, but there was to be no more fighting on the Lake Champlain front. When the news reached Europe that the invasion of New York had failed, the British were ready to make peace. The negotiations at Ghent dragged on until Christmas Eve before the treaty ending the war was actually signed, and even then, because of the inability to communicate swiftly across the Atlantic, the battle of New Orleans was still to be fought, but for Beaumont the fighting was over. His future was in the balance.

60. Officers of the Corps of Artillery to Tilton, October 10, 1814, Officers to Tilton, October 10, 1814, Beaumont to James Monroe, October 10, 1814, James Mann to Tilton, October 16, 1814, WD, AG, LR.

61. Melancton Smith to Tilton, October 23, 1814, WD, AG, LR.

THREE

A Plattsburgh Practice

IN THE WINTER OF 1814–1815, Beaumont remained attached to the artillery in Plattsburgh as acting surgeon. There was a shortage of medical personnel at the post, and he was kept very busy with his medical duties; he was able to use this as one of his excuses for not obtaining leave to visit Lebanon. He also used his old excuse of money; in this case probably with good cause. The war and the British blockade had created a financial crisis for the United States government, and in January 1815 Beaumont told his brother that he had not been paid for seven months. At the same time, he advised Abel to improve his time and his opportunities, and to keep clear from "the shackle of matrimony" and the influence of passion until "a well known worthy object" should attract his attention.

Less than a year earlier, Beaumont had encouraged Abel to give up farming, but with Abel needed to ease any obligations that he might have in Lebanon, he used the news of peace to suggest that farming might now become a profitable and honorable occupation. With the death of his father, Beaumont was clearly hoping that Abel could be persuaded to fill the role of provider and adviser for his mother and sisters, allowing Beaumont himself to continue to pursue his own career. He was still in touch with Margaret, his late brother's wife, but, like Abel, he had few kind words for her. He admitted she was bearing up well under the loss of her property at the time of the battle of Plattsburgh, but he did not like her. "She fawns, flatters & tries to curry favor," he told Abel, "but I am not moved by her freaks or her flatteries."[1]

---

1. Beaumont to Abel Beaumont, January 9, 1815, BP, YU.

In the winter of 1814–1815, Beaumont was more comfortable than he had been for much of the war. The British had not returned to Plattsburgh, and Beaumont, along with a fellow army medical officer, Dr. Peleg Mason, was boarding in a private house in the town. They were, said Beaumont, "constant companions, mess mates, & bedfellows." After news of the Treaty of Ghent had arrived, Beaumont was giving much thought to his future career, because it was yet unclear what military establishment the United States would retain in peacetime. More than anything else Beaumont was interested in whether he could achieve his promotion to surgeon.[2]

The future arrangements of the army were much on the mind of military men in early 1815. It was soon learned that the army was to be reduced to ten thousand men, with the army medical corps suffering badly. The office of surgeon general was abolished, and the number of physicians sharply reduced. There were far fewer regiments, but still only one surgeon and two mates were to be allocated to each, along with twelve post surgeons per division. The hospital corps was reduced to five surgeons and fifteen hospital mates. In March 1815 the secretary of war contacted commanders of the various units to ask them confidentially to rate their officers in three categories: highest, good, and moderate. Many who wanted to stay in the army would be forced to leave, and some who wished to stay would lose the brevet rank that they had acquired during the war.[3]

Late in March 1815, Beaumont was still waiting for news of the army's decision on its future composition, and for his pay, which was now ten months overdue. Fortunately his brother Abel was being helpful. He told Beaumont that no difficulties had arisen in the settlement of their father's estate, and he had no immediate need of money. With Abel taking responsibility, and not asking for money, Beaumont was happy to be cooperative. There were decisions to be taken regarding the final disposition of the land and property owned by his father, and Beaumont took the attitude that he would approve anything that was equitable and just, and would not make any difficulty. He told Abel that his share could be assigned for the benefit of the family, so long as he retained the title in case future adversity meant that he would need it for his own support.

Again Beaumont suggested to Abel that it would be best for him and the younger brother, John, to improve and cultivate the farm as effectively as

2. Ibid., February 26, 1815, BP, YU.

3. Gillett, *Army Medical Department, 1775–1818*, 186–87; Secretary of War to the C. O. of the 29th Infantry Regt., March 14, 1815, BC, WU.

possible until some opportunities arose to shift the property into some other line of business. There was no need, he wrote, for them to tie themselves as slaves to the plough, the hoe, or the ax, "but be content & industrious, diligent & persevering, prudent & economical, & you may be sure of an easy subsistence till better fortune befalls you." He suggested that a man be hired for six or nine months of the year–"at a reasonable price." If the expense was difficult, then they could call on him.

Abel would have to have been remarkably patient not to have felt some irritation at his elder brother who was free with his advice but short on practical help or money. Only the previous year, Abel had determined to commit himself totally to the study of Latin in the hope of improving his lot in the world, and leaving the farm as two of his brothers had done before him. It could only have been irritating to have his elder brother tell him that his task in Lebanon was "hard & confining, though not difficult." The extent of William's family duty was his continued involvement in the settlement of his brother Samuel's estate, a matter that still lingered in the spring of 1815.[4]

With the army at peace, its personnel had the time to bicker, and in the spring of 1815 Beaumont was involved in a bitter, public dispute with Captain George H. Richards of the artillery corps. Beaumont knew his adversary well. They had both served at the battle of Plattsburgh, and Richards was one of the artillery officers supporting Beaumont's request for promotion. The precise origins of this personal dispute are obscure, but it burst into public view in June when Beaumont had details of the entire affair printed and issued as a circular. It appears that Beaumont had originally been offended at remarks made about him by Richards. He had been so incensed that he had asked for a military tribunal to look into them. This had produced no satisfaction, and in private correspondence he had attacked Richards's character. Early in June, Beaumont sent a friend, Captain Henry Shell, to challenge Richards to a duel, and it soon became apparent that the surgeon's mate was more willing to resort to arms than the captain of artillery.[5]

Another lieutenant testified that he had been present when Shell delivered the note, and said that Richards accepted the communication, at least verbally, threatened Shell for bringing it, apparently half-apologized for using

4. Beaumont to Abel Beaumont, March 25, 1815, BP, YU.
5. The discussion of the Richards case in this and the following three paragraphs is based on the material in the circular issued by Beaumont on June 11, 1815. There is a copy of the original in BC, WU. It is printed in facsimile in Myer, *Beaumont*, 58–59.

derisory language about Beaumont, and seemingly was desirous of "burying the hatchet." After Shell had left, Captain Richards compounded his problems. He went to another officer, said that he had refused to accept the challenge from Beaumont, "on account of his not being a gentleman," and implied that he would accept a challenge from Shell. He said that he had documents in his possession that would convince Shell that Beaumont was no gentleman. After hearing Richards's explanation, the officer refused to take a note to Shell, and apparently Richards delivered it himself, leaving it on a table. It repeated the assertion that as Beaumont was no gentleman, Richards would not apologize, explain, nor fight him, but he would challenge Shell.

Beaumont was never a man to temporize, and having read Richards's own explanation of the events, he issued a brief statement: "I hereby proclaim to the world, that Captain G. H. Richards, of the corps of Artillery, is a contemptible *liar*, a base villain, and a poltroon." He printed this, along with an account of the affair, and strong endorsements from the officers in Plattsburgh, in his circular. Captain William Hazard of the Sixth Regiment stated that he had been intimately acquainted with Beaumont for two years, that he considered him a gentleman and a man of honor, and that Richards had lied when he quoted Hazard to the effect that Beaumont was no gentleman.

What was even more gratifying to Beaumont, and what must have been a major blow to Richards, was that the circular contained an endorsement of Beaumont's position signed by thirty-seven army officers, stating that Richards had disgraced himself and was "guilty of conduct unbecoming an officer and gentleman" when he attempted by cowardly means to evade Beaumont's challenge after having traduced and attempted to injure his character. They also stated that they believed Beaumont to have been actuated by no other principle than that which honor and justice dictated "to every gentleman" in such a situation.

The whole affair petered out after the circular, but Beaumont's actions in this matter were typical of his actions throughout his life. He was quick to anger, extremely protective of his rights and character, and quite extreme in language when irate. On this occasion, the original cause of the quarrel was compounded by Richards's repeated comment that this former farm boy and surgeon's mate was no gentleman. Since leaving Lebanon, Beaumont had been determined to rise in the world, and was already pleased at what he considered to be an important change in status achieved through his medical training. He even viewed his position as surgeon's mate with more pride than was typical among either successful physicians or the general public. Without the status of regular army officers, army surgeons were in an anomalous position that was unsatisfactory to many physicians who had pretensions to status in the world outside of the army.

Beaumont's hopes of further recognition by promotion to the more prestigious position of surgeon were dashed in June 1815, when he was offered the position of surgeon's mate of the Eighth Regiment. It was small consolation that this reflected extremely well on him. The army and its medical service was being slashed, and he had been chosen as one of those who could remain in the peacetime force. But the proposed rank was a major disappointment. Beaumont had set his heart on promotion to surgeon, and he was not prepared to accept less. He declined the appointment, and was officially discharged from the army on June 15.[6]

Though he would almost certainly have remained in the army if he had been promoted, he was probably also influenced in his decision to resign by the circle of friends he was acquiring in Plattsburgh and by his confidence that he could establish a successful practice there. The peaceful winter of 1814–1815 had been a pleasant one for Beaumont. He liked the Frelighs, the family he was boarding with, and he had a good friend in his fellow boarder, Dr. Peleg Mason. He had commented in March that in the course of the previous winter he had "enjoyed much satisfaction & friendly sociability."[7]

In June 1815, as soon as he left the army, Beaumont began the private practice of medicine in Plattsburgh. The town had been founded shortly after the end of the Revolution by Zephaniah Platt and a large group of associates. Although it had grown slowly, it was the most important town in large Clinton County, and substantial business was carried on there. As it was more than 150 miles north of Albany, and only 60 miles by water to Montreal, its most important commercial ties in its early years were northward to Canada. This had hurt the town badly in the years of economic coercion and war from 1807 to 1815, but it appeared that the town had excellent prospects for prosperity and would be a suitable location for a young doctor in the years after the war.[8]

At the last census, in 1810, Plattsburgh's population had been greater than three thousand, but many of its inhabitants were scattered outside the village proper, and the war had scattered some even farther. On the eve of the war, four physicians had catered to the population in Plattsburgh and the surrounding area, and the profession had begun to organize. In 1807,

---

6. Beaumont to the adjutant general, June 3, 1815, WD, AG, LR.
7. Beaumont to Abel Beaumont, March 25, 1815, BP, YU.
8. Palmer, *History of Plattsburgh*, 5–24; Morse, *American Gazetteer*, entry for Plattsburgh.

three Plattsburgh physicians had met with three others from the county and organized the Clinton County Medical Society. This society had continued to hold its meetings in Plattsburgh even during the years of war. Although Beaumont began the practice of medicine in Plattsburgh in 1815, he did not join the society until four years later.[9]

Beaumont's first summer in private practice was a busy one. In September he told his mother that the season had been "quite sickly," and that he was writing when he should have been out visiting his patients. Perhaps exaggerating a little, he said he was called out of bed nearly every night, and that three nights out of five he did not even undress. He was trying to impress her with the size of his practice, and, as usual, he was also making excuses for not finding time to visit Lebanon. He did, however, say that if he found it possible to leave his practice during the winter, he would come home, and if his mother gave her consent, he would bring one of his sisters back with him.

Beaumont perhaps thought it was necessary to make a future promise about one of his sisters, because once again he was apologizing for not sending any money; an apology made more difficult because in the same letter he was also bragging about the size of his practice. He said he was still trusting the management of the estate to Abel, and would have sent fifty or sixty dollars if it had been in his power earlier. It had not been possible, he wrote, because he had only just received his army pay. If Abel needed money he should write. He pointed out, however, that he was using his back pay to pay his debts. It was typical of Beaumont to be apologizing for not sending money in the past, promising to send it if needed in the future, but not sending any now.

As he was now able to say that he planned to make Plattsburgh his place of permanent residence, he suggested that perhaps his mother might consider selling up in Lebanon and making the family's home in Plattsburgh. How serious this suggestion was is hard to tell; he immediately followed it with the comment that though this would be in the best interest of the children, his mother presumably could never reconcile her feelings to leaving Lebanon.[10]

A very practical reason why Beaumont was not keen to send money home was that he was about to invest in a new business. Late in 1815 he went into partnership with Dr. German Senter, who had entered the army as a surgeon's mate in 1812 and had achieved promotion to the rank of surgeon

9. *History of Clinton and Franklin Counties,* 132–34, 13, 290; Palmer, *History of Plattsburgh,* 29, 33–40.

10. Beaumont to Lucretia Beaumont, September 5, 1815, BP, YU.

in 1814. Senter, like Beaumont, had left the army in mid-June 1815. The partnership involved more than a medical practice, for when in December 1815 Beaumont and Senter advertised that they had opened their office in the upper part of what had been a store in Plattsburgh, they also notified the public that they had opened their own store. This was to carry a general assortment of drugs, medicines, groceries, dye woods, and related articles. Medicines would be "put up with accuracy and care."[11]

The partnership with Senter was short-lived. In May 1816 Senter was reinstated in the army medical service as a post surgeon. Beaumont, however, quickly found a replacement. This was a former officer, Phineas Wheelock, who was not a physician. Presumably, the plan was for Wheelock to run the store while Beaumont handled the practice and the medicines. Their plans were quite ambitious. They announced in the *Plattsburgh Republican* in September 1816 that they had just received a large assortment of groceries, which included a variety of wines and liquors, molasses, tea, coffee, sugar, rice, spices, tobacco, pipes, fish, chocolate, "Spanish Segars," window glass, powder, and shot. They added, almost as an afterthought, that they also had a large assortment of drugs, medicines, and dye woods.[12]

Reality did not live up to the advertisement, and this store closed just about as quickly as the one Beaumont had opened in Champlain with Pomeroy before the War of 1812. In November there was an announcement in the *Plattsburgh Republican* that the late firm of Wheelock and Beaumont was "this day" dissolved. Those owing money were given only a week to pay before accounts would be placed in the hands of an attorney for collection.[13]

Beaumont was finding that Plattsburgh had not prospered to the extent that he had expected. A general lack of dramatic growth was compounded by special problems in 1816 and 1817. The summer of 1816 was a strange one, in which there was snow in the town as late as June 6. This was followed by a particularly severe drought, with no rain in August or September. Widespread fires throughout the country increased the distress, and in the winter of 1816–1817 bread was so expensive that many could not afford it.[14]

---

11. *Plattsburgh Republican,* December 6, 1815; Francis B. Heitman, *Historical Register and Dictionary of the United States Army,* vol. 1, 874.

12. *Plattsburgh Republican,* September 6, 1816; Heitman, *Historical Register,* vol. 1, 1025.

13. *Plattsburgh Republican,* November 16, 1816.

14. Palmer, *History of Plattsburgh,* 46–47; Cynthia DeHaven Pitcock, "The Career of William Beaumont, 1785–1853: Science and the Self-Made Man in America," 32–33.

A period of economic distress always made it difficult for physicians to collect their debts, and it was perhaps because of diminished prospects that in December 1816 Beaumont attempted to enter the medical service of the American navy. As usual, Beaumont sought the most influential support he could muster; in this case Thomas Macdonough, the naval hero who had commanded the American fleet at the battle of Plattsburgh Bay. In supporting Beaumont, Macdonough stated he had considerable acquaintance with him during the last war. Macdonough's support was not enough. The attempt to enter the navy was unsuccessful. As chance would have it, Beaumont remained on land and was eventually given an opportunity for fame.[15]

There are few detailed sources for Beaumont's medical practice in the years immediately following the war, but there are indications that Beaumont was still anxious to expand his medical knowledge. One way he apparently sought to do this was through dissection. In the summer of 1816, Beaumont was given the body of a man who had hanged himself in his cell to forestall the executioner. There was precedent in Plattsburgh for handing over for medical dissection the bodies of those who had been executed. During the War of 1812, the body of a soldier who was hanged for murder was given to the president of the Clinton County Medical Society.[16]

The memory of Beaumont and his body remained in local Plattsburgh lore throughout the nineteenth century. One resident told a story, most likely embellished, of Beaumont receiving the body of the murderer and hanging it up by a fireplace in a cellar kitchen, "to dry out like a piece of mutton." He said he never knew what became of the skeleton, but one of Beaumont's nieces later wrote that two skeletons that Beaumont had received from the local judge hung in a stairway leading to an unfinished attic in the inn of Beaumont's future father-in-law. One of them, she said, was "in armor of dark-red arteries and bright-scarlet veins," the other was "a stark corpse of naked bones."[17]

If these memories are correct, it is possible that Beaumont made use of the skeleton with marked arteries and veins as an aid in teaching his cousin Samuel Beaumont. Samuel was the son of Beaumont's uncle William. He apprenticed with Beaumont at this time, and in March 1819 was examined

15. Macdonough to the secretary of the navy, December 30, 1816, in F. L. Pleadwell, "William Beaumont and the Navy," 107.

16. Palmer, *History of Plattsburgh*, 43–44; *History of Clinton and Franklin Counties*, 120. See also Kellogg, *Recollections*, 20–21.

17. Myer, *Beaumont*, 67n.

by the Clinton County Medical Society and licensed to practice medicine and surgery. Beaumont himself had only been admitted to membership in the society two months before, and it seems likely that, at a time when he was expecting to leave Plattsburgh, he had joined the society for the benefit of his cousin. After gaining his license, Samuel, who had already been studying with Beaumont for about four years, assisted him in his practice.[18] Samuel was later to be of considerable help to Beaumont at the time he was publishing the results of his experiments on human digestion.

Given Beaumont's desire for recognition and status, one would have expected him to have joined the Clinton County Medical Society as soon as he began private practice in Plattsburgh. His apprenticeship, his Vermont license, and his army service were certainly sufficient credentials in this provisional settlement, or anywhere else. In view of his touchy personality and later record, it is possible, however, that the delay was due either to some personal quarrel or to some perceived slight. In November 1817 his stint as treasurer of a local debating society–The Forum–ended abruptly when he took offense at an action of the society that he believed reflected on his integrity. He submitted a letter of resignation to the president, carefully listing an income of $15.13 with an outlay of exactly the same amount, and a balance of zero. He then resigned with the hope that his successor would be "a person of adequate honesty and responsibility" to take care of the funds, and that he might not, "like his predecessor in that office, be indirectly impeached for a breach of trust by any unprecedented order of the Society without his knowledge or "the least shadow of a reason assigned for such an egregious imposition upon every honest and manly feeling." Beaumont had a very thin skin, and was particularly sensitive when the subject was money.[19]

Beginning in 1817, Beaumont again began to note in his journals cases that he thought particularly interesting, usually those in which there had been a recovery after extreme sickness. In February 1817, Beaumont described in some detail a case involving complications after childbirth. Having given birth to "a fine large healthy boy," his patient, within half an hour, complained of a pain in the pit of her stomach. She tried to treat it with paregoric, but the pain increased rapidly and led to violent retching of "monstrous foetid black bilious matter." After an hour of this, Beaumont gave a "gentle" emetic of ipecac and iron sulfate. It gave momentary relief, but had no

18. *History of Clinton and Franklin Counties,* 134; Myer, *Beaumont,* 67–68; Beaumont to Joseph Lovell, October 12, 1819, WD, AG, LR.
19. Statement of funds of the Forum, BC, WU; see also Myer, *Beaumont,* 63.

permanent effect. The patient now went into spasms "of the most alarming nature." These went on, at irregular intervals, for three days, depriving her of "reason or recollection." The spasms brought "a horrid distortion of the whole features," and ended in a general and violent convulsion, difficulty breathing, frothing at the mouth, and general exhaustion. These episodes left the patient comatose, until the onset of the next spasm.

Beaumont wrote that he administered the most powerful antispasmodics—large doses of opium, castor (a bitter substance taken from beavers), ether, amber, warm baths, friction, and "injections." All these were useless in preventing or easing the convulsions for about thirty-six hours. Beaumont claimed that he finally had results by administering eight grains of calomel and three grains of musk every two hours, along with blisters on the extremities, a large blister on the abdomen, and the use of "stimulating injections."

Forty hours after the initial attack, the patient experienced some relief, and Beaumont continued to use musk in smaller doses with camphor and ipecac every four hours. He also gave her daily purges, along with frequent injections of an infusion of senna, alternating with yeast or broth, and, for nourishment, arrowroot with a small quantity of wine and chicken broth. He noted that within a month the patient could ride a mile or two, and within five or six weeks resumed her domestic duties. Beaumont made particular note of the fact that when his patient began to regain her reason she had lost her memory of even important events for longer than the previous year, and her memory of this period only came back slowly as she regained her health and strength.[20] Beaumont described this case in detail, and was obviously proud of his patient's recovery.

There are indications that Beaumont's reputation was growing. In 1819 he was called in by another local physician, Dr. Benjamin Mooers, who was suffering from a "severe attack of fever." Arriving at midnight, Beaumont administered twenty grains of calomel—a very large dose—and applied cold vinegar to his head. Later, Beaumont bled sixteen ounces from his patient and gave him an enema. He continued with a cathartic of eight grains of calomel followed by ten grains of ipecac. After prolonged treatment, Beaumont noted, Dr. Mooers began a rapid convalescence.[21]

A case in which even Beaumont must have had some difficulty believing that his treatments had effected the cure was that of Mrs. Wheeler, who was

20. Miller, ed., *Beaumont's Formative Years,* 26–28, 35.
21. Medical and Physical Journal, commenced November 1, 1818, BC, WU.

bitten by a supposedly rabid cat. Beaumont was called to the patient one and a half hours after the incident, and found that she had a slight wound on her foot. He cut out the whole of the wounded part and dressed it with the leaves of Alysma plantago (the water plantain). In his personal papers Beaumont had a clipping from an English newspaper that described Alysma plantago as an "Effectual Cure for Hydrophobia," a cure that was said to have been once known only to a Russian peasant. Beaumont ordered the dressing to be kept constantly wet with salt, vinegar, and water. He also gave purges of ten grains of calomel, and later of calomel with rhubarb.

In two or three days the wound became very inflamed, swollen, and painful, and the patient was feverish. On about the fifth day Beaumont gave an emetic, and the fever went. The foot was now treated at night with a charcoal poultice with yeast, "sometimes alternated with carrots," and in the daytime was dressed with calomel and carbon. The wound was completely covered with scar tissue within a month, but the patient then felt sharp pains in the sore, and in her foot and leg, and piercing pains in her head. She also developed "a wild, glary appearance in her eyes," though she was perfectly composed and rational. The sore on the foot had ceased to discharge, and was "of a dark, livid color." Beaumont assumed these to be the approaching symptoms of hydrophobia and prescribed doses of calomel. He also told her to apply a charcoal or carrot poultice, and to keep the sore covered with calomel. He also made use of another plant–Scutellaria lateriflora (Skullcap)–which he said he had discovered a few days before. In the form of a strong decoction, the patient was to drink a gill of it in the morning, and then was to drink a mild decoction throughout the day. She was also to use it to wash the sore. Eventually, more than two months after the original bite, Beaumont pronounced her perfectly recovered.[22] Although the patient obviously never had rabies, presumably Beaumont's incision on her foot had become infected.

Even in the case of young children, Beaumont believed in rapid and large-scale intervention. To a one-year-old child with "Spotted Fever," Beaumont gave a variety of medications including two grains of calomel and grains of ipecac every three hours. Later he gave five grains of calomel and five grains of ipecac. He also applied blisters to the soles of the child's feet.[23]

Beaumont had been trained in an age of heroic medicine, and he continued to have faith in early and large-scale medical intervention, particularly in the

22. Ibid. Beaumont's account of this case is partially reprinted in Myer, *Beaumont,* 64–66.
23. Medical and Physical Journal, commenced November 1, 1818, BC, WU.

general use of purges and emetics. He also made use of botanical preparations, and there was a tradition among Beaumont's descendants that he had
acquired a knowledge of botanical preparations when he was an apprentice
under Dr. Chandler.[24]

Although Beaumont's attempt to join the naval medical service resulted in
failure, he was given new hope of reentering military service when in 1818
the army underwent a general reorganization. In this reorganization, a new
central medical department was put under the command of Joseph Lovell
as surgeon general. The positions of post surgeon, regimental surgeon, and
regimental surgeon's mate were retained, but those of hospital surgeon and
hospital mate were eliminated. Congress authorized, as before, one surgeon
and two mates to each regiment, and set a maximum of forty post surgeons.
Medical officers, however, were still left in an anomalous situation. They
were commissioned, but they had no rank.[25]

In June 1818 Beaumont wrote to Lovell asking for appointment as a post
or regimental surgeon, stating that he was "conscious of his just claims,
and adequate qualifications" and that he felt assured of Lovell's "friendship
and interest." He also pointed out that he had the backing of the army
officers stationed in Plattsburgh, and of the officers who were convened
there for the purposes of a court martial. Beaumont also wrote to Secretary
of War John C. Calhoun with the same request, stressing both the quality
of his recommendations and his nearly three years of "arduous service" as
surgeon's mate of the Sixth Regiment.[26]

Beaumont was backed by strong supporting letters from a variety of officers in Plattsburgh. Lieutenant Colonel Josiah Snelling of the Sixth Regiment
submitted a letter signed by himself and sixteen or so other officers, stating
that they had for a long time been well acquainted, most of them intimately,
with Beaumont as a physician and surgeon. They praised his service in
the war, his character as a gentleman, and his attainments. Colonel Henry
Atkinson of the Sixth Regiment recommended Beaumont "as a man of first
standing & respectability, both as a Gentleman and a Physician." It was as

24. See Deborah B. Martin, "Doctor William Beaumont: His Life in Mackinac and
Wisconsin, 1820–1834," 264–65.
25. Mary C. Gillett, *The Army Medical Department, 1818–1865*, 27–34; Wyndham D.
Miles, *A History of the National Library of Medicine: The Nation's Treasury of Medical
Knowledge*, 1–3; Edwin S. Marsh, "The United States Army and Its Health, 1819–1829,"
502–5.
26. Beaumont to Lovell, June 10, 1818, to John C. Calhoun, June 12, 1818, WD, AG,
LR.

though the officers in Plattsburgh remembered or had been told of the public dispute that had swirled around Beaumont's quarrel with Captain Richards of the artillery in 1815, and were as anxious to confirm Beaumont's status as a gentleman as to attest to his excellence as a physician.[27]

In writing to Surgeon General Lovell, Atkinson was even warmer in his support of Beaumont. He referred to "Our mutual friend," Beaumont, as a late "brother in arms," known by them both to possess "much merit & much skill in his profession." This was no cursory letter of recommendation.[28]

A recommendation, which is revealing of Beaumont's own feelings, was sent to Lovell by Lieutenant Colonel Abram Eustis of the artillery. He said he had become acquainted with Beaumont while he had been at Plattsburgh to take part in a court martial. "I find him here engaged in a very extensive practice," he wrote, "for which however he gets very little pay, & he is therefore desirous to return to the army as a Post or Regimental Surgeon." Eustis wrote that Beaumont's reputation for professional skill was greater than that of any other physician in that part of New York state in which he lived, and that his "anatomical preparations" offered abundant proof of his attention to the art of surgery. One can imagine Beaumont showing Eustis his office, while telling him of his extensive practice, his reputation, and the poor rewards. He may well have had trouble collecting his bills, but if his practice was really extensive it is questionable whether he would have wanted to return to the colors.

Eustis obviously had become impressed in his brief acquaintance with Beaumont. He said he was persuaded that Lovell would prefer to get "one such as Beaumont to a hundred *Waterhouses* & being sure that he would be of infinitely more service to the army." Benjamin Waterhouse, who was a well-known physician, had obviously rubbed Eustis the wrong way either in person or with his ideas, and this was an occasion when Beaumont's modest background, combined with active service, had much helped his cause.[29]

At first, Beaumont's application seemed to go well. He had excellent backing, and on the reverse of his letter to the secretary of war, Lovell added, "I know Dr. Beaumont to be well qualified." Also, in writing to Calhoun later in June, Lovell commented that "from a personal acquaintance with him I can recommend him," but there was a catch in his endorsement. He also

27. Josiah Snelling et al. to John C. Calhoun, June 12, 1818, Henry Atkinson to John C. Calhoun, June 12, 1818, WD, AG, LR.
28. Henry Atkinson to Lovell, June 12, 1818, WD, AG, LR.
29. Abraham Eustis to Lovell, June 13, 1818, WD, AG, LR.

stated that he had already recommended another physician as a candidate for the *first* vacancy as post surgeon. Lovell was a fair man who was later to give very great help to Beaumont, but there were few positions as post surgeon open, and there were more qualified applicants than were needed to fill them.[30]

For the time being, Lovell could not place Beaumont as a post surgeon, but he liked him and his work, and wanted to make use of him. He offered him a position as an assistant or clerk in his new office in Washington, D.C., at a salary of one thousand dollars a year. At first Beaumont accepted, but then he had second thoughts. He assumed that Lovell was offering him this position until he was able to place him elsewhere, but he was concerned about the future attitude of Congress toward the army and the medical department. He expressed these doubts to Lovell, and finally decided to remain in Plattsburgh, still hoping that something would open up for him in the army.[31]

In the winter of 1818–1819 the local military commandant, lacking a replacement for his surgeon, employed Beaumont to carry out the medical duties of the post. The Sixth Regiment had moved out, but they had left some of their sick behind. These men and a detachment from another regiment had no army physician to serve them. In the early spring Beaumont also received a commission as surgeon to the Fifteenth New York militia (cavalry), signed by Governor De Witt Clinton. Beaumont was a political supporter of Clinton and had placed his name on a long list of those urging Clinton's reelection.[32]

Beaumont's surgical experience in the War of 1812 had served him well, and for the rest of his career he was acknowledged to have a surgical specialty. In the spring of 1819 he was called in as consultant in the case of a woman with a rapidly growing breast tumor. The tumor he removed weighed some six ounces, and in his rough notes on the case he demonstrated that in this age of surgery without anesthetics he had difficulty in simply taking a detached medical view of his patient. He commented about "the life of a valuable human being in my hands," and wrote with feeling of the operation itself: "The operation was excruciatingly painful & protracted yet she endured

---

30. Joseph Lovell to John C. Calhoun, June 25, 1818, WD, AG, LR.
31. Beaumont to Lovell, December 18, 1818, War Department, RG 94, Office of the Adjutant General, Individual Medical Officers Folders (William Beaumont), National Archives, Washington, D.C. Hereafter cited as WD, AG, IMOF.
32. William Worth to Lovell, March 19, 1819, Beaumont to Joseph Lovell, August 3, 1819, WD, AG, IMOF. Beaumont's commission as surgeon in the New York militia, April 6, 1819, BC, WU.

it without a struggle, without fainting & without a murmur, & almost without a groan, bearing the most painful operation that can necessarily be performed on the human frame" with the fortitude of a Christian and the resignation of a Saint. In the week after the operation Beaumont's patient improved, but there are no notes of the eventual disposition of the case.[33]

War service had not deadened Beaumont to human suffering, but he was a man who combined considerable imagination with a certain pettiness in mundane matters. He took the time in February 1819 to advertise that the "person who took a small glass SAND BOX from the office of Doct. Beaumont, is requested to return it, and save their reputation, as it is well ascertained who the offender is."[34] Beaumont never forgot that he had to make his own way in the world, and that every penny counted.

As his years away from home increased, Beaumont was growing apart from his family in Lebanon. When writing to them in early 1819, he was obliged to apologize to them for not having written in about a year. He said he was in good health, "neither mad, nor crazy–in love–nor intoxicated," and commented that he had more business than he could attend to, "much of it perplexing–I have been embarrassed but hope soon to be extricated." What his embarrassment had been is not specified, though he seems to connect it with "business."[35] It is possible, however, that his problems were personal, which might explain his cryptic comments to the effect that he was not mad, crazy, in love, or intoxicated.

In June 1819 the editor of the *Plattsburgh Republican* printed a brief account to the effect that he had received a handbill, signed by Lucy Williams, "attacking the character of Dr. William Beaumont." She had asked all printers to insert it in their papers. The editor, a friend of Beaumont's, gave him his full support. His comment was that "living in the neighborhood of Dr. Beaumont, and having been intimately acquainted with him since his first settlement in this place–and knowing also the light in which this Miss Williams is generally regarded–we are much surprised that any printer could have been found, whom money would have induced to put so scurrilous a production in print."[36]

The editor did not repeat the accusation, but there is some much later evidence that Beaumont was perhaps not quite as innocent as the editor

33. Manuscript draft of 1818–1819 case [c. April 1819], BC, WU.
34. *Plattsburgh Republican*, February 20, 1819.
35. Beaumont to his family, February 21, 1819, BP, YU.
36. *Plattsburgh Republican*, June 19, 1819.

indicated. More than sixty-five years later, Mrs. Mary Torrey, a woman of ninety, was interviewed in Plattsburgh about its early history. Among her reminiscences, which their editor rightly comments have "the ring of truth," was the statement that "Bill Beaumont was a bachelor. He kept around a girl here till he ruined her. Her name was Lucy Williams." This was not included in any general attack on Beaumont, for she also said: "He was a good doctor. He doctored our family by the year for thirty dollars a year."[37]

Beaumont had very probably remained a bachelor with the specific intent of making his way in the world before taking on the financial and other obligations of a family. He had to live on what he earned, and until 1815 this had mainly consisted of what he had been able to make as a schoolteacher and as a surgeon's mate. He was always extremely careful with money, and his advice to his brother Abel had been to avoid any premature commitment until he had become established. Yet Beaumont was now thirty-three years old, and there are indications both in his letters and in his journals that his thoughts wandered a good deal from social mobility and medicine. It was about this time that between two cases in his medical journal he copied out several quotations from Robert Burns. The first was Burns's comment that there was no talking or writing "with an amiable fine woman, without some mixture of that most delicious passion, whose most devoted slave I have more than once had the honor of being." He also copied the comment, "To be feelingly alive to kindness & to unkindness, is a charming female character."

It is certainly possible that Beaumont's jottings were stimulated by thoughts of Deborah Platt, the woman he was going to marry–these were the years in which he was getting to know her–though he ends the series of quotes with a Burns comment beginning: "How wretched is the condition of one who is haunted with conscious guilt–& trembling under the idea of dreaded vengeance!"[38] It seems quite possible that as Beaumont was beginning to court the woman he was eventually to marry, he was also seeing Lucy Williams. Local gossip remembered Lucy Williams as "ruined" by Beaumont. It could mean she became pregnant, but it may simply have meant that she had confirmed the ruin of her local reputation, which the editor of the *Plattsburgh Republican* had questioned, by publishing a handbill advertising that she had been betrayed by Beaumont. Beaumont had considered the possibility of returning to military service since 1816. Now, with an angry and

37. Kellogg, *Recollections*, 22 and 22n.
38. Miller, ed., *Beaumont's Formative Years*, 28.

hurt woman publicly attacking his character in the small town of Plattsburgh, a military appointment undoubtedly seemed even more desirable.

In the previous year, when Beaumont had sought support for his attempt to reenter the army medical service, he had obtained a letter of recommendation from a personal acquaintance, Captain Nathan Towson of the artillery. In August 1819, Towson became paymaster general of the army, and Beaumont, knowing that his recommendation would now carry more weight, wrote to him again asking for his renewed support in seeking an appointment as a post or regimental surgeon in the army, or even as surgeon or mate in the navy. He was particularly interested in filling a vacancy for a light-artillery surgeon, and asked Towson to use his influence jointly with that of the surgeon general.[39]

By late November, Beaumont heard informally that his application had been successful. He was not given a position with the light artillery, but in December he received a formal offer of a position as post surgeon. He promptly accepted it. He had already announced in the *Plattsburgh Republican* that he was ending his practice, and asked for a settling of accounts. He also asked for debts outstanding to the old partnership of Beaumont and Senter, and even to the estate of his dead brother, Samuel. He recommended his old patients to the care of his cousin. Sam Beaumont had hoped to enter the army as a surgeon's mate, and Beaumont had recommended him, but he failed to secure an appointment.[40]

For much of his career in the army, Beaumont sought favors from Surgeon General Lovell, and it was appropriate that one of his first acts after appointment was to ask Lovell if it could be arranged for him to delay in reporting for duty. He said that he needed two or three months to settle his own and his late brother's business affairs.[41] Beaumont wanted maximum time to collect any money owed to him before he left town, but it is also possible that the request for delay was concerned with thoughts of marriage. He now had someone in mind, but she had been married before and was not yet free to marry.

The woman Beaumont had in mind was Mrs. Deborah Platt, née Green, whose father, Israel, owned an inn that figured prominently in the early history of Plattsburgh. It was often used for meetings, including those of the

39. Nathan Towson to John C. Calhoun, June 11, 1818, Beaumont to Towson, October 12, 1819, Towson to John C. Calhoun, November 10, 1819, WD, AG, LR.

40. Beaumont to C. Vandeventer, December 21, 1819, to Joseph, October 12, 1819, WD, AG, LR; *Plattsburgh Republican*, December 11, 1819.

41. Beaumont to Lovell, December 21, 1819, WD, AG, LR.

Clinton County Medical Society, and in July 1817, when President James Monroe arrived in the town, he received an address of welcome at Israel Green's inn. In the newspaper notice in which Beaumont announced that he was ending his practice in Plattsburgh, he also stated that his cousin Samuel had taken an office at Israel Green's.[42]

The Greens were of Quaker stock. Originally from Long Island, they had moved to Plattsburgh from Dutchess County, New York. Israel Green had two daughters. Deborah, who was born in 1787, was first married to Nathaniel Platt Jr., a member of the family who founded Plattsburgh. This marriage failed, but with divorce a rarity in the early nineteenth century, it was believed, or at least said among later Beaumonts, that Deborah was a widow at the time of her marriage to William.[43]

In northern New York in the first decades of the nineteenth century, women rarely returned to their father's home and sought a divorce as Deborah did. Perhaps Platt and Deborah were utterly incompatible (though that rarely doomed a marriage). There are some slight indications in mortgage foreclosures that Platt may have had some financial difficulties, but it is extremely unlikely that such problems sent her back to her father. Perhaps there were major sexual difficulties. Nathaniel married again and lived until 1858, but he had no children by either marriage. Mary Torrey, in her recollections sixty years later, had the surname of Deborah's first husband wrong, but she remembered that Deborah and her first husband did not have any children, that "he was jealous of her and accused her wrongfully," and that she returned to her original home. Whatever the reasons, this separation was made possible by a reasonably prosperous and tolerant father. "She went home," remembered Mrs. Torrey, "and her folks received her."[44]

If Mrs. Torrey's memories were accurate, Beaumont was boarding at Israel Green's when Deborah returned to her father, "and they got too close together." Although she had been married before, Deborah was a good catch for Beaumont. Mrs. Torrey was thinking of something else when she said that

42. *History of Clinton and Franklin Counties*, 132; Mrs. George Fuller Tuttle, comp. and ed., *Three Centuries in Champlain Valley: A Collection of Historical Facts and Incidents*, 231; Palmer, *History of Plattsburgh*, 49.

43. Tuttle, comp. and ed., *Three Centuries in Champlain Valley*, 327; Cassidy and Sokol, comps., *Index to the Wm. Beaumont Manuscript Collection*, 14; Charles Platt, *Platt Genealogy in America from the Arrival of Richard Platt in New Haven, Connecticut, in 1638*, 94.

44. *Plattsburgh Republican*, January 1, 1813, September 6, 1816; Kellogg, *Recollections*, 22.

"she made him an awfully good wife," but for a man who was cautiously but steadily rising in the world, Deborah had other than her personal attractions and attributes. Her father was a successful businessman, and Deborah's sister, Ann, had married one of the most prominent men in early Plattsburgh, Colonel Melancton Smith. In 1817, when President James Monroe came to Plattsburgh, Colonel Smith dined with him at Israel Green's inn, at the president's specific invitation.[45]

Beaumont's actual commission as post surgeon was signed by President Monroe on March 18, 1820; he was given rank from December 4, 1819, but he had already heard in February that his post was to be the distant and isolated Fort Mackinac in the northern lakes.[46] He was given permission to remain in Plattsburgh until the end of April, but was ordered to proceed to Mackinac in May. When a local French-born judge heard this, he noted in his diary that "it will really [be] a loss to this place." He also added other comments, which confirm the impression that Beaumont was fortunate in his prospective bride. On Washington's birthday (February 22), there was a grand ball at Israel Green's. "The room," said the judge, "was ornimented really with taste and elegance and neatness really Aunt Deborah is 'le je ne suis Quoy' . . . the simatry of the arrangements of the room were admirable. I never in Europe see such magisti of fancy." "Aunt Deborah," or more usually "Aunt Debby," was the name by which Beaumont's future wife was often affectionately known, at times even by Beaumont himself. This was not a deprecating title. "Aunt" was apparently a term used playfully and affectionately in Plattsburgh for young women. Beaumont used it with a young married woman he met in Detroit in a passage in which he commented on her beauty.[47]

If Beaumont's attempt at delay in reporting for duty had been in the hope of marrying Debby before he left, it had been unsuccessful. The long-memoried Mrs. Torrey's recollection of this was that when Beaumont was sent to Mackinac, he told Debby that if she could get a bill of divorce he would marry her. This was arranged, and he came back and did it. The details may not be quite right, but the general sense of it is. Beaumont was ready to go to Mackinac, but he intended to make the long trip back to marry Debby.[48]

45. Kellogg, *Recollections*, 22; Tuttle, comp. and ed., *Three Centuries in Champlain Valley*, 118, 233; Everest, *War of 1812 in the Champlain Valley*, 165.

46. Beaumont's commission is printed in facsimile in Myer, *Beaumont*, 70.

47. Harris A. Houghton, "Dr. William Beaumont: His Life and Associates in Plattsburgh, N.Y.," 296–98; Miller, ed., *Beaumont's Formative Years*, 60–61.

48. Kellogg, *Recollections*, 22.

Just before he left Plattsburgh, Beaumont took another step that he thought was important in achieving the respectability and status that was so important to him as a young man. The Mason's Lodge in Plattsburgh raised him to the rank of 7th degree Mason, and conferred on him the honorary degree of Mark Master Mason. He had been a member of the masons since before the War of 1812, and at times of change in his young career he asked his fellow masons for references.[49]

At the end of April, writing to Lovell, Beaumont told him that he intended to leave for Mackinac on the next steamboat, but he also took steps to improve his financial position. He said that he had been told by an officer acquainted with Mackinac that there was a need for medical service to nonmilitary personnel. Beaumont wanted to know if he would be able to engage in private practice on the island. In theory, the army medical department prohibited its surgeons from engaging in private practice, but exceptions were often made. Beaumont received the permission he desired, and he regularly engaged in private practice at the different posts in which he served.[50]

In this first part of his life, Beaumont always had a keen interest in new scenes and new faces, and he kept a journal of his long trip to Mackinac. He had decided to make it even longer by making a detour to visit his mother and family in Lebanon. His journal depicts his lively interest in what he sees along the way, but it also records his determination to start his renewed military life with the dedication to personal improvement that he had always urged upon his brother Abel.

He left Plattsburgh by steamboat at 3 A.M. on May 6, 1820. At Whitehall he continued by land, taking the coach for Albany, New York. On the way, he visited one of his uncles (Daniel) at Sandy Hill, New York, had breakfast with the family, and went to church with them. He was obviously enjoying the trip, and commented that they passed "through several most delightful Towns." He arrived cheerfully in Albany, although the women in his coach were "almost over come with fatigue." After staying overnight, he then proceeded through Hartford to his old home in Lebanon. He only stayed a few days, but took the time to visit relatives in the surrounding area.[51]

49. Certificates of the Masonic order, April 3 and 11, 1820, BC, WU.

50. Beaumont to Lovell, April 30, 1820, WD, AG, LR, IMOF. Gillett, *Army Medical Department, 1818–1865,* 33.

51. The account of the trip west here and in the following paragraphs is based on Beaumont's journal, printed in Miller, ed., *Beaumont's Formative Years,* 51–59. See also Beaumont to Abel Beaumont, May 30, 1820, in Annan, ed., "Early Letters of William Beaumont," 659–61; Nelson, *Beaumont,* 72–83.

Leaving his family, Beaumont returned through Albany to Utica, where he took passage on the new Erie Canal, on a boat pulled along the canal by two horses on the bank. The canal was in the process of construction, but the stretch from Utica to Montezuma was complete. Beaumont thoroughly enjoyed this part of the journey. He told his brother Abel that this was "a most delightful way of travelling," with the boat proceeding perfectly smoothly at about five miles an hour. In his journal, he enthusiastically wrote of this "Stupendeous work," which "astonishes a reflecting beholder & excites a solemn reverence—even for the ingenuity & perseverance of man." He wrote with all the enthusiasm of a promoter about the prosperous villages and the rich farms, and prophesied that if the canal were completed as planned from Albany to Lake Erie it would convert "the *once* Western wilds into a cultivated garden."

Beaumont always closely correlated beauty and utility, and in the course of his trip west—which he depicted in western New York as a smooth, majestic progress through a land flowing in milk and honey—he energetically visited every new and useful improvement as well as every "wonder of nature" that he could find. Beaumont was very much the nineteenth-century tourist gaining evidence of the wondrous works of God and man, not a military surgeon making an arduous trek to his first posting.

At Auburn he visited the state prison; at Rome, the United States Arsenal; at Clinton, Hamilton College. He admired them all, and when, on leaving the canal, he went by stage from Auburn to Buffalo, he continued to be impressed by "very pleasant & flourishing towns." His pleasure increased when the Reverend Jedidiah Morse and his son boarded the stage at Canandaigua. The well-known Morse was on his way to report on the western Indians. Beaumont anticipated "deriving much benefit & instruction" from the opportunity to travel with him.

The Reverend Morse also derived much satisfaction from having encountered Dr. Beaumont. He later commented that as his health was feeble it was providential that he met Beaumont, "a gentleman of much skill in his profession, and of most amiable and kind dispositions." He attributed not only his health, but probably even his life, to Beaumont's attentions and prescriptions.[52]

Arriving at Buffalo on Sunday, May 27, Beaumont went to the church where the young Morse was preaching, and on the following day accompa-

52. Jedidiah Morse, *A Report to the Secretary of War of the United States on Indian Affairs*, 17.

nied Morse and his son to Niagara Falls, visiting the War of 1812 battlefields of Chippawa and Lundy's Lane on the way. They viewed the falls in great detail from both the American and the Canadian side, and returned to Black Rock to board the steamboat for Detroit. Steamboat travel to Detroit had only begun two years before, and Beaumont was appreciably impressed at the speed of nine miles an hour.

That morning Beaumont, while reading an old newspaper, came across Franklin's *"project for attaining moral perfection"* and copied the whole extract into his journal. Franklin had listed thirteen virtues, ranging from temperance through chastity to humility. In the following months, Beaumont from time to time noted in his journal his attempts to live up to these ideal precepts. One wonders if Beaumont's private and public problems with Miss Lucy Williams had sent his eye in the direction of Franklin's moral principles.

At Detroit there was a delay. Beaumont arrived there early in June, but could not leave for Mackinac until the fourteenth. He spent much of his time reading, but also drew some maps and did some writing for the Reverend Morse. He also did what he could to assure his future prospects. He reported to the commander of the Fifth military district, Major General Alexander Macomb, and was invited to dinner. They had a good basis for conversation as Macomb had commanded the American forces at the battle of Plattsburgh. Beaumont also wrote to the surgeon general to repeat the request that he had made before leaving Plattsburgh that he should be given permission to carry on a private practice at Mackinac.[53]

Beaumont was disturbed to find "very strong symtoms [*sic*] of dissepation" among the officers of the garrison. Drinking was a prevailing vice among both officers and men at the lonely, isolated western garrisons, and Beaumont, like several other army medical officers, became extremely concerned in the following years at the problems caused by intemperance. He became even more concerned when his medical research allowed him to see the effects of alcohol on the human stomach.

In his comments on religion in Detroit, Beaumont well reflected his New England upbringing. He heard the Reverend Morse preach in the Presbyterian Church, but also attended the Catholic Church on the same afternoon. In the latter, he witnessed the annual ceremony of the celebration of "our Saviour," and commented that "it was a great ceremony & *I think,* a great burlesque on religion." Brought up in Lebanon, and living on the northern

53. Beaumont to Lovell, June 3, 1820, WD, AG, IMOF.

New York frontier, this was probably Beaumont's first attendance at any but a simple Protestant service.

For all Beaumont's interest in a new and virtuous life, Debby's absence meant that he had an acute awareness of all the young women he met. On the stage coach to Albany one of Beaumont's companions had been a Miss Charlotte Taylor. At Detroit, he took the time to write her "what I *called a friendly letter.*" When he accidentally ran into a married friend from Plattsburgh, and flustered her, he commented that this only "served to heighten her *beauty*–She blushed like the *rose*–so crimson was her *youthful* cheek, that it made even the *sun* look *pale.*"

Beaumont spent an evening reading the poetry of the American Samuel Woodworth, and copied out some lines regretting leaving those who were close, "while the moist eye bespeaks the aching breast," and, soon after he left Detroit, he jotted down a few faltering lines of his own about his longings for his future wife: "Oh–D–my heart a vacuum feels, Your image only I can see; And wheresoever my body reels, My spirit wings its way to thee."

On June 14, Beaumont, along with the Reverend Morse and General Macomb, boarded the steamboat for Mackinac. On Lake Erie, he had written out Franklin's project for achieving moral perfection; upon leaving Detroit he noted that he adopted the following maxim: "Trust not to man's honesty, whether Christian–Jew–or Gentile.–Deal with all as though they were rogues & villains, it will never injure an honest person & it will always protect you from being cheated by friend or foe. Selfishness, or villainy, or both combined, govern the world, with a very few exceptions." On June 16 the steamboat reached Mackinac. Here, Beaumont was to be given his chance for fame.

F O U R

Mackinac and Alexis St. Martin

ON JUNE 16, BEFORE leaving the steamboat, Beaumont wrote a quick letter
to his mother so that it could go back on the steamboat that had brought
him. It had been more than five weeks since he had left Plattsburgh, but
he still showed few signs of travel weariness. His journey, he wrote, had
been "a very pleasant one," his health good, his spirits tolerable, and his
hopes of seeing his friends within two or three years strong. He warned
his mother that because there was no communication with Mackinac in the
winter months, any letters she wrote would have to reach him by November
or they would be delayed until the spring. He told her not to worry. "I shall
make myself contented even in this cold & isolated country," he wrote, "under
the prospects that I am not always to be here & away from my friends."[1]

Situated on a small island that lay at the narrow strait separating Lake
Huron from Lake Michigan, Fort Mackinac was one of the most isolated posts
in the American army. The island itself is less than four miles in length, and at
its widest is only two miles across. At the south end, the inhabitants clustered
around the harbor, with the fort on the heights above them. There had long
been forts at the straits; the French and the British had forts on the adjacent
mainland, but in the Revolution the British had built a new fort on the island.[2]

The great importance of the island was for the fur trade. Indians were
numerous in the surrounding area, and they came to Mackinac in great

---

1. Beaumont to Lucretia Beaumont, June 16, 1820, BP, YU.
2. David Armour, *At the Crossroads: Michilimackinac during the American Revolution.*

numbers to trade with the Europeans. At the time Beaumont arrived the island was assuming particular importance as the western center of John Jacob Astor's American Fur Company. One of the partners, Robert Stuart, lived on the island to supervise day-by-day business, and in the spring when the great exchange of winter furs took place, Astor's chief manager, Ramsay Crooks, traveled to the post to oversee operations and visit lesser company posts in the region. In the summer of 1822, Crooks became ill while traveling by canoe, and on his arrival at Mackinac was treated by Beaumont. The doctor, he wrote, "laid a heavy hand on me." He was to become a good friend to Beaumont.[3]

While troops complained of the fort's isolation and the long, frigid winters, and drank to relieve their boredom, summer visitors, then as now, were usually struck by the beauty of the tiny island and its surroundings. The explorer Henry Schoolcraft was thrilled by Mackinac when he arrived in this spring of 1820. "Nothing can exceed the beauty of this island," he wrote. He thought its harbor was "a little gem." Around the harbor, Schoolcraft described a "little old-fashioned French town," which he thought had "a very antique and foreign look." The newest buildings were those erected since 1815 for the use of Astor's agents. In 1820 the whole island had fewer than five hundred permanent inhabitants, though this swelled considerably in the spring and summer from the influx of Indians and traders. Schoolcraft was told that there was no physician other than the one with the garrison, so the interests of Beaumont and the residents coincided to their mutual advantage.[4]

The scene that greeted Beaumont was more exotic than that provided by the frontier of northern New York. When Schoolcraft came to Mackinac, a few months before Beaumont, a great number of Ottawa and Chippewa Indians were encamped near the town. "The beach of the lake," he wrote, "has been constantly lined with Indian wigwams and bark canoes." The Indians were bringing in furs, maple sugar, moccasins, rush mats, miniature boxes to hold sugar, and a variety of other items made by the Indian women. Elizabeth Baird, who lived there as a girl in the early 1820s, even had pleasant memories of Mackinac's icebound winter. For about eight months, she said, the island lay dormant, but she remembered the feasting at Christmas and

3. John D. Haeger, *John Jacob Astor: Business and Finance in the Early Republic,* 206, 225–26; Alice Elizabeth Smith, *James Duane Doty: Frontier Promoter,* 39–40; David Lavender, *The Fist in the Wilderness,* 339 (quotation).

4. Henry S. Schoolcraft, *Summary Narrative of an Exploratory Expedition to the Sources of the Mississippi River in 1820,* 57–71.

the grotesquely dressed men who sang and danced from house to house on New Year's Eve.[5] Food, drink, and feast days took on a special meaning in the frozen north.

For Beaumont, it worked to his advantage that he had traveled from Detroit with the commander of the whole district, General Macomb. On the day after his arrival he accompanied Macomb in his inspection of the troops, and then dined with the post commander, Captain Benjamin K. Pierce. In the following days, he obtained two horses from Pierce and a private servant for his quarters.[6]

Beaumont took up his duties in the post hospital on the day after his arrival. The hospital was in a converted storehouse in poor condition, and needed to be replaced. In the fall of 1824, Beaumont, recommending a new building, described the existing structure as "wholly unfit"; it was "insupportably cold & smoky in winter," and open to "every Shower in Summer." In winter, the snow came into the sick wards. Conditions did not improve while Beaumont was at the post. In the summer of 1826 the hospital was described as "a perfect barn in ruins," and so leaky "that during a rain the bunks of the patients are moved about from place to place to avoid the wet." Beaumont made the best of what he had, and in 1824 was praised by the visiting inspector as "an officer of great merit."[7]

The immediate problem that confronted Beaumont was that the hospital was in urgent need of medical supplies, and there was nowhere to obtain them. He reported this immediately to Surgeon General Lovell and set about bringing order to medical affairs on the island. The man and wife who had been serving as steward and matron respectively had not been regularly mustered for the previous eight months, and he had to intervene with Lovell to get them paid.[8]

5. Elizabeth T. Baird, "Reminiscences of Early Days on Mackinac Island," 19–34. See also Mrs. John H. Kinzie, *Wau-Bun: The Early Day in the Northwest,* 5–9.

6. Miller, ed., *Beaumont's Formative Years,* 62.

7. Beaumont to Major Henry Stanton, September 20, 1824, War Department, RG 92, Office of the Quartermaster General, Consolidated Correspondence File, Fort Mackinac, 1819–90 (microfilm, Mackinac Island State Park Commission), hereafter cited as WD, QG; Francis Paul Prucha, ed., *Army Life on the Western Frontier: Selections from the Official Reports Made between 1826 and 1845 by Colonel George Croghan,* 69 (1826); Keith R. Widder, *Dr. William Beaumont: The Mackinac Years,* 29 (1824 quotation).

8. Beaumont to Lovell, June 17, 1820, WD, AG, IMOF; Beaumont to Lovell, August 1, 1820, War Department, RG 112, Office of the Surgeon General, Letters Received, National Archives, Washington, D.C. Hereafter cited as WD, SG, LR; Widder, *Beaumont: The Mackinac Years,* 4–5.

The question of the rank of medical officers was still a thorny one, and Beaumont pursued the question with Lovell. He had noticed in army regulations that subalterns were entitled to an additional ration, and he asked Lovell if post surgeons were regarded as subalterns. If not, he wrote, this should be righted at the next session of Congress. Post surgeons were treated as officers, but they had no real position within the official army hierarchy. Beaumont always felt extremely comfortable writing to Lovell, regarding him as a friend as well as a superior, and in writing from Mackinac Beaumont continued to press, without success, for an appointment for his cousin Samuel.[9]

Beaumont was obviously delighted to be back in the army and serving as post surgeon. He told a Plattsburgh friend that he was "highly pleased" with the post and its commander, and that he would not exchange his station "with any subordinate medical officer in the Army." After three months of a Mackinac summer, he painted the island in glowing colors: a "most delightful situation—serene, romantic & healthy," with a soil and climate that abundantly furnished fruits, flowers, and vegetables of excellent quality. He said that the island had everything that Plattsburgh had to offer except "political contentions." There were fewer people, but the society of the island was enlivened by a stream of visitors, there were frequent balls and dinners, and the residents amused themselves with billiards, backgammon, chess, riding, sailing, and walking.

The months from June to September had given Beaumont the best possible introduction to the island, but his pleasure in it was obviously enhanced by his improved financial position. He reported that, compared to Plattsburgh, money was more plentiful, *"and easier to be obtained."* Only three months after his arrival, he was able to say that he had "a considerable practice" in the village that provided him with "a handsome perquisite." He was not pressed for time in building his private practice, because there had been few sick in the garrison. The winter months were to bring more sickness among the troops, but Beaumont had the advantage of serving at one of the healthier army posts. Mackinac was not racked by the fevers that were a constant problem at more southerly stations.[10]

For Beaumont, Mackinac met all his needs except one. He missed Debby, and she figured very largely in his private journal in the summer and fall of 1820. He wrote of his thoughts being *"nightly and every night, & all the nights*

9. Beaumont to Lovell, August 1, 1820, WD, SG, LR.
10. Beaumont to Hon. Judge DeLord, September 1820, *North Country Notes* (Plattsburgh), 65 (May 1970); Gillett, *Army Medical Department, 1818–1865,* 40–42.

constantly with thee," and wished that he could fly as easily as his thoughts to lay his "glowing cheek" on her "swelling bosom." He was concerned about the progress of Debby's divorce from her first husband, and wrote that if his *"heart-sustaining prospects"* were cut off, he envisaged a "dark benighted world" and a "joyless life." Debby, he wrote, was the soul of his existence.[11]

Beaumont's nights as well as his days began to be dominated by his hopes and fears for his future with Debby. One night he asked "lovely Sleep" to stupefy his senses and ease his pain: "O D—I must bid you good night & retire to dream of you dreams of unsubstantial bliss–12 ock.–going-going-gone–to bed–to *sleep*–to dream. Oh! . . . D.D. where are you? 4 ock. *morn*–awake . . ." On another night he dreamt that Debby was wounded and sick, and that he strove to reach her in an open canoe on a stormy lake. But on finding a safe harbor, he met two friends from P[lattsburgh], who told him she was now well, had triumphed over her enemies, and there had been a happy result of her "affair in court." He was with her "mutually enjoying . . . *tender trembling & . . .* affectionate embraces of Love!" He awoke "in the extacey of joy," and expressed the hope that this was a happy omen of what was to come.[12]

Haunted by thoughts and dreams of Debby and her charms, Beaumont revived his interest in Benjamin Franklin's plan for attaining moral perfection. On September 9 he began a diary of conduct based on that plan. Possibly, in his inflamed state, he had decided that he needed all the help he could get if he were going to stay faithful to his Debby. In the coming winter, when he told Lovell that he intended to marry, he commented that "to live a bachelor & alone on this desert, isolated Isle, I am not content–to mingle with its Copper-Colored inhabitants I cannot." Many did have relationships with the local Indians, or with the daughters of fur traders and Indian wives. Captain Pierce had married a woman of mixed Indian and European ancestry.[13]

Several months after his arrival, Beaumont described one of his days. He rose at 6 A.M., completed his garrison duties and his calls on patients in the village by 9 A.M., settled his hospital accounts with the commandant, read the Scriptures and Pope's *Essay on Man* until the evening, received letters from Plattsburgh, and spent the rest of the evening happily reading them and in "fanciful sociability." Beaumont did not usually record the details of his days, and was usually not much given to perusing the Scriptures. One

11. Miller, ed., *Beaumont's Formative Years,* 62–63.
12. Ibid., 66–68.
13. Ibid., 64; Beaumont to Lovell, January 1, 1821, WD, AG, IMOF; Nelson, *Beaumont,* 85.

assumes that the particular pattern of this day was not unconnected with the previous day's decision to begin a diary of conduct based on Franklin's plan for attaining moral perfection. He noted at the end of this second day that there were "only 2 little blots on my Book."[14]

Whether from desire to follow Franklin's plan, a wish to improve his mind, or simply to relieve the loneliness of Mackinac and the absence of Debby, Beaumont read a good deal in the fall of 1820. It is likely this also stemmed from his thoughts of Debby, for though she never went to the theater, she very much enjoyed plays and poetry, reading Shakespeare aloud to her family and friends until a few weeks before her death in 1871. It was also said that "Irving, Scott, Cooper, even Byron were her familiar companions."[15]

Beaumont was dipping into Shakespeare in the fall of 1820, and copied, almost accurately, some of the lines that attracted him into his journal. From *All's Well that Ends Well,* he took "Love all, trust a few, Do wrong to none: be able for thine Enemy, rather in power, than use; & keep thy friend under thy life's key: Be checked for silence, but never taxed for speech." A few weeks later, reading *Twelfth Night,* his attention was caught by "I hate ingratitude more in a man, Than lying, vainniss, babbling drunkness [sic], or any taint of vice, whose strong corruption inhabits our frail blood." He also copied down brief passages from *A Winter's Tale* and *Henry V,* and a few lines from Byron.[16]

The reading was not simply for pleasure and Debby. Beaumont was also trying to broaden his knowledge in these first months in Mackinac. He copied extracts into his journal from Louis Pierre Anquetil's *A Summary of Universal History* and from Charles Rollin's *Ancient History,* and took notes on the spreading of Christianity under Constantine and on the tumultuous events following Constantine's death, as well as noting various bits of information on Rome, Carthage, Genghis Khan, and Assyria. He also wrote a passage on North American Indian dancing, but it was taken from a book rather than from personal observation.[17]

While the journals reveal an interest in literature and history, there is no indication that Beaumont was trying to expand his medical knowledge, or that he had access to books or journals that would have helped him to do so. He did, however, fulfill his routine duties as post surgeon with dedication.

14. Miller, ed., *Beaumont's Formative Years,* 64.

15. "Dr. William Beaumont," clipping from a Green Bay newspaper, by E[lizabeth] S[mith] M[artin], BC, WU.

16. Miller, ed., *Beaumont's Formative Years,* 64–66, 80.

17. Ibid., 68–73, 80–81.

These duties involved more than simply treating sick or injured soldiers. Because of the strong belief that there was an intimate connection between the state of the atmosphere and disease, post surgeons were required to keep a careful meteorological record. This had first been done, in somewhat desultory fashion, on the direction of Surgeon General James Tilton in the War of 1812, but after 1818 Joseph Lovell insisted that this part of the surgeon's duties should be carried out regularly and efficiently. Lovell's comment, on renewing Tilton's order, was that "the influence of weather and climate upon diseases, especially epidemic is perfectly well known." Lovell instructed surgeons to keep not only a diary of the weather but also a record of local topography, climate, prevalent complaints, and anything that might "tend to discover the causes of diseases, to the promotion of health, and the improvement of medical science."[18]

This read well, but at Mackinac Beaumont found that he did not even have a proper thermometer. Five months after his arrival, he complained that he had received forms to record the temperature, but no thermometer. He told Lovell that he felt "a deep sense of Chagrin" at being forced to submit such an imperfect diary of the weather. His most accurate observations were on the winds and the state of the atmosphere. Beaumont was a meticulous man with a strong sense of duty, and this was to serve him well when he ultimately began to record his scientific experiments. He might have been limited by lack of knowledge, but not by lack of care. He expressed his regret to Lovell that he was imperfectly acquainted with the science of mineralogy, and that he had no means in Mackinac for analyzing for signs of valuable metals. To compensate for this, he sent Lovell two pieces, metallic in appearance, that he had obtained on the island. He commented that whatever they were, more of the same abounded on Mackinac.[19]

The medical department at Mackinac had gained a vigorous advocate in Beaumont, and when within a few months of his arrival he learned that the Indian agent George Boyd had gained permission to build a new agency house on part of the post gardens, he waged a spirited resistance. In the spring of 1820 Boyd had tried to get permission for this, but Captain Pierce had refused him. Boyd had then gone over Pierce's head and appealed to General Macomb. Macomb had approved the request.

18. Hume, "The Foundation of American Meteorology," 202–8; Sargent, *Hippocratic Heritage,* 307–43, discusses the eighteenth-century interest in the maintenance of meteorological journals.
19. Beaumont to Lovell, September 30, 1820, WD, SG, LR.

This brought a bitter protest from Beaumont. He pointed out to Lovell that for twenty years or more the garden area had been developed at the expense of the officers at the fort for use as a vegetable garden for the troops, and also as a hospital garden for the specific use of the sick. The hospital garden, he wrote, was handsomely laid out in walks, alleys, and bowers, with a variety of plants and fruit trees. Beaumont was particularly irritated because he had brought with him to Mackinac the seeds of medicinal plants and "ornamental flowers," and these were now planted in the garden. Among the seeds he had planted were those of the *"Papaver Somniferum"* (opium) and the *"Marrubium Vulgare"* (horehound), which he said were efficacious in many diseases, particularly in the "obstinate pulmonary complaints" of the region. The garden already had *"Humulus Lupulus"* (hops). Beaumont said he was taking great pains with this because it provided a very healthy and pleasant beverage for the use of the sick. He also wanted to introduce it among the troops in general as a substitute for whiskey.

Beaumont was never subtle in his attacks, and he launched a vigorous assault on Indian agent Boyd. Boyd, he wrote, was sent to Mackinac to perform duties that, compared to those of the duties of military officers at the post, were *"nothing at all."* For this, wrote Beaumont, Boyd had a salary of $1,400 to $1,500 a year, together with another $500 or $600 in perquisites. There was no reason, Beaumont argued, why Boyd could not build his agency house on the abundant public ground, without putting out the military at the post. Beaumont excused the warmth of his arguments by stating that they were dictated by "an imperious sense of duty." The government would either have to supply the money to buy vegetables or stop this annexation of the gardens on this "isolated, barren Isle." Justice and humanity, he wrote, demanded it.[20]

The diet of soldiers was of considerable concern to the members of the medical department. Many were concerned that vegetables were not a part of the official diet, that too much poorly cooked meat was eaten, and that too much whiskey was drunk. During the War of 1812, Surgeon James Mann had complained of the amount of meat eaten by the soldiers, and said that it would be desirable if part of the meat ration could be commuted for beans and peas. Surgeon General Lovell had a special interest in diet, and thought it was of great importance to the army. He was disturbed that the army ration gave soldiers ample meat, bread, and a gill of whiskey a day, but no vegetables. For

20. Beaumont to Lovell, November 1, 1820, WD, SG, LR.

vegetables, the soldiers had to depend on the gardens that the commanders were expected to establish at the military posts.[21]

Soon after his appointment, Lovell had recommended a change in army rations to the Secretary of War Calhoun. He told Calhoun that it was essential for the health of the army that customary habits should be changed. It was not enough to provide food of good quality, he argued, it was also necessary that there be "a due mixture of animal and vegetable food," and as much variety as possible in cooking. Lovell wanted to encourage soups in place of the constant frying. He thought that the most important change needed was the addition of vegetables to the diet, but he also wanted to reduce or eliminate whiskey from the ration. Lovell's efforts did not produce any dramatic results, but in 1821 the ration was modified twice a week to include beans, peas, or rice, in place of half the meat ration.[22]

Beaumont was at least able to keep the Mackinac vegetable garden. His vigorous protest, supported by the rest of the military on Mackinac, was successful. Boyd's new agency house was built outside the area of the garden, and the troops continued to have their vegetables. Such a garden was a feature of most army posts in these years; officers usually provided modest financial support, while the men provided the labor.[23]

In his first months at Mackinac, Beaumont neglected his medical notebook. When he turned from his work, or from his reading, he was far more likely to write of his thoughts of Debby or to make notes from his general reading than to write up the mostly routine medical cases he was dealing with, but early in December he had a case that intrigued him. A private was hit on the head by a heavy club; the blow depressed the skull and produced a severe fracture running back from the area of the frontal sinus.

The private was in a daze—"appeared stupid." He would walk when compelled, but could say nothing except an occasional yes or no, and "looked wild with his Eyes." After twenty-four hours he was attacked "with severe spasms," mostly on the right side of his body; the left side "appearing rather paralytic than otherwise." This condition continued until Beaumont saw him

21. Gillett, *Army Medical Department, 1818–1865,* 16; Fanny J. Anderson, "Medical Practices in Detroit during the War of 1812," 271; Peter N. Barboriak, "Reporting to the Surgeon General: The Peacetime Practice of Military Surgeons in Antebellum America, 1818–1861," 249–50.

22. Lovell to Calhoun, August 22, 1818, in W. Edwin Hemphill, ed., *The Papers of John C. Calhoun,* vol. 3, 61–63, 273–74; Barboriak, "Reporting to the Surgeon General," 249–50.

23. Myer, *Beaumont,* 91; Nelson, *Beaumont,* 91.

for the first time, six days after the injury. He was brought in on a sleigh ten or fifteen miles in the snow, and when he arrived was wet and chilled through, was undergoing spasms every ten or fifteen minutes, appeared comatose, was breathing laboriously, and had a weak pulse.

In the post hospital, Beaumont had him washed all over in warm soap suds and rubbed with camphorated spirits. He administered ether, laudanum, and spirits of ammonia, with a warm infusion of valerian and castor "to restore the action of the extreme vessels & raise the circulation." This went on for two or three hours. Beaumont then bled the patient of ten or twelve ounces and gave him ten grains of calomel and five of valerian, twice repeated, together with an enema.

The spasms continued to increase in frequency over the next eighteen hours, and Beaumont decided to "perforate the cranium." He could not actually see the fracture, but presumed that there were fluids on the brain that needed to be relieved. He used a trephine, and found a fissure extending back from the sinus. A quantity of "dark, grumous blood" came out, and the spasms continued for twelve hours after the operation, until they became less frequent. Beaumont noted that the side opposite the injury was most affected by the spasms. The operation had been performed between three and four in the afternoon, and the patient was given an infusion of valerian and castor throughout the night.

On the following day, Beaumont cleansed the wound, "filled it with Carbon" (presumably charcoal), applied a carbon poultice on the whole area, had the patient rubbed all over with warm soap suds and camphorated spirits, administered "Spts Mindereri" (a solution of ammonium acetate) and soluble Tartar (potassium tartrate), and gave arrowroot and gruel for food. By the evening, the patient was becoming worse, and on the following day, he died. Three hours later, Beaumont "opened & examined" the head. He found an extensive fracture, and an abscess. Usually, Beaumont wrote in some detail in his medical notebook when he thought he had produced a striking cure. In this case, he was content to believe that the original damage was so extensive that nothing he could have done would have made any difference.[24]

In beginning his army career, Beaumont clearly retained the belief in heroic therapy that he had gained from his apprenticeship. His treatment for dysentery that first year was ipecac, tartar emetic, calomel, rhubarb, castor oil, and bleeding. By the time of the last years of Beaumont's career in the

24. Miller, ed., *Beaumont's Formative Years*, 29–31, 36.

1840s and 1850s, belief in heroic therapy had waned, but Beaumont was one of the physicians who continued to make use of therapies learned earlier in the century.[25]

Although Beaumont had suggested to his mother at the time of his arrival at Mackinac that he would be completely cut off during the winter months, there was some communication through the British possession of Drummond's Island, east of the American post. Beaumont sent letters out that way, and apparently near the end of the year he heard that Debby would be free to marry him if he returned in the following summer. At the beginning of January, he wrote to Lovell to request a sixty-day leave of absence because *"to marry I am resolved."* He wanted to go sometime between June and October, with the exact time to be left to his discretion. He told Lovell that if it was not possible for an army surgeon to stand in for him then he would, at his own expense, employ a civilian to attend to the medical needs of the garrison. He did not explain to Lovell how there could be a civilian available, although earlier in the year he had obtained permission to treat the local population because of the lack of physicians. Yet he could have given no clearer indication of his eagerness to marry than by suggesting he would spend his own money; something he avoided unless it was absolutely necessary. Even on this occasion he added the comment that a particular army surgeon who had passed through Mackinac in the previous summer had indicated he would willingly relieve Beaumont if he could be spared from his own regiment. Beaumont was ready to bring Debby back to Mackinac, but he made the request that if Plattsburgh became a permanent garrison, and needed a post surgeon, he would like to be transferred there.[26]

Beaumont obtained the leave he wanted, but his marriage came in a year of disappointing professional news. In 1821 Congress reduced both the army and the medical service. There were to be fifty-three, not sixty-four, medical officers, and medical officers would all be classed as surgeons or assistant surgeons, with the great majority (forty-five) assistant surgeons. Beaumont was still to serve the post of Mackinac, but it was to be as an assistant surgeon.[27]

When Beaumont left Mackinac on August 9, 1821, he had received private word from Lovell that his leave was to be granted, but no official orders. If

25. Barboriak, "Reporting to the Surgeon General," 108, 150–51. For changes in therapy, and regional variations, see Warner, *Therapeutic Perspective,* 83–161.
26. Beaumont to Lovell, January 1, 1821, WD, AG, IMOF.
27. Gillett, *Army Medical Department, 1818–1865,* 28–29.

he was to marry and return before winter set in, he could wait no longer,
and he decided to leave and apply for his official furlough at Detroit. There
was no army surgeon sent to replace Beaumont, and he paid for a civilian
physician to serve the post during his absence. At the end of 1821 there were
fewer surgeons in the army than there were posts and stations to be filled.[28]

Beaumont had a swift journey to Plattsburgh, and on August 28 he was
married to Mrs. Deborah Platt by a Presbyterian minister. Beaumont was
thirty-five, his wife was thirty-three. Mrs. Beaumont had a Quaker background and used "thee" and "thou" in her speech, but she was not a practicing
Quaker. Unlike her new husband, however, she was a churchgoer. Even after
his marriage Beaumont generally avoided churches, but he demonstrated no
active prejudice against religion. When in 1823 he heard of the death of his
sister Abigail, he wrote to his brother Abel that "the doings of God we are not
to criticize, or complain of—prais'd be his name, although we surely feel the
affliction of his providence."[29]

The newly married pair left for Mackinac soon after their wedding, taking
with them Melancton, the stepson of Debby's sister Ann. Ann's husband,
Colonel Melancton Smith, had died in August 1818, leaving his wife with
a year-old daughter and the young Melancton from his first marriage. The
boy, who was eleven at this time, stayed with the Beaumonts for several years,
entered the navy as a midshipman in 1826, and eventually reached the rank
of rear admiral.[30]

On October 11, Beaumont reported to Lovell that he was back on duty at
Mackinac. For his wife, Mackinac required considerable adjustment. Debby
was an innkeeper's daughter, and Israel Green's Inn at Plattsburgh had
been a center of activity for the county. At Mackinac, "society" for Mrs.
Beaumont was comprised of army officers, their wives, and the company
provided by American Fur Company agent Robert Stuart and his wife. There
were no more than ten women with whom Debby could mix socially. The
living quarters were simple, and there she made a home for her husband,
Melancton, and after June 8, 1822, her baby daughter Sarah.[31]

28. Beaumont to Lovell, August 8, 1821, WD, AG, IMOF; Ayars, "Some Notes on the
Medical Service," 508; Miller, ed., *Beaumont's Formative Years,* 73.

29. *Plattsburgh Republican,* September 1, 1821, facsimile in Myer, *Beaumont,* 98;
"Dr. William Beaumont," by E[lizabeth] S[mith] M[artin], clipping from a Green Bay
newspaper, BC, WU; Beaumont to Abel Beaumont, June 1823, BP, YU.

30. Tuttle, comp. and ed., *Three Centuries in Champlain Valley,* 260–61; Reuben G.
Thwaites, "Rear Admiral Melancton Smith, U.S.N."

31. Beaumont to Lovell, October 11, 1821, WD, AG, IMOF; list of family births,
William Beaumont Collection, Joseph Regenstein Library, University of Chicago. Here-

More than two years after Beaumont had brought his wife to Mackinac, Beaumont described some of the problems of her adjustment in a letter to her parents. Debby, he wrote, had periods when she mused on her separation from her family and friends, "and feels sad and sorrowful at the time, shedding tears of gratitude and affection most copiously." This, he said, was "only the impulse of a moment," and she quickly resumed her "usual cheerfulness and vivacity." Debby was a warm, kindly, and friendly woman, and at the various posts in which her husband served she had a reputation as a gracious and cheerful hostess for the young army officers. In a note added to her husband's letter, Debby apologized for not writing, but said she was kept busy with her household duties, with only "an invalid boy" to help her.[32]

The "invalid boy" who was helping Debby in the winter of 1823–1824 was to be Beaumont's source of fame. On June 6, 1822, two days before the birth of his first daughter, Beaumont was called to the American Fur Company's store. A French Canadian voyageur had been accidentally shot at the distance of no more than two or three feet. The whole of the charge–consisting of powder and duck shot–entered Alexis St. Martin's upper left abdomen, creating a wound more than the size of a man's hand. The sixth rib was fractured and partially carried away, the fifth rib fractured, the lower portion of the left lobe of the lung ruptured, and the stomach lacerated by a portion of the rib that was blown into it. The charge and the wadding were lodged in the cavity.[33]

For the course of events over the next eighteen months, the problem is not a paucity of sources, but an overabundance. Beaumont kept some notes at the time, wrote longer manuscript accounts while St. Martin was still recovering, apparently amplified and amended these accounts at a later date, and also used his original notes together with some rewriting to publish articles and then a book on the subject of St. Martin. The course of events is reasonably clear, but there are some minor contradictions. What is clear is that in the months after the accident, Beaumont devoted considerable effort to treating St. Martin's wound and attempting to close the hole in his stomach.[34]

---

after cited as BC, UC. Information from Sophie Beaumont, typed, in William Beaumont Papers, State Historical Society of Wisconsin, Madison, Wisc. Hereafter cited as SHSW.

32. Beaumont to Israel Green, December 18, 1823, BC, WU.

33. Notes of cases, BC, WU. See also Henry E. Hamilton, *Incidents and Events in the Life of Gordon Saltonstall Hubbard,* 117–18; Myer, *Beaumont,* 102–3; Nelson, *Beaumont,* 103–10.

34. Beaumont's manuscript journals for this period and later are in the BC, WU. The most detailed account of the medical history of St. Martin in the six months following the accident was originally written by Beaumont in late November or early December 1822, when he apparently used his earlier notes and his memory to describe the course

Beaumont described St. Martin as a Canadian lad about nineteen years old, and often referred to him as a boy, but in reality St. Martin was twenty-eight at the time of the accident. He had been born at Berthier, in Lower Canada, on April 18, 1794, and his full name was Alexis Bidagan dit St. Martin. Apart from the fact that he had become a voyageur and worked for the American Fur Company, nothing is known of his life until the day that he received his horrible wound.[35]

Beaumont arrived less than thirty minutes after the accident. He found a lacerated and burnt portion of the lung protruding through the external wound, and below this a portion of the stomach with a hole in it "large enough to receive my forefinger." Some of the food St. Martin had eaten that morning was now lodged in his clothing. There seems no reason to doubt the statement that appears in Beaumont's most detailed handwritten account of the case that "I considered any attempt to save his life entirely useless." He cleansed the wound and gave it a superficial dressing. When he tried to ease back the protruding portions, he found that the lung was caught on a sharp point of the fractured rib. He clipped off the point of the rib with his penknife and was able to replace the lung, but each time St. Martin coughed the lung came out again.[36] St. Martin was moved, and in about one hour Beaumont again tried to deal with the wound. He took out fragments of the ribs, parts of his clothing, the wad, and the shot, replaced the lungs and stomach as far as was practicable, and treated the wound with "a carbonated fermenting poultice" composed of flour, hot water, charcoal, and yeast, which was changed periodically. He also kept the area constantly bathed with a solution of muriate of ammonia in spirits and vinegar, and gave liberal internal doses of a solution of ammonium acetate and camphor water. He said his intention was to excite reaction on the surface as soon as possible and obtain a sloughing off of "contused, lacerated and burnt muscles and integuments."[37]

Within twenty-four hours St. Martin had the symptoms of violent pneumonia and fever, accompanied with a "distressing cough." To treat this,

---

of recovery and treatment. In December he made regular journal entries detailing St. Martin's progress, and he continued with sporadic entries until June 1823. Later, in September 1824, he wrote out another account to send to Surgeon General Lovell. This is printed in Myer, *Beaumont*, 107–25, and for convenience I cite it in my following description of the period following the accident.

35. See Edward H. Bensley, "Alexis St. Martin," 738–41.
36. Myer, *Beaumont*, 107–8.
37. Ibid., 107.

Beaumont took twelve or fourteen ounces of blood and gave a mild cathartic. Beaumont's comment was that the bleeding gave relief, but the cathartic had no effect because it escaped through the wound in the stomach. Treatment continued to consist of treating the wound with a carbonated poultice. It was also washed with spirits and water, though the muriate of ammonia was now omitted. Camphor water was given internally.

The fever continued for eight or ten days, the wound became "very fetid," and Beaumont wrote that St. Martin had no bowel movements because anything he took into his stomach was either absorbed or came out through the wound. During this period, St. Martin was fed by means of anal injections. This situation continued for about two weeks while there was a sloughing off of the pieces of the lung and stomach that protruded, the wound became healthier, and Beaumont was able to use compresses and an adhesive strap to retain food in the stomach.

The stomach instead of falling back into its natural position adhered to the intercostal muscles, and the hole in the stomach was kept in contact with the external wound. This enabled dressings to be applied. About the fifth week, the external wound began steadily to scar and contract, and the stomach remained attached to the intercostal muscles, but the hole in the stomach showed no sign of closing. In the two months after the accident, more debris from the wound worked its way out, and Beaumont had to cut off the sixth rib about halfway between the sternum and the spine. He had "a very narrow, short saw made for the occasion."[38]

In his notes, Beaumont gives a detailed description of his attempts to close the wound, and of his failure to achieve this. At first he made repeated attempts to close it by trying to get adhesion between the lips of the wound. This did not work, and he could not proceed by simply drawing together the external wound because while doing that there was no way of keeping food in the stomach. If a lint plug was kept in to stop the food coming out of the stomach, then this lint prevented the external wound from closing.

Recovery was a long and difficult process. Four months after the accident, an abscess formed about two inches below the wound, brought with it a fever, and the wound was infected. Beaumont first used poultices, and then lanced the abscess; for weeks bits of bone and cartilage were discharged. Other setbacks arose, and St. Martin was in a weakened condition. Beaumont gave him diluted muriatic acid and wine as a tonic.[39]

38. Ibid., 107–10.
39. Ibid., 111–12.

At the beginning of December, the hole in the stomach was still visible and had contracted very little, but St. Martin's general health was now much better. Beaumont realized that he had a fascinating and unusual case of survival on his hands, and that survival seemed particularly unusual because of the hole in the stomach. Beaumont showed no sign at this point, however, of realizing that he had been given a most unusual opportunity for research. He had no research experience and little formal training, and his increased knowledge in the years since the War of 1812 had been practical rather than theoretical.

On December 2, Beaumont posed the rhetorical question: "Can the puncture of the Stomach be successfully closed by mechanical means until the granulations have time to form over and across it?" In the following days St. Martin continued to improve, but the stomach still had not closed. On December 13, Beaumont tried a different method of closing it. He believed that the constant pressure of the compresses that he was using to keep the food in was preventing the formulation of granulations that would close the puncture of the stomach, so he used a piece of lint tied to a ligature; putting the lint into the stomach wound, and drawing up the ligature so that food was sealed in from the inside. He also tried inserting "a small silver canula" but found that it did not work as well as the lint suspended on a string.[40]

From the middle of December 1822 to the end of May 1823, St. Martin continued to improve, but Beaumont found that food still came out whenever the dressings were removed. On May 30, St. Martin complained of a pain in the head and nausea. Beaumont gave him a cathartic, "administered, it is presumed, as never medicine was before administered to man since the creation of the world—to wit, by pouring it in through the ribs at the puncture into the stomach." It was administered as a dry powder, and it worked as a cathartic within two hours.[41]

In the spring of 1823 St. Martin was recovering, though still with a hole in his stomach, but he now had no means of support. Since December, the county commissioners of Mackinac County had provided for him as a pauper; in that month Beaumont had received thirty dollars from the commissioners for his medical services, and in 1823 he was paid another fifty dollars.

40. Ibid., 112–13.
41. Ibid., 113–14. Numbers, "Beaumont and the Ethics of Human Experimentation," 114, suggests that this was the occasion when the idea of using St. Martin for scientific purposes first seemed to have occurred to Beaumont. Pitcock, "The Career of William Beaumont," 47–48, 54, suggests that the realization was a gradual process over a long period of time.

Beaumont continued to see St. Martin constantly, as from April 1823 St. Martin was able to work as the family's general handyman.[42]

A crisis arose when the county commissioners decided that the time had come to remove St. Martin from the pauper roles and send him back to Montreal. Beaumont protested, arguing that St. Martin could not stand the rigors of the long boat trip, and after the local authorities refused to support him any longer, Beaumont took St. Martin into his own home, where he continued to work as a servant. Some ten years later, in applying to Congress for reimbursement for his years of research and in the hope of getting support for future work, Beaumont omitted the role of the commissioners of Mackinac County in supporting St. Martin and paying medical fees.

While Beaumont later claimed that his action in taking in St. Martin was simply out of charitable interest in a patient who had needed so much of his attention, it seems more likely that even if he was not yet thinking specifically of scientific research, he had become fascinated by the stomach that would not close and wanted to continue to observe the case with the possibility of writing it up for publication. With St. Martin in his household, he could now observe the progress of the wound, and his wife would have a servant who, although "an invalid boy," could now perform rough household duties. The attitude of the Michilimackinac authorities in this and other cases rankled with Beaumont. "Were I reduced to the necessity of existing upon the charity of this Borough," he wrote later, "I would commit suicide without scruple or hesitation."[43]

While Beaumont had devoted considerable time to St. Martin's case since June 1822, he had of course continued with his usual military duties as well as his private practice among the inhabitants of Mackinac. Beginning in the summer of 1822, Beaumont had also contracted with agent George Boyd to render service to the Indians of the Mackinac district for one hundred dollars a year. Beaumont later affirmed that under this contract, he had pre-scribed and administered medicine "to diverse and sundry individuals." He also stated that he had vaccinated between six hundred and seven hundred Indians, "most of whom underwent the genuine Kinepox disease." In all, he said he had received more than $250 for his services.[44]

42. Minutes of the County Commissioners of Mackinac County, Mackinac Island State Park Commission (microfilm); Widder, *Beaumont: The Mackinac Years,* 26; Joseph Lovell [William Beaumont], "A Case of Wounded Stomach," 18; Myer, *Beaumont,* 116.

43. This is in a journal of cases in BC, WU. It is reprinted in Myer, *Beaumont,* 116.

44. Statement of William Beaumont, June 10, 1828, George Boyd Papers, SHSW; Nelson, *Beaumont,* 93.

At first, St. Martin's case was simply entered into Beaumont's private journals along with others that seemed of special interest, and in the same notebook in which he originally recorded St. Martin's case he also thought two other cases were worth recording. As yet, they could be linked with St. Martin, because St. Martin was, at first, just another interesting case.

Both of the cases that Beaumont was dealing with while he was treating the desperately wounded St. Martin illustrated the degree to which Beaumont, like most early-nineteenth-century physicians, was called upon to fulfill a variety of roles. For a military surgeon at an isolated post, the normal round of fevers, diarrheas, and dysenteries was interspersed with fractures, wounds, amputations, and the general run of most surgical procedures that could be carried out at the time.

The first of the cases that Beaumont thought worth recording along with that of St. Martin turned out to be surprisingly simple. In November 1822, a private fell from one of the platforms on the south side of Fort Mackinac and sustained a fractured skull as well as leg and arm fractures. Beaumont gave him medicine to ease the pain, but even in this case he followed his usual practice of bleeding the patient. The head injuries were presumably less severe than Beaumont had initially feared, because by mid-January he recorded that his patient was walking about on crutches.[45]

A more unusual and more complex case was that of a deserter from Fort Mackinac, who in February 1823 attempted to reach Drummond Island across the ice. He became lost, wandered for a week in temperatures that were often below zero, and was brought to the hospital when he was found unconscious in the snow. His left foot and ankle, the toes and the bottom of the heel of the right foot, all his fingers, and both his thumbs were frozen solid. His ears, nose, and the whole surface of his face was severely frosted.

Beaumont had his patient's hands rubbed with snow, and his feet placed in ice water for ten hours; only then could his stockings be removed. He gave opium to relieve the pain, and had a strong solution of camphorated muriate of ammonia and vinegar and a carbonated fermented poultice applied to his hands and feet. There was no way of saving all the extremities, and several weeks later Beaumont amputated the fingers on the left hand and the whole of the left foot. The patient had been brought in to the hospital in mid-February; by the beginning of April he had been released.[46]

---

45. Notes, BC, WU; Widder, *Beaumont: The Mackinac Years,* 23–25.
46. Notes, BC, WU; Widder, *Beaumont: The Mackinac Years,* 25.

In 1823–1824, Beaumont's life seemed to settle into what was becoming his usual pattern. He was enjoying married life, and in March 1824 the birth of a son added to his domestic pleasures. His letters in these years talk affectionately about his wife and children. He obviously took great pleasure in his little daughter Sarah, who he described in December 1823 as having "the cheerfulness & vivacity of her mother's disposition." He built her a dog cart, equipped it with a harness brought from New York, and used two Indian dogs to pull it. His pleasure extended to his wife's nephew, who he described as a fine, interesting, and remarkably intelligent boy.[47] While ambitious, Beaumont did not have the unhappiness of expecting too much from life. He was able to take pleasure in the moment, while attempting to turn the future to his advantage. He was not beset with self-doubt. From his earliest years away from Lebanon, he believed that he was making a success of his life.

Beaumont also protected his own happiness, and that of his immediate family, by continuing to avoid wider personal obligations. In the spring of 1823 he had heard that his family in Lebanon had been sick, and that his sister Abigail had died. In responding, Beaumont had to apologize for his long silence. As before, a long silence involved money. Abel had apparently asked for one hundred dollars, and Beaumont had not responded. He now gave the explanation that at the time he could have sent it there was no safe means of forwarding it, and since then he had been obliged to pay an old debt incurred during his business partnership. This may have been true, but in any event it provided an excuse to send nothing. He told Abel that he had expended all the cash he had to spare "for a year or two hence." To Abel's news that he was thinking of leaving teaching to farm the old place in Lebanon, Beaumont replied that agriculture was one of the happiest, most permanent, and sure pursuits of life, and also that before many years had passed he was convinced he would give up his present profession to engage in it.[48] There is not the slightest evidence that he had any such intention.

In the fall of 1824, Beaumont set on foot a chain of events that was to make him far more than an army surgeon satisfied in his work and happy in his family. In September of that year he wrote up a careful account of the St. Martin case and sent it to Surgeon General Lovell. Lovell, a physician with broad interests, wanted his surgeons to send him accounts of unusual cases.[49]

47. Charles S. Osborn, "Beaumont–Citizen," 589; Beaumont to Israel Green, December 18, 1823, BP, YU.

48. Beaumont to Abel Beaumont, June 1823, BP, YU.

49. Barboriak, "Reporting to the Surgeon General," 108.

Beaumont's statement was for the most part a straightforward account of the original wound, Beaumont's treatment, and St. Martin's recovery, but in his last few paragraphs, Beaumont indicated that the way in which the wound had healed had gradually suggested to him the possibility of using St. Martin for experimentation.

A year after the accident, Beaumont wrote, the injured parts were all sound with the exception of the stomach, which was much the same as it had been six weeks after the wound had been inflicted. The wound in the stomach was "about the size of a shilling piece," with its edges "firmly attached" to the pleura and the intercostals. Food and drink came out continually unless the wound was covered with a "plug, compress, and bandage." In September 1824, Beaumont wrote, St. Martin was "in perfect health." He was able to perform any kind of labor, "from that of a house-servant to chopping wood or mowing in the field." He was eating and digesting as well as he ever did. Since April, Beaumont said, St. Martin had not had any sickness sufficient to prevent him from performing his duties.

Beaumont concluded his article by commenting on the stomach itself and the possibilities that it provided. He first pointed out the openness of the stomach by noting that if St. Martin drank a quart of water, or ate a dish of soup, it would immediately pass out of his stomach if the compress were removed. Beaumont wrote that he could "look directly into the cavity of the stomach, observe its motion, and almost see the process of digestion." He could pour in water with a funnel, or put in food with a spoon, and take them out again with a syphon. Although he had not begun any systematic experimentation, he had already realized the possibilities presented by this gastric fistula. "I have frequently suspended flesh, raw and roasted, and other substances in the hole," he wrote, "to ascertain the length of time required to digest each; and at one time used a plug of raw beef, instead of lint, to stop the orifice." He found that in less than five hours it was "as smooth and even as if it had been cut with a knife."

Beaumont's concluding paragraph demonstrated that his lack of formal training or research experience had not prevented him from realizing the implications of what it might be possible for him to do. "This case," he wrote, "affords a most excellent opportunity of experimenting upon the gastric fluids, and the process of digestion." He said, optimistically, that it would cause no pain, "nor cause the least uneasiness," to extract a gill of gastric fluid every two or three days. Various digestible substances might be introduced into the stomach, said Beaumont, and they could easily be examined during the whole process of digestion. "I may, therefore," he concluded, "be able hereafter to give some interesting experiments on these subjects."[50]

In 1823 and 1824, Beaumont had obviously become interested, in a non-systematic way, in observing facets of the process of digestion through the hole in St. Martin's stomach, and had dangled meat in the cavity to find out how long it took to digest. He had not begun any systematic research, because what he knew of human digestion was simply what he had learned from the limited reading that had been possible in medical textbooks in Champlain and St. Albans. He had not had previous contact with those engaged in research, but his curiosity had been aroused, he thought there was a possibility that there was something useful to be learned, and he was testing the waters by describing what was, even without experiments, a fascinating case. And he was anxious to know what Surgeon General Lovell thought of the case and his tentative suggestions for possible lines of investigation.

Lovell was always a good, supportive friend of Beaumont's, but he now also demonstrated that he conceived of his duty of superintending the army medical service in broad terms. He responded enthusiastically to the report on St. Martin and described Beaumont's account as a "valuable communication." He said he would follow Beaumont's suggestion and submit it to the *Medical Recorder* for publication. The only change he intended to make was to include a part of Beaumont's accompanying letter that described the present state of St. Martin.

It was important for Beaumont, and for research on the physiology of digestion, that Lovell was a man of imagination, that he believed that problems connected with diet were of great importance to the army, and that he responded favorably and with encouragement to Beaumont's suggestion that St. Martin provided an excellent opportunity for research. He said he would try to send Beaumont a book of experiments on the gastric juice to guide him in his own observations. Lovell had already read enough himself to suggest possible lines of research for Beaumont. It was said, he told Beaumont, that if several different articles of food were taken into the stomach at the same time, the stomach would digest all of one kind first, then the next kind, and so on. If one ate too much, then by the time the stomach had disposed of eight or ten items it would become exhausted, and the last items would remain

50. The manuscript account written by Beaumont in September 1824 is in the BC, WU. The published account is "A Case of Wounded Stomach." The quotations are taken from the printed article.

undigested, ferment, and produce indigestion. Lovell asked Beaumont if he could make experiments to ascertain if this were true, and also to find out the digestibility of various items of food. Lovell said he would be happy to receive an account of any experiments, and thought that they would be acceptable to the public.[51]

This was exactly what Beaumont needed. The surgeon general had given him great encouragement, and even sketched a possible line of research. There is no indication in Beaumont's notes or letters that Lovell carried out his promise of sending a work dealing with research on human digestion, but from the questions that Beaumont tried to answer it seems most likely that he did. In his research, Beaumont was quickly to add to his interest in the length of time it took to digest different items of food the more vital research question of the process by which food was digested in the stomach, particularly the key question of whether the process was chemical in its nature.

It has been suggested that Lovell may have sent Beaumont Nathan Ryno Smith's *A Physiological Essay on Digestion*, published in New York in 1825.[52] Its date of publication certainly makes it appropriate, but Beaumont's approach does not particularly suggest the influence of Smith's work. It is possible, but not likely, that Beaumont remembered some of the details of the ongoing controversies about human digestion from his reading during his apprenticeship fifteen years before. What was essential, however, was that Beaumont now knew that the surgeon general would welcome any results he could obtain from experimentation on St. Martin's stomach.

The fate of Beaumont's first attempt to add to published medical literature was less happy. When the article appeared in the January 1825 issue of the *Medical Recorder*, it appeared under the name of Joseph Lovell, the man who had submitted it. This was not a deliberate theft on Lovell's part–he was too generous for that–and he quickly gave a correction to the editor. Later in the year, the editor of the journal printed a correction with the comment that it should have been mentioned that the case had been reported by Dr. William Beaumont, and that it had occurred at Mackinac. Trying to compensate for his error, the editor also commented that he would be obliged if Beaumont would send any further details of the case, "which was considered as highly interesting, instructive, and well drawn up."[53]

51. Lovell to Beaumont, November 9, 1824, BC, WU.
52. Jerome J. Bylebyl, "William Beaumont, Robley Dunglison, and the 'Philadelphia Physiologists,'" 10–11.
53. The correction is printed in Myer, *Beaumont*, 120.

Beaumont's disappointment at the failure of his name to appear on his own article was somewhat assuaged even before the correction appeared in the journal. In February 1825, the Medical Society of Michigan met in Detroit and unanimously elected Beaumont as an honorary member.[54] If Beaumont could find time, gain St. Martin's acquiescence, and surmount the problems of his lack of knowledge of basic research techniques, he now had a chance to rise higher in the opinion of his contemporaries. It was something that he had always wanted.

It would not be easy. Army medical officers usually spent much of their time in lonely frontier posts, and there were frequent moves for all except those with considerable seniority. In the spring of 1825, Beaumont was ordered to report to Fort Niagara. In April, when he received this order, Beaumont informed Lovell that he intended to leave for Niagara in two or three weeks, but that on arriving there he would like to have a leave of six or eight weeks to conclude private business in Plattsburgh.[55]

If Beaumont hoped to experiment when he was settled in his next post, he must have experienced considerable frustration. The move of the troops was delayed, and it was not until June that Beaumont was established at Fort Niagara. When he later published his book on his experiments on St. Martin, Beaumont stated that he began his first series of gastric experiments at Fort Mackinac in May, but these must have been preliminary attempts such as he described in first reporting the case. Both in his book and in a brief article he published describing his first experiments, he listed his first formal experiment as being carried out at Fort Niagara on August 1, 1825. He did, however, entitle this brief article as "Further Experiments."[56]

Research and writing for publication was all very new to Beaumont, and undoubtedly while at Mackinac, as he came to realize that St. Martin had a permanent stomach fistula, he tried various dressings, observed what he could of the actions of the stomach, and used various means to introduce food through the opening. This became easier, because as St. Martin recovered, "a small fold or doubling of the coats of the stomach" appeared, blocking the hole into the stomach and making it unnecessary to use a compress

54. John Whitney to Beaumont, March 3, 1825, BC, WU; Nelson, *Beaumont,* 121.
55. Beaumont to Lovell, April 1825, WD, AG, IMOF.
56. Beaumont to Lovell, June 2, 1825, WD, SG, LR; William Beaumont, *Experiments and Observations on the Gastric Juice and the Physiology of Digestion,* 17, 125; William Beaumont, "Further Experiments on the Case of Alexis St. Martin, Who Was Wounded in the Stomach by a Load of Buckshot, Detailed in the Recorder for Jan. 1825," 94.

and bandage to retain the stomach contents. Although this was firm enough to keep in the contents of the stomach even when the stomach was full, it could easily be depressed with a finger. In his book, published in the 1830s, Beaumont stated that this natural valve appeared in the winter of 1823–1824, but it seems likely that it was later, since in writing his first description of St. Martin's case for publication in September 1824, Beaumont refers to St. Martin removing the compress and letting out the contents of the stomach.[57]

Before he could begin any systematic experiments, Beaumont had to take charge of the post hospital at Fort Niagara, which was situated at the junction of the Niagara River and Lake Ontario. Beaumont had become quite familiar with the region during the War of 1812. At Fort Niagara, as at Mackinac, Beaumont found that his small army hospital offered few conveniences for the care of the sick. A few years later an inspector noted that the building used as the hospital was very ill-suited to that function. It was on the second floor, it leaked, it was very cold in winter, and it could only be reached by steep uncovered steps on the outside of the building.[58]

At Niagara, as at Mackinac, Beaumont was ready to make requests of Surgeon General Lovell. In July he reiterated his request for two months' leave to visit his friends and transact private business, and he also asked permission to engage in civilian practice among the inhabitants in the vicinity of Fort Niagara. It was typical of Beaumont's view of his own affairs that he asked: "Can there be any objection to granting the above requests?"[59] Beaumont had no doubt that the answer was "no," and luckily for him, Lovell was cooperative. He granted the necessary permission. Before Beaumont went on leave, he managed to find time for his first formal experiments on St. Martin. He had taken his first steps on his meandering road to physiological fame.

57. Beaumont, *Experiments,* 17; Lovell [Beaumont], "A Case of Wounded Stomach," 18.

58. War Department, RG 159, Office of the Inspector General, Inspection Reports, 1814–1842, National Archives, Washington, D.C., Fort Niagara, October 1, 1831 (microfilm, SHSW). Hereafter cited as WD, IG, Reports.

59. Beaumont to Lovell, July 10, 1825, with notation of approval of leave, WD, AG, IMOF.

William Beaumont in uniform. The date of the portrait is unknown, but it probably was made around the time of his marriage in 1821.

William Beaumont and his family, c. 1833 (courtesy of the Joseph Regenstein Library, University of Chicago)

Alexis St. Martin (courtesy of the Archives, Washington University School of Medicine)

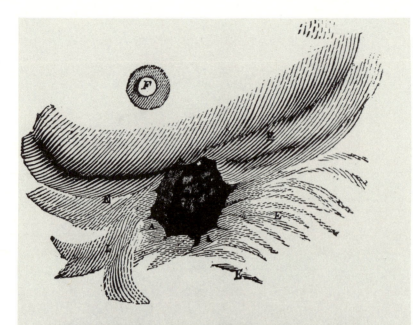

This engraving represents the appearance of the aperture with the valve depressed.

A A A Edges of the aperture through the integuments and intercostals, on the inside and around which is the union of the lacerated edges of the perforated coats of the stomach with the intercostals and skin.

B The cavity of the stomach, when the valve is depressed.

C Valve, depressed within the cavity of the stomach.

E E E E Cicatrice of the original wound.

F The nipple.

Alexis St. Martin's wound (from Beaumont, *Experiments and Observations on the Gastric Juice and the Physiology of Digestion*, 1833)

Mackinac (pencil sketch by Seth Eastman, courtesy of the Peabody Museum, Harvard University, photograph by Hillel Burger)

Fort Crawford, Prairie du Chien, 1829 (pencil sketch by Seth Eastman, courtesy of the Peabody Museum, Harvard University)

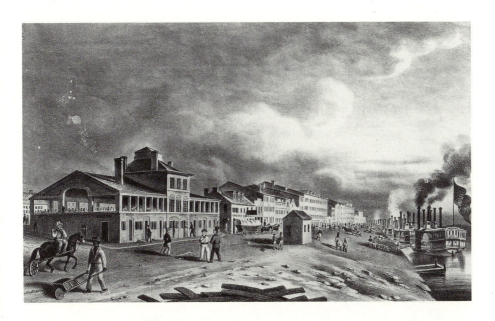

View of Front Street, St. Louis, 1840 (lithograph by J. C. Wild, courtesy of the
Missouri Historical Society, St. Louis)

William Beaumont as a successful St. Louis private physician (courtesy of the Archives, Washington University
School of Medicine)

FIVE

The Problems of Research

THERE IS NO INDICATION in Beaumont's correspondence, nor in his notes, that Beaumont had found the time or opportunity to engage in reading to expand his medical knowledge since his qualification in 1812. In Plattsburgh from 1815 to 1820, he might well have had access to some volumes to look up points that puzzled him about specific cases, but in Mackinac he expanded his practical rather than his theoretical medical knowledge. The reading he had undertaken in Champlain and St. Albans while preparing for a medical career would have left him with the idea that much about human digestion was unknown, and what was known was in dispute. What Beaumont lacked, and this was ultimately to be to his advantage, was a commitment to any one of the basic theories that had been advanced to explain the process of digestion. When he conducted his experiments, he wanted to see how digestion occurred, but he was not trying to confirm a preconceived theory.

Since the age of classical Greece, physicians had exhibited an interest in the process of human digestion. At different times in the past, digestion had been explained in terms of the heat of the stomach, putrefaction, grinding (trituration), and fermentation.[1]

---

1. Anthony M. Kasich, "William Prout and the Discovery of Hydrochloric Acid in the Gastric Juice," 340–41; George Rosen, *The Reception of William Beaumont's Discovery in Europe*, 13–16; Edward Atwater, " 'Squeezing Mother Nature': Experimental Physiology in the United States before 1870," 318; Walter R. Steiner, "Dr. William Beaumont: An Appreciation," 413.

During the seventeenth and eighteenth centuries, the physiology of the digestive process had attracted considerable attention, and while other theories were still advanced, much of the debate had evolved into an argument between those who argued that digestion was a chemical process and those who argued that it was a mechanical, grinding action.[2] Research was still far away from understanding that digestion was a process of great complexity involving the whole gastrointestinal tract, and that changes that took place in the stomach were only one part of that process.

Those who defended the chemical nature of the digestive process traced their origin to the work of the seventeenth-century researchers Jean Baptiste van Helmont and Franciscus Sylvius. Van Helmont had argued that food was digested by chemical action that produced fermentation. His work influenced Sylvius, who ultimately became a far more influential figure. Sylvius also stressed chemical action and fermentation, but unlike van Helmont, he discussed stages in fermentation and also placed considerable emphasis on the action of saliva. Sylvius believed that saliva swallowed with the food was of great importance in the process of fermentation in the stomach, and also believed that in a later stage bile and pancreatic juice played an important part before chyle could be absorbed.[3]

The basis for contending that digestion was a mechanical process had been laid by Sanctorius and Gian Alfonso Borelli. Borelli attempted to explain the human body in mechanical terms. He saw digestion as a process of grinding (trituration) in the stomach, and his followers went even further in denying the role of chemical action in the process of digestion.[4]

In the eighteenth century a variety of attempts were made to add to existing knowledge of the digestive process, but the most useful work for those who thought of digestion as a chemical process was the research of the Frenchman René Antoine Ferchault de Réaumur and the Italian Lazzaro Spallanzani. Spallanzani was ultimately to be the researcher Beaumont most admired, and whose work he endorsed and helped to prove.

Réaumur and Spallanzani went beyond what had often at an earlier date been general speculation to ground their conclusions in actual research. Réaumur used a bird—a kite or buzzard—for his experiments. From the point

2. Michael Foster, *Lectures on the History of Physiology during the Sixteenth, Seventeenth and Eighteenth Centuries,* 55.

3. Ibid., 120–56; Rothschuh, *History of Physiology,* trans. Risse, 59–61.

4. Foster, *Lectures,* 55–82, 159–65; Rothschuh, *History of Physiology,* trans. Risse, 76–82.

of view of studying digestion, the kite has the advantage that it regurgitates food it cannot digest. Réaumur obtained gastric juice from the kite by having it swallow perforated metal tubes containing sponges. When the bird regurgitated the tubes, he squeezed the juice out of the sponges. This juice, he demonstrated, was acid in nature and could dissolve food.[5]

Spallanzani went beyond Réaumur in the breadth of his research. He experimented on a number of different animals—birds, sheep, dogs, and cats among them—and on himself. To experiment on himself, he swallowed sponges tied on strings and pulled them back up, or regurgitated linen bags. After obtaining gastric juice, he was able to demonstrate that it would dissolve food in vitro (outside the body), that the process could be speeded up by the use of heat, and that food placed in it did not putrefy. He also demonstrated that the process was not one of fermentation. Spallanzani submitted some of the gastric juice to one of his colleagues—the chemist Giovanni Scapoli—for analysis, and Scapoli reached the conclusion that gastric juice contained sal ammoniac and was neither acid nor alkaline. Spallanzani accepted the idea of the "neutral" quality of gastric juice, and thus left its nature in much doubt.[6]

Réaumur and Spallanzani had done much to prove that digestion was a chemical rather than a mechanical process, but this did not end the argument. The British surgeon John Hunter undertook experiments similar to those of Spallanzani, but in the 1780s he launched a strong attack on Spallanzani's views. Hunter was strongly influenced by the idea of "vitalism." The vitalists believed that human processes could not be conceived of in strictly chemical or mechanical terms.[7]

Even if one believed that gastric juice acted as a solvent, and that digestion was a chemical process, there were still additional difficulties. Spallanzani had done much to show how gastric juice acted on food, but he denied the existence of acid in the stomach. Some thought acid was there but that it came from the food in the process of digestion; others asked why, if acid

5. Kasich, "William Prout," 342–43; Atwater, "'Squeezing Mother Nature,'" 318; Rothschuh, *History of Physiology*, trans. Risse, 132.

6. Arnold I. Walder, "A Historical Review of the Nature of the Gastric Fluid," 547; Kasich, "William Prout," 342–43; Atwater, "'Squeezing Mother Nature,'" 318; Rothschuh, *History of Physiology*, trans. Risse, 132–33; Alfred H. Whittaker, "Observations of Some Physiologists Who Preceded Beaumont," 751–52; Donald G. Bates, "The Background to John Young's Thesis on Digestion," 354–56.

7. Rothschuh, *History of Physiology*, trans. Risse, 133–34; Bates, "Background to Young's Thesis," 345–49; Bylebyl, "Beaumont, Dunglison, and the 'Philadelphia Physiologists,'" 3–5.

was present, it did not dissolve the stomach itself. The vitalists contended earnestly for the presence of some vital principle in the human body that acted outside the normal bounds of chemical or mechanical action. Others still thought that a mechanical process of grinding was involved, or that fermentation was part of the process.[8]

In America, research in physiology did not have a long history, and had not produced any great names or all-encompassing theories in the European manner. What research had been done, had largely been carried out at the University of Pennsylvania in the late eighteenth and early nineteenth centuries and was mostly in the form of student theses. The interest in digestion was partly the result of the influential Benjamin Rush, who earlier in his own career had written a thesis on digestion, in which he had supported the theory of fermentation.[9]

One of Rush's students, John R. Young, who also worked with Benjamin Smith Barton and dedicated his work to him, submitted a thesis on digestion in 1803 in which his work was based on research on frogs and on himself. By using litmus on the gastric juice of frogs, and on partially digested food that he regurgitated, Young reached the conclusion that acid was present in gastric juice, although he misidentified it as phosphoric. He did, however, give support to Spallanzani's defense of gastric juice as a solvent.

Young's mentors reacted differently to his work. Barton, a vitalist, refused to believe that acid was present in a normal stomach, but Rush in his lectures reversed his own original belief in fermentation and accepted the presence of acid in the gastric juice. If Young intended to continue his research, he had no chance, for he died of tuberculosis in the year following the publication of his dissertation.[10]

The work of Réaumur and Spallanzani was well known in Philadelphia, and another early-nineteenth-century student, Oliver H. Spencer, who wrote his graduate dissertation on digestion, gave a description of their work in presenting his own efforts at research, which was mainly based on the stomach of dogs. All of the research, in Philadelphia or elsewhere, was thrown into doubt by the lack of adequate access to the human stomach

8. Bates, "Background to Young's Thesis," 344–56; Rosen, *Reception*, 15–16.

9. Bates, "Background to Young's Thesis," 356–57; Atwater, "'Squeezing Mother Nature,'" 315–19; William S. Miller, "William Beaumont and His Book: Elisha North and His Copy of Beaumont's Book," 156.

10. Kasich, "William Prout," 343–44; Atwater, "'Squeezing Mother Nature,'" 318–19, 327n48; Bates, "Background to Young's Thesis," 356–57.

and its gastric juice, and the dependence on the stomachs and gastric juices of a variety of other animals.[11]

In Europe, interest in the process of digestion continued to be strong in the late eighteenth and early nineteenth centuries, and in spite of Spallanzani's work there was still bitter controversy. Vitalism enjoyed a great vogue in late-eighteenth- and early-nineteenth-century France. Arguing that digestion had to be the result of the direct action of a living stomach, the vitalists contended that what was produced by the use of gastric juice in vitro was not the same as the chyle produced by human digestion. A. Jenin de Montegre argued in 1812 that gastric juice was not a solvent, that there was no true digestion in vitro, and that any acid in the stomach came as a result of the process of digestion or from saliva. This conclusion was widely accepted in France, and it also was the basis of the conclusions regarding the stomach in François Magendie's well-known textbook on physiology.[12]

The argument about digestion was of such wide interest that in the mid-1820s the French Academy of Science sponsored a contest on the process of digestion in animals. The most important results that came out of this were the findings of the Germans Friedrich Tiedemann and Leopold Gmelin, and to a lesser extent those of the Frenchmen François Leuret and Jean Lassaigne. The Germans argued that gastric juice was acid in nature, that it was muriatic (hydrochloric), and that it was secreted only when the stomach had been stimulated. They also produced digestion outside the stomach, in vitro, and did much to discredit the work of Montegre. The two Frenchmen, who based their conclusions on research on horses and dogs, argued that gastric juice was ninety-eight parts water, and that the acid that was present (with other ingredients) in the other two parts was lactic.[13]

Almost contemporaneously with the work of Tiedemann and Gmelin, the Englishman William Prout also demonstrated the chemical nature of digestion. In 1824 he published his conclusion that hydrochloric acid was present in the gastric juice. Leuret and Lassaigne attacked Prout's conclusions; Tiedemann and Gmelin not only agreed with him but also acknowledged that his work, in this particular respect, took precedence over their own.[14]

11. Whittaker, "Observations of Some Physiologists," 753.
12. Bylebyl, "Beaumont, Dunglison, and the 'Philadelphia Physiologists,'" 5–8; Walder, "Historical Review of the Nature of Gastric Fluid," 546–48.
13. Kasich, "William Prout," 350; Bylebyl, "Beaumont, Dunglison, and the 'Philadelphia Physiologists,'" 9, Walder, "Historical Review of the Nature of Gastric Fluid," 548–52.
14. Kasich, "William Prout," 340–58.

With his limited, provincial training, Beaumont had no way of knowing, when he began his research on St. Martin, the full extent of the controversy in the field he was entering, nor could he have realized from his limited background the intense interest there was in the subject of digestion. He was entering this area of physiological research as an innocent, but he was entering it with an advantage lacking in Paris, London, or Berlin. He had an accessible human stomach, and could observe digestion both in the stomach and in vitro.

Although medical literature contained a few previous cases of patients with gastric fistulae, there had been no sustained and methodical research. In the eighteenth century, only in one of the handful of cases had a doctor even considered performing experiments, and he had not been able to do so before the patient died. In the early nineteenth century there were again a few cases, but very limited experimentation. The most systematic, but not very productive, experiments were those of the Austrian physician Jacob Helm. Between 1798 and 1802, Helm conducted experiments on a woman with a gastric fistula and published the result of his researches. He fed his patient through the fistula, observed that he could use his finger to stimulate the production of gastric juice, and made observations on the times it took to digest different items of food. He also made practical suggestions regarding diet and the best ways to have healthy digestion. He said chewing food and saliva were important, and that the stomach should not be overloaded. Although he confirmed Spallanzani's observation that food was digested better the longer it remained in the stomach, his results were limited, and he did not delve with any great effort into the vexed question of the nature of the gastric juice. He was far more interested in problems of diet than he was in the physiology of the stomach.[15]

Helm's work was known in the United States from the first decade of the nineteenth century, but it did not make any great impact. Although Helm had read much of the main earlier research on digestion, such as that of Réaumur and Spallanzani, he did not ask the right questions, nor conduct any systematic pattern of research to answer the questions that were perplexing those engaged actively in research on digestion.[16]

15. Bruno Kisch, "Jacob Helm's Observations and Experiments on Human Digestion," 311–28; Bruno Kisch, "Jacob Anton Helm and William Beaumont," 54–74; Walter B. Cannon and George Higginson, "The Book of William Beaumont after One Hundred Years," 569–71.
16. Kisch, "Helm and Beaumont," 75–81; Kisch, "Helm's Observations," 327; Numbers and Orr, "Beaumont's Reception," 609.

Lovell had suggested that Beaumont might investigate whether the stomach, as some thought, digested food one item at a time, and that it would also be useful if he could ascertain the digestibility of different items of food. That Beaumont went beyond this probably reflects that Lovell had fulfilled his promise of sending reading pertaining to research in human digestion.[17] Beaumont made mistakes, but he was able, without research training and without contact with those engaged in research, to proceed in an orderly and consistent manner, and to ask many of the right questions. He also learned quickly from his mistakes.

Beaumont's first effort was extremely brief. The series consisted of just four experiments, which he published in the following year in the *Medical Recorder*. The first was a false start, but he quickly learned from it. He began at noon on August 1, 1825, when he suspended various items of food along the length of a silk string and dangled them through the cavity into the stomach. In his inexperience, he put in a variety difficult to digest–"a piece of high-seasoned *alamode beef,* a piece of raw *salted lean beef,* a piece of raw salted *fat pork,* a piece of raw lean *fresh beef,* a piece of boiled *corned beef,* a piece of *stale bread,* and a bunch of *raw cabbage.*" Each piece consisted of about two drachms (a quarter of an apothecary's ounce). St. Martin then went about his normal domestic duties.[18]

At one, two, and three o'clock Beaumont pulled out the string, and observed the rate at which the different items were digesting. By three o'clock the stomach had an unhealthy appearance, and St. Martin was complaining of pain and discomfort. This created problems for Beaumont as well as for St. Martin, because Beaumont's research obviously depended upon St. Martin's cooperation. By five o'clock St. Martin was complaining of "considerable distress at the stomach," general debility, and a headache. Beaumont pulled out the remaining food and found the stomach fluids "rancid and sharp." Because of St. Martin's complaints, he did not return the food into the stomach.[19]

On the following day (August 2), St. Martin complained of nausea, headache, and costiveness, and Beaumont could observe numerous white spots ("or pustules") spread over the inner surface of the stomach. Beaumont was later to realize that this physical evidence of indigestion did, in itself, constitute a valuable observation. At the time, he reacted as one might expect of a practical, early-nineteenth-century physician trained in the heroic

17. Lovell to Beaumont, November 9, 1824, BC, WU.
18. Beaumont, "Further Experiments on the Case of Alexis St. Martin," 94.
19. Ibid., 94–95.

therapeutic mode. Through the cavity into the stomach, he dropped in "half a dozen" calomel pills, of four or five grains each. In about three hours the cathartic effect of the calomel, wrote Beaumont, had restored St. Martin to health and the stomach to a normal condition.

It was not until August 7 that Beaumont renewed his experiments, this time with more success. After having St. Martin fast for seventeen hours, until 11 A.M., he used a glass thermometer to ascertain the temperature of the stomach. The mercury rose to one hundred degrees, and remained stationary. This procedure would suggest that he had access to a book concerning research on digestion, for the question of heat and digestion had occasioned much discussion.[20]

Beaumont then used a procedure that was, throughout the period of his research, to give him a marked advantage over other researchers. With a gum-elastic syphon, he drew off an ounce of "pure gastric liquor" into a vial. The main eighteenth-century researchers into digestion—including Réaumur and Spallanzani—had been obliged to undertake their research on the gastric juices of animals, or to use whatever gastric juice they thought present in what they could bring up from their own stomachs.

At this very first stage of his research, Beaumont now ran a test that went to the heart of the eighteenth- and early-nineteenth-century controversy over digestion and the role of the gastric juice—he compared digestion in vitro with digestion in the stomach itself. Into a vial he placed a piece of *"corned boiled beef,* large as my little finger." Later, after years of work and more reading, when he wrote his book on these experiments, he described this as placing into the vial "a solid piece of *boiled, recently salted beef,* weighing three drachms." He apparently had realized that his description of a piece as "large as my little finger" was not in the best tradition of scientific research. Although Beaumont was to be systematic in his research, the problem of failing to weigh and to list exact quantities remained with him throughout his work.[21]

Beaumont may not have been exact in describing amounts, but in this, his second formal experiment, he both demonstrated that he already knew some of what he needed to look for and he also achieved significant results. He now proceeded by corking the vial containing the gastric juice and beef, warmed it to exactly one hundred degrees in a saucepan of water, and kept it at that

20. Ibid., 95.

21. Ibid., 95; Beaumont, *Experiments,* 128; Bylebyl, "Beaumont, Dunglison, and the 'Philadelphia Physiologists,'" 10.

temperature in a sand bath. In a sand bath, the vial was protected from direct heat by a layer of sand. He observed that in forty minutes digestion had begun over the surface of the meat, in fifty minutes the liquid was cloudy, with the external texture beginning to break loose, and in one hour chyme began to form. Beaumont regularly examined the vial throughout the afternoon and early evening, and he noted that by 9 P.M. the meat was completely digested. When taken from the stomach, the gastric juice was as clear as water; by 9 P.M. it was "about the colour of whey." After it had been at rest for several minutes, a fine sediment the color of meat settled in the bottom of the vial.[22]

At the same time that Beaumont began this process of digestion in vitro, he also suspended an identical piece of beef through the fistula into St. Martin's stomach. By withdrawing it for examination, he discovered that the effect of the gastric juice on the piece of meat suspended in the stomach was the same as that in the vial, except that the meat in the stomach digested much more quickly. By 1 P.M. the meat was completely digested. Both in vitro and in the stomach, he noted that digestion began on the surface of the meat. Agitating the vial accelerated the process by removing the outer coat and giving the gastric juice access to the undigested portions. In Beaumont's first day of real research with St. Martin and his gastric fistula he had achieved more significant results than the Viennese doctor Jacob Helm had achieved in four years of research on his similar subject.

On the following day, August 8, Beaumont drew off one and a half ounces of gastric juice and placed it in a vial with two pieces of boiled chicken. He followed the same procedures as on the previous day regarding temperature. He pointed out that in this case digestion was slower than for the beef, because the texture of the chicken was firmer and the juice had more difficulty in penetrating below the surface. After digestion in the vial was complete, the fluid was grayish-white and more resembled a milky fluid than whey, and the sediment was of a lighter color. Otherwise, digestion had proceeded in every way in a similar manner to that of the beef on the previous day.[23]

Beaumont in the last section of his brief report on these experiments again demonstrated that he knew what to look for. He noted that he kept the contents of both vials tightly corked from August 7 and 8 to September 6, and that for that whole period the contents did not become putrid in any way. Only then did the beef become putrid; the chicken remained the same

---

22. Beaumont, "Further Experiments," 95–96.
23. Ibid., 97.

as before.[24] This confirmed Spallanzani's conclusions regarding gastric juice retarding rather than promoting putrefaction.

Eight years later, when Beaumont included these experiments in his book, his greater experience, additional reading, and additional research enabled him to draw the conclusions that were implicit in his earlier report. In his book, he noted that these experiments had demonstrated that the stomach secreted a fluid that possessed solvent properties, and that solid substances were affected too rapidly for it to be accounted for on the principle of either maceration or putrefaction.[25]

The last sentence of Beaumont's report published in January 1826 revealed the difficulties he was to have for the rest of his life when wanting to continue his research on digestion with St. Martin. "The man absconded to Canada," Beaumont wrote, "and it is to be regretted that the experiments have, on that account, been suspended."[26]

In the week before he had begun his research, Beaumont had received approval for the sixty-day leave he had requested, and in September, when he traveled to Plattsburgh, he took St. Martin with him. This trip took St. Martin very close to his old home on the St. Lawrence, and he took the opportunity to leave the Beaumont family and return to Canada. When Beaumont submitted his brief article on his experiments to James Webster, the editor of the *Medical Recorder*, he apologized that he could not send fuller results but said that St. Martin was "unwilling to be experimented upon, though it caused him but little pain or distress." This, of course, was not completely true; Beaumont's first unwise effort, on August 1, had caused St. Martin considerable discomfort, and St. Martin may well have thought this would be repeated. He may, of course, have just been homesick.[27]

It was to be nearly four years before Beaumont saw St. Martin again. In the meantime St. Martin set about pursuing a more normal life, a life that had been totally disrupted since he had received his terrible wound more than five years before. In October 1826 he was married. He was to have children, and for a time he again traveled west as a voyageur.[28]

24. Ibid., 97.
25. Beaumont, *Experiments,* 130.
26. Beaumont, "Further Experiments," 97.
27. Beaumont to Lovell, August 15 and September 15, 1825, WD, AG, IMOF; Beaumont to James Webster, [c. November 1825], BC, WU (this letter is printed in Myer, *Beaumont,* 122, quotation).
28. Bensley, "Alexis St. Martin," 739.

Beaumont had obviously enjoyed seeing his name in print and corresponding with the editor of a major medical journal. When he wrote to Webster to send the result of his experiments, he also mentioned that he had other interesting cases in his journals that he would be happy to send if the readers might like to see them.[29]

The visit to Plattsburgh brought Beaumont a much greater sadness than the departure of St. Martin. His baby son William died on October 8.[30] The death of a baby was so common as to be usual in the early nineteenth century, but it was still difficult for a physician to accept. For Beaumont, it could only reveal the deficiencies of an art in which he was usually so confident.

Back at Fort Niagara, Beaumont, on the day after Christmas, responded to a circular from the surgeon general's office asking assistant surgeons to give their preferences for postings. Beaumont preferred to be with the Second Regiment, but most of his choices were frontier posts in the Great Lakes region. He would have been happy to return to Fort Mackinac, or to some other post in Michigan Territory. There are strong indications in the list that Beaumont's early years of marriage on isolated Fort Mackinac had been happy ones, and that if he could not be in Plattsburgh, which he now regarded as his home, then he preferred northern frontier posts. His very brief taste of research had not inspired him with any strong wish to locate in posts near eastern cities with scholars, books, hospitals, and universities, and unsurprisingly, he had no great desire to be near his own original home and family in Lebanon. Fort Trumbull at New London was only seventh on his list. On Mackinac Island, Beaumont had successfully combined his military duties with a private practice and a happy home life, and he seemed content to continue living in isolated frontier posts.[31]

Beaumont spent the winter of 1825–1826 at Fort Niagara. In November, with his hopes of further research on St. Martin at least temporarily frustrated, he sent his description of the few experiments he had carried out to the *Medical Recorder*. The publication of this article in January 1826 was some consolation for the loss of St. Martin, but in the immediate future his thoughts were dominated by a crisis in his military life that had arisen as a result of his medical actions in the case of a suspected case of malingering.

29. Myer, *Beaumont,* 121–22; Beaumont to James Webster, [c. November 1825], BC, WU.
30. Tuttle, comp. and ed., *Three Centuries in Champlain Valley,* 66.
31. Beaumont to Lovell, December 26, 1825, WD, AG, IMOF.

In June 1825, shortly after Beaumont had arrived at Fort Niagara, Lieutenant Edmund B. Griswold reported sick. Beaumont bled him, and soon removed him from the sick list. Griswold apparently did not agree that he was well, and so neglected his duties that complaints were made to the commanding officer of the post. To justify himself, Griswold, on July 2, returned to Beaumont and said that the arm from which he had been bled was so sore that he could not wear his uniform coat. Although Beaumont later said he could find nothing wrong with the arm, Griswold insisted on being placed on the sick list.[32]

Beaumont was becoming suspicious that Lieutenant Griswold was malingering, and apparently became convinced of this when he saw Griswold enjoying himself on July 4. When Griswold once again reported sick, Beaumont decided that he would test whether Griswold was actually sick. He left Griswold "an emetic-cathartic" of fifteen or twenty grains of calomel, and five or six grains of tartar emetic. He did not stay to see if Griswold took it, but visiting him frequently in this quarters that day found no signs that Griswold had taken the medicine. Griswold, Beaumont wrote later, was reading or writing, "appearing very comfortable and undisturbed." Later in the day he saw Griswold walking about outside in cloudy, damp weather. "If Mr. Griswold had taken medicine as I directed him that morning," Beaumont commented, "he would have swelled jaws and a sore mouth for his imprudence."

On the next morning, when Beaumont visited Griswold, he saw no signs that the medicine had been taken and no soreness of his mouth or throat. From this, and from his previous examinations of Griswold, Beaumont decided that Griswold had not been sick at all, struck him off his sick report, marked him fit for duty, and reported him to the commanding officer.[33]

As a result of Beaumont's report, Griswold was court-martialed and sentenced to be dismissed from the service. A complication in the trial was that the two officers who had originally complained to the commanding officer of Griswold neglecting his duties reversed themselves, and testified on behalf of the prisoner. The case appeared to be over, but early in 1826 Beaumont's actions were challenged, and the decision of the court-martial was reversed at the very highest level. On examining the recommendation of the court-martial, the president of the United States, John Quincy Adams, intervened

32. Myer, *Beaumont*, 123–28; Nelson, *Beaumont*, 123–27, has a full discussion of the Griswold case.
33. Myer, *Beaumont*, 122.

personally on behalf of Griswold and reprimanded Beaumont. On February 18, 1826, an order was issued reversing the decision of the court-martial. President Adams argued that the evidence did not warrant the dismissal. The decision of two of Griswold's fellow officers to testify for the man they had originally complained about was of key importance in the reversal, for they had stated that Griswold could not perform his duties because he was ill.[34]

Griswold's conviction, argued Adams, rested on the testimony of Beaumont, which was more an expression of his professional opinion than a statement of facts. Moreover, his testimony, Adams stated, had been shaken by the testimony of the two officers. Adams went on with statements that, coming from the president of the United States, could have shattered a general, let alone an assistant surgeon. "The testimony of Brevet-Major Thompson and that of Assistant Surgeon Beaumont," wrote Adams, "both bear internal marks of excited feelings, impairing their credibility." He went on with even more damning comments. He reprimanded Beaumont for having made an experiment "of more than doubtful propriety in the relations of a medical adviser to his patient. A medicine of violent operation, administered by a physician to a man whom he believes to be in full health, but who is taking his professional advice, is a very improper test of the sincerity of the patient's complaints, and the avowal of it as a transaction justifiable in itself discloses a mind warped by ill-will, or insensitive to its own relative duties."[35]

For a man who was still an obscure assistant surgeon in the United States Army, Beaumont's brief stay at Fort Niagara was quite remarkable. He had begun experiments that were to give him a permanent name in the history of science, and he was publicly chastised by the president of the United States for abusing the doctor-patient relationship. Adams had told the world, or at least the army world in which Beaumont existed, that he had a mind "warped by ill-will, or insensitive to its own relative duties." For an insecure man, this could have been a crushing blow, but Beaumont survived without any apparent blight on his army career or to his own self-esteem.

Beaumont was always confident of his own rectitude, and never lacked courage. He tried, without success, to obtain a court of inquiry into his conduct, and then, informing his superiors that he was required "by every principle of honour and feeling of manliness" to reply to the president's accusation, he issued a long circular defending his conduct. In it he claimed that

34. Ibid., 125.
35. Ibid., 125.

the principle of "Equal rights in a free Government," and his right to justice within the army, gave him the right to defend himself. "My reputation," he wrote, "is dear to me." He addressed Adams's attack on his conduct as a doctor by stating that whether the course he had adopted was justifiable "either in a moral or professional point of view" he would leave to medical men and "candid judges" to decide. Beaumont claimed that he never expected Griswold to take the strong cathartic-emetic he had prescribed because he was convinced that he was quite healthy, and that he was proved right when Griswold obviously did not take it. What is more, Beaumont stated, if he were placed in the same situation a hundred times, he "would do as in this case I have done." He complained of the officers who had reversed their original statements when called to testify, and he asked for reconsideration because his reputation had been "stigmatized throughout the army" by the president of the United States.[36]

Beaumont's conduct toward Griswold would clearly be unacceptable in a modern context, but it was not exceptional in the early-nineteenth-century army. Mary Gillett, in her history of the army medical department in these years, comments on the recommendations of army surgeon Jabez Heustis. In his work on the diseases of Louisiana, published in 1817, he maintained that blistering was a good test to find out if a man was really sick. If a man was not sick, he was unlikely to submit to the pain of blistering a second time. Beaumont himself was obviously convinced that Griswold was malingering, and he copied pages of extracts on malingering into his notebooks.[37]

What Beaumont perceived as the injustices of this case rankled in him for many years. His family in Lebanon must have been surprised when, two years later, Beaumont broke a long silence with a letter in which he commented that he had "received the *unjust* censure of the President of the U States for having acted openly & independently in the discharge of my official duty." President Adams had written with remarkable candor in giving his opinion of the acts of an assistant surgeon, but he was not petty. In February 1828 he signed the commission that promoted Beaumont to the rank of surgeon, with the rank to take effect from November 26, 1826.[38]

Beaumont did not take the opportunity of his temporary posting at Fort

36. Ibid., 126–28.
37. Gillett, *Army Medical Department, 1818–1865,* 192. Beaumont copied some fourteen pages of extracts on the subject of malingering, BC, WU.
38. Beaumont to Lucretia Beaumont, May 3, 1828, BP, YU; Commission, signed by President John Quincy Adams, February 15, 1828, BC, WU.

Niagara to visit his family in Lebanon. Abel, having observed his brother's progress, had at last broken away from the farm, and had begun his own medical studies in New York City. Beaumont told Abel that he was willing to renew his earlier offer that Abel should study with him between lecture sessions if he remained at a post in the East, but this would not be possible if he was ordered west, which he expected to happen within a month. In this event, he suggested Abel should do what he had done himself, and apprentice himself to a physician who would accept work for part of the fee. Beaumont was pleased with the way his own apprenticeship had worked out, and wanted Abel to follow a similar path.

More surprisingly, Beaumont said he should be able to help pay for Abel's second course of lectures in the following winter. In that event, however, he said Abel should transfer from lectures in New York, which Beaumont considered "extravagant & extortionary." He also suggested that Abel might earn some money in the hospitals and asylums of the city, and the possibility that he might join the apothecaries department of the United States Army. One often has the impression that Beaumont would have been happy if his conscience would have permitted him to forget completely about his old family in Lebanon. It was not that he was ashamed of them; he simply did not want to spend money on them.[39]

A few weeks after writing to Abel, Beaumont received orders to accompany the Second Regiment to Fort Howard, Green Bay, which at that time was in Michigan Territory. Late in March, when he acknowledged receipt of this order to Surgeon General Lovell, he also asked for a fresh supply of smallpox vaccine, because he feared there would be none at Green Bay when he arrived. Since 1818, the army had required that all its soldiers be vaccinated against smallpox. The Indian agents also tried to ensure vaccination of the Indians in their districts, and Beaumont had vaccinated many Indians at Mackinac. Beaumont was able to take the vaccine with him.[40]

Before leaving for Fort Howard, Beaumont also requested permission to practice among the civilian population at Green Bay, stating that they depended on the military surgeon for help. As at Mackinac, Beaumont was able to combine a civilian with a military practice.[41] It is quite possible that

---

39. Beaumont to Abel Beaumont, March 6, 1826, BP, YU (I used the typed copy of this letter in the BC, WU).
40. Beaumont to Lovell, March 29, 1826, WD, AG, IMOF; Beaumont to Lovell, April 21, 1826, WD, SG, LR. See also Gillett, *Army Medical Department, 1818–1865,* 15.
41. Beaumont to Lovell, March 31, 1826, WD, AG, IMOF.

Beaumont showed a preference for distant western posts in small communities because it was easier for him to argue the necessity of having a civilian practice. This provided a very valuable addition to his income.

The Green Bay settlement, which was chiefly inhabited by French Canadians, stretched about six miles on either side of the Fox River, from near the entrance to the bay to the De Pere rapids. Many of the French Canadians were retired voyageurs who had intermarried with the Menominee Indians, who lived in the region. In the French fashion, their houses were scattered along the six-mile stretch of the river, with the cleared land stretching back about half a mile or less. There were some five hundred inhabitants. The soil was fertile, and produced good crops.[42]

There had been an old French fort, La Baye, near the mouth of the Fox River, and after the War of 1812, American troops built a new American one on the old site. When Henry Schoolcraft visited Green Bay in 1820, he described the fort as situated on a handsome, fertile plain near the mouth of the Fox, and said it consisted of a timber stockade thirty feet high enclosing barracks and a parade ground. Schoolcraft described the fort as whitewashed and presenting a neat military appearance, but when a military inspector visited in 1828, he was somewhat shocked that the timber stockade had the appearance of one of the old western forts built as rallying points in the event of Indian troubles; with "stables, hen houses, cow houses, *private* workshops, root houses, wash houses in any number and without any order." The fort personnel took advantage of the excellent soil, and to the north of the fort had a large garden, which produced an abundance of vegetables.[43]

In 1820, a commander who was dissatisfied with the existing fort began to build a new one, Camp Smith, some two and a half miles up the river. This had been abandoned, but not before a "Shantytown" had grown up around it. Some of the early American residents had begun to settle upriver from "Shantytown." One of them, Daniel Whitney, became a major entrepreneur throughout the whole region, a good friend of Beaumont's, and a useful

42. Samuel Stambaugh, "Report on the Quality and Condition of Wisconsin Territory, 1831," 402–4; Lockwood, "Early Times and Events in Wisconsin," 104–5; Morgan L. Martin, "Narrative of Morgan L. Martin," 386; Schoolcraft, *Summary Narrative*, 189–90.

43. Francis Paul Prucha, *Broadax and Bayonet: The Role of the United States Army in the Development of the Northwest, 1815–1860*, 14; Schoolcraft, *Summary Narrative*, 190; Elizabeth T. Baird, "Reminiscences of Life in Territorial Wisconsin," 206–7; "Fort Howard (1824–1832)," *Green Bay Historical Bulletin* 4 (1928), 3–19; Prucha, ed., *Army Life*, xxxi, 38–39 (quotation).

adviser in land speculation. With the abandonment of Camp Smith, the fort built near the mouth of the river was to be continually garrisoned until the 1840s.[44]

In the late spring of 1826, when Beaumont reached Fort Howard, he reported to Lovell that the hospital lacked everything but medicines. He asked that the hospital equipment at Sackett's Harbor be transferred to Fort Howard. This was carried out. He had to make use of a temporary hospital and temporary quarters, because the previous garrison and its surgeon had not yet moved out. They were in the throes of an influenza epidemic.[45]

The temporary hospital was "an old stable (fitted up in as comfortable a manner as possible without changing too materially its original features)." Fortunately, in the month after Beaumont's arrival with four companies of the Second Regiment, there were very few sick. When an army inspector examined the temporary quarters late in July 1826, he noted that a requisition of hospital stores had recently been received, but the boxes had not been opened for lack of room to put anything away. Although all the usual hospital ledgers had not yet been provided, the inspector noted that such as there were, along with the various memoranda, gave proof of a wish "to meet not only the spirit, but the exact letter of the book of regulations." Beaumont always sought a practice outside the garrisons he served, but he also had a very meticulous sense of his army duties and army regulations.[46]

The hospital and living quarters that Beaumont moved into later in the summer had been built a little away from Fort Howard. They had been kept in very good order by the previous surgeon, but in 1826 the complaint of the military inspector was that it would have been more comfortable for the sick if less space had been allotted to the living quarters of the medical director and more to the hospital wards. The commander of the Second Regiment, presumably advised by Beaumont, was already talking of putting up a new building with a better allocation of space, and nearer to the fort, so that the sick could reach it more easily and so that they would be under the eye of the sentinel to prevent them "from straying." As was usually the case, these plans for improvement were deferred, but the Beaumonts were at least able

44. Prucha, *Broadax and Bayonet*, 114; Albert G. Ellis, "Fifty-Four Years Recollections of Men and Events in Wisconsin," 215–17; Kinzie, *Wau-Bun*, 15n; William L. Evans, "The Military History of Green Bay," 137–39; Smith, *James Duane Doty*, 66–69; Alice E. Smith, "Daniel Whitney: Pioneer Wisconsin Businessman," 283–304.

45. Beaumont to Lovell, June 18, 1826, WD, SG, LR; Nelson, *Beaumont*, 135–39.

46. WD, IG, Reports, Fort Howard, 1826 and 1828. These are reprinted in "Fort Howard (1824–1832)."

to take advantage of roomy living quarters. They had good use for these, as in August 1827 Debby gave birth to another child–a daughter, Lucretia.[47]

Fort Howard had been regarded by Beaumont's predecessors as a healthy post, and Beaumont commented in his first meteorological report, "The Climate had ever been considered Salubrious." Perhaps because of his previous experience in northern New York and Mackinac, Beaumont had a somewhat optimistic view of what to expect from Green Bay. Reporting in the fall of 1826, before he had experienced a Green Bay winter, he was able to state that "the Seasons are serenely pleasant, temperate, & uniform." Beaumont reported that the summer and early fall had brought "a regular continued fever of a slow nervous kind, generally inclining & frequently running into the typhoid state," both among the soldiers at the fort and among the citizens of Green Bay. Patients were slow to recover, and quick to relapse. He had also had frequent cases of dysentery and diarrhea. Beaumont still believed in rapid and vigorous medical intervention, and he wrote that these diseases very readily yielded in a few days to bleeding, twenty or thirty grains of calomel, or an emetic, followed by antidysentery pills containing opium and ipecac.[48]

Bleeding was resorted to by Beaumont for a variety of conditions. Early in December 1826 when one of the soldiers had his back crushed and was brought into the hospital in a "painfully distorted condition," Beaumont used the lancet with regularity. In a month his patient was walking about. Early in the following summer, when another soldier reported sick with a severe pain in his left side, difficulty in breathing, pain in the head, and a sick stomach, Beaumont took sixteen ounces of blood and gave him an emetic of antimony, potassium tartrate, and ipecac; a cathartic of calomel and jalop; and raised a blister on his side. After two days, when the patient complained of severe pain in the region of his liver, Beaumont applied another blister and gave him a powder of potassium nitrate, ipecac, and camphor every three hours. In a week, the patient was convalescent.[49]

When Beaumont wrote his quarterly report in March 1827, he was less sanguine about the healthy location and climate than he had been on his arrival. Like others before him, he had decided that the fort would be better off farther up the river, where the land was higher and there were fountains

47. Ibid.; genealogical material from Sophie Beaumont, Beaumont Papers, SHSW.

48. Fort Howard, September 30, 1826, War Department, RG 112, Office of the Surgeon General, Records of the Weather Bureau (microfilm, SHSW). Hereafter cited as WD, SG, Weather Records.

49. Case Book and Aphorisms, December 1826–, BC, WU.

of good spring water. The fort, he had now observed with more care, was near the mouth of the river, on a low sandbank, surrounded by swamps and prairies. In the warm seasons, he had learned, the water from the river was "very impure," unfit for any use other than washing. He pointed out that because of the good health that had generally prevailed among the soldiers and citizens, it was obvious that there was nothing in the soil and climate that was deleterious to health. Yet for the past year there had been more sickness than had ever been known before over such a length of time.[50]

The typical imprecision of the period in identifying specific diseases was evident in Beaumont's report of the sicknesses that had prevailed in the previous year. "Fevers," he reported, had been the main disorders. At first they had resembled "regular intermittents," but had generally become "continued, low, and protracted." He thought that the most probable cause of prevalent fever over the past six months had been "the excessive heat and drouth during the summer and fall." This had led to unusually low water, and had produced "exhalations from the decaying vegetable animal & vegetable matters spread on the adjacent swamps and prairies." Diarrhea, he thought, had mostly been caused by drinking too freely of the bad river water. Dysentery, he wrote, had generally come from careless or unavoidable exposure to a damp atmosphere, wet clothes, or night air after vigorous exercise in unusually hot weather, and from drinking too much bad water made worse by the addition of ice. Beaumont attributed the rheumatism during the past winter to the same causes as the fevers. The seeds of the disease, he wrote, had lain dormant until stimulated by variable and inclement autumn weather.

At the end of June 1827, Beaumont continued to connect the weather and disease. He wrote that the weather in the past three months had been "peculiarly variable," with sudden changes from extreme heat to a damp and chilly atmosphere. June had been unusually wet, with excessive heat and chilly air following in close succession. His conclusion was that local inflammations, dysenteries, and diarrheas had "almost invariably & immediately followed these changes."[51]

After the Griswold affair at Fort Niagara, and censure by the president, one would have expected Beaumont to be keen to avoid personal controversies, but within a year of arriving at Fort Howard, he was again involved in a dispute. In this posting, Beaumont had a fellow assistant surgeon, Thomas S.

50. Fort Howard, March 31, 1827, WD, SG, Weather Records.
51. Ibid.

Bryant, who had only received his appointment in October 1825. In February 1827 Bryant applied a splint to the thigh and leg of a soldier who had been kicked by an ox. The patient experienced considerable distress for two days or more, and within a month Bryant was arraigned before a General Court-Martial to answer charges of malpractice, incompetency, and neglect of duty for applying a splint to a leg that was simply contused. Beaumont could have had a much more peaceful time if he had not always been ready to challenge the conduct of his fellow officers, but when he believed he was right he did not remain quiet. Bryant was found guilty of malpractice and neglect of duty, but once again President Adams intervened to overturn a court decision. This time, however, he intervened on technical grounds and did not enter into the merits of the case. The case became well known to the medical department not because of the quarrels at Fort Howard, but rather because medical officers questioned whether medical competence should have been decided by a court consisting solely of line officers.[52]

Beaumont's quickness to perceive weaknesses and faults in those he worked with caused difficulties throughout his stay at Fort Howard. Early in 1828 he complained, in writing, that his commanding officer, Major William Whistler, had been drunk on duty. Whistler was not an efficient officer and had other problems besides drinking, but Whistler's superiors were apparently more irritated that the question had been raised than disposed to solve it. Beaumont's charges, however, must have brought tense months at Fort Howard, particularly as counterattacks were launched against Beaumont himself. This did not dissuade him, and he even continued to harass his old nemesis, Lieutenant Griswold. He now claimed that Griswold had been embezzling money, and he gained some support in his charges from officers of the Second Regiment.[53]

It was not that Beaumont launched false charges—over the years it frequently came out that what he said was true—but he certainly was unable to keep quiet about what he thought were faults or derelictions of duty among those with whom he worked closely. Beaumont made some very good and close friends throughout his life; he also made some bitter enemies. It is to his credit that his close friends were often men of considerable ability and

52. Harvey E. Brown, *The Medical Department of the United States Army from 1775 to 1873,* 133–35; Nelson, *Beaumont,* 139–40; Heitman, *Historical Register,* vol. 1, 257.

53. See discussion in Nelson, *Beaumont,* 151–54. Most of the relevant documents are calendared in Newton D. Mereness, *The Mereness Calendar: Federal Documents on the Upper Mississippi Valley, 1780–1890,* vol. 2, 756–58.

worth, while his enemies were frequently badly flawed. Beaumont's problem was that he never knew when to turn a blind eye to the flaws of those he had to work with.

Beaumont's first summer at Green Bay had been unusually dry, but in the following year he had the opportunity of observing the effects of one that was unusually wet as well as exceptionally hot. The river was very high, and overflowed the marshes and the prairies. Beaumont continued to report that sudden changes from excessive heat to damp, cool conditions had produced disease—in this case dysenteries, catarrhs, and rheumatism. He had also treated "colics" resulting, he wrote, from excessive drinking of iced water when the system was overheated.[54]

There was still no new hospital, and Beaumont remained some way from the garrison in buildings that had enough room for his family, limited room for the patients, and stabling for cows. The buildings were repaired because of weather damage in the summer of 1827, but the commandant reported that a new hospital was needed. More minor damage from the wind and the weather was sustained in the fall. Again the buildings were repaired, but in the quarterly report they were described as only "tolerable."[55]

Although Beaumont had arranged to take smallpox vaccine to Green Bay, an accident left him with none that was usable. In September 1827 he urged Surgeon General Lovell to send him a fresh supply of vaccine before the close of lake navigation. He wrote that it was particularly necessary in an area like Green Bay, where there was a constant danger of smallpox being introduced by the continued passing and repassing of Indians and voyageurs.[56]

Lovell sent the vaccine, but because winter had closed lake navigation, it did not reach Green Bay until January 1828. It had been sent by land from Detroit through Chicago. The virus arrived in two separate packages at different times, and when Beaumont used vaccine from the first package it did not take effect. He suggested to Lovell that frost might have destroyed the vaccine, and asked for more to be sent as soon as navigation opened on the lakes in the spring. Lovell complied with this request, but worried whether Beaumont was using it properly and gave detailed instructions for using the

54. Fort Howard, September 30, 1827, WD, SG, Weather Records.
55. Quarterly Reports on Buildings, September 30 and December 31, 1827, War Department, RG 92, Office of the Quartermaster General, Consolidated Correspondence File, Fort Howard, National Archives, Washington, D.C. (microfilm, SHSW).
56. Beaumont to Lovell, September 18, 1827, WD, SG, LR; Miller, "William Beaumont, M.D.," 38.

vaccine. He said that the puncture should be allowed to bleed "pretty freely" before introducing a small portion of the crust softened with a little warm water. An alternative method he suggested was to make half a dozen "pretty deep incisions with the edge of the lancet," to cut across the incisions in the same way, and to cover them well with the vaccine matter.[57]

Amid the daily round of medical duties in an increasingly dilapidated frontier military hospital, Beaumont was thinking of how he could renew his experiments on Alexis St. Martin. His residence at Mackinac had given him not only St. Martin but also the opportunity to make influential friends among the tight-knit little fur-trading community that lived there. Beaumont kept in contact with Robert Stuart, who continued to live on the island. Also, an even more influential figure in the company, Ramsay Crooks, who was based in New York but made annual tours to the West, became a good friend, and proved very willing to help Beaumont.[58]

Beaumont had asked his friends in the American Fur Company to help him locate St. Martin, and in August 1827 he received a letter from William Matthews, a Canadian agent of the company who worked out of Montreal, and who was in Mackinac. Matthews told Beaumont that he had located "your ungrateful Boy." He was now married, wrote Matthews, and was living in Lower Canada, some fifty miles or so from Montreal and about twelve miles from Berthier, a place that was to figure much in Beaumont's correspondence for the rest of his life. Matthews reported that St. Martin was "poor and miserable beyond Description," and that his wound was worse than when he had left Beaumont. Matthews said that he had done all he could to bring St. Martin up country to Mackinac, but could not persuade him to come. The efforts had cost him fourteen dollars, and he asked Beaumont to let him know immediately whether to continue trying to get St. Martin, and also, as it would not be paid by the American Fur Company, how he would get his fourteen dollars.[59]

For once, Beaumont did not quibble about money. He wrote immediately, sending the money and expressing his interest in getting St. Martin back. Matthews was equally prompt in reply, and said there would be no difficulty at getting St. Martin back at a reasonable price, providing "you will employ his Wife!!!" Matthews emphasized that St. Martin was very poor, and would

57. See Myer, *Beaumont*, 131–32.

58. See Beaumont to Robert Stuart, November 18, 1826, BC, UC; Myer, *Beaumont*, 132–33.

59. William Matthews to Beaumont, August 13, 1827, BC, WU.

remain so unless he came back to Beaumont. He suggested that Beaumont should write requesting Matthews to engage St. Martin and his wife to stay with Beaumont for one or two years. He could then bring them up to Mackinac in one of the company's boats, charging the lowest possible price.

Matthews gave Beaumont considerable hope, but he also revealed that there might be competition. He reported that another doctor had seen St. Martin when he was last in Montreal, and had shown a great interest in him. The possibility that other physicians might gain control of St. Martin remained a worry of Beaumont's for the rest of his life. If St. Martin attracted the attention of physicians with major reputations and became the subject of research in some well-known institution, then his own hopes of gaining recognition through research and publication were likely to be thwarted.[60]

News of St. Martin revived Beaumont's interest in his own research, and he sent the report of his experiments to the Michigan Territory Medical Society in Detroit. In March, the secretary of that organization transmitted a resolution thanking him for his "able & luminous report."[61] If Beaumont wanted to rise above the petty military squabbles in isolated posts, he needed St. Martin.

Beaumont, however, had at least found St. Martin again, and could expect the cooperation of the American Fur Company in getting him from Lower Canada. In October he told Lovell that unless Detroit was made a post for an assistant surgeon, his first choice in a post for the next two years was Mackinac. His next choice was Green Bay.[62] If Matthews persuaded St. Martin to come up country, he would be brought to Mackinac; from there was easy communication by water to Detroit and Green Bay.

More research now seemed to be possible, but Beaumont was busy with his usual round of routine army medicine. The main complaints in the last months of 1827 were inflammation of the joints, abscesses, and sore and pained muscles. Beaumont blamed the diseases he was treating on "the common causes of this & similar complaints"–sudden changes in the weather, moving from warm, crowded rooms to the damp, cold outside, and wet feet and damp clothes. There had been frequent changes from warm, damp days to days of chilling cold, sudden changes in the wind, and much rain. Beaumont thought that variable weather accounted for some of the medical problems, but for wounds, contusions, and sprains he had

60. Ibid., August 18, 1827, BC, WU.
61. R. S. Rice to Beaumont, March 20, 1828, BC, WU.
62. Beaumont to Lovell, October 20, 1827, WD, SG, LR.

another explanation. These, he wrote, had their "causes chiefly, and almost invariably, in the abusive use of whiskey."[63]

Beaumont, along with Surgeon General Lovell and many other army surgeons, was concerned about alcohol abuse in the army, and for the rest of his life counseled moderation. Excessive drinking was a constant problem at army posts. The gill of whiskey a day contributed to this, and soldiers employed on manual labor for ten days or more were given an extra gill a day. There was also ample whiskey for sale around all military posts. Lovell was particularly keen to root out heavy drinking, and Beaumont agreed with him, but the army did not abolish the daily whiskey ration until 1830. This, of course, did not stop heavy drinking, and Beaumont continued to stress excessive use of alcohol as one of the basic causes of illness and injury among the soldiers.[64]

Beaumont's promotion to surgeon, which was signed by President Adams on February 15, 1828, led to another posting. Beaumont was ordered, as soon as he was relieved of his duties at Fort Howard, to report to the head-quarters of the Fifth Regiment in St. Louis. Because of the usual military delays, Beaumont's stay at Fort Howard stretched through the spring and into the summer. Rumors of Beaumont's quarrels at the post had reached his family in Connecticut, and in May, in writing to them, he denied that "some unpleasantness" was causing him to move to another place. He said he was having some difficulties with the officers at Green Bay, but that he would be moving because of his promotion to surgeon. Beaumont felt no pressing need to get away from the tense situation brought about by his challenge to the competency of those around him. He told Lovell that though he was preparing to report to St. Louis, he would like to proceed with his present command to the new post that was being established in Maine.[65]

Shortly before he left Fort Howard, in July 1828, Beaumont, at the request of the surgeon who was replacing him, Dr. Lyman Foot, warned of the dangers of employing the soldiers in procuring hay on the prairies around the post. Beaumont stated that in past seasons the use of men to procure hay had increased the number of sick. The prairies, he wrote, were generally wet,

63. Fort Howard, December 30, 1827, WD, SG, Weather Records; Gillett, *Army Medical Department, 1818–1865,* 15.

64. Ayars, "Some Notes on the Medical Service," 511–13; Marsh, "The United States Army and Its Health," 511–12; Prucha, ed., *Army Life,* 100n2; Gillett, *Army Medical Department, 1818–1865,* 15; Barboriak, "Reporting to the Surgeon General," 109, 237.

65. Commission as surgeon, February 15, 1828, BC, WU; Beaumont to Lucretia Beaumont, May 3, 1828, BP, YU; Beaumont to Lovell, May 7, 1828, WD, AG, IMOF.

and covered with mud and water from three to eight inches deep. When the men worked there, he argued, they were exposed to the deleterious effects of the poisonous roots, plants, and reptiles, became diseased and in some cases developed chronic problems with their joints, rheumatism, and swellings of the legs.[66]

At the end of his stay in Fort Howard, Beaumont revealed to an army inspector both the extent to which his work with St. Martin and writing for publication had stimulated an interest in medical research and the utmost seriousness with which Beaumont still took his army duties. Some army medical officers simply sank into a stupefying round of drinking, card-playing, and hunting on their lonely western posts, but Beaumont never did. He had always been proud of being an army medical officer, and pursued what he thought were the best interests of the service. His zeal in this, combined with the degree to which he perceived most matters through the blinkers of his own self-interest, was the cause of much of the friction with those who took a more relaxed view of their army duties and who had a more generous view of human foibles. Later, when his army duties became less central to his life, he expected from others a tolerance that he had not been prepared to give himself.

Usually, military inspectors commented on the state of the hospital structure, the way the books were kept, and the degree of efficiency of the surgeon. On this occasion, however, the inspector noted in his report that his attention had been called to the medical library, in which there appeared to be sufficient volumes (each post tried to keep on hand a small shelf of basic texts), but, the inspector said, they possessed little variety. Clearly, the complaint was Beaumont's, not the inspector's. The inspector even listed the existing items—"the Surgeon's Vade Mecum" (eight copies), "Thomas' Practice" (four copies), "Bell on venerial," (seven copies), and a few other titles. He went on, obviously primed by Beaumont, to suggest that in addition to the standard works now furnished, the best medical journals and the best works on mineralogy and botany were much wanted at all the frontier posts. The former were needed, he wrote, so that it might be within the power of the surgeons "to keep pace with the improvements and discoveries that are daily taking place in the science of medicine," the latter as reference books to enable the surgeons to report accurately on the mineral and botanical

66. Beaumont to Lyman Foot, July 3, 1828, WD, QG, Consolidated Correspondence File, Fort Howard.

wealth of their areas. One can hear echoes of Beaumont's own words when the inspector asked, "whether or not the government could be a loser by even the most liberal appropriation towards this purpose."

There was even a suggestion from Beaumont regarding the surgical instruments that were kept at each station assigned a surgeon or assistant surgeon. The inspector reported that there were perhaps a dozen sets of surgical instruments at Fort Howard, each set including instruments for amputation, trephining, and the like, and that in Beaumont's opinion not one of them was fit for use. They were to be sent to New York for repair. The inspector stated that it had been suggested (obviously by Beaumont) that to save the government money, and to "avoid the torture of a dull knife," every surgeon and assistant surgeon should be furnished with complete sets of instruments for use during his period of service, and for which he would be held individually responsible.[67]

Although Beaumont was to spend the latter part of his life in St. Louis, he did not, as he expected, go there in 1828. With his wife and children, he set out for St. Louis by way of the Fox-Wisconsin river system, but on August 5, 1828, when he reached Fort Crawford at Prairie du Chien, the commander there ordered him to remain to allow their medical officer to proceed on leave. Beaumont was to remain in Prairie du Chien for four years, and in this unlikely spot he was to carry out a substantial part of the research that gave him his permanent reputation.

---

67. Fort Howard, WD, IG, Reports. This is reprinted in Prucha, ed., *Army Life,* 70–72, with an identification of the books in the library.

Hope Revived

FORT CRAWFORD WAS A decrepit, weakly garrisoned military post in a small, flood-beset village. It was also the site of some of William Beaumont's best work. The problems he faced in conducting research there were well revealed in his first meteorological report. He kept meticulous records on the local temperature from his arrival until September 15, but then he noted that someone had removed the thermometer from its usual position at the hospital, thrown it on the ground, and broken it. Temperature reports were now missing because he had no thermometer and no way to replace it. Conducting research in Prairie du Chien was to be unlike research in Philadelphia, Paris, or Vienna.[1]

Situated at the point where the Wisconsin River joins the Mississippi, Prairie du Chien had long been known for its trading and strategic importance. As at Green Bay, French Canadian voyageurs and traders had settled there, often with Indian wives. Settlement at Prairie du Chien was not as compact as at most French Canadian settlements. Along a street some half a mile in length, which ran parallel to the river, there was a scattering of homes, stores, workshops, and stables, and there were other homes sprinkled across the prairie around the village. In all, there were less than forty dwellings, less than twenty in the main part of the village. The houses were mostly built of logs and plastered with mud and clay. Visiting in 1817, an army officer had commented that some of the homes were comfortable "but none

---

1. Fort Crawford, September 30, 1828, WD, SG, Weather Records.

of them exhibiting any display of elegance or taste." About half a mile behind the village was a large farm area where the inhabitants grew corn, wheat, barley, oats, potatoes, and other vegetables, but many of the inhabitants were still engaged in hunting or trade.[2]

When Henry Schoolcraft visited Prairie du Chien in 1820, he said that the village "has the old and shabby look of all the antique French towns on the Mississippi, and in the great lake basins; the dwellings being constructed of log and barks, and the courtyards picketed in, as if they were intended for defense." The village experienced much difficulty from chronic flooding. One comment, just before the War of 1812, was that in essence the village had been built on an island about three miles long and a mile broad, except that in low water the back channel was dry except where it formed small ponds or lakes. The village was described as surrounded by numerous Indian tribes. A visitor in the summer that Beaumont arrived commented that the river was higher than ever before, and that the village site had been made an island by the high water.[3]

The fort at Prairie du Chien had suffered attack from both sides in the War of 1812, but when American soldiers arrived there in the summer of 1816 they had simply taken over and repaired the old fort. In August 1826 the military inspector reported "a new work must be erected, for the present one is in ruins." The hospital, he wrote, was under good regulation, and sufficiently supplied, but "the Building like every other within the fort, in a state of ruin." In the following year, it was reported that the fort was much decayed and "not fit to inhabit except extensive repairs are made." The floors and the lower timbers were decayed, partially due to the regular flooding.[4]

One aspect of the location that was of prime importance to Beaumont was that the post had the reputation of being one of the unhealthiest in the nation. An earlier surgeon at the post had reported that when the river rose in the spring, the water spread over the low ground for about six weeks. When it withdrew, it left ponds of stagnant water and "a large quantity of vegetable substance exposed to putrefaction." These sources of miasma, he wrote, were added to by the low fertile islands in the Mississippi itself. Intermittent and

2. Peter L. Scanlan, *Prairie du Chien: French, British, American,* 181–82 (quotation); Smith, *James Duane Doty,* 48–59; Lockwood, "Early Times and Events in Wisconsin," 112–30.

3. Schoolcraft, *Summary Narrative,* 167–68; John H. Fonda, "Reminiscences of Wisconsin," 235.

4. Prucha, *Broadax and Bayonet,* 18; Scanlan, *Prairie du Chien,* 133–34 (1827 report); WD, IG, Reports, Fort Crawford, August 1826.

remittent fevers were common during the summer months, and there was also diarrhea and dysentery. Although given other names, the main problem at Prairie du Chien was malaria, spread by the mosquitoes swarming in the flooded areas around the fort.[5] In the summer of 1830, nearly three-quarters of the troops at Fort Crawford suffered from this disease. In the 1840 report from the surgeon general's office on medical conditions at army posts in the previous decades, it was stated that at Prairie du Chien, "the diseases arising from the general epidemic constitution of the atmosphere, assumed chiefly a dysenteric form, followed by intermittent fever."[6]

Between 1829 and 1838, intermittent and remittent fevers affected on average more than one-third of the soldiers at the fort in each year. The condition of the troops was worsened by the ruinous state of the fort itself. In the month before Beaumont arrived, the officer who assumed the quartermaster's duties at the fort stated that the condition of both the quarters and the public storehouses was a matter of deep concern both for the security of the public property and the comfort of the troops, and that the garrison had already been twice flooded that season.[7]

The construction of a new Fort Crawford began in 1829. Because of the problems with the previous fort, it was built of stone. For most of Beaumont's service in Prairie du Chien, this new post was under construction and a scene of considerable confusion. The healthy troops were able to move into the new fort in December 1830, but Beaumont and the sick were left in the hospital at the old fort. The new hospital and Beaumont's new living quarters were not ready for occupancy until late in 1831.[8]

At Prairie du Chien, as elsewhere, Beaumont engaged in private practice, as well as caring for the officers and men of the garrison, their wives and children, and transient military personnel. Because of fears of Indian hostilities the garrison varied in number during Beaumont's stay, increasing from little more than a hundred in 1829 to more than 250 in the summer of

5. WD, SG, Weather Records, Fort Crawford, c. June 1820.

6. Peter T. Harstad, "Frontier Medicine in the Territory of Wisconsin," 14; *Statistical Report on the Sickness and Mortality in the Army of the United States . . . from January, 1819, to January, 1839,* 39 (quotation), 155.

7. Peter T. Harstad, "Sickness and Disease on the Wisconsin Frontier: Malaria, 1820–1850," 91–92; Louis Jamison to Thomas Jesup, July 13, 1828, War Department, RG 92, Office of the Quartermaster General, Consolidated Correspondence File, Fort Crawford, National Archives, Washington, D.C. (microfilm, SHSW).

8. Scanlan, *Prairie du Chien,* 137–41; Edward P. Alexander, "Surgeon Beaumont at Prairie du Chien," 1009.

1831. The local inhabitants who were reluctant to call on Beaumont's services could turn to the nurse and midwife, Mary Ann Menard, who was of mixed African and European ancestry. She had long acted as the local midwife, and used herbs to treat the local diseases. Undoubtedly for the normal run of complaints, some of the local residents would have avoided Beaumont, his bleeding, and his purging, and sought Mrs. Menard and her herbal drinks.[9]

Although Prairie du Chien was not the most comfortable spot for Beaumont to bring his family, he and his wife were to find compensation in the strong friendships they made there. The most important of these was Captain Ethan Allen Hitchcock, who arrived at the post in November 1828 on his way to Fort Snelling. He was delayed for several months because of the icy conditions on the Mississippi, and never continued his journey because he was called back to be commandant of West Point.

Hitchcock, who was the grandson of the famous Revolutionary hero Ethan Allen of Vermont, was a most unusual army officer. He was deeply interested in philosophy, and wrote several books on philosophical subjects, as well as a book on Shakespeare's sonnets. He was also a keen amateur musician. When in Europe in 1850, he attended a meeting of the World Peace Society in Frankfurt. But he also had a distinguished army career. Although he questioned the morality of the war against Mexico, he was twice awarded brevet rank for gallantry in that conflict. Hitchcock became an intimate friend of both William and Debby Beaumont, was later to regard their home in St. Louis as his own home, and in every way was treated by the Beaumonts as a member of the family. It tells a good deal of Beaumont that he could become the intimate friend of a man of Hitchcock's caliber. Beaumont gave his friendship to Hitchcock with all the enthusiasm he usually threw into his quarrels with more obviously flawed individuals.[10]

Two other officers—Lieutenant James Kingsbury and Lieutenant Joseph H. LaMotte—also became close to the Beaumonts during their stay at Prairie du Chien. Kingsbury was a good friend for many years, and LaMotte was eventually to propose to Beaumont's daughter Sarah—a girl toward whom

9. Post Returns, Fort Crawford, 1828–1832, WD, AG; *Statistical Report*, 156–57; Scanlan, *Prairie du Chien*, 198–99; Lockwood, "Early Times and Events in Wisconsin," 125–26; Kinzie, *Wau-Bun*, 318.

10. See Ethan Allen Hitchcock, *Fifty Years in Camp and Field: Diary of Major-General Ethan Allen Hitchcock, U.S.A.;* Heitman, *Historical Register,* vol. 1, 532; Hitchcock to [Beaumont?], August 27, 1850, G. P. Putnam to Hitchcock, June 11, 1855, Hitchcock Family Papers, Missouri Historical Society, St. Louis, Missouri. Hereafter cited as MHS. Nelson, *Beaumont,* 159–60.

the much older Hitchcock also had more than avuncular feelings. The few officers at Prairie du Chien were a very close-knit group, and Beaumont did not get into one of the major feuds that so often punctuated his life.[11]

A few years later, writing to a civilian acquaintance from these years, Beaumont said that it was "with peculiar pleasure & satisfaction" that he reflected "upon the scenes of social enjoyment, incident to our residence at the Prairie." A visitor who knew Beaumont later recalled Prairie du Chien in the summer of 1830. The officers gave a large dancing party in the unfinished stone fort. Only the walls were up; the windows were not in, and the doors had not been hung, but the floor was smooth for dancing, and she thought the party was "a delightful one." Another visitor who came to Fort Howard just after Beaumont left arrived as the soldiers were putting on a play—an English comedy. He said that the small group of officers and their families formed a tight-knit circle in their new fort, about half a mile from the "antique-looking timber-built houses" of the village. Apart from the library, most officers devoted much of their time to hunting and shooting, making use of the many "high-bred dogs" kept at the post.[12]

Beaumont neither had the time nor the inclination to throw himself into the hunting and shooting, but he enjoyed the social life. It was as well that he did, for the winters were long and the post was very isolated. In January 1829, Beaumont reported that he could not forward the medicines and stores sent via Prairie du Chien for Fort Howard, as there was no snow for sleighing and the rivers were not yet frozen hard enough for traveling.[13]

The advantage of the long winter for Beaumont was that the troops were generally healthier and he was less on call. He needed this break in his first winter, because the summer of 1829 was to be one of great excitement at the post—both generally and personally. For the general population and troops, the main excitement was that Indians were to come to the post in considerable numbers to negotiate with the government. For Beaumont this council was overshadowed by the return of St. Martin, and by Debby giving birth to a son—Israel Green Beaumont—at the end of August.[14]

11. See James Kingsbury to Beaumont, July 14, 1833, BC, WU; Kingsbury to Madame Cabanne, May 1, 1831, James W. Kingsbury Collection, MHS.

12. Beaumont to Thomas Burnett, January 7, 1833, in Thomas P. Burnett Papers, SHSW, Area Research Center, University of Wisconsin-Platteville; Baird, "Reminiscences of Life in Territorial Wisconsin," 232–33; Charles F. Hoffman, *A Winter in the West by a New Yorker,* vol. 2, 1–13 (quotations, 7, 11).

13. Beaumont to Lovell, January 15, 1829, WD, SG, LR.

14. Genealogical material from Sophie Beaumont, BC, UC.

The Indian council took place in July. Caleb Atwater, who came for the treaty, commented favorably on "Dr. Beaumont and his amiable and accomplished lady," and the other officers and their families at the post. He thought it "an interesting sight, to see such persons located as they are, in a fort, on the very verge of civilized life, educating a family of young children." Atwater also praised the reading habits of the officers and noted the library and reading room established at their own expense. Among the books were works on chemistry and on other scientific subjects.[15]

Although the Indian council brought Beaumont much additional work, it also helped him financially. He received two hundred dollars for his services to the Indians and officials attending the conference. He was so busy that the arrival of Alexis St. Martin and his family late in June could not deflect him from his general medical duties. The agents of the American Fur Company had carried out Beaumont's wishes, and St. Martin and his family had come out from Montreal in the company canoes. It was late in the year before Beaumont found the time to renew his experiments.[16]

The fall of 1829 began with Beaumont treating dysentery, sore throats, and mild influenza. In November the main problems came from "inflammatory" diseases, but in December, when the weather was mild, dry, and healthful, Beaumont was able to report that no disease had prevailed during the month. The winter continued to be "pleasant, mild, & dry." Beaumont still had the army routine to carry out–there were always some sick, and there were always reports to turn in–but the pressure of the summer months had at last lessened. On December 6, 1829, Beaumont was able to renew his experiments. He worked in the log hospital that was in the same ruinous condition as the rest of the old fort.[17]

From December 1829 to April 1831, Beaumont carried out fifty-six experiments at Prairie du Chien. The first group, from December 1829 to March 1830, were few and far between. He carried out experiments on eight days in December, on three days in January, and on three days in March. This meant that in the first nine months that St. Martin was back with him, Beaumont experimented on only fourteen days. He never explained why the time he devoted to experiments was so limited. One can only assume that the pressure of his regular military duties, other calls on his medical services, his family,

15. Caleb Atwater, *Remarks Made on a Tour to Prairie du Chien: Thence to Washington City in 1829*, 178–79.

16. Scanlan, *Prairie du Chien*, 163; Beaumont, *Experiments*, 131.

17. Fort Crawford, December 31, 1829, WD, SG, Weather Records.

and perhaps St. Martin's reluctance to be the subject of experimentation may
have contributed to the many days Beaumont could not devote to research.
For Beaumont, in these years in Prairie du Chien, self-motivation was everything. He had no colleagues asking him about the progress of his research, no
laboratory, no research library. Even the earlier encouragement of Surgeon
General Lovell did not count for much on those cold winter days in the old
decrepit army hospital on the banks of the Mississippi.[18]

Beaumont's research objectives in this first winter at Prairie du Chien
were summarized in the book he published in 1833. He tried to ascertain
whether variations of stomach temperature were brought about by changes
in St. Martin's system and by different weather conditions, and whether
gastric juice accumulated in the stomach during periods of fasting or from
the immediate and direct influence of hunger. He also tried to ascertain
the difference between natural and artificial digestion by demonstrating
digestion out of the stomach with gastric juice, and also the degree to which
the natural process continued when some of the stomach contents were taken
out during the period of chymification.[19]

To pursue his first objective, Beaumont, from December 1829 to March
1830, at different times, on different days, in different weather conditions,
introduced a glass thermometer into St. Martin's stomach. He did it when the
stomach was healthy and empty, an hour after St. Martin had breakfasted on
pork and bread, and before and after breakfasting on meat, biscuit, butter,
and coffee. Beaumont concluded that a dry atmosphere increased stomach
temperature and a humid one diminished it. He estimated the ordinary
temperature of a healthy stomach at one hundred degrees Fahrenheit, but
he warned that allowance should be made for imperfect instruments.[20]

To ascertain whether gastric juice accumulated during the stomach when
fasting or from the immediate and direct influence of hunger, Beaumont
made widely separated experiments in December 1829 and in March 1830.
On December 5, after St. Martin had fasted for twelve hours, Beaumont
introduced "a gum-elastic tube" into the stomach. He was able to draw off
only a dram or two of gastric juice, and reached the false conclusion that there
was no accumulation in the stomach when fasting. A week later, he decided
that the two or three drams that he could draw off was simply a result of the
irritation of the tube. On December 14 he reached the same conclusion. After

18. Beaumont, *Experiments,* 131–45.
19. Ibid., 131, 134, 139.
20. Ibid., 131–34.

St. Martin had fasted for eighteen hours, Beaumont drew off one and a half ounces of gastric juice, but decided that there was no accumulation in the stomach at the time the tube was introduced.[21]

These particular experiments were renewed in March 1830. On the thirteenth he introduced the tube, but could obtain no gastric juice. It began to flow when he put a few bread crumbs on the inner surface of the stomach. On the eighteenth he obtained one and a half ounces of gastric juice, but again reached the conclusion that it was the irritation of the tube that caused the juice to flow, and that there had been no accumulation of juice in the stomach.[22] Beaumont was to renew these experiments in the spring of 1831, but this was one of the areas in which he continued to reach false conclusions.

Some of Beaumont's most important work was in demonstrating that digestion could take place in gastric juice outside of the stomach, and many of his experiments from December 1829 to April 1830 were directed toward aspects of this problem. He was interested in a direct comparison of digestion in the stomach and in vitro, and he was also interested in ascertaining whether digestion would continue in gastric juice outside of the stomach when the process of chymification had already begun.[23]

He began, on December 14, by drawing out one and a half ounces of gastric juice. This was after St. Martin had fasted for eighteen hours. He put the juice in a vial with twelve drams of boiled, salted beef, placed it in a basin of water on a sand bath, and kept it at the temperature of one hundred degrees Fahrenheit. After twenty-four hours he separated the undigested from the chymous portion, and found that about half of it had been digested. He said that he tried to keep the temperature as regular as possible, but that it varied from ninety to one hundred degrees during the time of his experiment.[24]

Two days later, St. Martin had "an ordinary dinner" of boiled, salted beef, bread, potatoes, and turnips, with a gill of water. Twenty minutes later, Beaumont took a gill of the stomach contents into a vial. He noted that digestion had already begun. The vial was placed in a basin of water on a sand bath and kept at ninety or one hundred degrees for five hours. Digestion, which had already begun when it was removed from the stomach, continued until the whole was "completely chymified." At this time, Beaumont removed

21. Ibid., 134–35.
22. Ibid., 135–36.
23. Ibid., 139.
24. Ibid., 139–40.

from St. Martin's stomach "a gill of pure chyme." There were no particles of undigested food. He found very little difference between that in the vial and that from the stomach, except that the food had digested a little faster in the stomach, and more perfectly than in the vial.[25]

Beaumont continued this aspect of his experiments on January 11, when St. Martin ate eight ounces of recently salted lean beef, four ounces of potatoes, four ounces of boiled turnips, and bread. On this occasion Beaumont recorded the exact quantities, but frequently, in his inexperience, he omitted such data, making his tables of the comparative times needed for the digestion of different items of food much less useful than it otherwise would have been. Again, as in his experiment in the previous month, Beaumont took out a portion of the food. But now he took out portions at more than one time in the process of digestion. Again he used a vial in a sand bath, and he compared the rate and nature of digestion inside and outside the stomach. To conclude these experiments he had St. Martin drink half a pint of milk, and after fifteen minutes compared digestion in the stomach to digestion of milk that he had mixed with gastric juice outside the stomach. As Beaumont did not publish these experiments for several more years, he was later able to draw on much more extensive reading before reaching his conclusions from what he had observed.[26]

In these 1829–1830 Prairie du Chien experiments, it is clear that Beaumont already knew enough, from his early reading or from materials sent by Lovell, to try to address some of the main problems that had divided those interested in the process of human digestion. He even undertook a few crude experiments to try to find out the effects of bile and pancreatic juice on the chyme produced by digestion in the gastric juice. As he could not obtain human bile in a pure state, Beaumont made use of "beef's gall," and for human pancreatic juice he substituted diluted hydrochloric acid. His reason for using hydrochloric acid was that he noticed a resemblance in taste between that acid and pancreatic juice.[27] Although he achieved no useful results from these particular experiments, they demonstrated that he already understood some of the problems that beset those who were attempting to understand human digestion.

The sporadic experiments of the winter of 1829–1830 ceased with the coming of warmer weather and the sickness that came with it. There was

25. Ibid., 141.
26. Ibid., 142–46.
27. Ibid., 163–66.

high water in June that caused flooding over the areas around the fort, and when the water withdrew in the first part of July it left the marshes and ponds in a "foul condition." A visitor to Prairie du Chien in the spring reported that the village was inundated, and that she had to use "dug-outs" to reach some places. Beaumont reported that the cattle and swine became diseased, and many of them died. July and August were very hot and dry, but late in July the river once again flooded over the flats. It subsided by the second week in August, leaving marshes and shallow ponds covered with dead fish and decomposing animal and vegetable matter. As a result of all this, Beaumont reported, intermittent fever sprang up with violence, and "became universal" among the soldiers and civilians. September brought frequent changes in the weather, from oppressively hot to chilly with heavy rainstorms. By late September the sloughs and ponds were covered with slime, and "nauseating gas" rose in bubbles. Beaumont concluded that the prevailing sickness stemmed from these conditions.[28]

Beaumont was so impressed by the general sickness of this summer of 1830 that he contemplated writing an article on the subject. He began a "History of the Intermittent Fever, as it Prevailed at Prairie du Chien in the Summer and Fall of 1830," but he never finished it.[29] It is clear, however, that Beaumont was constantly busy in the summer and fall, and his experiments on St. Martin, which even in the winter months had been sporadic, now ceased.

At the end of the year, shortly before Christmas, the troops moved into their still unfinished fort, but Beaumont and his family were left in their old quarters in the old hospital building. The shell of the new hospital was up, but it still needed a good deal of work. In the middle of winter, and more than a mile from his officer friends in the new fort, Beaumont found time to renew his experiments on St. Martin. The troops were healthy in these early months of 1831, and Beaumont's main problems were caused by their excessive drinking.[30]

On January 25, Beaumont restarted his research. For this first effort, after a nine-month break, he simply decided to observe the normal course of

28. Fort Crawford, September 30, 1830, WD, SG, Weather Records; Baird, "Reminiscences of Life in Territorial Wisconsin," 232–33; Harstad, "Sickness and Death on the Wisconsin Frontier: Malaria," 92.

29. His unfinished history is in the BC, WU.

30. Fort Crawford, March 31, 1830, WD, SG, Weather Records; Jonathan Garland to Thomas Jesup, September 1, 1830, Col. Morgan to Thomas Jesup, November 12, 1830, WD, QG, Consolidated Correspondence File, Fort Crawford.

digestion within the stomach. At 1 P.M. St. Martin ate a dinner of roast beef, potatoes, beets, and bread, and during the afternoon went about his usual work as house servant. At different times, Beaumont examined the stomach contents. By 5:30 P.M. the stomach had nothing in it except a little gastric juice. Beaumont noted that the chyme formed from the dinner appeared to have all passed out of St. Martin's stomach.

On the following two days, Beaumont again experimented on the state of the fasting stomach. He drew gastric juice from St. Martin's empty stomach, noting that the application of bread crumbs to the inner coat of the stomach immediately produced a free flow of gastric juice. He was again leaning toward the false conclusion that the stimulus of the tube or of food produced the juice, and that it did not accumulate in a fasting stomach.[31]

More than a month later, Beaumont returned to this question, and for more than a week conducted regular experiments. He continued to extract one and a half or two ounces of gastric juice from an empty stomach, but concluded that in a normal stomach gastric juice was produced by the presence of food. In his book, he stated that any digestible or irritating substance produced gastric juice when applied to the internal coat of the stomach.[32]

In the early months of 1831, Beaumont again concentrated much of his attention on comparing digestion inside and outside of the stomach. He also began to take a greater interest in the digestibility of different foods. He had already done much to show the solvent nature of gastric juice by his experiments with gastric juice in vitro. He had digested food in gastric juice in a vial standing in a sand bath at a temperature as near as possible to one hundred degrees, and had shown that the results only differed from digestion in the stomach by being somewhat slower, and, at times, less complete. He now extended his efforts by comparing results at different temperatures, and also tried to demonstrate the action of gastric juice on food by comparing it with food simply placed in water.

On March 9, Beaumont drew off two ounces of gastric juice, separated it into two vials, and put in equal quantities of roast beef. One of the vials he put on the sand bath at ninety-nine degrees; the other he put in the open air at thirty-four degrees. He also placed the same quantity of meat in an equal amount of plain water and put it in the open air. At the same time he had St. Martin breakfast on the same kind of meat, together with warm biscuit,

31. Beaumont, *Experiments*, 136.
32. Ibid., 136–38.

butter, and a pint of coffee. One hour later, Beaumont removed a portion of this meal from the stomach and placed it in a vial on the sand bath, noting that the meat already in a vial on the bath had digested about as much as that taken from the stomach. He also noted that the meat in the cold gastric juice was much less advanced, and that in the water was merely macerated and had no signs of digestion.[33]

Beaumont found that the meal in the stomach digested first, but when he added more gastric juice to the vials on the sand bath, digestion recommenced. He examined all four vials after twenty-four hours, noting that the vial containing the food taken from the stomach after one hour had the most advanced digestion and that the meat in the cold gastric juice and in the water had not digested. When he put the vial with cold gastric juice on the bath, digestion recommenced. From these experiments he was to draw the conclusions that heat was necessary for the gastric juice to work, and that digestion would stop not only if the gastric juice was cold but also if there was insufficient juice; digestion would restart with heat and additional gastric juice. He concluded from this that gastric juice was discharged into the stomach gradually, in the amount needed to digest the amount of food that was swallowed.[34]

In this second series of experiments in Prairie du Chien, Beaumont extended his range. He gave St. Martin a variety of foods to eat, and there are some indications that St. Martin was becoming impatient, and probably experiencing discomfort, particularly as Beaumont frequently removed partially eaten food from his stomach. On March 12, St. Martin breakfasted on fat pork, bread, and potatoes. Beaumont took out a portion after four hours and found it was in a completely chymous state, but it was also "considerably tinged with yellow bile." Beaumont assumed this was the effect of "violent anger," which occurred about the time he was removing this portion of food.[35]

Again, two days later, there are signs in Beaumont's notes that St. Martin was becoming impatient. At 8:15 A.M. Beaumont put two ounces of rare roast beef, suspended on a string, into St. Martin's stomach. He pulled it out to examine it every hour until noon. He also put two ounces of the same meat in a vial and had St. Martin keep it close to his chest. Beaumont compared the two, and decided that the meat in the stomach digested badly because it was too much confined in a lump by the string and had not been freely

33. Ibid., 149–50.
34. Ibid., 150–53.
35. Ibid., 153.

moved by the motions of the stomach. But he also decided that the process of digestion might have been interrupted by the "anger and impatience, which were manifested by the subject, during this experiment." Either because of St. Martin's increasing impatience, Beaumont's other duties, or perhaps simply Beaumont's inclinations, his experimenting was sporadic. He experimented on three days in January, none in February, ten in March, and three in April.[36]

In these experiments, Beaumont made efforts to test the times needed for the digestion of a variety of foods: on March 6 St. Martin breakfasted on venison, cranberry jelly, and bread; on the twelfth he had meals of roast beef, biscuit, butter, and coffee; and fat pork, bread, and potatoes. On the thirteenth he dined on roast beef, bread, and potatoes; on the fourteenth at noon he had a pint of milk and four ounces of bread; on the fifteenth a breakfast of fresh sausage, pancakes, and coffee; on the sixteenth fresh meat, vegetable hash, bread, and coffee; and at 2 P.M. on the same day salted lean beef, pork, potatoes, carrots, turnips, and bread; on the eighteenth breakfast was soused tripe, pig's feet, bread, and coffee. In this last case, Beaumont noted with some surprise that the breakfast apparently had all digested within one hour; even the portion he took out of the stomach after thirty minutes digested just about as quickly in gastric juice on the sand bath. Over the three days that Beaumont experimented in April, St. Martin ate eggs, pancakes, apples, pork, wild goose, boiled dried codfish, potatoes, parsnips, bread, and drawn butter.[37]

The experiments Beaumont carried out in Prairie du Chien from December 1829 to April 1831 plainly demonstrated the solvent nature of gastric juice. The juice appeared to have somewhat slower digestive powers outside of the stomach, but Beaumont believed that this stemmed from his difficulties in keeping it at the right temperature. He was still a long way from publication, but carrying out his research in the most difficult of circumstances, with primitive equipment in a building in the last stages of ruin, he had firmly established the chemical nature of the digestive process. In the month following the end of this series of tests, Beaumont reported to Surgeon General Lovell that he had lost a large quantity of his medicines. His hospital shelves, attached to a rotten, decayed wall, had collapsed.[38]

There were increasing signs in this winter of 1830–1831 that St. Martin was becoming impatient with the inconvenience and discomfort of experimentation. Perhaps for this reason, he indicated in the spring of 1831 that

36. Ibid., 154–55, 136–69.
37. Ibid., 147–62.
38. Beaumont to Lovell, May 15, 1831, WD, SG, LR.

he needed to return to Canada with his family for a time. Beaumont later stated that he provided an outfit for the family for the trip, and that St. Martin promised to return when required. St. Martin took his family in a canoe down the Mississippi to the Ohio River, up that river to the state of Ohio, across that state by means of its rivers and a portage to Lake Erie, through Lakes Erie and Ontario to the St. Lawrence, and down the St. Lawrence to Montreal. They arrived there in June. Clearly, St. Martin's gastric fistula had not severely weakened his talents as a voyageur.[39]

Beaumont was anxious to ensure St. Martin's cooperation, because by April 1831 he had become interested enough in his research to request a one-year leave of absence to pursue it more systematically. He wanted to visit medical centers both in the East and in Europe, and asked that the leave should begin on or before September 30.[40]

Beaumont's vision was extending far beyond that of the typical provincial army surgeon. He now believed he could advance both scientific knowledge and his own prospects by his research on St. Martin and human digestion. His only real outer stimulus in this had been the support and encouragement given him by Surgeon General Lovell, and that had been of great importance. If Lovell had taken the position that Beaumont should have been devoting all his attention to his strictly military medical duties, he might well have doused the flicker of interest that had begun to grow in Beaumont since the mid-1820s. St. Martin had opened up a whole range of new intellectual possibilities for a man who had once been extremely pleased that he had achieved enough training to be accepted as a surgeon's mate in the War of 1812.

When Beaumont requested leave, the army medical department was still insufficiently staffed for the duties it had to perform, but Surgeon General Lovell was, as usual, cooperative. Late in May he informed Beaumont that, when possible, his request would be granted. Lovell was faced with a shortage of medical personnel, and it was difficult to know when it would be possible to find a replacement to go to Prairie du Chien. Lovell, however, said that he would try to find one so that Beaumont could begin his leave by the time he had requested—on or before September 30. Lovell clearly intended to act when he could, for he expressed an interest in seeing St. Martin when Beaumont came to the East.[41]

39. See Beaumont, *Experiments,* 19; Meyer, *Beaumont,* 139.
40. Beaumont to the Secretary of War, April 6, 1831, WD, AG, IMOF.
41. Lovell to Beaumont, May 23, 1831, BC, WU.

With the coming of the summer months, Beaumont found that the regular demands on his services were increased because of tension among the Indians in the region. This brought about a frequent movement of troops in and out of Prairie du Chien. It also delayed the completion of the new fort, and Beaumont was still living in his old quarters and working in the old hospital. When the army inspector visited the post in July, he reported that there were twenty-nine sick in the hospital. He attributed most of the sickness to exposure when the troops had been sent to Rock Island for a show of force against the Indians. The inspector reported that the old hospital was inconvenient and uncomfortable. As there were insufficient bunks, some of the sick were sleeping on the floor. Difficulties were compounded because Beaumont himself was sick. He was bearing up, the inspector reported, because he was hoping that he would soon be able to move to the new hospital, and in spite of his illness was exerting himself "to promote the comfort & convenience of the sick." Beaumont told a friend in Green Bay that he was receiving help from another physician until he recovered.[42]

The Indian unrest of these years was a cause of considerable anxiety in the Beaumont household. While the Beaumonts had been at Fort Howard, troops had been called out because of the killing of a settler near Prairie du Chien, and in 1830 and 1831 further tension arose because of clashes between Indian tribes in the vicinity of Fort Crawford. In the spring of 1830, a party of Fox Indians was ambushed some fifteen miles away from the fort, and in July 1831 the Sac and Fox retaliated by killing twenty-five Menominee within a half-mile of the old, wooden fort.[43]

Beaumont and his wife were still in their old quarters, but the main garrison had moved into the new stone structure. Deborah Beaumont felt extremely vulnerable when she saw warriors passing by, holding high poles festooned with enemy scalps. Elizabeth Smith Martin, who lived with the Beaumonts a few years later, commented that Debby had passed sleepless nights "with a great and hourly dread of attack from a Savage foe," and that she saw Indian women and children who had been gashed and mangled. Over half a century later, Mrs. Martin said that these events "proved

---

42. John Garland to Thomas Jesup, July 28, 1831, WD, QG, Consolidated Correspondence File, Fort Crawford; WD, IG, Reports, Fort Crawford, July 20, 1831; Nelson, *Beaumont,* 181–82.

43. Roger L. Nichols, *General Henry Atkinson: A Western Military Career,* 119–36; Scanlan, *Prairie du Chien,* 146–47; Lockwood, "Early Times and Events in Wisconsin," 170–71.

disastrous to her nervous system," and that it took her years to overcome her fears.[44]

On July 13, 1831, an assistant surgeon was ordered to report to Prairie du Chien to relieve Surgeon Beaumont, so that Beaumont could proceed on his leave. The order stated that Beaumont's leave of absence included permission to visit Europe, and in the following month Lovell informed Beaumont that he would be relieved before the end of September. This was not to happen. The medical department was already stretching to meet its obligations, and there were concerns that additional troops would be needed along the Mississippi because of the Indian unrest. On October 24 an order rescinded Beaumont's leave, stating that the public service required his presence at his post.[45] For the immediate future Beaumont would remain in Prairie du Chien.

In the winter of 1831–1832, Beaumont at last moved into his new quarters and new hospital in the stone barracks, but the hospital had been poorly planned. The best part of the new facilities were the living quarters for the surgeon and his family, but there was insufficient space for the sick. A year later when the army inspector visited the post, he pointed out that the hospital was inadequate for the twenty-three men who were at that time sick. He suggested that the living quarters for the surgeon, no longer Beaumont, should be converted into wards, and the surgeon given quarters within the fort. But in the following years, no action was taken.[46]

After a long Prairie du Chien winter without leave and without St. Martin, Beaumont was showing signs of frustration. Lovell had informed him that it was unlikely that there would be any army surgeons available to relieve him in the spring, and had asked if it might be possible to find a civilian substitute. In writing to Lovell, Beaumont poured out his frustrations and made every effort to enlist the surgeon general even more ardently in his cause.

After complaining that in an election year Congress would probably have neither the time nor the inclination to help the medical department, Beaumont laid his own case before Lovell. He said that he had been banished from society, and compelled to live outside "the pale of civilization" for twelve or

44. Elizabeth Smith Martin Diary, August 1835, Morgan Martin Papers, Neville Public Museum, Green Bay, Wisconsin; "Dr. William Beaumont," by E[lizabeth] S[mith] M[artin], clipping from a Green Bay newspaper, BC, WU.

45. Special Orders #78 and #127, July 13 and October 24, 1831, Lovell to Beaumont, August 8, 1831, BC, WU.

46. Richard Mason to Thomas Jesup, with enclosure, October 19, 1831, WD, QG, Consolidated Correspondence File, Fort Crawford; WD, IG, Reports, Fort Crawford, October 15, 1833, and August 21, 1834; Scanlan, *Prairie du Chien,* 144–45.

fourteen successive years, constantly on arduous duties. Privation, hardship, and injustice, he wrote, was imposed on a few medical officers long stationed on the extreme frontier. Officers of every other section and department of the service were freely and frequently granted indulgences; the officers on the northwestern frontier should occasionally get the same. In reality, Beaumont had not found frontier service quite this onerous, but he wanted his leave and he had practical suggestions for achieving it.

Even if Congress should not provide extra help for the medical department, Beaumont thought that arrangements could be made for him to come east. He suggested that Assistant Surgeon Lyman Foot, who had expressed a willingness to serve in Prairie du Chien, should be relieved at Jefferson Barracks, near St. Louis, by another surgeon, now in St. Louis, who had very limited duties. It was typical of Beaumont to say that, as he had *"just claims"* for leave for a specific purpose, he could see no reasonable objection to this arrangement. Beaumont knew and liked Dr. Foot, and said he knew no officer in the army to whom he would rather surrender his hospital; a hospital that he now thought to be "one of the finest Hospital establishments in the army."

Beaumont even had an alternative. If the plan with Foot was considered inappropriate, then he said use could be made of his hospital steward, C. H. Badger, a man he described as young and proficient. Beaumont said he would feel more confident entrusting the medical duties of the command to him than any citizen to be found in the region. He saw no real prospect of employing anyone in the vicinity. There were only "itinerant, speculating Doctors, in whose talents, or integrity I could neither repose confidence, nor even recommend to the employment of government, with half the cheerfulness & safety as I could young Badger."[47]

Beaumont was pressing for his leave at a particularly inconvenient time, both at Prairie du Chien and for the army in general. At Prairie du Chien, the commander, Colonel Willoughby Morgan, was dying in the spring of 1832. Beaumont's efforts were to no avail. On April 4, Colonel Morgan died.[48]

Beaumont must have felt that fate was against him in the following summer. The fears of Indian troubles that had existed in Prairie du Chien for several years came to a head. Black Hawk's desire to bring some of his Sac and Fox back to the homeland from which they had been forced was interpreted

47. Beaumont to Lovell, April 18, 1832, WD, AG, IMOF.
48. Nelson, *Beaumont,* 189; Scanlan, *Prairie du Chien,* 151.

as a military threat. In the spring and early summer, regular troops were sent into the region from other areas, and militia were called into service. There was no real threat, except to the Indians, but western Wisconsin and the adjacent areas were in turmoil.[49]

For the medical department of the army, the Black Hawk war brought many problems. By the latter part of June, sixteen additional surgeons had been ordered into the region, and medical personnel had to be recalled from leave. Their services became highly necessary when the troops from the East brought cholera into the region. Cholera had appeared in Montreal early in June, spread in the East, and traveled into the Old Northwest with General Winfield Scott's army. Beaumont, who had so often argued that disease emanated from peculiar weather conditions, in this case brought in psychological factors to account for the death rate. He commented in his notebook that the greatest proportion of deaths was caused by fright and the presentment of death.[50]

A threatened smallpox outbreak added to the medical difficulties. Early in May, Beaumont had asked that fresh vaccine be sent as soon as possible. He had doubts about the efficacy of the supply he had on hand, and though smallpox had not yet reached Prairie du Chien, he said it seemed to be approaching from every direction. There was to be a major outbreak of smallpox among the Indians of Wisconsin in the winter of 1832–1833.[51]

It says a great deal for Surgeon General Lovell's support of Beaumont that, in the middle of a crisis, an order granting Beaumont a leave of six months was issued on June 6. It was specifically stated that the leave included permission to visit Europe. Pressing army needs had reduced the leave from a year to six months, and it was stated that the leave should take effect only when Beaumont's services could be dispensed with. Yet Lovell had even managed to arrange the specific relief that Beaumont had suggested. On August 1, Beaumont reported to Lovell that Foot had arrived to relieve him of his duties.[52]

49. Francis P. Prucha, *The Sword of the Republic: The United States Army on the Frontier, 1783–1846*, 225; Nichols, *Atkinson*, 152–69.

50. Gillett, *Army Medical Department, 1818–1865*, 50–52; Charles E. Rosenberg, *The Cholera Years: The United States in 1832, 1849, and 1866*, 23–34; Peter T. Harstad, "Disease and Sickness on the Wisconsin Frontier: Cholera," 207; Beaumont's notebooks, BC, WU.

51. Beaumont to Lovell, May 6, 1832, WD, SG, LR; Peter T. Harstad, "Disease and Sickness on the Wisconsin Frontier: Smallpox and Other Diseases," 254.

52. Special Order #79, June 6, 1832, BC, WU; Beaumont to Joseph Lovell, August 1, 1832, WD, AG, IMOF.

Before he left, Beaumont had one other duty to perform. The last tragic act of Black Hawk's return was being played out, and early in August the steamboat *Warrior* proceeded up the Mississippi to take part in the last engagement of the Black Hawk war near the mouth of the Bad Axe river. As the Sac and Fox attempted to flee across the river, they were overtaken, and many of them were killed. It appears that Surgeon Beaumont was on board the *Warrior,* and that he tended the wounded after the engagement. It was his last duty before his furlough. On August 22 he was ordered to begin it by accompanying wounded militia from the hospital at Fort Crawford to St. Louis. They traveled by steamboat.[53]

Beaumont was still hoping that he could use his leave to visit Europe, and while he was on the boat traveling to St. Louis, he asked a friend who was a passenger to write a letter of introduction to his uncle in Paris. The writer said that Beaumont was about to leave for Europe, that he would spend some time in Paris, and that he was taking with him "a man who is said to have recovered from the most extraordinary wound ever known up to the present time." He spoke warmly of Beaumont, describing him as "a lovable and dignified man possessed of great knowledge." Lovable was a side of Beaumont usually known only to his close family and intimate friends. Surprisingly, in view of Beaumont's considerable contact with St. Martin over the previous years, and his residence in Mackinac, Green Bay, and Prairie du Chien, the writer warned his uncle that Beaumont spoke no French.[54]

While Beaumont was on his way east, the secretary of war received a letter from one of Beaumont's brothers—John—who was trying to find him. "I have not heard any thing from him for more than three years past," wrote John, "and I am entirely ignorant of his Station." The family in Lebanon needed to contact Beaumont, but they had no way of reaching him. The ties with Lebanon had long been tenuous; in Prairie du Chien they were broken.[55]

Beaumont arrived in Plattsburgh late in September and reported to Lovell that within a few days he intended to leave for Canada to find St. Martin. If all went well, he intended to travel to Washington to try to secure an extension of his leave; he had decided that six months was too short a time to travel to Europe.[56]

53. Nichols, *Atkinson,* 171–73; Frank E. Stevens, *The Black Hawk War,* 223–28; Philip St. George Cooke, *Scenes and Adventures in the Army, or, Romance of Military Life,* 188; Nelson, *Beaumont,* 192–94; Special Order #20, August 20, 1832, BC, WU.

54. James Soulard to Benjamin Soulard, August 24, 1832, in Myer, *Beaumont,* 145.

55. John Beaumont to the secretary of war, September 6, 1832, WD, AG, LR.

56. Beaumont to Lovell, September 30, 1832, WD, AG, IMOF.

St. Martin fulfilled his promise and returned into Beaumont's service, but with hopes of research both in the East and in Europe, Beaumont wanted to make sure that St. Martin would be available for research during the whole period of his leave and even beyond. On October 16, at Plattsburgh, a formal contract was drawn up between the two men. St. Martin contracted that for one year he would "serve, abide, and continue" with Beaumont, wherever he went. During that time he was contracted to "perform such service and business matters and things whatsoever as the said William shall from time to time order, direct, and appoint to and for the most profit and advantage of the said William."

In addition to the general obligation to serve as Beaumont should direct, St. Martin also contracted himself specifically to be the subject of medical experiments. At all times during the term of the contract, St. Martin, when directed by Beaumont, would "submit to, assist and promote by all means in his power such Physiological or Medical experiments as the said William shall direct or cause to be made on or in the Stomach of him, the said Alexis, either through or by means of the aperture or opening thereto in the side of him, the said Alexis, or otherwise, and will obey, suffer and comply with all reasonable and proper orders or experiments of the said William in relation thereto." He also agreed to cooperate with Beaumont in the exhibiting of his stomach, its powers and properties, and its contents. The contract stated that it was understood that his stomach would be exhibited or used by William "for the purposes of science and scientific improvements" and "the furtherance of knowledge in regard to the powers, properties and capacity of the human Stomach."

In return for these commitments, Beaumont promised to provide room, board, and apparel for St. Martin, and would pay him $150; $40 on signing the agreement, and the other $110 at the end of the period of service. Beaumont was clearly trying to protect against St. Martin fleeing before the year was up, although in the following April he gave another $40 of the agreed sum. The contract, on which St. Martin had to make his mark, was signed by three witnesses.[57]

There is no better indication of the importance that Beaumont now attached to his research than the commitment of $150 to St. Martin. Even though he was no longer hard-pressed for money, he still watched every

57. Articles of Agreement, October 16, 1832, BC, WU. The agreement is printed in Myer, *Beaumont*, 147–49; Harris A. Houghton, "The Beaumont–St. Martin Contract and the Descendants of Dr. Beaumont," 564–66.

penny. Beaumont's finances had undergone a marked improvement since he had reentered the army. He had managed to supplement his army pay with special services to the Indian department, and he had also carried on private practice in all of his military posts. At Prairie du Chien this had allowed Beaumont to begin to make a modest investment in property. In the spring of 1830 he had bought, for three hundred dollars, a farm lot of some 140 acres, with a house and a small stable. Like so many others in this era of rapidly increasing western speculation, he was hoping for a rapid and great increase in value. While waiting for its expected rise, he was renting it out. At the end of 1833, he estimated its worth at twelve hundred dollars.[58]

Beaumont had also, through his friend Daniel Whitney, invested in property in Green Bay. Whitney, who had come to Green Bay in 1820, had in the course of the 1820s become a very successful investor in a variety of western enterprises. In 1826 he obtained title to a large tract of land at the mouth of the Fox River, opposite Fort Howard. In 1829, on this tract, he laid out the town site of Navarino. During their stay in Green Bay, Beaumont and his wife had become quite close to the Whitneys, for "society" at the Bay was small and tight-knit. Debby Beaumont was a particularly good friend of Emmeline Whitney, and in the summer of 1831 the Whitneys had traveled to Prairie du Chien to visit their old friends.[59] As at Prairie du Chien, the expected dramatic boom had not yet arrived, but Wisconsin investors lived in expectation of a sudden and dramatic escalation in the value of their properties. Beaumont as yet was an extremely modest investor, but he had achieved the financial stability he had long sought.

In November 1832, Beaumont left Plattsburgh for Washington, D.C. At last he was to have the chance to take his research out of the frontier isolation in which he had conducted it into contact with others who had long been far more interested than Beaumont himself in the problems of human digestion and physiological research. All the previous research on digestion of any international importance had been carried out in Europe, but there were physicians and chemists along the eastern seaboard who had a great interest in the problems that Beaumont had been addressing.

Beaumont left his family in Plattsburgh, and on his departure he penned "Pill Cochie's Parting Admonition to his Dear old Wife, Deb." Pill Cochie was

---

58. Indenture between Hercules L. Dousman and Beaumont, April 24, 1830, BC, UC; Memo of assets, December 8, 1833, BC, WU.

59. Memo of assets, December 8, 1833, BC, WU; Deborah B. Martin, "Navarino," 11–20; Alice E. Smith, "Daniel Whitney," 283–304; Baird, "Reminiscences of Life in Territorial Wisconsin," 237.

a pet name for Beaumont. One of Beaumont's daughters later said that it was her father's habit, on leaving home, to leave "loving missives" around the house for members of the family. This letter was written in a gently comic tone of religious instruction. He told Debby to take good care of herself and her children, to be sociable with all her friends, to take tea and dinner with them when she had a chance, and not to be melancholy or depressed at his absence. He told her to drive "evil forebodings" from her mind, and to look forward to his return in the spring. She was to make all around her happy by her "natural vivacity & cheerfulness of disposition."

Beaumont also gave specific advice regarding each of his children. He asked Debby to give Sarah a good share of her care; he thought she could "scarcely be too vigilant in the daily observance for the improvement of her mind & morals," and in correcting every irregularity of her disposition. She was not to be too much indulged, and her companions were to be watched. He was also concerned that his other daughter—Lucretia—should not be "too much *petted.*" Debby was told to check "her natural vanity and affection." Of Israel—young "Bud"—his advice was not to let the *"young gentleman"* get the upper hand. Debby was to "apply the rod effectually when necessary to coerce obedience" to her authority.[60]

Though he wrote of using the rod, Beaumont was no tyrannical nineteenth-century patriarch. His letters, and contemporary and later comments, show him to have been, at least by all outward signs, a loving husband, and an affectionate and, in a nineteenth-century context, fairly indulgent father. His quick temper and tightness with money were generally shown in dealing with the world outside his immediate family and outside his small but very close circle of friends. There is every indication that when Beaumont left for Washington, D.C., with his hopes of greater medical success and reputation, his family looked forward to his return. Beaumont himself was about to enter a world of education, research, and politics that was provincial by European standards, but was heady stuff for a Connecticut farm boy and Vermont medical apprentice who had tried to rise in the world as a surgeon's mate in the United States Army.

---

60. Pill Cochie's Admonition, November 1832, BC, WU; Myer, *Beaumont,* 150n; Nelson, *Beaumont,* 171.

SEVEN

Success in the East

WHEN BEAUMONT REACHED WASHINGTON, D.C., it soon became clear to him that he had no chance of obtaining an extension of his leave to one year, and he abandoned his dream of taking St. Martin to Europe. Encouraged by Lovell, he decided to take full advantage of the books available in the capital, and to read extensively about research in the history of human digestion while continuing his experiments on St. Martin.

For Beaumont, this was a unique period in his life. His usual routine was broken. Living in lodgings in Washington, D.C., he devoted most of his time to work, but Lovell also saw that he dined with, or at least was introduced to, a variety of influential Washingtonians, including the president. Though he had spent the last dozen years in lonely western posts with his wife and family, Beaumont was not thrilled by his temporary bachelor status in the nation's capital. Writing to an old Prairie du Chien friend early in January, he was nostalgic for the "social enjoyment" he had experienced in the little village on the Mississippi. The "ingenuousness & magnanimity of soul" he had found there, he wrote, was "widely different from that produced by the commonplace, everyday, *poorly disguised*, cold, hollow-hearted, affectedness of fashionable society, of which this place is the seat & centre, & than which nothing can be more discordent to the present state of my feelings."[1]

---

1. Beaumont to Thomas Burnett, January 7, 1833, Thomas P. Burnett Papers. The Beaumont Collection of Washington University contains various social invitations from this period.

When not experimenting on St. Martin, much of Beaumont's time was taken up by his reading. It was in these months in the East that Beaumont laboriously compiled for his own purposes a "Synoptical Index of Different Authors on Digestion." In this he tried to give some order to his copious notes from a variety of authors. Some, such as Spallanzani, were of key importance in the history of the physiology of digestion, but he included other major figures such as Blumenbach and Broussais. Beaumont was never one to fritter away his time. He had always worked hard, and he tried to make use of every moment in these months away from his regular duties.[2]

As before, Beaumont received complete cooperation from Surgeon General Lovell. Lovell introduced him to those who would be helpful in his work, entertained him in his home, and took the most unusual step of arranging for St. Martin to receive an army appointment. This was presumably in the hope of making him more subject to Beaumont's control, as well as to ease the costs connected with St. Martin. In December 1832 it was arranged for St. Martin to enlist for a five-year stretch in the United States Army. He was assigned as a sergeant in the detachment of orderlies stationed at the War Department, with pay of $12 a month, an allowance of $2.50 for clothing, and ten cents a day for subsistence. In practice, St. Martin's duties consisted of making himself available to Beaumont for the purposes of experimentation.[3]

Beaumont had already, in his experiments at Prairie du Chien, reached the most important results that were to come from his research, but he now threw himself enthusiastically into a whole series of experiments that confirmed and somewhat broadened his earlier findings. He began on December 4, 1832, and was able to work far more consistently than he had earlier. This must have caused considerable irritation and discomfort to St. Martin, and there are indications in Beaumont's notes that at times St. Martin was drinking heavily. Beaumont experimented with great regularity: twenty-three days in December (including Christmas Day), nearly every day in January, and sixteen days in February. He completed this set of experiments on two days late in March.[4]

In these months, Beaumont was particularly interested in testing the time taken for digestion by a variety of different foods, and he also attempted to ascertain any differences that might arise in digestion because of changes in

2. Beaumont, Synoptical Index . . . , BC, WU.
3. Entry for Alexis St. Martin, enlisted December 1, 1832, in WD, AG, Descriptive and Historical Register of Enlisted Soldiers of the Army. Additional Material in BC, WU.
4. Beaumont, *Experiments,* 170–234.

weather conditions or because of differences in St. Martin's movements and exercise. As in Prairie du Chien, Beaumont made determined efforts to vary St. Martin's diet: on December 4 he ate beef soup, meat, and bread; on the fifth, raw oysters and crackers, roast turkey, potatoes, bread, and sausage; on the sixth, bread, butter, coffee, sausages, and bread; on the seventh, corn and wheat bread, butter, coffee, mutton, and potatoes; on the eighth, fried sausage, toast, and coffee. Beaumont repeated his efforts to show that food that had begun to digest in the stomach would restart digestion when removed, placed in a vial, and kept at the correct temperature in a sand bath. He also again demonstrated that when digestion ceased in a vial, it could be restarted by the addition of fresh gastric juice.[5]

Very early in his experiments, Beaumont had realized that gastric juice had a solvent, chemical action, and in Washington he continued to build up proofs of that assertion; comparing digestion of foods in the stomach itself with the same foods in gastric juice in a vial on a sand bath, and the same foods in water on a sand bath. He also refined this a little by comparing masticated and unmasticated meat.[6]

The constant experimentation was a considerable strain on St. Martin, and when Beaumont drew off gastric juice for experiments in vitro, Alex often complained of "sinking" and "vertigo." This feeling subsided in a few minutes. But periodically, St. Martin's stomach showed signs of sickness. When he noticed this on December 7 and 8, Beaumont dropped six grains of "blue pill" (a preparation containing about one-third mercury) directly into the stomach, and he sprinkled five or six grains of calomel onto the stomach's surface. Beaumont noted that when parts of the stomach and the tongue appeared diseased, digestion was protracted, and that "oil" was particularly hard to digest.[7]

On December 22 he noted that the coats of St. Martin's stomach had not appeared healthy for several days, that digestion was slower, and that St. Martin was constipated. On the following morning, Beaumont put six grains of calomel directly into the stomach to act as a cathartic. Eight hours later, as this had not worked, he put in an additional twelve grains. This produced the desired result. Before that happened, noted Beaumont, "the stomach was in commotion," full of white frothy liquid "like fermenting beer from a bottle."[8]

5. Ibid., 170–73.
6. Ibid., 176–81.
7. Ibid., 172–74, 194–95.
8. Ibid., 182–83.

On Christmas Day, Beaumont experimented, and St. Martin breakfasted on *"boiled, salted, fat pork, corn bread* and *coffee."* Beaumont observed the process of digestion on these items after St. Martin had walked two and a half miles. Earlier in the month, he had compared digestion when St. Martin walked and when he was recumbent. There is no indication in Beaumont's observations that either of them celebrated Christmas in any formal way. Possibly, Beaumont was invited out for a meal in the afternoon, as he made observations on St. Martin from 8 A.M. to 1 P.M., but not again until 9 P.M. that night.[9]

For the rest of December, and throughout January, Beaumont continued daily experiments and observations. He repeatedly demonstrated the solvent properties of the gastric fluid, directly rebutted the arguments of those who had contended that food was digested by a process of maceration, and observed that gastric juice retarded rather than caused putrefaction. To test the solvent properties of gastric fluid, he placed a piece of the rib bone of a hog in a vial, and added gastric juice to it to the extent necessary for digestion. He concluded that it required fourteen and a half drams of gastric juice to dissolve ten grains of solid bone. In these Washington experiments, it became more common for Beaumont to precisely record the weights of the items used in his experiments.[10]

By mid-January, Beaumont was quite convinced that gastric juice was a solvent that could digest food both inside and outside of the stomach, and he had also satisfied himself that neither putrefaction nor maceration accounted for the digestive process. These were results of basic importance in the disputes concerning human digestion, and Beaumont now tried to refine his basic experiments. He compared the solvent powers of gastric juice and saliva by placing equal amounts of beef in their respective vials. In concentrating on the gastric juice, Beaumont failed to understand the importance of saliva. He simply stated that it facilitated putrefaction.[11]

A few days later, Beaumont attempted to ascertain where the human sense of hunger resided, and whether a sense of hunger could be allayed without food passing through the esophagus. He had St. Martin fast from breakfast time until 4 P.M., and then placed three and a half drams of beef directly into the stomach. St. Martin's feelings of hunger immediately subsided. On another day, when St. Martin complained of being quite hungry, Beaumont

9. Ibid., 183.
10. Ibid., 184–203.
11. Ibid., 203–6.

put twelve raw oysters directly into his stomach. Beaumont's conclusion was that the sensation of hunger was allayed, and St. Martin's appetite was as satisfied as if he had swallowed the oysters.[12]

Throughout the experiments, Beaumont continued to show interest in the effect of exercise on digestion. Frequently, he had St. Martin take walks between tests, and drew off gastric juice before and after St. Martin exercised. He reached the conclusion that exercise promoted the discharge of gastric juice.[13]

Although Beaumont, except for his attempts to ascertain the function of saliva, did very little experimentation on aspects of digestion other than that by gastric juice inside and outside of the stomach, he did compare the digestive powers of pure gastric juice with that of gastric juice tinged with bile. He did this by placing such a mixture in two vials with ten grains of raw suet. His conclusion was that oily or fatty food was sooner digested when there was a small admixture of bile with the gastric juice.[14]

Until the middle of January 1833, Beaumont was still proceeding alone, but he continued to ask many of the right questions. From the time he had begun his research at Fort Niagara, he had tried to answer the questions that had most concerned researchers in Europe in the previous one hundred years. In Washington, Beaumont had the advantage of personal encouragement from Surgeon General Lovell and the new knowledge brought by extensive reading, but he was still very much his own man, and unsurprisingly for one who had done so much alone, anxious that no one should share the credit for his research.

Late in January, Beaumont for the first time came into direct contact with a physician and scholar of some eminence—Dr. Robley Dunglison, professor of medicine at the University of Virginia. Born in England, Dunglison, after an apprenticeship in Cumberland, had studied in London, Edinburgh, and Paris, and had begun his practice of medicine in London. In the mid-1820s he had been recruited to serve as a professor in Thomas Jefferson's recently founded university. He had become not only the prime mover in shaping medical education at Virginia but also Jefferson's physician, and had treated Jefferson for an enlarged prostate, visited him regularly at Monticello, and stayed there during Jefferson's last illness.[15]

12. Ibid., 208–9, 211.
13. Ibid., 175, 183–84, 191, 193, 199, 200, 209.
14. Ibid., 203–6, 209.
15. See Samuel X. Radbill, ed., "The Autobiographical Ana of Robley Dunglison, M.D.," 3–4, 7–32.

In 1832 Dunglison published his basic textbook, *Human Physiology,* which was to go through seven editions by 1850. In this work Dunglison threw his support behind the work of Spallanzani and the more recent research of Leuret and Lassaigne, and Tiedemann and Gmelin. He defended the idea of gastric juice as a solvent. Yet the whole subject of human digestion was still highly controversial, and in the same year that Dunglison published his work, Samuel Jackson of the University of Pennsylvania defended vitalistic doctrines in his work on physiology. The influential medical school of the University of Pennsylvania still had an important group that rejected the idea that human digestion could be explained simply in chemical terms.[16]

Early in January 1833, Dunglison received through a friend an invitation from Lovell to visit Washington to work with Beaumont in experimenting on St. Martin. On January 12 Dunglison wrote to Lovell, apologizing that he had been unable to respond and take part earlier but expressing a great interest in the ongoing research. Dunglison assumed that Lovell was associated with Beaumont in this work, and commented that several years ago he had seen their article on this subject. He said he had not included notice of the work in his book on human physiology because he had mislaid the article, but he remembered it had confirmed the views of Spallanzani and others.[17]

In his letter to Lovell, Dunglison suggested lines of research. Among these was the suggestion that it would be useful to test the effects of saliva outside the body, to discover whether that fluid possessed the sole agency in digestion, as supposed by Montegre, or was simply an adjunct influence "as presumed by the best Physiologists." He also suggested that it would be interesting to learn the comparative digestibility "of the great chemical divisions of Aliments," as well as individual items, both in the stomach and artificially.

In discussing the gastric fluid, Dunglison gave a strong indication of why Beaumont's work was to have such an important impact both in the United States and in Europe. He wrote that there had been great discrepancy in the experiments that had attempted to determine what were the fluids, known collectively as gastric juice, found in the stomachs of fasting animals. Dunglison wanted to know the general result of the research on St. Martin—whether

16. Ibid., 48–49; Bylebyl, "Beaumont, Dunglison, and the 'Philadelphia Physiologists,'" 12–13.

17. Radbill, ed., "Autobiographical Ana of Dunglison," 50; Dunglison to Lovell, January 12, 1833, BC, WU. The letters between Beaumont and Dunglison at this time are printed in Myer, *Beaumont,* 154–68.

litmus paper indicated the presence of any free acid or alkali. If it was acid, he wanted to know if by burning they could discover whether it was muriatic or acetic, or whether the fumes of ammonia showed either was present, and whether a solution of nitrate of silver indicated the presence of the former. He went on to suggest various more detailed chemical tests that he would like to perform on pure gastric juice. These tests, while clearly indicating the limitations of chemical analysis in the 1830s, were also tests that for the most part were not within Beaumont's experience or expertise.[18]

Dunglison was not certain he could get to Washington–he complained of the abysmal condition of the Virginia roads–but his curiosity had obviously been aroused, and before the end of the month he was there. He stayed only briefly, but he later stated that he obtained a microscope and collaborated with Beaumont on a number of experiments. In his book, Beaumont listed four microscopic examinations made in the presence of Professor Dunglison and Captain H. Smith of the United States Army. These were respectively an examination of the gastric juice itself, of "the chymous product" of gastric juice of beef, gastric juice and albumen, and gastric juice and veal. The observations were brief, and the results meager. Of the gastric juice itself, it was noted that it exhibited the appearance of water, except that a very few minute globules were perceptible in it; of gastric juice and veal, that it exhibited numerous minute, fleshy particles. Beaumont's comment on these observations was that they showed "no very satisfactory results are attainable from Microscopic examinations of Chyme."[19]

The meeting of Beaumont and Dunglison did not turn out entirely satisfactorily. While Dunglison was a man of far wider experience and more general knowledge than Beaumont, and knew a lot more about chemistry, he was more a physician, a teacher, and an author than he was a researcher. The accident to St. Martin had given Beaumont a chance for basic research that, whatever Beaumont's original limitations, he had taken up successfully. When the two men met, Dunglison seemed a little jealous that this frontier army doctor should have been given such an opportunity, and Beaumont was worried that this well-known Virginia professor would somehow take some of the credit for his work.

In writing of these events at a later date, Dunglison was rather deprecating in regard to Beaumont while exaggerating his own participation in the

18. Dunglison to Lovell, January 12, 1833, in Myer, *Beaumont,* 154–58.
19. Beaumont, *Experiments,* 233; Radbill, ed., "Autobiographical Ana of Dunglison," 53.

experiments. "Dr. Beaumont," he wrote, "was neither by his nature or his stars well fitted for the investigation of any profound physiological subject. He was most persevering, however; and his zeal and industry compensated in some degree for his deficiency in ability." There is a good deal of truth in this judgment, but Dunglison placed Beaumont's strengths in the most unflattering light possible. Dunglison exaggerated the extent of his contact with Beaumont by stating that he was "associated with him in the prosecution of numerous interesting experiments."[20]

Dunglison could hardly have been associated with Beaumont in "numerous interesting experiments," because on January 12 he was in Charlottesville, complaining of the state of the roads, and indicating a doubt whether he would come to Washington, and by January 25 he had been to Washington and was about to return to Charlottesville. On that day Beaumont left a bottle of gastric juice at Dunglison's Washington hotel. He said he was leaving the gastric juice for chemical analysis in the hope that Dunglison would obtain satisfactory results, and send a detailed report.

While Beaumont asked for Dunglison's help in performing a chemical analysis, there are indications in his letter that Dunglison had patronized him, and also worried him by indicating that he was anxious for it to be known that Beaumont's research on St. Martin had bolstered the Spallanzani view of digestion that Dunglison had supported in his own book. Beaumont said that he would ever be grateful for the aid and instruction Dunglison had provided, but added he felt confident that Dunglison would never by premature publication in any periodical "improperly" anticipate his own intention to publish his experiments.[21]

A few days later Dunglison, now back in Charlottesville, wrote a letter thanking Beaumont for the gastric juice, and for allowing him to examine St. Martin and be associated with him in his experiments. He also assured Beaumont in regard to the question of premature publication, and was gracious in his praise. "The praiseworthy manner in which you have entered your experiments demands my thanks," wrote Dunglison, "as well as those of every lover of science, and I have no doubt when complete they will add largely to our amount of useful knowledge."

Though Dunglison promised, "I shall not anticipate you," he was obviously anxious to associate himself with experiments on which Beaumont had spent

20. Radbill, ed., "Autobiographical Ana of Dunglison," 51.
21. Beaumont to Dunglison, January 25, 1833, in Myer, *Beaumont,* 159.

years. He said he would, with pleasure, afford Beaumont every facility in communicating his results to the public, and would be quite satisfied "to perform a secondary part." Dunglison had made suggestions, had spent a few days with Beaumont, and had promised to make a chemical analysis of the gastric juice, but he was apparently hoping that he might appear as a collaborator in Beaumont's eventual publication.[22]

Dunglison acted with great promptness in trying to analyze the gastric juice. On February 10 he reported that in association with his colleague, Professor John P. Emmet, he had found the juice contained "free muriatic and Acetic acid," together with various other substances. He said that though they had been satisfied in Washington that free muriatic acid was present, he had no idea until the analysis was made that there was so much of it. The disappointing aspect of the report, however, was that Dunglison said they did not have enough juice to estimate the precise amounts of the various ingredients; surprisingly he said that he did not think that this was of great importance. He said that he thought it was probable that the acetic acid was the "great disinfecting agent." If Beaumont could supply half a pound of the juice, then Dunglison thought they could proceed further.

Dunglison was particularly pleased by the results of Beaumont's work, because the conclusions he had drawn in his own recent book were being challenged. A reviewer in the *American Journal of the Medical Sciences* had sided with Samuel Jackson and the Philadelphia vitalists, and the vitalists were still active. Beaumont's work was to deal them a deathblow, and for Dunglison it had the advantage of being produced by a man who had no axe to grind in the arguments that had divided better-known physiologists. Dunglison commented that the conclusions he could now draw from the research on St. Martin would have been challenged as special pleading, but for the fact that he had been associated with Beaumont and Emmet. Beaumont was completely unknown to the world of physiological research until the accident to St. Martin had created the opportunity for his research. That Beaumont should publish soon was important to Dunglison, and he suggested that a report should be sent to the *American Journal of the Medical Sciences,* which was edited by his friend Dr. Isaac Hays.[23]

Dunglison did not tell Beaumont that on the previous day he had written an account of the St. Martin case to Dr. Hays, saying that he was gratified

22. Dunglison to Beaumont, January 29, 1833, ibid., 159–60.
23. Dunglison to Beaumont, February 6, 1833, ibid., 160–61.

that it supported the deductions he had made, from less evidence, in his own book. The St. Martin case, wrote Dunglison, supported the conclusions of Tiedemann and Gmelin, who also found that the secretion of acid began as soon as the stomach received the stimulus of a foreign body, and that it consisted of muriatic and acetic acids. It was as well that Beaumont had warned Dunglison about premature publication, for Dunglison told Hays that his letter should not be made public until after Beaumont had published. His later comment was that Beaumont's urging not to publish first was, of course, needless, "although savouring somewhat of a want of delicacy." Beaumont, wrote Dunglison, "had long been observing and experimenting, although in a somewhat desultory manner, on the Canadian, and it was but right he should have all the credit to which he was legitimately entitled."[24]

Having been warned off by Beaumont, Dunglison did not publish anything on the St. Martin case before Beaumont's own book appeared, but Dunglison's obvious desire to share in what he knew to be highly important research leads to the conclusion that Beaumont, indelicately or not, did well to issue the warning. When the Scots phrenologist George Combe visited the United States at the end of the 1830s, he recorded in his published journal that at a dinner he attended, Professor Dunglison mentioned in regard to Beaumont's experiments on St. Martin "that he had suggested and also performed the experiments at Washington, which are recorded in Beaumont's work." Dunglison published a correction in the *American Medical Intelligencer*, saying that this was a "singular injustice" to Dr. Beaumont, although he had made certain suggestions and performed certain experiments in Washington with him.[25]

When Dunglison recollected these events in his autobiography, he commented that it was strange a man so sensitive about priorities in publication should have omitted all mention of Dunglison's help in his published book. This was simply untrue. The modern editor of Dunglison's autobiography has pointed out that Beaumont made "frequent respectful allusions" to Dunglison throughout his book. Beaumont probably was right to fear that Dunglison might put something in print quickly so that he could share in the glory; it seems likely that but for Beaumont's specific request, the letter to the editor of the *American Journal of the Medical Sciences*, written immediately after Dunglison had been to Washington, would have been public rather than private. On March 11 a notice appeared in the *Washington Intelligencer*, denying

24. Radbill, ed., "Autobiographical Ana of Dunglison," 51–52.
25. Ibid., 52–53; George Combe, *Notes on the United States of North America during a Phrenological Visit in the Years 1838–9–40,* vol. 1, 187–88.

a previous announcement that Dunglison and Beaumont were planning to write a history of the case together.[26]

Whatever Dunglison's blind spot in trying to enhance his role in the experiments on St. Martin, one anecdote he remembered about Beaumont has the ring of truth. He wrote that soon after the appearance of Beaumont's book, he ran into Beaumont in Baltimore, and that as Beaumont did not present him with a copy he offered to buy it. Beaumont, he wrote, said "he thought under all the circumstances, I *ought* to have a copy gratuitously; but took the money." That sounds like Beaumont. Also having the ring of truth is that when Dunglison on this occasion said he hoped to see more of their cooperation, Beaumont replied "that he did not think I would care to be associated with so humble an individual as himself."[27] Dunglison's manner clearly irked Beaumont.

For all Beaumont's legitimate concern that Dunglison might exaggerate his role in the St. Martin experiments, he responded quickly to Dunglison's specific suggestions, reported the results to him promptly, and paid extravagant compliments to Dunglison's "pre-eminent qualifications." Dunglison had suggested in his letter of January 29 that Beaumont should mix saliva and diluted muriatic acid, and saliva and diluted acetic acid, to test some of Montegre's conclusions. Beaumont replied that he had done this, stating that he had judged by sense of taste when they approximated the acid flavor of the gastric juice. He tested these mixtures on foods in vials on a sand bath for several days, and noted very little progress in real digestion. He then tried the acids mixed together, with about the same result. He sent the results to Dunglison for examination, observing that he could send more such experiments but thought they would not be of sufficient importance to excite Dunglison's attention. In his book, Beaumont drew out of this unsuccessful attempt to reproduce the gastric juice the correct conclusion that gastric juice probably "contains some principles inappreciable to the senses, or to chemical tests, besides the alkaline substances already discovered in it."[28]

While Beaumont also promised to send Dunglison more gastric juice, he did not react with any enthusiasm to Dunglison's suggestion of publishing in the *American Journal of the Medical Sciences*. He said that he was planning in

26. Radbill, ed, "Autobiographical Ana of Dunglison," 52 and 52n.
27. Ibid., 52.
28. Beaumont to Dunglison, February 10, 1833, in Myer, *Beaumont*, 161–64; Beaumont, *Experiments*, 227–28; Bylebyl, "Beaumont, Dunglison, and the 'Philadelphia Physiologists,'" 20–21.

the near future to send an abstract report of his experiments to the surgeon general, while reserving the entire series of experiments for "other and future arrangements." The latter project seemed to Beaumont "an herculean labor."[29]

When just nine days later Beaumont sent more gastric juice to Dunglison, he told him that he had experimented on masticated meat and gelatin with gastric juice, and with dilute muriatic and acetic acids as Dunglison had suggested. He enclosed the results, and expressed the hope that Dunglison would excuse "the awkward and unscientific manner in which they were made and here attempted to be described." He noted, however, that he appeared to be confirming the principles of gastric function enunciated by Dunglison in his book on physiology.[30]

Beaumont's experiments on St. Martin went on practically continuously from early December 1832 to late February 1833. Dunglison's visit and suggestions did not seriously deflect him from the course he was already pursuing. Late in January he became particularly interested in the variations in temperature he observed in moving the thermometer up and down inside the stomach, and in the following days he recorded such differences. He also at this time devoted attention to the internal motions and contractions of the stomach, and began to comment more particularly on what he observed at its "pyloric" and "splenic" ends.[31] Beaumont was now attempting to vary what, at quite an early stage in his investigations, had become his basic and most important results—the plain evidence that gastric juice was a solvent, that gastric juice had a chemical action, and that digestion could proceed in gastric juice outside as well as inside the stomach.

One of the reasons that Beaumont was working relentlessly in January and February was that his furlough was coming to an end. He knew that he would soon be leaving Washington, and did not know whether circumstances would allow him to continue his work on any consistent basis. In reality, given the general limits of research in human digestion in the early nineteenth century and Beaumont's own limitations in training and knowledge, he had done about all he could do. His most important results had been achieved even before he began his Washington research.

---

29. Beaumont to Dunglison, February 10, 1833, in Myer, *Beaumont*, 164; Bylebyl, "Beaumont, Dunglison, and the 'Philadelphia Physiologists,'" 13–17, discusses Dunglison's participation in the experiments.
30. Beaumont to Dunglison, February 19, 1833, in Myer, *Beaumont*, 164–65.
31. Beaumont, *Experiments*, 213–23.

Beaumont was anxious to learn more about the composition of the gastric juice, which he had decided was the key to digestion, but in this he was limited by not only his own inability to undertake the necessary chemical analysis but also the limitations in chemical analysis in his period. Dunglison, who was one of the few men in the United States to whom he could turn, had told him very little more than he already knew. Beaumont had hopes that Dunglison would do more with the additional quantity of gastric juice he had supplied, but soon after he left Washington he had a disappointing response. Dunglison's report on his latest attempt to analyze the gastric juice was that its precise contents, besides muriatic and acetic acids, might never be known. He simply told Beaumont that he believed that his experiments tended to show that the main gastric action was one of solution, not of chemical conversion. He suggested other experiments, but this was not what Beaumont wanted.[32]

While still in Washington, Beaumont, probably through Lovell, had been brought into contact with Dr. Thomas Sewall of the Columbian College of that city. Early in February, Sewall had provided him with a letter of introduction to Dr. J. K. Mitchell of Philadelphia. The letter stated that Beaumont had "charge of the boy with an open orifice," and said that he was seeking an analysis of the gastric juice. Beaumont was still hoping to get better results than he had received from Dunglison. Beaumont also gave samples of gastric juice to a colleague of Sewall's at the Columbian College, and sent some to Baltimore in his attempts to get an answer regarding its chemical composition.[33]

Beaumont had impressed Dr. Sewall enough that he had decided to take steps to have him awarded the honorary degree of Doctor of Medicine. This was of far more importance for a military surgeon who had gained his medical education in a small town in northern Vermont than it would have been for any of the main figures in American medicine. Beaumont was obviously a little worried that his official credentials could not bear comparison with those of the eastern medical establishment. On March 1 he sent Sewall such testimonials as he had, with the comment that he hoped they were good enough. Though of the first respectability, he wrote, "their forms, & the authorities from which they emanate, may not be of so high & classical

32. Dunglison to Beaumont, March 23, 1833, in Myer, *Beaumont,* 167–68; see also Atwater, "Squeezing Mother Nature," 327.
33. Thomas Sewall to J. K. Mitchell, February 5, 1833; Beaumont to Sewall, n.d. [c. September 1833], BC, WU.

an order, as may be required by the laws of your Institution." Of an official nature, he had little more than his certification from the state of Vermont and his honorary membership in the Michigan Medical Society. He need have had no worries. On March 6, the Columbian College awarded Beaumont his honorary degree, although Beaumont had already left the city.[34]

Early in March, shortly before he left Washington, Beaumont gave Surgeon General Lovell an abstract report of his work with St. Martin. In it, he went to the heart of why his results were to receive such contemporary acceptance. "I can truly assert," he wrote, "that no favorite *theory, system,* or *hypothesis*–preconceived opinions or partiality for popular authority have had any influence in making or recording them." He also made no bones about his own inexperience in carrying out experiments: "a mere tyro in science with a mind free from every bias, I commenced them, as it were, by accident."[35] Few researchers can have begun research of such major importance knowing so little about the detailed arguments revolving around their subject.

Beaumont now needed time to prepare his manuscript for publication, and, if possible, to obtain an effective chemical analysis of the gastric juice. The pressing problem was that his leave was ending, and an immediate posting to some distant western post would create great difficulties. Once again, Lovell came to his aid, and was entirely cooperative. For the time being, he arranged for Beaumont to be posted to New York, where there was a temporary vacancy owing to the absence of Surgeon Thomas Mower. Beaumont's duties in New York were to be light; he examined recruits and arranged for the shipment of medical supplies. Lovell was simply making every effort to ensure that Beaumont would have the time to complete his work.[36]

Lovell's influence was also enough to secure a special order from the Adjutant General's Office giving St. Martin a leave of three months from his supposed duties with the detachment of orderlies in Washington. It is perhaps an indication of Beaumont's realization of the importance of Lovell's remarkable support that as soon as he reached New York, he sent a musical instrument (most likely a flute) and music as a gift to Lovell's daughter, Eliza.

34. Beaumont to Thomas Sewall, March 1 and July 31, 1833, Sewall to Beaumont, July 24, 1833, BC, WU; Myer, *Beaumont,* 177–78.
35. Draft of report to Joseph Lovell, [c. March 1833], BC, WU, partly reprinted in Myer, *Beaumont,* 165–66.
36. Beaumont to Lovell, March 19, 1833, BC, WU; Beaumont to Lovell, March 31, 1833, WD, SG, LR.

What to some men would have been a casual act was for Beaumont a major gesture.[37]

In New York, Beaumont took lodgings in lower Manhattan on Broadway, and was able to spend time with another old and valuable friend, Ramsay Crooks of the American Fur Company. Crooks, who in the following year was to succeed John Jacob Astor at the head of the company, entertained Beaumont in his home and also advised him on financial matters. While in New York, Beaumont, on Crooks's advice, deposited five thousand dollars at interest. Beaumont had achieved a comfortable living by combining a private practice with his military duties, but this deposit was made possible by his caution in spending money.[38]

As Beaumont began to write up a more detailed account of his experiments on St. Martin, his main concern, apart from what seemed to him the formidable task of getting it ready for publication, was the question of the exact nature of the gastric juice. After hearing the disappointing news that Dunglison thought its exact composition might never be known, and discovering that he could get no help in New York City, Beaumont determined to consult the famous Professor Benjamin Silliman of Yale, one of the few American chemists who might be able to help him. On April 1 he traveled to New Haven and met with Silliman and some of his colleagues.[39]

In his notebook, near to his cryptic account of this trip, Beaumont copied (perhaps at about the same time) two pieces of verse; one fairly typical of what usually attracted him, one untypical. The typical one seems to reflect that he was about finished with his experiments on St. Martin. It begins:

> The work is done! nor Folly's active rage,
> Nor envy's self shall blot the golden page.

The other perhaps reflects that he was missing Debby, whom he had not seen since leaving for Washington the previous November. It was in Latin, and was translated:

> Wine, women, warmth, against our lives combine
> But what is life, without warmth, women, wine?[40]

---

37. Special Order regarding Alexander St. Martin, March 4, 1833, BC, WU; Eliza Lovell to Beaumont, March 23, 1833, BC, WU.

38. Ramsay Crooks to Beaumont, March 20, 1833, Beaumont's memo of assets, December 8, 1833, BC, WU; Haeger, *John Jacob Astor*, 241–43.

39. Notebook, April 1, 1833, BC, WU.

40. Ibid.

Beaumont was gratified to find that Professor Silliman and his fellow professors took a great interest in his work. Silliman accepted gastric juice for analysis, and also arranged to have Beaumont send gastric juice to the eminent Swedish chemist, Professor Jacob Berzelius. Soon after Beaumont's visit, Silliman wrote to Berzelius and told him that Beaumont would send him, through the Swedish consul at New York, gastric fluid from the stomach of a healthy man. He said that he intended to make a few tentative experiments himself, but doubted whether he was likely to discover "the peculiar agent" that worked such wonders in the human system.[41]

Silliman sent a copy of this letter to Beaumont, along with a letter to the Swedish consul asking him to deliver the bottle of gastric juice to Berzelius. To Beaumont, Silliman recommended sending Berzelius "a pretty liberal supply" of the fluid, and told him that, when he had time, he would try some experiments himself. Physiological chemistry, however, was not a field in which Silliman had any particular expertise, and he placed more hope in Berzelius.[42]

In mid-April Beaumont sent the gastric juice to Berzelius, together with a long letter describing the case and his articles from the *Medical Recorder*. He described how he used a rubber tube to extract the juice, and gave a brief description of the experiments that he had carried out. He emphasized that though he had submitted gastric juice for analysis to "some of the most eminent practical chemists" in the United States, none had obtained complete and satisfactory results, and only Dunglison had managed to provide anything useful or important on the subject. He said he hoped to publish in the coming autumn or winter, or when he could get a satisfactory analysis of the fluid.[43]

By the time he wrote to Berzelius, Beaumont was tired of New York and very anxious to see his family in Plattsburgh. He told Lovell that he had not been able to do much in experimenting since he had been in the city, "so numerous & increasing are the calls of the curious–the social–the scientific & the professional." He admitted that his official duties were very light and would not interfere with his experiments if he could avoid "the *vexatious* social intercourse to which I am perpetually exposed in this City." He said he was determined to finish his experiments soon, even if he had to write

41. Benjamin Silliman to Jacob Berzelius, April 10, 1833, BC, WU.

42. Silliman to Beaumont, Silliman to Mr. Gahn, April 10, 1833, BC, WU.

43. Beaumont to Jacob Berzelius, April 17, 1833. See also Erik M. P. Widmark, "William Beaumont Och Jons Jacob Berzelius," [1941], proofs of article in Pharmacy Library, University of Wisconsin, Madison. This is in Swedish, with letters in English.

shut up with St. Martin in a convent or in the country. He was still frustrated by his inability to secure an analysis of the gastric juice, and told Lovell that the professional men of New York had too many personal, political, and commercial matters on hand to attend to physiological chemistry.[44]

In preparing for publication, as in undertaking his research, Beaumont ultimately acted with little professional help. It was as though, having been solely responsible for the research, he wanted even this last aspect of his work to be under his own control. He accepted help only from his cousin Samuel. Although he told Lovell that when he had assembled all the materials for publication he would send them "for correction," this was never done. Part of the problem was, as was typical of Beaumont, money. While Beaumont and St. Martin had been in Washington, he had obtained colored drawings of the wound.[45] In New York, Beaumont checked the cost of having them engraved, thought it would be too expensive, and decided to omit them. Crude, simple drawings took their place. He was hoping that by winter he would be ready for publication, but he still had not contacted a publisher, and asked Lovell if he thought Philadelphia would be a good place for publication.

Beaumont was now so confident of the personal support and friendship of the surgeon general that he did not even bother to exaggerate the little amount of time that was taken up by his official duties. He simply said that he had very little to do, and that he was constantly beset by the social and other obligations incidental to his residence in New York. He even informed Lovell, without first submitting a formal request, that within a few days he was going to visit his family in Plattsburgh. He said he had arranged for Dr. Joseph Russell to take care of his official duties during his absence, that while in Plattsburgh he hoped to go forward with his experiments, and that he hoped all this met with Lovell's approbation.[46] Beaumont had become increasingly used to obtaining special concessions. This continued to be possible while Lovell was in charge, but Beaumont was developing a pattern that could and would be dangerous with a different surgeon general.

Beaumont did not experiment on St. Martin during this visit to Plattsburgh. St. Martin had heard that his family was sick and that one of his children was dying, and Beaumont gave him permission to go to Canada. By June 1, however, when Beaumont was back in New York, St. Martin had returned from Canada and was in Plattsburgh with Beaumont's family.[47]

44. Beaumont to Lovell, April 16, 1833, BC, WU.
45. See *Boston Medical and Surgical Journal* 9 (September 18, 1833), 94–95.
46. Beaumont to Lovell, April 16, 1833, BC, WU.
47. Beaumont to Lovell, June 1 and 10, 1833, BC, WU; Myer, *Beaumont,* 174.

In Plattsburgh, Beaumont had learned that his cousin, who early in his career had worked in newspaper printing and publishing, was willing to help in the publication of the book. Beaumont told Lovell that he already had a rough manuscript written, which together with the experiments would make a book of about three hundred pages. He thought that he and his cousin could get this ready for typesetting in three or four weeks, and that it could be published as well at Plattsburgh or Burlington as in New York or Philadelphia for half the cost of publication elsewhere. "I find it an immense job to make *a Book*, & I heartily wish it were done, & *publicly approved* of & *well sold*–& I were snugly established at the Arsenal near St. Louis in regular performance of my offl duties again." In mid-April, Beaumont had expressed a wish that on his return to regular duty he should be posted to St. Louis.[48]

Beaumont, having learned in New York of the expense of having engravings made, and possibly hearing on further enquiry that a publisher might require a subvention from him for a book on this topic, decided that he would have greater control of the costs, and perhaps would be able to make a profit, if he and his cousin handled the publication themselves. This was a bad decision–the book came out with far too many typographical errors and without the imprimatur of a major Philadelphia publisher–but is understandable in the light of Beaumont's fears of spending money and his lack of experience in the world of research and publication.

To organize the details of publication, Beaumont now made yet another exceptional request of Surgeon General Lovell. He asked Lovell if it would be possible to relieve him of his duties from June to November. Lovell, as ever, was cooperative. He replied immediately, saying that if Dr. Russell would again substitute for him in the continued absence of Dr. Mower, and if the commanding general would give his consent, then he could return to Plattsburgh. He also told Beaumont that Edward Livingston, who was about to go to Paris as the American minister, wanted Beaumont and St. Martin to come to Paris. Lovell was sure that Livingston would find people there to pay all the expenses.[49]

A week later the question of Plattsburgh was settled. The commanding general gave permission, and Dr. Russell agreed to substitute. On June 10, Beaumont told Lovell that in about another week he would leave for Plattsburgh "to rush the execution of the Book as fast as possible." He said that

    48. Beaumont to Lovell, April 16 and June 1, 1833, BC, WU; Nelson, *Beaumont*, 53, 211.
    49. Beaumont to Lovell, June 1, 1833, Lovell to Beaumont, June 3, 1833, BC, WU.

he had arranged to have the drawings made in Washington engraved in New York, and would take them with him. In reality, he abandoned the plans for professional etchings made from skilled drawings and had three simple, rather primitive-looking plates made in Plattsburgh. Beaumont also made another of his usual requests. He had heard of the possibility that the recruiting station at Middlebury, Vermont, might be moved to Plattsburgh or Burlington. If that was to be the case, he asked to be posted to examine the recruits at either of those places. If so, he said that he assumed he would get all the allowances he was now receiving. Also, he said that an official position would relieve him from the embarrassment he felt in receiving an allowance while absent from duty carried out by Dr. Russell. He did not mention that he presumably could have easily relieved himself of the embarrassment by making a private payment to Dr. Russell in the amount of his allowance.

Money was also involved in Beaumont's request to Lovell regarding St. Martin. He had asked that St. Martin's furlough should be extended, but had heard nothing. He suggested to Lovell that if it could be "constantly continued" it would relieve him of St. Martin's constant requests for money. Beaumont hoped to reengage St. Martin for three or four more years of experiments, and thought that there would be no difficulty as St. Martin liked the idea of going to Paris. After all this, Beaumont could hardly have done less than ask Lovell if he would have any objections to having the book dedicated to him. But that was not the end of the letter, for Beaumont still remembered to ask Lovell about some requests he had made for extra allowances for transportation.[50] Lovell must have been a remarkably patient and understanding man.

Lovell had in fact already made the necessary arrangements regarding St. Martin, and they were all that Beaumont could possibly have hoped for. Beaumont was informed by the Adjutant General's Office that in the future Sergeant Alexis St. Martin would be considered on duty with him, and would be subject to his orders. He would be dropped from the rolls of the detachment of orderlies in Washington, D.C., and would now be mustered by Beaumont, who was to report monthly to the Adjutant General's Office until further orders.[51]

From the time that Beaumont had arrived in Washington, Lovell had done a remarkable job of bending the army system to suit Beaumont's wishes in

50. Beaumont to Lovell, June 10, 1833, BC, WU.
51. S. Cooper to Beaumont, June 10, 1833, BC, WU.

regard to himself and St. Martin, and even Beaumont's request for a new posting in what had become his hometown of Plattsburgh was to be met, but it took a few weeks for Lovell to manage. On July 1 Beaumont wrote to Lovell to say he was disappointed and discouraged at not receiving an order to repair to Plattsburgh or Burlington, and suggested he would go without a formal order if Lovell would give him permission. He said he would prefer an order, as it would be "unpleasant" to go without. The unpleasantness presumably was that without a formal order Beaumont would not receive the allowances payable on moving to a formal new posting. Beaumont placed a little additional pressure on Lovell by suggesting that St. Martin was not entirely happy in Plattsburgh, and would return to Canada if Beaumont did not arrive soon.[52]

Lovell obliged again. On July 8 he told Beaumont that the adjutant general had made the necessary arrangements. A special order had been issued requiring Surgeon Beaumont to repair to Plattsburgh without delay, and to report to the recruiting officer. Russell had been ordered to take over Beaumont's New York duties.[53]

As Beaumont left for Plattsburgh to complete his researches and his book, he was given another boost. The Connecticut Medical Society informed him that they had made him an honorary member because of his dedication to the improvement of medical science. They also told him that the honor had been conferred on only twenty-seven individuals since 1792.[54] The honor presumably reflected the impression that Beaumont had made on Benjamin Silliman and his colleagues at Yale.

Back in Plattsburgh, even while the main part of his manuscript was being prepared for the press, Beaumont carried out a fourth series of experiments. The sixty-two experiments he completed from July 9 to November 1 added nothing of major importance to what he had already accomplished. In July and August he was mainly concerned with the temperature and appearance of the interior of the stomach. In this period, Beaumont was able to note that the stomach itself could appear unhealthy even when there were no outside symptoms. His opportunity for this came because St. Martin was now drinking heavily. On July 28 Beaumont indicated that St. Martin had been drinking "ardent spirits, pretty freely, for eight or ten days past." In the following days, Beaumont noted the morbid condition of the stomach while

---

52. Beaumont to Lovell, July 1, 1833, BC, WU.
53. Special Order, July 5, 1833, Lovell to Beaumont, July 8, 1833, BC, WU.
54. Charles Hooker to Beaumont, July 10, 1833, BC, WU.

there were no marked external symptoms, and concluded that inflammation of the stomach could exist even in an *"apparent* state of health."[55]

In these months in Plattsburgh, Beaumont continued to observe the times taken for the digestion of a wide variety of foods, and he continued to compare digestion in the stomach with digestion in gastric juice in vials. Of greatest interest in Beaumont's conclusions from this group of experiments is the extent to which Beaumont was coming to realize that gastric juice alone was not the complete answer to human digestion. In writing on the slow digestibility of oil, he emphasized the importance of bile: *"bile* accelerates the solution of oil, by the gastric juice; and I have no doubt, it facilitates the chymification of all fatty and oily aliments; and is required, and necessarily called into the stomach *only* for that purpose."[56]

These last experiments in Plattsburgh seem to have been as much with the purpose of bringing the book to what Beaumont deemed a suitable length as with the hope of securing any new data. They also seem to have been dedicated to broadening the appeal of the book by enabling him to draw more conclusions on the digestibility of different items of food. On October 2 he noted that stimulating condiments (strong mustard and vinegar) were prejudicial to a healthy stomach, and on October 20 that a breakfast of boiled sago with sugar was "peculiarly grateful to the surface of the stomach." His experiments in Plattsburgh, in both natural and artificial digestion, enabled him to expand his charts on the digestibility of various items of food.[57]

Beaumont's biggest disappointment in preparing for publication was that he was unsuccessful in obtaining a satisfactory chemical analysis of the gastric juice. His long awaited report from Professor Silliman came in August, and it was a great disappointment. The long letter would have been a lot more use to Beaumont in the fall of 1832, or even earlier, for it consisted more of an academic survey of the literature than a report of a precise analysis of the gastric juice. Silliman surveyed the contributions of Spallanzani, Montegre, Tiedemann, Gmelin, and others who had contributed to the study of human digestion, and the particular properties of gastric juice, but the analysis added nothing to what Beaumont had learned from Dunglison. Silliman regretted that he was unable to contribute something important to previous knowledge, and admitted that there was much in physiology that eluded the scrutiny of chemistry. He said that the pressure of his other engagements prevented him

55. Beaumont, *Experiments*, 235–40.
56. Ibid., 264.
57. Ibid., 24–72.

doing more, but he urged Beaumont to delay publication until he heard from Berzelius.[58]

The prospect of an early reply from Sweden seemed to have disappeared, however, for at about this time Beaumont heard from the Swedish consul in New York that he had difficulty in finding a way to send the container of gastric juice, and that it had not left New York until June 27.[59] Beaumont now decided to make another effort in the United States. On August 9 he sent gastric juice to Dr. Franklin Bache in Philadelphia, saying he would like to have an analysis as soon as possible because he was going to press in three or four weeks. On the same day he also wrote to Dunglison in Virginia, wanting to know if Dunglison had obtained additional results from the second batch of gastric juice he had supplied. He told Dr. Sewall of Washington, who had given him a letter of introduction to Dr. Bache: "I am determined not to cease my efforts to obtain a thorough analysis of the juice."[60]

It took Bache a month to reply, and his reply was as disappointing as Silliman's. He said that he did not have the apparatus to make the detailed test requested by Beaumont. He hoped to be able to discover the principle constituents of the gastric juice, but not their relative proportions. He also said that animal analysis was the most difficult department of chemistry, and that there were only a few living chemists—Thenard in France, Berzelius in Sweden, and Prout in England—who could perform a complete analysis of the gastric juice. In reality, no one, not even Berzelius, was able to give Beaumont the analysis he desired.

In writing to Bache, Beaumont had enclosed a prospectus of his book. Bache had made arrangements for subscriptions, but gave a warning that Beaumont must have been sorry to receive. "I presume you do not intend to print your work in Plattsburgh," wrote Bache, "as I am sure that it cannot be done there in that handsome style which is so essential to its success."[61] This was not what Beaumont wanted to hear, but it did not dissuade him from the course he had decided upon. In the late summer and fall of 1833, while completing his last experiments on St. Martin, he worked continually with his cousin Samuel both to prepare his book for the printer and to promote it.

58. Benjamin Silliman to Beaumont, August 2, 1833, BC, WU.
59. Memo from the Swedish Consul, July 30, 1833, BC, WU.
60. Beaumont to Franklin Bache, to Robley Dunglison, August 9, 1833, to Thomas Sewall, [c. August 1833], BC, WU.
61. Franklin Bache to Beaumont, September 12, 1833, BC, WU.

EIGHT

Experiments and Observations

ON JULY 23, 1833, Beaumont filed the copyright for his book title, and from that time he moved with all possible speed to get the book published. As was quite common at the time, he decided to try and sell his book by subscription, and in the middle of August he had a prospectus printed. The prospectus, which had space for subscribers to enter their names, described the accident to St. Martin, the experiments, and the general format of the book. The book, it was said, was to be printed on fine paper with perfectly new type bought expressly for the purpose, would contain three engravings, would be bound in boards, and would sell for three dollars a copy. An earlier draft written in Beaumont's hand had referred to St. Martin as "a *sort of living walking miracle,* now in *perfect health, athletic* & *vigorous,*" but Beaumont had decided that this was a little too undignified for the scholarly book he was announcing. Beaumont's scholarly and monetary instincts were somewhat at conflict in the actual planning for the book, but for the most part the scholarly won out.[1]

Beaumont, however, obviously did have hopes that by appealing to public interest in digestion and diet, he would be able to reach a market that would be unavailable to a purely scientific treatise. He very much wanted scientific recognition, but he also very much wanted his book to sell. He began his prospectus with a paragraph he hoped would be of general appeal:

1. Certificates of copyright, July 23 and December 20, 1833, draft of prospectus, and prospectus, August 15, 1833, BC, WU. A facsimile of the prospectus is printed in Myer, *Beaumont,* 184–85.

The great subject of digestion, a correct knowledge of which must materially conduce to the health and happiness of all, is one which cannot fail to commend itself to the understanding and interests of physiologists, physicians, men of science, and the whole community. These experiments and observations, the author believes, comprise a body of facts, in relation to this subject, which are of vital importance, and are submitted to the public with a confident hope that they will essentially subserve the cause of science and medicine, and ultimately become the means of ameliorating the condition of suffering humanity.[2]

Beaumont hoped that the book would give him a major scientific reputation and become a standard source for information on correct diet.

In the late summer and fall of 1833, Beaumont wrote to a variety of medical men and friends, both military and civilian, asking them to secure subscribers. Lovell sent copies of the prospectus to friends in Philadelphia and also kept two copies in Washington in the hope of helping Beaumont's sales. He said that when the book came out, it would be best to contact the French journals by sending a copy or two of the book, via the State Department, to Edward Livingston, the American minister in Paris, because he already had expressed great interest in Beaumont's work.[3]

Beaumont also received practical advice regarding the marketing of his book from his friend Ramsay Crooks. Crooks said that the medical men to whom he had shown the prospectus had said that it should have included testimonials from distinguished colleagues, and that even now, if there were time, they should be provided. Crooks, like Lovell, was a good friend to Beaumont, and told him that he had decided to employ a competent man to visit the principal physicians in New York, and later to call on those of lesser note. While disclaiming any knowledge of bookmaking or bookselling, Crooks advised getting the book out as soon as possible, sending it to those respectable journals that would help the work, and putting it into the hands of an able bookseller in each of the principal cities. He advised Beaumont to be suspicious of subscription lists. He said some were willing to sign to get their name listed with their "betters," but were not so willing to pay when called upon. Crooks may have disclaimed knowledge of bookselling, but he was a successful businessman.[4]

2. Prospectus, BC, WU.

3. Beaumont to Dr. Samuel DeCamp, September 5, 1833, DeCamp to Beaumont, October 4, 1833, lists of subscribers, Lovell to Beaumont, September 13, 1833, BC, WU; Myer, *Beaumont*, 187.

4. Ramsay Crooks to Beaumont, September 29, 1833, BC, WU.

Copies of the prospectus were sent to newspapers throughout the country, and many of them printed announcements in praise of the forthcoming volume. Beaumont carefully clipped these and kept them in his private papers. Although the book was scientific, it was helped in attracting attention by its subject and by the emphasis Beaumont had given at the beginning of the prospectus. All agreed that the stomach and human digestion were topics of general concern, though it was suggested that the book's price was rather high. One newspaper even helped Beaumont by making it clear that the book contained nothing a woman could not read; the book, it was reported, was suitable and valuable reading for either sex.[5]

The type of scientific and professional notice that Beaumont desired was provided in the *Boston Medical and Surgical Journal.* It included praise of Beaumont and his work from Dr. Thomas Sewall, his friend and supporter in Washington, D.C. He reported Beaumont's ongoing attempts to obtain a chemical analysis of the gastric fluid, from men such as Silliman of Yale, Bache of Philadelphia, and Emmett and Dunglison of Virginia. These were the types of men with whom Beaumont wanted to be associated, and Sewall stated that Beaumont was still hoping that an analysis by Berzelius would be available before the book was issued.

There is also an indication in this brief notice that Beaumont was preparing the way for an attempt to secure money from Congress. Sewall commended Beaumont for supporting St. Martin and his family for eight years at his own private expense. This was an exaggeration, but it was a view that Beaumont wanted to have disseminated at a time when he was planning to approach Congress for money.[6]

With the book's publication imminent, Beaumont had developed a taste both for research and the growing renown that it was bringing him, and on November 7 he entered into a new contract for St. Martin's services. This time it was to be for two years rather than one, but the agreement was essentially the same. St. Martin was to make himself available to Beaumont for research, and Beaumont was to pay St. Martin four hundred dollars for the two years of service and experimentation. Again, payment was to be staggered; Alexis received forty dollars on signing.[7]

Working closely with his cousin Samuel on the details of production, Beaumont had his book printed by F. P. Allen of Plattsburgh. It was ready by

5. Clippings and extracts from various newspapers and journals, BC, WU. There is a selection of them in Myer, *Beaumont,* 188–91.

6. *Boston Medical and Surgical Journal* 9 (September 18, 1833): 94–95.

7. Articles of agreement, November 7, 1833, BC, WU.

December, and though clearly printed its general appearance reflected the fact that it had been readied for publication not by experienced professional publishers in Philadelphia or New York but by Beaumont and his cousin, and that it had been printed by a provincial printing establishment. It lacked a famous publisher's name on its title page, had numerous typographical errors, and included only three simple illustrations depicting the wound, but it was able to surmount its provincial origins. Whatever the limitations of its production, this book of 280 pages carefully described Beaumont's experiments on St. Martin and drew conclusions that gave Beaumont a permanent place in the history of human physiology. The book was dedicated to Joseph Lovell, and no dedication was ever more richly deserved.[8]

In his brief, effective preface, Beaumont disclaimed any "originality in my opinions, as it respects the existence and operation of the gastric juice." He said that his experiments confirmed, with some modifications, the doctrines taught by Spallanzani, and "many of the most enlightened physiological writers," and had been suggested not by his desire to follow a particular doctrine, but rather simply by the opportunity placed in his path. "I had no particular hypothesis to support," wrote Beaumont, "and I have therefore honestly recorded the result of each experiment exactly as it occurred." The preface began modestly, but it ended with a confidence that Beaumont had often exhibited in his private life. "I submit a body of facts that cannot be invalidated," he wrote. "My opinions may be doubted, denied, or approved, according as they conflict or agree with the opinions of each individual who may read them; but their worth will be best determined by the foundation on which they rest–the incontrovertible facts."[9]

The thirty-page introduction was essentially a description of St. Martin's accident, the wound itself, how Beaumont had treated it, and the manner in which it had healed. Beaumont said little about St. Martin himself, and some of what he said was wrong. St. Martin was twenty-eight at the time of the accident, not eighteen as Beaumont believed. In these years, the "boy" St. Martin was regularly described as younger than his actual age. The general chronology that Beaumont gives in the preface agrees for the most part with that which can be obtained from his personal papers, although he states that he began his first series of experiments at Mackinac in May 1825. This presumably refers to preliminary efforts at learning something from

8. Beaumont, *Experiments.*
9. Ibid., 5–7.

the wound in the stomach, for his notes and publications give his formal experiments as starting later that year at Niagara. Beaumont emphasized that during the whole time following the spring of 1824 St. Martin had been in good health, had perhaps had less disease than most, and had been "active, athletic, and vigorous."[10]

At the end of the introduction, Beaumont gave a description of how he extracted the gastric juice and of the practical details of dealing with the gastric fistula. He emphasized that when St. Martin was placed on his side and the rubber tube inserted, the stomach was *"usually* entirely empty," and he said that normally he could draw off from four drams to one and a half ounces of fluid. He mentioned here, as he sometimes did in his actual description of experiments, that extracting the gastric juice usually produced a sinking sensation in the pit of St. Martin's stomach, and some degree of faintness. Beaumont also described how, by moving St. Martin onto his back, turning him on his left side, and pressing with his hand on the hepatic region, he could bring out "bright yellow bile" through the tube.[11]

Beaumont also described how he had easy access to the stomach. As St. Martin recovered and became active, a "small fold or doubling of the coats of the stomach" had appeared, and had increased in size until it filled the aperture into the stomach. This "valve" made it unnecessary to use a compress and bandage to hold in the stomach contents. When the stomach was full, Beaumont was able to obtain contents of the stomach by pressing down on the valve; when he did this the contents flowed out "copiously." He also wrote that when the stomach was nearly empty, "the interior of the cavity," when distended by artificial means, could be examined to a depth of five or six inches, and food and drink observed entering through the ring of the esophagus.[12]

Although the largest section of Beaumont's book—more than 140 pages—was devoted to a detailed account of the actual experiments, Beaumont introduced this with some ninety pages of preliminary observations. Also, after the experiments, he included a four-page table of the time needed for digesting different foods, two pages on the temperature of the stomach at different times of the year and day, four pages listing fifty-one inferences, and a statement that he had been unable to obtain an analysis of the gastric juice from Berzelius before publication. He noted in the introduction to his

---

10. Ibid., 9–20, 20 (quotation).
11. Ibid., 21.
12. Ibid., 1, 22.

observations that he had "been led to conclusions opposite to the opinions of many who have been considered the great luminaries of physiology, and in some instances from all professors of this science."[13]

The fifty-one "inferences" that ended the book were not ranked in order of importance, nor did Beaumont attempt to separate conclusions that were of major importance for the long-existing scientific debate over the nature of digestion from general comments on diet.[14]

Of key importance in the scientific debate were Beaumont's conclusions regarding the chemical nature of digestion: that gastric juice was the agent of chymification; that, like other chemical agents, it began its action on food as soon as it came into contact with it; that it contained free muriatic (hydrochloric) acid as well as "some other active *chemical* principles"; that it acted as a solvent on food; that it worked better because of the warmth and motions of the stomach; and that it was secreted from vessels distinct from the mucous follicles. He noted that gastric juice checked the progress of putrefaction, that it coagulated albumen, and afterwards dissolved the coagulate. He also noted that the gastric juice and the mucus in the stomach were *"dissimilar* in their *physical* and *chemical* properties." A false inference he drew was that gastric juice was not present in the gastric cavity unless brought there by the introduction of food or some other irritant. He also wrongly assumed that hunger was "the effect of *distention* of the vessels that secrete the gastric juice."

Reinforcing his assertion of the chemical nature of digestion was his conclusion that "the processes of *mastication, insalivation* and *deglutition"* did not affect the digestion of food. He stated that food introduced directly into the stomach in a finely divided state, without these previous steps, was as perfectly digested as it was when these steps had been taken.

Although Beaumont asserted in these inferences that "the *first* stage of digestion is effected in the stomach," he was unable to say much about the other complex processes of digestion. His contribution centered on the stomach. He examined, but did not understand, the function of saliva, and made only passing comments on the rest of the process of digestion. He drew the inference that bile was not ordinarily found in the stomach, and was not commonly necessary for the digestion of food, but that it assisted in the digestion of oily food. Chyle, he wrote, was formed in the duodenum and small intestines, by the action of bile and pancreatic juice on the chyme. He

13. Ibid., 31–122 (preliminary observations), 269–78 (tables and inferences), 31 (quotation).

14. The "inferences" discussed in the following five paragraphs are in ibid., 275–78.

also stated that the chyle was further changed by the action of the lacteals and the mesenteric glands, but noted that this was merely an inference from the other facts; it had not been the subject of any experiment.

Beaumont also commented on the physical appearance of the stomach itself and on the way in which its motions facilitated digestion. He described its inner coat as pale pink in color, constantly sheathed with a mucous coat when healthy, but of an essentially different appearance when diseased. The motions of the stomach, both transversely and longitudinally, he wrote, produced a constant churning of its contents and a resulting mixture of food and gastric juice. He also concluded that the action of the stomach and its fluids were the same on all kinds of diet.

Mixed in with Beaumont's conclusions of great interest to physiologists were conclusions that, while of interest to physiologists, were primarily intended to give the general reader and the physician advice on eating and drinking. His first inference was that animal and farinaceous foods were more easily digested than vegetables; that digestion was facilitated by the minuteness and tenderness of the fibers, and retarded by the opposite; that usually more food was taken than needed, and that if this was persevered in it produced "functional aberration" and disease of the coats of the stomach; that bulk as well as nutriment was needed in the diet; that oily food was difficult to digest; that stimulating condiments injured the healthy stomach; and that "the use of *ardent spirits always* produces disease of the stomach if persevered in." He also concluded that "gentle exercise" facilitated the digestion of food.

Beaumont's conclusions regarding the time needed to digest different food-stuffs were weakened by his failure to maintain detailed records of the quantities of food involved in all of his experiments. In his list of inferences, he noted that although the time required for the digestion of food varied according to quality and quantity, and the state of the stomach, the time ordinarily required for the disposal of a moderate meal of meat and bread was from three to three and a half hours. Beaumont here was clearly thinking of the time it took the gastric juice to act on the food received in the stomach. In his detailed table of the time required for the chymification of a variety of articles of diet, Beaumont did not list specific amounts, but stated at the end of the table that the times gave the average, as near as practicable, for the digestion of one dram of alimentary matter in one dram of gastric juice. In his table, Beaumont compared the time of digestion in the stomach with the time needed for digestion in vials. The latter was usually more than twice as long.[15]

15. Ibid., 269–72, 275.

While there was a great deal that Beaumont did not know about digestion, the value of his work was that after his carefully reported experiments, the earlier advances of Spallanzani, Tiedemann, Gmelin, and Prout could not be seriously challenged. It was not only that Beaumont had a human subject but also that the very inexperience with which he began his work, his total lack of a connection with any of the main schools of thought advocating one or other views of digestion, convinced most of those who read his work that here was an honest reporter. It was possible to quibble with Beaumont's techniques, or to complain about the way in which he mixed major scientific conclusions with general advice on eating and drinking, but it was very difficult to question the thoroughness with which he had demonstrated that gastric juice was a solvent that dissolved food inside and outside of the stomach. Rather than pursuing a course of research specifically designed to back up a certain theory, Beaumont had realized where his experiments fitted into the current scholarly debate as his research progressed.

During this hectic fall of 1833, Lovell had arranged for Beaumont to have only limited military duties. Beaumont's assignment in Plattsburgh was to examine recruits, and he carried out this not too onerous task with his usual care, reporting monthly to Lovell on the performance of his duties and becoming enough involved in it to complain of doctors and recruiting officers who to increase recruitment would accept anyone who volunteered. He said that none but healthy, active young men would "pass the ordeal of my examination."[16]

Late in November, when his work on the publication of his book was completed, Beaumont was ordered to report to the surgeon general in Washington, D.C. Lovell told him to report as soon as practicable as his services might be required with troops ordered to Fort Mitchell, Alabama. By the second week in December Beaumont was ready to leave, but he asked Lovell if he could stay for two or three days in New York to arrange for the distribution and disposal of his book, which he now received from the printer. There were already one thousand copies in print, and this edition was eventually to sell some three thousand copies.[17]

16. Beaumont to Lovell, September 1, 1833 (quotation), November 1 and December 2, 1833, WD, SG, LR.

17. A. Van Buren to Beaumont, November 23, 1833, Special Order #177, November 25, 1833, Lovell to Beaumont, November 23, 1833, Beaumont to Lovell, December 7, 1833, BC, WU; Beaumont, *The Physiology of Digestion with Experiments on the Gastric Juice,* corrected by Samuel Beaumont, 5.

When Beaumont left Plattsburgh, his family and St. Martin stayed behind. St. Martin seems to have given little concern to his formal status as a sergeant in the United States Army, although Beaumont filed official reports on St. Martin's location with the Adjutant General's Office throughout the fall and even after Beaumont arrived in Washington.[18]

Shortly before leaving Plattsburgh, Beaumont drew up a list of his assets: his 140-acre farm at Prairie du Chien (valued at twelve hundred dollars), which was rented out; a city lot at Navarino at Green Bay; a mortgage on farms and property belonging to one of his deceased relatives; five thousand dollars on deposit in New York City; his library, surgical instruments, notes of experiments, drawings and engravings of the stomach, and the like, which he had left with his cousin, along with instructions for superintending the distribution of the book; and various deeds, mortgages, and papers, left in a trunk. He noted that he was "not aware that I owe any body a cent," except for the binding of his books; those in boards were to be eight cents each, those in full sheepskin fifty cents each. The sheepskin volumes were presumably to send to those figures he considered of influence, men such as Martin Van Buren, Lewis Cass, Edward Livingston, Edward Everett, and Thomas Hart Benton. Included in the memo of assets was the financial status of St. Martin. Beaumont owed him ten dollars on his old contract, and the new one at two hundred dollars a year had begun on December 1. St. Martin had also been drawing his pay as a sergeant; twelve dollars a month, $2.50 a month for clothing, and ten cents a day for subsistence.[19]

Beaumont stopped in New York to make arrangements for the distribution of his book, and then traveled on to Washington. Soon after he arrived there, his wife sent on a request for a book that had come in from Tennessee, and took advantage of the two blank pages on the request to bring Beaumont up to date on the state of his family. Beaumont and his wife had been apart a good deal in the past year, but they were still close, and Debby was clearly ready for a return to family life. After saying how delighted she was at the praises bestowed on his book by the public, she said her prayer was that he would see all his wishes accomplished and be ready to settle down quietly with his family, "who all love you so much." His cousin Samuel, Debby reported, was relieved at the welcome given to the book, because he thought neither of them were scholars.

18. Beaumont to the adjutant general, August 29, September 30, October 31, December 31, 1833, WD, AG, LR.
19. Memo of assets, December 8, 1833, BC, WU.

In writing of their children, Debby perhaps again hinted at the desirability of them making a family home again. She said all the children were anxious for his return, and that their son at times flew into a "violent rage" at those he thought were keeping him away. But she also said his general conduct was good, and that his sister Lucretia was "almost faultless." Debby had been invited to visit friends in Middlebury, Vermont, and wanted to go, but did not want to leave the children. Beaumont had a happy marriage, and the forbidding front he often showed to those who displeased him in the outside world was seldom present at home.[20]

In the course of worrying about the costs involved in research, and in producing a book, Beaumont had decided to try to persuade Congress to support his research. Lovell's advice was that a memorial sent directly to Congress would have little chance of success, and that he needed to secure the help of individual members to press the matter. Beaumont followed this advice by writing to those he thought had a knowledge of the political scene or had influence in Washington. Among those he contacted was Azariah Flagg, a past editor of the *Plattsburgh Republican* who had become influential in New York politics, and the so-called Albany Regency. In December, Flagg told Beaumont that he had written to Silas Wright, the New York Democratic Senator, and also emphasized to Beaumont that his memorial should be in a form that would be "easily *digested*" by Congress.[21]

In any circumstances, obtaining money from Congress would have been a difficult task, as Congress was extremely loathe to vote money for individual purposes, but in Beaumont's case this was particularly difficult, because he was a surgeon in the United States Army who had carried out research while on his military salary. If the medical department of the army was as overburdened as it claimed, how was it that one of its surgeons had been able to carry out an extensive course of experiments and produce a large book? To help his case, Beaumont tried to enlist the aid of prominent medical men. Dr. Franklin Bache of Philadelphia gave him his support, and even Robley Dunglison, who was displeased that Beaumont had not more directly involved him in the credit for his book, endorsed the idea of Beaumont receiving public funds, although he later wrote that he believed such a request was of doubtful propriety.[22] Beaumont, of course, could expect to get

20. Deborah Beaumont to Beaumont, January 2, 1834, BC, WU.
21. Lovell to Beaumont, September 13, 1833, Azariah Flagg to Beaumont, December 19, 1833, BC, WU.
22. Franklin Bache to Beaumont, January 24, 1834, letter of Robley Dunglison, January 25, 1834, BC, WU; Radbill, ed., "Autobiographical Ana of Dunglison," 53.

support from the medical establishment, because they would like the idea of the federal government advancing funds for medical research.

The memorial was submitted to the Senate in January. Beaumont was hoping for not only reimbursement for past costs but also support for future research. He began by stating that a most favorable opportunity had arisen for improving the science of medicine and physiology, and for ascertaining and testing the powers of the human stomach, and then immediately went on to recount the great expense that he had incurred in his relations with Alexis St. Martin. After a brief account of the wound and of St. Martin's slow recovery, Beaumont described how, when St. Martin was destitute, he had taken him into his home to prevent him from being sent back to Lower Canada. Omitted was the role of the authorities of Mackinac in paying for the support of St. Martin and the payment to Beaumont for the medical services provided to the wounded man. Beaumont also failed to mention that St. Martin for more than a year had been enrolled as a sergeant in the United States Army.[23]

Beaumont described how he had kept St. Martin, at times sought him out in Canada, expended money to keep him in his service, and supported his wife and family for more than three years. Extra expense, he claimed, had been incurred traveling with St. Martin in the East, prosecuting the experiments, and publishing the book. The book itself, Beaumont stated, would not be of interest to the general reader, and would hardly cover the costs of production. All of this, he said, had been done while performing his regular services as an army surgeon, and without additional remuneration.

For money paid in supporting St. Martin and keeping him available for experiments since 1822, Beaumont asked the government for four thousand dollars. For professional medical attendance since St. Martin was wounded, Beaumont requested one thousand dollars. In addition, Beaumont asked Congress to grant him an extra allowance of $1.25 a day for time spent in actually attending St. Martin and restoring him to health, and in making the experiments. From June 1822 to May 1825, he requested $1,323.75, from January 1830 to January 1834, $1,825. In all, Beaumont was asking Congress to grant him eight thousand dollars for work already completed. He also requested funds to enable him to pursue future research, and asked that the government support St. Martin in the future.[24]

23. See the discussion of Beaumont, St. Martin, and the Mackinac authorities in Numbers, "Beaumont and the Ethics of Human Experimentation," 114–15.
24. Draft memorial, January 1834, BC, WU.

Late in January Beaumont's petition was formally presented in the Senate, and was referred to the Committee on the Library of Congress. For a time, it seemed to be going well. Beaumont's friends, including Surgeon General Lovell, rallied to give him support. Thomas Sewall wrote to testify to the importance of Beaumont's research by stating that no "subject in Physiology has been more extensively investigated, or received a larger share of the attention of medical men, than the functions of digestion."[25]

On March 11, in the committee of the whole in the House, Edward Everett of Massachusetts moved an amendment to the army appropriation bill, to provide compensation for Beaumont. Beaumont's claim had already, in the course of committee action, been whittled down to less than two thousand dollars, but at this preliminary stage he still had reason to hope that he would receive some compensation. Everett, confused about St. Martin's status at the time of the accident, stated that Beaumont had performed a series of experiments on the stomach of a wounded soldier. Although there were objections to using the appropriations bill for private purposes, and to the principle of the federal government making such grants, the amendment was passed by a vote of 80 to 53.[26]

On March 14 the amendment adopted in the committee of the whole was considered in the House, and the proposal immediately ran into trouble. Thomas Hall of North Carolina went to the essence of the first objection when he said that, whatever the intrinsic merits of the individual appropriation, it was entirely out of place in the appropriation bill. But he also made it clear that he objected to the award itself, because the grant would introduce a new principle "of very objectionable character." Since 1789, many congressmen had been determined to restrict the role of the federal government in matters that they believed should not concern it. To them, the support of private research opened a Pandora's Box of potential federal expenditures, and they wanted nothing to do with it.[27]

There was some support for Beaumont, and it was suggested that the

25. *Senate Journal,* 23d Cong., 1st sess., 116–17; Thomas Sewall to Asher Robbins, January 20, 1834, BC, WU; Myer, *Beaumont,* 215–16.

26. Letter of Dr. Thomas Henderson, February 10, 1834, of Dr. Abel Huntington, et al., February 11, 1834; *American Journal of Arts and Sciences* 26 (1834), extract, BC, WU; *Register of Debates,* 23d Cong., 1st sess., 2954–55.

27. *Register of Debates,* 23d Cong., 1st sess., 2990–91; A. Hunter Dupree, *Science and the Federal Government: A History of Policies and Activities to 1940,* 1–43, discusses the difficulties encountered in the early years of the century by those wanting to participate in scientific endeavors.

award might be granted if it were in a separate bill, but the general opinion was negative. Several members brought up the constitutional objections to such an award, and one suggested that the only constitutional way the House could reward Beaumont was for each member to buy one or two copies of the book. Even John Quincy Adams, who was more willing than most to see the Constitution interpreted broadly, objected to the "mode and form" by which the grant was proposed. Adams was jealous of the House's prerogative to originate all bills making appropriations of money, and this appropriation had originated in a petition to the Senate. He said he had no constitutional objection to Congress granting rewards for discoveries in science, but such awards should only be granted on memorials presented to the House.[28] One wonders if Adams remembered that as president, he had censured Beaumont for his medical conduct toward a fellow officer at Fort Niagara.

In Adams's speech, as in some of the others, there was continuing confusion concerning St. Martin's position. In his petition, Beaumont had not mentioned St. Martin's enlistment in the army because he had wanted to give the idea he had been St. Martin's sole support, but Everett had mistakenly assumed that St. Martin had been a soldier at the time of the experiments. This, however, did not become a major issue.

The idea of an appropriation for Beaumont died in a typical Congressional debate in which some objected constitutionally, some objected to the form in which the request had been made, and some simply did not like it. The amendment to the army appropriation bill was defeated by a vote of 129 to 56.[29]

On April 1 Everett explained the defeat to Beaumont. He said he was "mortified" by the failure, "but not much disappointed." His strategy had been to try to get the appropriation through the House "without exciting its attention," once it was noticed, and the constitutional issue raised, he knew he was in trouble. Beaumont's failure to clarify the question of St. Martin's army status had left Everett as well as other members of Congress in some confusion. Everett acknowledged to Beaumont that some members of Congress thought St. Martin had been a soldier. He said that at first he had thought so himself. Some members, said Everett, would have preferred St. Martin to have been a soldier. The crux of the matter, however, was constitutional. Though Everett conceded that some members might have

28. *Register of Debates*, 23d Cong., 1st sess., 2991–93.
29. Ibid., 2993; *House Journal*, 23d Cong., 1st sess., 406. The correct vote is given in the *House Journal*.

objected to the manner in which the petition was introduced, he feared that the true objection lay deeper. "The great difficulty here," he stated, "is the theoretical objection to the appropriation by Congress of money for any scientific or philanthropic purpose whatever."

Everett still held out some hope. He suggested that Beaumont might submit a memorial substantially the same as present, setting forth what he had expended and asking for some compensation, "but not proposing an appropriation for the Continuance of the Experiments." Even this, however, was not a suggestion in which Everett placed much faith. He told Beaumont that his reliance would have to be on the curiosity and intelligence of the medical profession and the general public. The book, he thought, would eventually have a large sale, larger still if the price was lower.[30]

Beaumont's jaundiced view of Congress, and of public life in Washington, D.C., was stated succinctly in June 1834, just before he left the city, when he told his Congressman cousin Andrew: "Hold fast yr political integrity against the combined attack of wealth, power, fraud, flattery, force or fear—the world, the flesh or the devil."[31]

Beaumont's attempt to seek public compensation for his research on St. Martin gained enough public notoriety in the national capital to be deemed worthy of satirical comment. The Washington *Evening Star* printed a piece signed "Medicus," stating that Beaumont had treated a man with a wound in his side, but did not heal the wound, and was thus able to watch the operation of the stomach. He had reported on his observations, but the writer asked whether this displayed "such science and genius" as to entitle the doctor to national remuneration by the special act of Congress. The writer pointed out that Beaumont was already paid as a surgeon in the army, and was protected by the law of copyright. In any case, stated the writer, who had some knowledge of research in the physiology of human digestion, there was a fallacy in the whole business. Digestion was a chemical process, the same in animal and human stomachs. Far more satisfactory experiments had already been made on dogs, and published to the world years ago.[32]

It was probably not purely coincidental that in the same month as Beaumont's memorial was rejected by the Senate, Beaumont was trying his hand at drafting a promotional piece to increase the sales of his work. He drafted

30. Edward Everett to Beaumont, April 1, 1834, BC, WU.

31. Memo to Andrew Beaumont, June 8, 1834, BC, UC, printed in the *Journal of the American Medical Association* 99 (July 1932): 57.

32. This is printed in Myer, *Beaumont*, 219.

it as though it were written by someone who had read and been impressed by the book. There is no evidence that it was ever used, but it demonstrates the way in which Beaumont's scientific and medical interests were always entwined with a desire for profit as well as greater reputation. The draft was headed "Physiology of Digestion–Dyspeptics Take Notice," and went on to say how important it was to pay close attention to a daily diet. These reflections were said to have been inspired by Dr. Beaumont's book, which should be read by physicians, invalids, and valetudinarians; it "ought to have a place in *every* Physician's Library, & on the dining table of every Family." Beaumont probably thought better of this piece of self-promotion, but his hopes of making money as well as a reputation never died.[33]

Beaumont was disappointed that Congress had not rewarded him for his research, but he had the consolation in these months, and in the following years, that his book attracted widespread attention in the United States and abroad. American scientific and medical journals quickly reviewed it. There was some lavish praise, but there also was criticism, particularly by those who saw their vitalistic doctrines sustaining a severe, ultimately a fatal, blow. The review in the *Boston Medical and Surgical Journal* described Beaumont's book as "a work of rare interest and value–a work that will doubtless find its way to the table of every medical practitioner in this country, and be republished abroad, and translated into the various languages of continental Europe." The reviewer differed with Beaumont on some of his details, and questioned Beaumont's conclusions that saliva had no function other than softening and lubricating the food, but he generally accepted Beaumont's arguments. He pointed out that Beaumont had provided evidence to refute those who believed digestion only began an hour after the food was received into the stomach, who believed that newly eaten food was never mixed with old, and that bile was always present in the stomach.[34]

The review in Benjamin Silliman's *American Journal of Science and Arts* was all that Beaumont could have desired. His book was described as "to say the least of it, equal in interest to any one on the subject, that has ever been presented to the public." Beaumont was praised for having had the ability to take advantage of a rare opportunity. The public and the medical profession were counted as fortunate that "it fell into the hands of one who appreciated its value, and who possessed the requisite intelligence, perseverance, and

33. Draft, [March 1834], BC, WU.
34. *Boston Medical and Surgical Journal* 9 (January 15, 1834): 365–68.

candor to make the investigation which it afforded, and to state the results of such investigation, in a plain, simple, intelligible manner, without bias from preconceived opinions, or fanciful hypotheses." After summarizing Beaumont's conclusions, the review ended with the praise that the book contained "more *facts*, plainly and honestly stated, upon the subject of digestion in the human stomach, than can any where else be found."[35]

For the most part, even those who criticized aspects of Beaumont's work felt obliged to testify to its importance. In the *American Journal of the Medical Sciences* the reviewer expressed disappointment at what had not been investigated, suggested that Beaumont did not know enough about other research on the subject of digestion, and regretted that the opportunity had not fallen to "some one better qualified," but was obliged to testify to its importance. He suggested, like the reviewer in the *Boston Medical and Surgical Journal,* that Beaumont had wrongly dismissed the importance of saliva in the digestive process, but he also acknowledged that after Beaumont's work the solvent power of the gastric juice could never again be in dispute. Even more important for Beaumont's reputation was that even this reviewer who was clearly irritated at the fate that had given such an opportunity to an obscure army surgeon, and who would have preferred that the research had produced different results, felt obliged to state that Beaumont's report of his experiments constituted "unquestionably, in many particulars, the most important work ever published on the physiology of digestion."[36]

Attacks could be expected because the different theories regarding human digestion had gained ardent adherents, and the vitalists were strong in the United States, but there was solid support for the view that Beaumont had produced the most important work on human digestion ever published in the United States. He had not made any startling new discoveries, but in conclusively demonstrating the chemical nature of the digestive process he had settled important questions that had long been in dispute in Europe and the United States.

With praise ringing in his ears, and given his combative approach to life, Beaumont could not have been expected to sit quietly when the *Western Medical Gazette* of Cincinnati published a scathing attack on his book. Beaumont arranged for one of his friends to submit a rebuttal. It was written out by the friend, but it appears from Beaumont's papers that he probably wrote it.[37]

35. *American Journal of Science and Arts* 26 (July 1834): 193–202.
36. *American Journal of the Medical Sciences* 14 (May 1834): 117–49.
37. Response to review in *Western Medical Gazette*, BC, WU; also Myer, *Beaumont*, 221n6; Nelson, *Beaumont*, 231.

Beaumont's book also attracted a good deal of popular newspaper interest. He had tried to shape it to say something to the general public as well as to the scientists, and he had succeeded. In an age of heavy drinking and heavy, unselective eating, supposedly authoritative statements on diet and digestion were of considerable interest. A great many individuals were interested in his comments on the digestibility of different items of food and his tables listing digestion times. Also, newspapers helped Beaumont's reputation by summarizing his conclusions. One newspaper commented that Beaumont had settled conclusively Spallanzani's argument that the stomach secreted a gastric juice that exercised a solvent power on food.[38]

Beaumont's work rapidly found its way into American medical textbooks and into the lectures at medical schools, and remained there for the rest of the nineteenth century. American physicians routinely learned of the research of the first great American physiologist. Also, because of Beaumont's emphasis on the importance of diet, he became known on a more popular level. General works on physiology and hygiene included Beaumont's experiments, along with his observations on the comparative digestibility of different foods. Even books on hygiene intended for children included Beaumont's work.[39]

While Beaumont's warnings regarding moderation in eating and drinking, and of the value of exercise, became an accepted part of American dietetic advice for the rest of the nineteenth century, vegetarians were perturbed by his assertion that meat was easier to digest than vegetables. Some vegetarians, including Sylvester Graham, tried to get around Beaumont's conclusions by arguing that slowness of digestion could be an advantage.[40]

The scientific impact of Beaumont's book was greater in Europe than in the United States, for there were more experimental physiologists eager to pursue research avenues that he had clarified. For the rest of the nineteenth century, Beaumont's work influenced research both on human and on animal subjects. Yet the first European response was disappointing. Soon after his American publication, Beaumont attempted to interest London publishers in bringing out a British edition of his work. He found they were not interested. It was said that the publishing trade was in depression, but it was also suggested (and this undoubtedly went to the heart of the matter) that the merits of this man and his work were unknown. Because of his earlier articles, Beaumont's

38. See Numbers and Orr, "Beaumont's Reception," 600–602; clippings from various newspapers, BC, WU.

39. Numbers and Orr, "Beaumont's Reception," 597–98; Atwater, "Squeezing Mother Nature," 313–14.

40. Numbers and Orr, "Beaumont's Reception," 600–603.

name was known to some research physiologists in Europe, but he had no general reputation. British medical publishers undoubtedly did not wish to risk the publication of a work by an unknown army surgeon across the Atlantic.[41]

Yet for all the reluctance of British publishers, Beaumont's book soon began to be noticed. The London *Athenaeum,* which reported on the work in April 1834, was unusual in the degree to which the reviewer empathized with St. Martin. Commenting on Beaumont's first attempts at experimentation, in which he inserted a variety of food and produced an upset stomach, the reviewer commented that Beaumont, in his haste to make experiments, forgot he was operating "on a living, irritable human stomach." The result was that "science was to benefit even by Dr. Beaumont's errors." The reviewer did not agree with all of Beaumont's conclusions, "some of which are drawn with great looseness indeed," but praised his perseverance. He added, however, that equally admirable was the temper of St. Martin in so long submitting to the experiments.[42]

The ethics of the experiments on St. Martin never concerned Beaumont himself, and the references to St. Martin in the *Athenaeum* were unusual in showing sympathy for him. Beaumont himself was far more apt to complain about St. Martin's unreliability than to worry about how he was bearing up under the experiments, and those who discussed Beaumont and St. Martin usually did not question Beaumont's assumption that the only problem was to try to make sure St. Martin was available. This was typical of the age. The southern physician J. Marion Sims developed his famous procedure for treating a vesicovaginal fistula by operating numerous times on slave women who were taken under his control specifically for the purpose of developing a treatment.[43]

From the time of Beaumont's first articles describing his experiments on St. Martin, his work had been noticed by European researchers, although some confusion was caused by the first account appearing under Lovell's name. A German medical magazine published in Hamburg had first brought

41. Harry Renshaw to W. Miller, February 1834, A. Vail to Beaumont, March 2, 1834, Thomas Jones to Beaumont, April 14, 1834, letter from S. Highley, N.D., BC, WU.

42. Extracts from *Athenaeum,* June 4, 1834, BC, WU.

43. See Numbers, "Beaumont and the Ethics of Human Experimentation," 113–35; Reginald Horsman, *Josiah Nott of Mobile: Southerner, Physician, and Racial Theorist,* 315; Todd Savitt, "The Use of Blacks for Medical Experimentation and Demonstration in the Old South," 344–46; Deborah Kuhn McGregor, *Sexual Surgery and the Origins of Gynecology: J. Marion Sims, His Hospital, and His Patients,* 40–68.

the case to European attention, and by 1828 Beaumont's work had also received mention in Edinburgh and Paris. The first German edition of his book was published in Leipzig in 1834, and Beaumont's conclusions soon found their way into influential German textbooks of physiology. There was similar early interest in France and Great Britain, and the work ultimately attracted attention in other parts of Europe.[44]

Lovell sent copies of the book to Edward Livingston, the American Minister in Paris, and in March Livingston reported that he had given a copy to the French Academy of Science. The academy had referred the book to a committee to discover if additional experiments were needed, and whether it might be expedient to send for St. Martin or to have the experiments done in the United States.[45] British interest in Beaumont's work was immediate, and most of the comments were more favorable than those that appeared in the *Athenaeum*. The book's conclusions were incorporated in standard British texts on physiology by 1837, and in 1838 the well-known British physiologist Andrew Combe published the first British edition of the work. Combe admired Beaumont's research and had referred favorably to it in one of his own books on dietetics in the previous year.[46]

Beaumont had achieved far more than he could possibly have expected when he had first realized that St. Martin's permanent stomach fistula had presented him with the opportunity of attempting some experiments. The encouragement and advice of Lovell had been invaluable, but it had also required his own persistence, his ability to learn by trial and error, and his willingness to work under a variety of conditions unfavorable for the pursuit of scholarly research.

In the early months of 1834, as he saw his hopes of Congressional reward disappearing, Beaumont was hoping to continue his research on St. Martin, but he was also planning to continue his army service. In March he gave Lovell his list of preferences for a posting. He had apparently developed a taste for eastern life in the past year, for his first choice was Governor's Island in New York Harbor, whenever a depot should be established there.

44. Numbers and Orr, "Beaumont's Reception," 604–11; Rosen, *Reception*, 26–37; Genevieve Miller, review of Rosen, *Reception*, in *Bulletin of the History of Medicine* 13 (1943), 11–13.
45. Letter of Edward Livingston, March 16, 1834, BC, WU.
46. F. N. L. Poynter, "The Reception of William Beaumont's Discovery in England: Two Additional Early References," 511–12; Myer, *Beaumont*, 246; Beaumont, *Experiments and Observations on the Gastric Juice and the Physiology of Digestion*, reprinted with notes by Andrew Combe, M.D. (Edinburgh, 1838), v–xii.

One suspects it was the financial rather than the research opportunities that attracted him to New York, for in the previous year he had complained about the lack of cooperation he was getting from New York physicians in his research objectives. Yet if it was not to be New York, then Beaumont was ready to go west again. After New York, his choices were Fort Crawford at Prairie du Chien, Fort Howard at Green Bay, and Jefferson Barracks near St. Louis. His last choice was West Point, New York.[47]

While Lovell served as surgeon general there seemed good reason to expect that Beaumont would receive every encouragement in continuing with his research and that Lovell would do all he could to give him favorable postings, but for the time being Beaumont remained in Washington, and was given special assignments as the need for an army surgeon arose. In March he was detailed to sit on a three-man army medical board that was examining recruits for the service. The members of the board took their duties with the utmost seriousness. On March 5 they examined a candidate in anatomy, physiology, surgery, theory and practice of physic, materia medica, chemistry, and obstetrics. He passed at 7 P.M. after nine hours of "close & critical examination." They immediately proceeded to examine another candidate. He also passed, and the board adjourned at 1 A.M. They were to examine another candidate on March 7, but he failed to appear; perhaps he had heard about the proceedings on the fifth.[48]

Beaumont's next temporary assignment was a tour of inspection of the hospitals at the forts in New England. He was told that when that tour was complete his services would be required at Jefferson Barracks, near St. Louis. Beaumont was able to travel home before beginning his tour, and though he had been ordered to make it "with convenient dispatch," he did not begin it until April 16. Before the tour began, he took St. Martin from Plattsburgh to Boston to be examined by the physicians of the city. There was no time for experiments, but the physicians observed how water drunk by St. Martin "passed freely through the orifice." The *Boston Medical and Surgical Journal* reported that Beaumont intended to pursue further investigations. Beaumont also took St. Martin to New Haven, and was thanked by the Connecticut Medical Convention for his "interesting exhibition."[49]

47. Beaumont to Lovell, March 8, 1834, WD, AG, IMOF.

48. Special Order, March 4, 1834, Beaumont's notes of proceedings of the army medical board, March 5 and 7, 1834, BC, WU.

49. The order to inspect hospitals is printed in Myer, *Beaumont,* 222. See also *Boston Medical and Surgical Journal* 10 (1834): 163; Milo L. North and Edward P. Terry to Beaumont, May 15, 1834, BC, WU.

While he was in Boston, Beaumont left a vial of gastric juice for the well-known Dr. Charles T. Jackson to analyze. Jackson reported late in May that he had obtained an acetic acid, but could not ascertain its precise quantity. He said that he was now examining for lactic acid, which he suspected existed in the juice, and for hydrofluoric acid, which Berzelius had suggested might be in it. Jackson had also used the gastric juice to digest food in vitro, and had successfully repeated Beaumont's experiments. He asked Beaumont to send more fluid, and also urged him, if possible, to come himself and assist in the experiments; he suggested they could "do something handsome" if they had St. Martin there. He had spoken to other physicians in Boston, and said there would be no difficulty in getting up a subscription to support St. Martin while experiments went on under Beaumont's direction. Beaumont himself could perhaps be paid for lectures. Jackson said he would be happy to perform the part of the labor that Beaumont assigned to him. This was a generous letter, and Beaumont must have been considerably flattered to receive it.[50]

Beaumont carried out his inspection tour with great care. Although he was getting very used to special privileges, he had not yet grown careless in the performance of his army duties. In this particular tour, he was less critical than he often was in dealing with his fellow surgeons, possibly because, having experienced the problems of a ruinous hospital at Fort Crawford, he was anxious to have on the record that army surgeons needed better facilities.

The first hospital he visited, at Fort Constitution, in Portsmouth, New Hampshire, Beaumont described as old, leaky, inconvenient, uncomfortable, "and wholly unfit for the use of the sick." Fortunately, the troops were healthy, but he recommended a new hospital. Traveling on to Maine, Beaumont visited Fort Preble in Portland, Hancock Barracks in Houlton, and Fort Sullivan near Eastport. He was satisfied both with the hospitals and the army surgeons at Fort Preble and Fort Sullivan, but criticized the civilian physician who had been employed to attend the sick at Hancock Barracks and the hospital he presided over.[51]

The Hancock physician, Beaumont wrote, was too much occupied with his own concerns, and "not very well qualified to perform the duties required of him." The meticulous Beaumont was concerned that no hospital books, except a diary of the weather kept by the steward, had been maintained from

50. Charles T. Jackson to Beaumont, May 23, 1834, BC, WU.
51. For Beaumont's tour discussed in this and the following three paragraphs, see Beaumont to Lovell, May 17, 1834, BC, WU; Beaumont to Lovell, May 17, 1834, WD, SG, LR.

the time that the last physician had left. There had been few sick. The three or four who were confined to the hospital had afflictions of the knee, hip, and abdomen, probably caused, said Beaumont, by the bad habits of the patients and by the omission of prompt "Anti-phlogistic" treatment at the beginning of the diseases. He thought that the post badly needed both an experienced medical officer and a new hospital.

From Maine, Beaumont went to Rhode Island to inspect Fort Wolcott, and then into Connecticut to Fort Trumbull at New London. He was satisfied with conditions at the former, but thought the latter needed either an improved or a new hospital. He took the opportunity of his visit to New London to give Dr. Elisha North a quantity of gastric juice.[52]

In general, Beaumont concluded from his tour of inspection that he had not found reasons why different types of disease should have arisen, except for drunkenness, dissipation, or imprudence, and even these were much less frequent than they had been in the past. Beaumont, who had consistently deplored the effects of heavy drinking in the army, had been brought to a new realization of the problems caused by alcohol from observing St. Martin's stomach. He said that the moral and physical condition of the men appeared to have been vastly improved by the abolition of the whiskey ration: "Sobriety, contentment, Cleanliness, & good order, now generally prevail," where almost constant drunkenness, riots, and mutinous conduct formerly abounded in the army. Although there had no doubt been an improvement since the whiskey ration had been abolished in 1830, there was not the stark contrast that Beaumont drew here. He was probably influenced by his service in isolated, bitterly cold western posts, where drinking was an even bigger problem than in the East.

At the end of April, when he was still on his tour of inspection, Beaumont received his long-awaited posting. He was to report to Jefferson Barracks, near St. Louis, but Lovell allowed Beaumont to proceed at a very measured pace.[53] After completing his tour, Beaumont returned to Washington, D.C., and while there made another attempt to have at least indirect official support for his book. Early in June he wrote to the secretary of war and the secretary of the navy suggesting that because of the expenses he had incurred, and because of the value of the book, each of them should buy one hundred copies for his department. He suggested that this would prove of value to

52. Miller, "Beaumont and His Book," 173.
53. Special Order, April 30, 1834, BC, WU.

both the sick and the well. It would encourage a wholesome diet, and promote temperance in eating and drinking. Beaumont was again disappointed.
Secretary of the Navy Levi Woodbury pointed out to him that he had already
bought twelve copies of the book to supply hospitals and navy yards, and
that it had not been deemed expedient to buy medical books for each of the
vessels in commission. He did, however, suggest that it would be considered,
and if there was any change Beaumont would be informed.[54]

In Beaumont's last days in Washington, it became apparent that Charles
Jackson had been very serious when he suggested that Beaumont should
bring St. Martin to Boston and direct further research in human digestion.
On June 10 Edward Everett and Gorham Parks called on Secretary of War
Lewis Cass to leave a petition, signed by more than two hundred members
of Congress, stating that as the eminent chemist Charles Jackson needed the
presence of Beaumont and St. Martin to proceed with experiments to analyze
the gastric fluid, they requested that Beaumont should be stationed in Boston
or in its vicinity. Apparently, this was a genuine attempt at facilitating his
research by Jackson, not something worked up by Beaumont himself, for
two days later the secretary of war answered that he would have paid close
attention to such an impressive list of signers, but that the surgeon general,
with Beaumont's agreement, had already arranged for him to be ordered to
St. Louis, and he was already on his way. It would not be advisable, he wrote,
to change these orders.[55]

After more than a year in which he had spent much of his time away from
home, Beaumont was hoping at last to satisfy his wife's heartfelt wish that
they should once again settle down as a family. He was obviously thinking
of this, and of again taking a more active role as a parent, when he took time
to write to his daughter Sarah, who was now almost eleven years old. Sarah
both played the piano and sang, and her father sent her some music, chosen,
he said, by her friends Lieutenant Joseph LaMotte and Major James Hook.
Beaumont urged his daughter to learn her lessons, to improve her mind "in
everything useful, virtuous, & becoming," and to become "an amiable *Lady*"
in her early youth. For the St. Louis trip he asked her to prepare her "little
Library, maps, charts and all the little travelling paraphernalia you can collect

54. Beaumont to the secretary of the navy, to the secretary of war, June 2, 1834,
secretary of the navy to Beaumont, December 30, 1833, June 3, 1834, BC, WU.
55. Edward Everett and Gorham Parks to the secretary of war, June 10, 1834,
enclosing petition of June 5, 1834, secretary of war to Everett and Parks, June 12,
1834, BC, WU.

to amuse and instruct yourself and the children on our journey through the Lakes & canals." She was to kiss her mother and the other children for him, and was asked to feel assured of "the doating [*sic*] love and tenderest affections of a father anxious for your health & happiness, and eager to be with you." It was an affectionate, loving letter, and had little of the forbidding atmosphere often generated by the Victorian father.[56]

His wife's niece, Elizabeth Smith, had been acting as a tutor to Sarah, and Beaumont told Sarah that Elizabeth was to prepare to go with them to St. Louis, to be her "preceptress & my female protege till she can find a more agreeable protector." To Elizabeth, Beaumont wrote a separate letter, apologizing for not previously answering her letters to him, and saying he understood the wrench it would be for her to leave her mother to go with them. He said, however, that she would be "one of a family whose constant desire will be to make you happy and contented." He admitted he was in a preaching mood, "more inclined to *poetry* than *politics*," asked her to kiss Aunt Debby and the children for him, and to drill Sarah in the piano. He signed as her "truly affectionate uncle."[57]

Beaumont's year and a half of eastern prestige had pleased and flattered him, but he was not a man who sought prestige as an alternative to the more intimate pleasures of family life. He had achieved the recognition he had sought since leaving Lebanon before the War of 1812. He had not earned or received, nor would he ever earn or receive, enough money for him to feel completely comfortable financially, but he was now quite content to renew the intimate ties of family and close friends that gave him most pleasure. He did, however, want to continue his research on St. Martin.

In mid-June Beaumont arrived back in Plattsburgh, turned in the report necessary for St. Martin to receive his pay for the previous three months, and planned to leave promptly for St. Louis. There was, however, a snag; it was to be a problem that plagued Beaumont for the rest of his life. St. Martin had gone to Canada to visit his wife, with the understanding that he would return to accompany the Beaumonts to St. Louis. He was not back when Beaumont returned from Washington, and after a delay, Beaumont left without him.[58] Establishing a family home was yet again delayed. Beaumont went alone to make arrangements for housing his family in St. Louis, but it is also possible

56. Beaumont to Sarah Beaumont, May 29, 1834, BC, WU.

57. Beaumont to Elizabeth Smith, June 4, 1834, Morgan Martin Papers.

58. Beaumont to Major Kirby, June 15, 1834, Beaumont to Lovell, July 31, 1834, BC, WU.

that he left his family to give him an excuse to apply for leave to return east to fetch them. In this way, he could try to contact St. Martin, find out if there was any chance of Congress changing its mind on giving him support, and check in person on the reception his book was receiving.

A letter from St. Martin caught up with him on his way to St. Louis. In it, St. Martin said that his wife did not want him to leave; she thought he could do a lot better if he stayed at home. He said he had actually started for Plattsburgh, but had fallen sick at St. John's and returned home. Although St. Martin's army duties had always been ambiguous, he could now have been listed as a deserter. Presumably, Surgeon General Lovell's private influence prevailed, because he was ultimately given a regular discharge as though he had served his five years.[59] Beaumont never lost his interest in St. Martin, or his hope of pursuing further research, but St. Louis was to deflect his life along a different path.

59. St. Martin to Beaumont, June 26, 1834, Beaumont to Lovell, July 31, 1834, BC, WU; Entry for Alexis St. Martin, WD, AG, Descriptive and Historical Register of Enlisted Soldiers of the Army.

NINE

St. Louis

ON THE STEAMBOAT THAT took Beaumont from Buffalo to Chicago, he had ample time to revive his interest in the West and its prospects. He was traveling with his good friend Daniel Whitney of Green Bay, a man who was deeply involved in the frenetic speculation of the mid-1830s. Like most others with any money to invest, Beaumont was soon to be caught up in the prospect of making money in land. Yet on this trip westward, Beaumont was still absorbed in the excitement of the publication of his book, and even before they called at Mackinac, his talk was of St. Martin and his research. He gave Episcopal Bishop Jackson Kemper a description of St. Martin's history and the interior of his stomach, told him that the natural stomach temperature was one hundred degrees, and, being Beaumont, sold him a copy of his book.[1]

He arrived at Jefferson Barracks on July 29, 1834, and took over the duties previously carried out by his old friend Lyman Foot. He reported his arrival in both official and private letters to Lovell, stating that he had been delayed in Plattsburgh by his hopes that St. Martin would arrive, and by sickness on the way. One wonders if the sickness might not have been a desire to visit old friends.

Beaumont also had to report that Sergeant Alexis St. Martin was now absent without leave. The appointment had succeeded in Lovell's objective of freeing Beaumont from additional financial obligations, but if intended to make St. Martin more amenable to orders, it was now proving to be a

1. Jackson Kemper, "Journal of an Episcopalian Missionary's Tour to Green Bay, 1834," 394, 396–99, 410, 448.

failure. In his private letter to Lovell, Beaumont poured out his frustrations, suggesting that St. Martin's objective had been to get Beaumont to come to Canada. There, where Beaumont would have difficulty enforcing his agreement, he would have extorted more money. Beaumont stressed the difficulty in enforcing his contract with St. Martin, not St. Martin's military status. Apparently Beaumont, like St. Martin, did not take St. Martin's military status very seriously. He told Lovell that, for the time being, he intended to ignore St. Martin. By fall, Beaumont prophesied, St. Martin would have spent all the money that had been advanced to him, and having "become miserably poor and wretched," would be "willing to recant his villainous obstinacy and ugliness, and then I shall be able to regain possession of him again, I have no doubt."

The object in regaining St. Martin was not simply research. Beaumont had strong hopes that Edward Livingston would arrange for them to be invited to Paris. He feared that if St. Martin did not return to him, he would sell his services to Canadian physicians and in that way come under the control of English doctors. Whatever happened, however, Beaumont wanted leave to return east in the fall, if not to go to Paris, then in the hope of bringing his family west to a permanent station at Prairie du Chien.[2]

Only two days after laying out his frustrations and hopes to Lovell, Beaumont pressed him more urgently about his desires in regard to a future post. Few, if any, surgeons general can ever have received so many special requests with such graciousness and accommodation as Lovell showed toward his friend. On this occasion, Beaumont's confidence in his relationship with Lovell was such that he also tried to make special arrangements for his friend, Surgeon Foot. Beaumont commented that Foot was particularly unhappy with his situation at Jefferson Barracks; his health and spirits were being affected by the climate and by his private circumstances, and Beaumont argued that from his long service Foot deserved a choice of stations before his juniors. Foot wanted to be stationed at Fort Howard at Green Bay.

Arguing that his own decided choice was Fort Crawford at Prairie du Chien, Beaumont demonstrated that his friendship for Foot was genuine by saying that if Foot could not be given Fort Howard or some other northern post, and if it were deemed expedient to assign Foot *"temporarily"* to Fort Crawford to rescue him from an undesirable location, then Beaumont would

---

2. Beaumont to Lovell, July 31, 1834, WD, AG, IMOF; Beaumont to Lovell, July 31, 1834, Private, BC, WU. Most of this private letter is reprinted in Myer, *Beaumont,* 227–28.

go along with it. This would be temporary, he assumed, until circumstances would make it possible for him to assume the Fort Crawford post "as a matter of acknowledged right." Even to a surgeon general as amenable as Lovell, this was strong language. He went on to say his superiors in the medical department all had their choice of posts, why could not he and Foot have theirs? "Surely," he wrote, "Justice *will not* be refused us."[3]

Jefferson Barracks, which was situated some ten miles from St. Louis, was a more elaborate military post than Beaumont was used to. It had been started in 1826 to replace the old Fort Bellefontaine, and was intended to serve not only as an army post but also as an infantry school. Building went on until 1840. A visitor in the year that Beaumont arrived was highly impressed by the barracks, "romantically situated" in an open wood on a high bluff. The barracks were built around three sides of a large parade ground, with the fourth side fronting on the Mississippi. The visitor took enjoyable rides on good horses, browsed in "a very good library" belonging to the post, lounged in the music room where the band was practicing "well-executed" pieces from a modern opera, and in the evening, at General Henry Atkinson's ample quarters, listened to musical pieces performed by the wives and daughters of the officers.[4]

The hospital was completed early in the history of the fort, and was built with the intention of being large enough to serve two regiments. It was a substantial building of brick, and the inspector's report in the summer of 1831 stated that "this Hospital as a building is the best arranged and most roomy of any other on the frontier." Two years later, it was reported that the patients were well provided for "in every respect." The inspector stated that at no other post had he seen "so good a hospital, or one in which a more perfect system and order prevailed."[5]

This was a far more comfortable western post than Beaumont had ever served in, but he was not happy with his situation. Fort Crawford at Prairie du Chien, though smaller, also had a new brick hospital and had the great advantage of being close to the local residents. A major difficulty for Beaumont at Jefferson Barracks was that it was about ten miles south of St. Louis, which would make it very difficult for him to carry on his usual private practice.

---

3. Beaumont to Lovell, August 2, 1834, WD, AG, IMOF.

4. Hoffman, *A Winter in the West*, vol. 2, 99–108; Nichols, *Atkinson*, 11–18; Henry W. Webb, "The Story of Jefferson Barracks," 199–200; Richard E. Mueller, "Jefferson Barracks: The Early Years," 7–17.

5. Jefferson Barracks, August 6, 1831, WD, IG, Reports.

For the time being, however, Beaumont settled into a bachelor routine at Jefferson Barracks and waited for what he hoped would be his reassignment to Fort Crawford. Duties were light, but the usual routine was broken in 1834 by fears of a cholera epidemic. Cholera was much feared in the St. Louis region in the early 1830s, and when any sickness that had symptoms at all like cholera appeared, there was usually general fear. This was unwarranted in 1834, for there were only a few cases. When the inspector visited the hospital at the barracks in August, he found Beaumont in charge, and commented that "no hospital in the country civil or military" was under better regulation.[6]

Beaumont had still not heard of the disposition of his request for a different post, but he decided early in September to ask Lovell for permission to travel east, hoping that he would be able to return, with his family, to Prairie du Chien. Although he did not say so in his official request, he told Lovell in a private letter that he hoped to use the trip east to contact St. Martin. Assuming that the possible trip to Paris had fallen through, he said that he wanted to continue his experiments on St. Martin at a more convenient post. He did not say so, but the inconvenience at Jefferson Barracks, with its better facilities, was not for research but for carrying on a private practice.

Beaumont told Lovell that he had not much doubt that, given the time and opportunity, he could obtain control of St. Martin again in the fall, and once again used this possibility as a reason for asking Lovell for help. He asked, in view of the financial sacrifices he had already made for his research, whether Lovell might not arrange it so that his private trip to bring his family might not be at least partially paid for by the government. He also repeated his request for an assignment to Fort Crawford, unless it was decided to put a surgeon at Fort Columbus, New York.[7]

Lovell had already met part of Beaumont's wishes. On September 4 he had written to inform him that he would be reassigned to Fort Crawford as soon as another surgeon could be found to relieve him. Surgeon Foot was not given Fort Howard, but he got the next best thing. He was assigned to Fort Winnebago at the Fox-Wisconsin portage.[8]

While Beaumont waited for Lovell's reply to his request to come east, he found Jefferson Barracks a little too quiet. Late in the month, he told one of

6. Ibid., Aug. 30, 1834; Mueller, "Jefferson Barracks," 21; Nelson, *Beaumont,* 232.
7. Beaumont to Lovell, September 6, 1834, WD, AG, IMOF; Beaumont to Lovell, September 6, 1834, BC, WU.
8. Lovell to Beaumont, September 4, 1834, BC, WU.

his friends that it was "rather dull times here since the Cholera left us."[9] A few days later, life became much livelier, and Beaumont was again into one of the periodic disputes that punctuated his army life.

Beaumont was delighted on September 27 to receive a special order from the Adjutant General's Office ordering him to report to Fort Crawford at Prairie du Chien. The same order directed Surgeon Clement Finley to relieve Beaumont at Jefferson Barracks. Finley had been farther west at Fort Leavenworth, and did not yet know of his new assignment. When on September 30 he arrived at Jefferson Barracks with a detachment of men, it was not to relieve Beaumont but simply because he was on his way east. He was eagerly looking forward to seeing his family. His mood quickly changed when Beaumont told him of the order directing him to relieve Beaumont at Jefferson Barracks. He wanted no part of it. He took the attitude that if Beaumont had not told him, he would have received an official order *after* he had seen his family in the East, and then could have taken up his post at Jefferson Barracks. Finley decided to leave without delay. He obviously decided the order would be official when he received his own formal notification, not when told by Beaumont.

Beaumont blew his top, and wrote an impassioned letter to Lovell, accusing Finley of desertion. He said Finley had refused either to see or acknowledge the order that Beaumont wanted to show him, rushed "headlong," like "a *scared Snake*" on board a steamboat lying at the wharf, and left for Philadelphia. Beaumont said that he tried to tell Finley that he needed to proceed east and return to Fort Crawford before the dead of winter, but Finley would not listen. Finley, wrote Beaumont, did not stay thirty minutes at the post, although it would have taken him less than a day to have signed the necessary documents to take over, and that within five days General Atkinson would "doubtless" have given him permission to go for his family. He then, wrote Beaumont, could have gone east, leaving the medical duties to a physician who assisted Beaumont at the post.

Beaumont poured out his indignation and his sense of injustice. "I could not permit Selfishness, *Nostalgic pains,* nor even affianced and filial affections to overcome & confound my sense of public duty, official fidelity or manly obedience," Beaumont wrote, "and induce me to evade an order, which I well knew was intended and ought properly to be obeyed!" Beaumont said he had been too long in the service of Mars "to be duped or controlled by *tamed Cupids,* or wheedled from the path of official duties, by the blandishments of

9. Beaumont to Thomas P. Burnett, September 24, 1834, Medical Envelope, MHS.

Love, either social, Self, or Sexual." Upon every principle of justice, he wrote, Finley ought immediately to be ordered back, not only to relieve him, but as an example to others.[10]

Beaumont simmered at Jefferson Barracks for several weeks before he received word that Surgeon Finley had been ordered to proceed immediately to the Barracks to await trial on charges to be preferred against him; Beaumont was to appear as a witness.[11] While waiting, Beaumont wrote to his cousin, Andrew Beaumont, who was a member of Congress, to try to enlist his aid in a renewed attempt to obtain recompense from Congress for his work on St. Martin. In the spring he had followed Edward Everett's advice and revised the memorial by omitting any reference to future Congressional support of his research. He now simply asked for reimbursement for what he said he had expended earlier. The new petition came up in December. Beaumont had asked Senator Lewis Linn of Missouri, a physician, to present the petition. In writing to his cousin, Beaumont was his usual practical self. He said he was willing to take what he could get; if five thousand dollars was not possible, then he would take $1,825, though it would not pay a third of his expenses pertaining to St. Martin. He expressed a hope of continuing his experiments and perhaps going to Europe, though his *"rascally Frenchman"* had absconded to Canada.[12]

All Beaumont's attempts to enlist political support were of no avail. This time the memorial did not even proceed to debate. It was quietly shelved.[13]

Late in October Beaumont at last received a three-month leave of absence to travel east.[14] He went to Plattsburgh by way of Washington, D.C. After traveling on the Mississippi and Ohio Rivers as far as he could, he took the stage over the Alleghenies through what is now West Virginia. Beaumont showed the same delight in these new scenes as he had when first traveling west to Mackinac nearly fifteen years before. In mid-November, writing to his wife less than an hour after arriving in Washington, he told her that crossing the Alleghenies by starlight was "the most sublime & beautiful scene I ever witnessed." He was gratified with his reception by the medical faculty at the

10. Beaumont to Lovell, October 1, 1834, BC, WU; Myer, *Beaumont,* 232.

11. Lovell to Beaumont, October 21, 1834, BC, WU.

12. Beaumont to Andrew Beaumont, October 21, 1834, in *Journal of the American Medical Association* 85 (1925): 632–33; draft of Beaumont's memorial, May 27, 1834, Beaumont to Finance Committee, June 3, 1834, BC, WU.

13. *Senate Journal,* 24th Cong., 1st sess., 61, 72. The relevant entries are printed in Myer, *Beaumont,* 239.

14. Beaumont to Lovell, October 28, 1834, WD, AG, IMOF.

University of Virginia, and he saw both Monticello and Mount Vernon. His only regret, he wrote, was that his wife and children were not with him. He sent his wife petals he had plucked from a rose in the garden at Mount Vernon, and said he had a rosebud for her that he was trying to preserve.

Beaumont was always a good traveler. He delighted in new scenery, enjoyed his fellow travelers, and displayed a zest for living. What to some would have been the major inconvenience and delay brought about by low water was to Beaumont an enjoyable experience. He told his wife that the change in plans had delayed him a day or two, but had allowed him to see a very romantic part of the United States. He wrote of excellent roads, fine horses, elegant carriages, and good dinners. In Washington, his main concern was to see Lovell, and he was hoping to get away within a few days. He told his wife he was writing to appease her anxiety, and to prepare her for the reception of her "ever affectionate William." After a summer at Jefferson Barracks and two weeks on rivers and roads, Beaumont was relaxed and happy to be going home to his family.[15]

When Beaumont talked with Lovell, it was apparently decided that Beaumont would return to Jefferson Barracks rather than Fort Crawford. It seems likely that in private discussions with Lovell, Beaumont received a go-ahead to pursue a private practice in St. Louis. To do so, he would have to make arrangements either to have a separate residence in St. Louis itself, or to locate at the military arsenal that was some seven miles closer to the city.[16]

Beaumont had decided to try to settle permanently in the West, and around this time he drew up a proposal for a chain of "commercial hospitals" on the inland waterways to serve old soldiers, inland sailors, and old craftsmen. He hoped that Congress would appropriate money for buildings to be located throughout the Mississippi Valley and the Great Lakes, but particularly at points linking the lakes and the navigable rivers; his old haunts of Green Bay and Prairie du Chien were two good examples. He proposed that the hospitals should be placed under a commission appointed by the president, and the commission would appoint a board of trustees for each hospital. In turn, the trustees would appoint resident physicians and surgeons, and control admissions. Beaumont suggested that the institutions should be founded on a system of manual labor and should be self-supporting.

Beaumont's plan was not acted upon, though he made an attempt to enlist

15. Beaumont to Deborah Beaumont, November 15, 1834, BC, WU.
16. See Lovell to Beaumont, December 26, 1834, BC, WU.

political support. A Congress that had balked at supporting his research was not ready to enter into appropriations for a whole chain of hospitals. It seems likely that Beaumont was inspired by thought of hospitals at Green Bay and Prairie du Chien, both of which would need resident physicians, and who better than the man who had thought up the idea, and who had gained extensive experience in western posts?[17]

While in Washington, Beaumont also continued his efforts to boost the sales of his book. He wrote to one of his agents to say that he would probably recall all unsold copies from the East to supply the western market, as copies there were nearly all sold out. The season was late, travel was becoming more difficult, and it was December before Beaumont reached Plattsburgh. It was a bad time to travel west, and when he left, early on the morning of January 9, he again went without his family. He did not ask for permission to delay because he had been ordered to appear as a witness in the court martial of Surgeon Finley. Leaving his family also gave him the excuse to return yet again in the spring in hope of obtaining the continued services of St. Martin.[18]

Shortly before Christmas, St. Martin had written from Lower Canada, saying that he was disturbed that he had received no direct answer to his letters; only word through the old fur trader William Morrison that Beaumont expected him to return. He used the excuse of sickness to explain why he had not come, but the main sticking point was St. Martin's family, and St. Martin's hope of obtaining more money. He said he would be glad to join Beaumont, with his family, if Beaumont would send money, which he said was still due to him. To exert a little pressure, he said he was thinking of cultivating his land if he did not soon hear from Beaumont. Beaumont made no new offer to St. Martin. He was hoping that St. Martin would run out of money and return to fulfill his original contract.[19]

The only answer St. Martin received at this time was written by Samuel Beaumont. He told St. Martin that his cousin had left for Jefferson Barracks and would not be back again until the spring. If St. Martin agreed to come without his family, he should meet Beaumont in Plattsburgh in the middle of April. Beaumont sent word that if St. Martin would not come without his

17. "Suggestions for a Plan of Regulation of Commercial Hospitals," n.d., William Mason to Beaumont, January 2, 1835, BC, WU.

18. Beaumont to H. Howe, November 19, 1834, File 1834, SHSW; Beaumont to Lovell, December 15, 1834, and January 8, 1835, WD, AG, IMOF.

19. St. Martin to Beaumont, December 19, 1834 (in French), BC, WU. This letter is reproduced and translated in Arno Luckhardt, "The William Beaumont Collection of the University of Chicago," 550–51.

family, or asked for more money, he could simply stay in Canada and expect no more assistance. The message was that there were to be no more advances of money until St. Martin returned.[20]

In January 1835, Lovell was able to tell Beaumont that his desire of being closer to St. Louis was likely to be fulfilled. The department was contemplating placing a medical officer in St. Louis, or at least at the nearby arsenal. The duties would not be particularly onerous: care of the army personnel and their families at the arsenal, treatment of the military men passing through the town, and purchasing medical supplies for the western department. Lovell was writing to make sure that Beaumont still wanted to be stationed in St. Louis.[21]

Even before he received official word that he was to be posted to the arsenal, Beaumont had heard, on the highest authority, that this posting was to be made. Late in January the commander in chief of the army, Alexander Macomb, wrote privately to him with the request that he should befriend and support George Johnson, the hospital steward at the arsenal. Johnson was the son of a physician of very respectable family in Georgetown, and his friends had asked for Macomb's support. Beaumont received other letters about Johnson, but not from so important a figure.[22]

Knowing that his official posting to St. Louis was imminent, Beaumont quickly sought another favor from Lovell. He told him that the order would reach him at Jefferson Barracks "too soon for my convenience & interest." As he had been unable to bring his family west in the middle of winter, he had been granted leave to return to get them in the spring. This would have been at his own expense. He asked Lovell if he could arrange for the new order to reach him in Plattsburgh; if that happened he could take his family to his new post at the public expense.

Although Beaumont had rushed back to Jefferson Barracks to testify against Surgeon Finley, when he arrived he found that there were long delays in beginning the court martial. Beaumont's anger against Finley had not diminished. He told Lovell of Finley's "selfish arrogance and obstinacy," and he testified against him in the middle of March. The decision to find Finley not guilty was taken after Beaumont left for the East.[23]

20. Samuel Beaumont to St. Martin, January 12, 1835, BC, WU.
21. Lovell to Beaumont, January 6, 1835, BC, WU.
22. Alexander Macomb to Beaumont, January 26, 1835, BC, WU.
23. Beaumont to Lovell, February 27 and March 17, 1835, BC, WU; Beaumont to Lovell, March 18, 1835, WD, AG, IMOF.

Beaumont took time in the first week in April to write a long letter to Lovell complaining of the great number of defective men admitted to the army through recruiting depots. He said that it was not uncommon to find a fourth or fifth of those sent to western posts to be more or less defective, with varicose veins, "diseased testes," incipient consumption, drunkenness, and a variety of other ailments. Beaumont suggested that examining surgeons should be paid so that half the money was withheld, to be forfeited if the recruit that had been admitted proved unfit.[24]

In mid-March Beaumont left Jefferson Barracks, and arrived in Plattsburgh about a month later. While in the East, he learned that the chemical analysis of gastric juice was proving intractable. In the previous summer, Berzelius had at last written to Benjamin Silliman describing his efforts to analyze the gastric juice sent by Beaumont, and, in January, Silliman's *American Journal of Science and Arts* printed extracts from the letter.

Berzelius had failed in his efforts at detailed analysis. One problem, though not the basic one, was that it had taken from April to August for the gastric juice to reach Sweden, and Berzelius stated that he was not sure that the juice had remained the same as when syphoned from St. Martin. The biggest problem, however, was in the limitations of chemical analysis in the 1830s. Berzelius reported that the juice proved to be strongly acid when tested with litmus paper, but when he began to evaporate it in a vacuum at room temperature, he encountered a problem he admitted he had been unable to solve. How was he to make a plan of analysis, he asked, when the nature of the substance to be separated was unknown? A single mistake would destroy the whole, and he had no more. He suggested that a great many experiments, chemical and physiological, should precede the analysis, and for this he would need almost daily supplies of the gastric juice.[25]

Although St. Martin had not arrived in Plattsburgh, and there was no word from him, Beaumont stuck to his plan of making no concessions. He simply wrote to William Morrison in the hope that he would be able to use his influence.[26] A major stumbling block in Beaumont's hopes of renewing his research on St. Martin was that he did not want to spend any more money than he had already agreed to. He had failed in his efforts to obtain

24. Beaumont to Lovell, April 6, 1835, BC, WU.
25. Beaumont to Lovell, April 16, 1835, BC, WU. Beaumont copied the relevant sections from the *American Journal of Science and Arts* 28 (January 7, 1835): 405–7, BC, WU.
26. Beaumont to William Morrison, April 18, 1835, BC, WU.

governmental support, and, from his own point of view, he believed that he had already arranged a generous contract with St. Martin, as well as having provided him with an army sinecure. He wanted St. Martin, but he did not want St. Martin's family. This would mean paying their travel expenses, and presumably lead to more demands for money later.

St. Martin clearly hoped, however, that given his unique situation he could succeed in the difficult task of prizing more money out of Beaumont so that his family could come with him to whatever post Beaumont was assigned to. With a man who was less tight with his money than Beaumont he probably would have succeeded, but ultimately Beaumont valued money over additional research. This ruined Beaumont's chance of visiting Europe and demonstrating his experiments on St. Martin to distinguished European researchers, but it probably did not have a major effect on Beaumont's scientific contribution. Beaumont had accomplished his most important work quite early in his research on St. Martin, and given what he was capable of, there was probably not a great deal more of scientific importance that he could have learned from further experiments.

For a work of science published in obscurity in Plattsburgh and quite expensive, Beaumont's book had sold quite well. He was eventually to sell some three thousand copies of his first edition. Given the spartan way in which the book had been published by Beaumont and his cousin, this probably meant that the book ultimately made money based on its production costs. Beaumont, however, very much thought of the costs of his book in terms of his whole history with St. Martin, even though for all of that time he had received his regular army salary. Even though Beaumont boarded St. Martin and had made modest personal payments to him under their contracts, he had also received the services of St. Martin as a general handyman around the house. Beaumont, however, was ever conscious of his costs and his perceived rights, and before he returned to St. Louis, he gave his cousin Samuel power of attorney to ask, demand, and sue for money due from a firm of Boston booksellers on account of five hundred copies of his book that they had received for distribution, and for which they had been slow in making payment.[27]

On this eastern trip in the spring of 1835, Beaumont also bid what was apparently his last farewell to his old Lebanon family. He still had brothers

27. Beaumont, *Physiology of Digestion*, 5; Power of Attorney to Samuel Beaumont, May 21, 1835, BC, WU.

and sisters alive, and he wrote to them from Plattsburgh, commenting that they had not exchanged letters for a long time. He told them of his constant moves in the past thirty months, but stated that he expected to be stationed in St. Louis for at least several years. After so many years in which he had largely neglected his Lebanon family, he still found it necessary to make vague promises for the future. When he got well settled, he wrote, he hoped that he could find some opportunity for his widowed sister Lucy's boys, because, he said, he had her and her children's future much at heart. If his brother John, or any of the others, should feel a migratory spirit, he would be on the lookout for them. But he did not mention money, said it would be a year or two before he could get fairly established, and asked them not to be impatient for such an event: *"Time & patience* are indispensable to the due accomplishment of all laudable undertakings."[28]

His only concrete suggestion for their future was singularly impractical. He said that the culture and manufacture of silk was becoming a subject of national and international attention, and that perhaps the long experience of the girls in making items of silk might be of mutual advantage. Beaumont said he was taking mulberry seeds with him to the West with a view to beginning the growth of trees. At this time of his life, Beaumont had a bee in his bonnet on the practicality of making money by growing mulberry trees, and in his plan for self-sustaining hospitals in the West had suggested experiments in the cultivation of such trees.[29]

Beaumont would have liked to have been helpful to his old family in Lebanon—many young men simply faded away into the West, and were never heard from again—but he did not want to spend a penny that he did not regard as essential for himself or for his own family circle. As a result, he usually wrote supportive and encouraging letters when there was little chance of having to do anything. After 1835, even this apparently stopped.

Beaumont, Debby, and the children finally left for St. Louis on May 22. Beaumont had been successful in having their costs paid by the government. His wife's niece, Elizabeth Smith, then in her teens, went to live with them, and her widowed mother, Ann, traveled with them as far as Green Bay. The Beaumont ties to Green Bay were strong. They had liked it in the 1820s, and had helped persuade a number of Plattsburgh residents that it was a good place to settle. Debby's brother, Thomas Green, had moved out there with his

---

28. Beaumont to John Beaumont, April 22, 1835, BC, WU.
29. "Suggestions for a Plan for Regulation of Commercial Hospitals," n.d., BC, WU.

family in the previous year. Elizabeth, after living with the Beaumonts in St. Louis, in the summer of 1837 married the important entrepreneur Morgan Martin, and settled permanently in Green Bay.[30]

The Beaumonts, after being delayed for a week in Buffalo waiting for a steamboat, were in Green Bay by June 12. Five days later, Beaumont wrote to Lovell to report that he had been sick with fever and ague on arrival, was now recuperating, but would be late returning from his leave. His lateness presented no problem, for after writing to Lovell he discovered that the secretary of war, Lewis Cass, was at Green Bay, and he obtained an extension of his leave from Cass.[31] Whether or not Beaumont was too sick to continue, he undoubtedly took good advantage of his stay in Green Bay to find out as much as possible about the prospects for growth in the region. The lakeshore region of Wisconsin was about to experience its first great rush of settlers, and like the rest of the West was experiencing feverish speculation in the mid-1830s. A group of men—Morgan Martin, Daniel Whitney, and James Doty—used Green Bay as a base to invest and speculate throughout the region. Beaumont knew all three, and was a good friend of Martin and Whitney. A land office opened at Navarino in August 1835, and in the following months there was a rapid sale of lots, not only in Navarino but also in a variety of other areas in eastern Wisconsin.[32]

Beaumont had already bought one lot in Navarino several years before, and in the mid-1830s he became a more substantial investor when he bought a tract of land across the river from Fort Howard. It was the site of the Washington Hotel. Like practically all other purchasers in these hectic years, Beaumont did not have to find all the money at one time. The Washington House had been built by Whitney in the early 1830s. When Beaumont took it over, he installed as its proprietor his brother-in-law Thomas Green, who had gained his experience in his father's noted inn in Plattsburgh.[33]

From Green Bay, the Beaumont family traveled along the Fox-Wisconsin river system to Prairie du Chien. This part of the journey almost proved disastrous. Beaumont, along with some of his luggage, was swept into the

30. Henry Stanton to Beaumont, April 28, 1835, Beaumont to Lovell, April 16, May 1, June 17, 1835, WD, AG, IMOF; "The Beaumont Homestead," 1–9; [Reuben G. Thwaites], "Sketch of Morgan L. Martin," 380–84; Martin, "Doctor William Beaumont," 277.

31. Beaumont to Lovell, June 17 and 23, 1835, to the secretary of war, June 26, 1835, WD, AG, IMOF.

32. Martin, "Navarino," 1–5; Smith, *James Duane Doty*, 177.

33. Martin, "Navarino," 2–4, 18–20; Nelson, *Beaumont*, 240–42, 278; Martin, "Doctor William Beaumont," 278–79.

water by the branch of a tree. Beaumont could not swim, but he managed to hold onto another branch, and survived to continue his career in St. Louis. He was hoping to find living quarters in the city, for he was anxious to begin his civilian practice, but St. Louis was booming and crowded. The family moved into quarters in the arsenal, and Beaumont had to make do with an office in the city, about three miles away. This he used both for his official duties and as a location from which he could carry on a private practice.[34]

By the following spring Beaumont had moved his family to "a small modest cottage" amid fields on the edge of the city. The center of St. Louis was dirty and tumultuous, but the city offered many more distractions than the lonely frontier posts that the Beaumonts had lived in for most of their married life. That spring they attended a private reception that had Daniel Webster in attendance and Italian opera singers providing the entertainment; a thrill that for their niece was tainted by the thought that the brother-in-law of their hostess had become well known for extreme cruelty to a slave. Beaumont was now living in a slave state.[35]

Beaumont settled in St. Louis at an ideal time for an ambitious physician. The town was beginning a period of great expansion, and it was a town that was developing a notorious reputation for ill health. In the next twenty years, this was to make it a mecca for physicians. St. Louis at first had grown only slowly after its foundation in the eighteenth century, and even the economic progress brought about by its key role in the western fur trade had not brought any dramatic growth in the years before 1830. Its population in that year was still less than six thousand, and about a fifth of its residents were slaves. This proportion of slaves was to decline sharply in the next thirty years. Beaumont had been able to observe slavery in his brief residences in Washington, D.C., but this was the first time that he had lived in a slave area.[36]

A visitor in the spring of 1834 referred to St. Louis as "once the ultima thule of western adventure, and still the depot of the fur trade, and the bureau of Indian affairs." Physically, it consisted of an older area of French "broad steep-roofed stone edifices" and Spanish "tall stuccoed" dwellings, and a newer area where the Americans lived in houses of brick. There were substantial streets close to the river, but the effect was spoiled by the filth that gathered in

34. Elizabeth Smith Martin Journal, Morgan Martin Papers; Beaumont to Lovell, August 1, 1835, WD, AG, IMOF; Myer, *Beaumont*, 238.
35. Elizabeth Smith Martin Journal, Morgan Martin Papers.
36. James N. Primm, *Lion of the Valley: St. Louis, Missouri*, 135–38; Lloyd A. Hunter, "Slavery in St. Louis, 1804–1860," 236–37.

them. In summer the general impression was one of dirt, dust, overpowering heat, and clouds of mosquitoes. The area suffered a great deal from flooding, cellars were often full of water, and there was no sewer system until the 1850s. A German visitor in 1834 reported that almost all the residents suffered from stomach troubles.[37]

From 1835 to 1840 the population of St. Louis doubled, reaching more than 16,400 in the latter year, and in the 1840s the population more than quadrupled, to nearly 78,000. Moreover, the permanent population of St. Louis was only a portion of the vast number of people who passed through the city, or settled there temporarily, on their way to new settlements. In one week in early April 1836, more than five thousand newcomers landed in St. Louis.[38]

Beaumont now had the possibility of a private practice that exceeded anything that had been possible before, and he threw himself vigorously into treating private patients. He did not neglect his military duties, but they were not burdensome. The garrison at the arsenal was small, the transient military personnel did not overwhelm him, and he could easily handle his purchasing responsibilities. Beaumont never wasted time, and he was now able to build a substantial private practice while satisfying his military obligations. There are indications, however, that as his military duties became less central to his existence, he began to construe them more narrowly.

After a year in St. Louis, Beaumont told Lovell that he had "a very handsome, lucrative and respectable private practice, with 6 or 8,000 dollars a year, a reputation far above my deserts, and a professional popularity more than commensurate with my best practical skill or abilities." This was an income far above anything he could have hoped to receive if he had remained in private practice in northern New York. In the 1830s, country doctors in New England found it difficult to earn more than five hundred dollars a year.[39]

Beaumont had quickly slipped into the regular medical life of St. Louis, and clearly his position was not that of a military surgeon with a few private patients. Within a few months of settling there, his patients ranged from

37. Hoffman, *A Winter in the West*, vol. 2, 63, 82; Charles Van Ravenswaay, *St. Louis: An Informal History of the City and Its People*, 296–300; Edward J. Goodwin, *A History of Medicine in Missouri*, 66.

38. Primm, *Lion of the Valley*, 147–53; Jeffrey S. Adler, *Yankee Merchants and the Making of the Urban West: The Rise and Fall of Antebellum St. Louis*, 23–27.

39. Quotation from Myer, *Beaumont*, 240–41. See also Barnes Riznik, *Medicine in New England, 1790–1840*, 15; see also Barboriak, "Reporting to the Surgeon General," 61–62.

transient indigents to the prominent trader William Sublette, his family, and slaves. The indigent patients he quickly referred to the mayor, recommending that they be admitted to the local Charity Hospital.[40]

Sublette was impressed by Beaumont, and said of him in January 1837 that he was "much pleasd with him and think him an Excelent Serjent [Surgeon]." Beaumont had been calling on him every few days, and had operated on him for an anal fistula. For many years, Beaumont continued to treat the Sublette household. The bill for one period from March 1839 to April 1841 was $185.10.[41]

There were many physicians in St. Louis, but the more prominent citizens knew Beaumont as an experienced army surgeon with influential friends and a well-known book. It helped separate him from the general run of physicians, and once he gained patients, they were impressed by his hard work and enthusiasm. He still believed in vigorous dosing, but though part of the public had turned to alternative medicines, many still believed that they needed doctors with the confidence to prescribe with certainty.

In 1835 and 1836 Beaumont was also benefiting from a western boom that was reaching a peak before its crash the following year. Money was easily available, speculation was rampant, and Beaumont increasingly became caught up in the general euphoria. He already had a substantial investment in Green Bay and a more modest one in Prairie du Chien, and he became interested in the potential development in both these places, as well as at other locations in the Old Northwest. Many believed that both Green Bay and Prairie du Chien, situated at either end of what had been the vital Fox-Wisconsin waterway, were destined for dramatic growth. Green Bay was to achieve a little of what had appeared to be its potential, but Prairie du Chien never fulfilled the expectations of those who invested there.

Beaumont's main source of information for prospects at Prairie du Chien was his old friend Hercules Dousman, agent for the American Fur Company but also an extensive dealer in land. He also was in touch with the family friend Lieutenant Joseph LaMotte, who was stationed at Fort Crawford. When LaMotte went from St. Louis to Prairie du Chien in August 1836, he sent back a report to Beaumont on the list of land sales made to various speculators, and

40. Beaumont to J. F. Darby, November 12, 1836, and undated [1836?], John F. Darby Papers, MHS.

41. William Sublette to Hugh Campbell, November 21, 1836, and January 1, 1837, Account of Beaumont and Sykes, 1841, Sublette Papers, MHS; John E. Sunder, *Bill Sublette: Mountain Man*, 192, 198, 217, 218; Nelson, *Beaumont*, 315.

told him that Daniel Whitney's company was talking about cutting a canal in the area. Two months later, LaMotte was pessimistic about the future of Prairie du Chien, and expressed the opinion that neither of them would live to see a big city there.[42]

LaMotte did not deter Beaumont, and Beaumont began to make additional land deals in Prairie du Chien and elsewhere, some of them, at least on paper, producing a very good profit. His first main speculative sale must have convinced him that he had found a new and even more effective way of making money than pursuing a private practice. The land he had bought from Dousman in the early 1830s for three hundred dollars he sold in two parcels for a total of eighteen hundred dollars. Although most of the purchase price was still owed to him, Beaumont quickly invested in more land. In the spring of 1837 he bought scattered lands from Dousman, some of them lands in which Dousman held only a partial interest; for eight hundred dollars, payable on November 1, 1837, he bought a town lot in the town of Winnebago, Illinois, and for two thousand dollars he bought Dousman's interest in various Wisconsin lands, most of them not far from Prairie du Chien.[43]

With his large and expanding private practice, his rapidly increasing interest in land speculation, and his regular military duties, Beaumont was stretched to the limit in his first years in St. Louis, and he could hardly expect to take on much more. It was thus with less than his usual enthusiasm that he greeted yet another opportunity that arose in the fall of 1836, even though it was an opportunity that was an indication of his new status. St. Louis University was about to establish a medical department, and on October 4 the Secretary of the Board of Trustees, the Reverend William Greenleaf Eliot, wrote to Beaumont to tell him that the trustees had elected him to the chair of surgery. Beaumont replied that as he could not accept the appointment without first obtaining the consent of the surgeon general, and as he assumed they needed a prompt reply, he would have to decline.[44]

Beaumont had always made strong efforts to make sure that his army obligations did not prevent him from doing what he wanted to do, and it seems likely that this quick rejection of the offer stemmed more from his very

42. Joseph LaMotte to Beaumont, September 2 and November 16, 1836, BC, WU.
43. Beaumont bought Hercules Dousman's interest in a number of landholdings in Wisconsin in 1837, see memo, April 1837, in Beaumont Papers, SHSW; deeds, 1837, in BC, UC.
44. William Eliot to Beaumont, October 4, 1836, Beaumont to Eliot, October 6, 1836, BC, WU.

full, profitable days rather than from the reasons he gave. He had, however, left a loophole. Eliot wrote back to him to say that the trustees were willing to wait until he received an answer from the surgeon general. This was possible because it seemed likely that regular lectures would not begin until the fall of 1837.[45]

Beaumont now wrote to Lovell, saying that he would like his advice both official and private, but that he would prefer, in Lovell's reply, "a good excuse for nonacceptance." Beaumont's stated reason for this was that he felt "extreme diffidence" in his "qualifications & fitness for the appointment." Beaumont certainly had an unusual background for a potential professor of surgery at a medical school, and he was somewhat defensive about his early professional training, but with Beaumont, money is a more likely reason than diffidence. He was engaged in a very lucrative and growing private practice, and it seems most likely that he did not want to interrupt it with other obligations.[46]

Beaumont never received the expected answer from Surgeon General Lovell, for his great friend and patron had died on October 17. Beaumont's letter was delivered to a new, more impersonal surgeon general's office. For a time, it appeared that Beaumont was still fortunate in that the acting position was given to Dr. Benjamin King, who was another friend, but when new arrangements were finally made, Beaumont was to be shocked by the stance of the permanent appointee, Dr. Thomas Lawson, who was another old acquaintance.[47]

Because of the changeover in the surgeon general's office, Beaumont's expected excuse for declining the chair did not arrive, and he found himself under considerable pressure to accept. The secretary to the trustees, the Reverend William Greenleaf Eliot, became a close family friend of the Beaumonts in these years in St. Louis. Eliot, a Unitarian who had come to the city in 1834, rapidly became one of the city's most prominent ministers, active in a variety of philanthropic and social causes. Deborah Beaumont attended his church, and while Beaumont himself still shunned formal religious observance, he became Eliot's close friend and personal physician.[48]

Not hearing from Washington, and being pressed to give a favorable answer, Beaumont in February 1837 accepted the chair of surgery, adding the

45. William Eliot to Beaumont, October 12, 1836, BC, WU.
46. Beaumont to Lovell, October 21, 1836, BC, WU.
47. Brown, *Medical Department*, 155, 158–59.
48. For William Eliot, see Charlotte C. Eliot, *William Greenleaf Eliot: Minister, Educator, Philanthropist*, xv–xvi, 1–126; Van Ravenswaay, *St. Louis*, 303–5.

proviso that should he fail to gain permission from the medical department, he would have to withdraw.[49] As it happened, the problem never arose because the medical department of St. Louis University did not open for several years. By that time, Beaumont's circumstances were different, and he never took up the position in the medical school.

Beaumont had no need of a chair of surgery, for his practice continued to flourish. In the following years, physicians settling in St. Louis often were interested in entering into a partnership with him. Beaumont, with good reason, was worried about how he would work with another physician, and was reluctant to share the profits, but he was so busy he needed help. He sought it from someone he thought he could work with—his cousin Samuel Beaumont. Sam was later recalled by Plattsburgh residents as "slow-going," and "a nice man." To have any chance of working with William Beaumont, it was certainly better to be slow-going and nice than volatile and nasty. In the summer of 1837, Beaumont briefly brought Sam to St. Louis as an assistant in his private practice. It did not work out. Sam was not happy working as an assistant to his cousin, found him too tight with money, and missed his family, who remained in Plattsburgh. He decided that they would not be happy in St. Louis. Sam quickly returned to Plattsburgh. The cousins remained friends.[50]

While pursuing what seems to have been in everything but name a full-time private practice, Beaumont was still a military surgeon, and the death of Lovell in October 1836 meant that his sheltered and privileged status was about to end. For a time, potential difficulties were averted because of the situation in the surgeon general's office. Thomas Lawson, who was appointed to succeed Lovell, took a considerable time to assume his new duties. He did not arrive in Washington until late in the spring of 1837, accompanied retired President Jackson to Tennessee, and then was absorbed by duties relating to the Seminole War. It was 1838 before he could act effectively as surgeon general. In December 1837 Benjamin King, as acting surgeon general, privately returned "papers" that Beaumont had sent to Lovell, commenting that as they were "strictly private," he had not placed them in the files of the office.[51]

49. Beaumont to the Secretary of the Board of Trustees, February 10, 1837, BC, WU.
50. Beaumont to Samuel Beaumont, April 4, 1846, Samuel Beaumont to Beaumont, April 24, 1846, BC, WU; Kellogg, *Recollections*, 23, 46; Nelson, *Beaumont*, 246–47.
51. See Mary C. Gillett, "Thomas Lawson: Second Surgeon General of the U.S. Army: A Character Sketch," 17; Brown, *Medical Department*, 158–59; Benjamin King to Beaumont, April 20, 1836, December 6, 1837, BC, WU.

In the meantime, Beaumont purchased supplies, examined recruits, and treated military personnel, both at the arsenal and in St. Louis. There are indications that Beaumont found his continuing duties at the arsenal, some three miles away, somewhat irksome. In the spring of 1838 he wrote to King to warn him of a potential difficulty. It seemed likely that Lieutenant Woodburne Potter at the arsenal would request compensation be made to a private physician.[52]

Beaumont told King that he had been called urgently to the arsenal to treat a supposedly very sick Lieutenant Potter. When Beaumont got there, he found that Potter was sitting comfortably and chatting with company. He examined him, found no marked symptoms, and gave him "mild purgative pills" to be taken at discretion if he fell sick. Beaumont said that there had been numerous previous calls that had demonstrated mental weakness more than physical disability. The next day, Beaumont said, Potter was seen riding in the town with his wife. Two days later, after dark, Beaumont was again summoned to attend Potter at the arsenal. He decided not to go until the following morning, and received a note from Potter's wife stating that they had been helped by another physician, and that Beaumont's services would not be required until Potter was informed by the proper department "whether the Public practice is to yield to the convenience of Private."[53]

For Beaumont, this may have been impatience with an officer he thought was malingering, but from the tone of the note from Potter's wife, there also appears to have been resentment at the arsenal at the way in which Beaumont carried on an extensive and lucrative private practice in St. Louis. The resentment was to reach the new surgeon general in Washington, and he was a man who was as much a soldier as he was a physician.

In spite of working long hours, Beaumont had still not given up hope of renewing his experiments on St. Martin, though at times he seemed as anxious to prevent others conducting independent research on St. Martin as he was to carry it out himself. He continued to seek news of St. Martin through William Morrison, and late in April 1837 Morrison had responded to Beaumont's queries by reporting that St. Martin was willing to go to Beaumont "at a moment's warning," provided that his family could go with him. He was even willing to engage for a longer term than was called for in the existing contract. Morrison warned Beaumont that he did not think St. Martin would go unless his family went with him.[54]

52. Beaumont to Benjamin King, May 24, 1838, BC, WU.
53. Ibid.; also note from Woodhouse Potter, n.d., note from Potter's wife, n.d., BC, WU.
54. William Morrison to Beaumont, April 26, 1837, BC, WU.

Fully occupied with his private practice and military duties, and unwilling to have St. Martin's family, Beaumont made no move to respond to Morrison's letter. But a few months later he was stirred to action by a letter from the American Physiological Society in Boston. This society had no connection with the later, more famous, society that was founded in New York in 1887. It was headed by William A. Alcott, and had been organized to promote vegetarianism, particularly the ideas of Sylvester Graham. The society expressed an interest in conducting experiments on St. Martin; presumably they hoped to produce results that would modify or reverse Beaumont's conclusion that meat was easier to digest than vegetables.[55]

Beaumont may not have known the membership or objects of this American Physiological Society, but he reacted in his normal manner at the prospect that St. Martin might be experimented upon by any other researchers. He quickly tried to convince the society that this would only be possible with his cooperation. St. Martin, he wrote, if not on his way to join Beaumont for the renewal of experiments, was in Lower Canada. He was under contract, said Beaumont, but partly from his family situation, and perhaps more from "the natural obstinacy of his disposition and unwillingness to submit himself for public experiments," he had been reluctant to come to St. Louis. To convince the society that it could only act through him, he stated that St. Martin was now willing to join him and that he had made arrangements for St. Martin to come with his family. In reality, for a considerable time, the whole sticking point had been Beaumont's unwillingness to have St. Martin with his family.

To try to ensure that the society would not contact St. Martin directly, Beaumont stated that he presumed nothing would induce St. Martin to engage himself to the physiological society, or any other society, without Beaumont's personal participation. Beaumont said that he had always wanted to put St. Martin in some scientific physiological institution where more might be done in experiments than was possible for him to do, but St. Martin had always refused any such arrangement. His own object, said Beaumont, was to carry out experiments on St. Martin with some of the best physiological societies and scientific men in the West, until it was possible to go to Europe.[56]

---

55. See Stephen Nissenbaum, *Sex, Diet, and Debility in Jacksonian America: Sylvester Graham and Health Reform*, 14, 143–45; John Brobeck, Orr E. Reynolds, and Toby A. Appel, eds., *History of the American Physiological Society: The First Century, 1887–1897*, 11–13.

56. Beaumont to the American Physiological Society, August 29, 1837, BC, WU.

Beaumont, of course, had not agreed to bring St. Martin and his family to St. Louis–he was still trying to get St. Martin alone–but he was hoping that he could dissuade the American Physiological Society from acting alone to seek out St. Martin for research. Ultimately, he learned that this tactic did not work, for in the following summer he heard from St. Martin that he had been contacted by the society, and that they wanted to engage him for a term of from three to six months for experiments by an eminent physician. St. Martin said that he would not accept without Beaumont's approval, and that he would like to know whether Beaumont wanted him to come, or did he approve of the other offer. But then came the sticking point. St. Martin said that he was ready at any time to join Beaumont–if he could bring his family.

While Beaumont tried to dissuade other researchers from using St. Martin for research, there was truth in his assertion that St. Martin wanted Beaumont to conduct the experiments. St. Martin was used to Beaumont. He had known him since 1822, for long periods had been the subject of Beaumont's experiments, and had lived with and worked for his family. Although he was to live until 1880 and was to receive other offers, only once did he actually go to someone else, and that produced no real research.[57] Yet St. Martin kept dangling the possibility of going to others for experiments because he knew that this worried Beaumont, and he wanted to persuade Beaumont to let him bring his family to St. Louis.

In the following year, St. Martin's tactic almost worked. Beaumont, at last willing to concede that he might have to bring St. Martin with his family, decided to seek the help of his old friend Ramsay Crooks. In January 1839 he told Crooks that he was anxious to get St. Martin again, *"without* his family, if I can, but *with it* if I must."* If possible, he would have liked St. Martin to fulfill the terms of the two-year engagement he had signed in 1834, but if not, he said he was prepared to engage him on the best terms possible. Remarkably for Beaumont, he gave a modest blank check, saying that he authorized "any reasonable sum necessary" for St. Martin to leave his family in comfort or to bring them to St. Louis.[58] Beaumont obviously trusted Crooks.

Crooks commented to Hercules Dousman that he would with much pleasure exert himself to engage St. Martin "for our much esteemed friend Dr. Beaumont," and he went out of his way to try to meet Beaumont's wishes. He

57. In 1856, St. Martin toured in the United States with a charlatan who went by the name of Dr. G. T. Bunting. See Edward H. Bensley, "Alexis St. Martin and Dr. Bunting," 101–8.
58. Beaumont to Ramsay Crooks, January 23, 1839, BC, WU.

promptly contacted his agents in Canada, urging them to make every effort to secure St. Martin and telling them that St. Martin could be sent up country through the Lakes with one of the company's outfits.[59]

Once again plans to obtain St. Martin collapsed, partially because of St. Martin himself, but also because of Beaumont's fears of wasting money. Morrison was at first optimistic. He talked to St. Martin and his wife. They were very poor, and did not have the proper clothing for the trip, but they were willing to go with their three children to St. Louis. Morrison did not think it practical to send the whole family in the company's boats, but suggested that if Beaumont could send one hundred dollars he could arrange for them to travel through the Great Lakes via Cleveland.[60]

Another of Crooks's agents was less optimistic. He reported that the family was in a very poor situation, and that St. Martin was "a Drunkard." His wife said that no money could persuade her to stay in Canada without St. Martin, and that she wanted the family to go together by steamboat. This agent thought that one hundred dollars was not enough. They needed at least sixty dollars to rig them out, and the remaining forty dollars would not get them beyond Buffalo. In any case, he thought it a great risk to advance St. Martin even one hundred dollars; some of it he would probably use to get clothes for his family, but he would probably drink the rest. He recommended that one hundred dollars be provided to Morrison or another agent to take St. Martin and his family to Montreal, pay the fares, and get them on a boat. They could be provided with another sixty dollars on the way. Crooks concluded from all this that Beaumont would almost certainly lose any money he advanced, and that St. Martin was "utterly worthless," but that if Beaumont was determined to have him then arrangements would be made to send him through Cleveland.[61]

Morrison, who had the most regular contact with St. Martin, continued to believe that if Beaumont would send the money, he could arrange for St. Martin and his family to go, without putting any money directly into the

59. Ramsay Crooks to Hercules Dousman, March 25, 1839, to Messrs. Vallee, Boyer, & Co., March 27, 1839, to Clement Beaulieu, March 27, 1839, to William Morrison, March 30, 1839, in Henry D. Janowitz, "Newly Discovered Letters Concerning William Beaumont, Alexis St. Martin, and the American Fur Company," 824–27.

60. Morrison to Crooks, April 6, 1839, in Janowitz, "Newly Discovered Letters," 828–29; Morrison to Beaumont, April 9, 1839, BC, WU.

61. C. H. Beaulieu to Crooks, April 12, 1839, in Janowitz, "Newly Discovered Letters," 829–30; also Vallee, Boyer, & Co. to Crooks, April 26, 1839, Crooks to William Morrison, May 8, 1839, ibid., 831.

hands of St. Martin. The passage money would be paid in advance, and at Buffalo the agent there would send him on—"the same as baggage."[62]

This unfortunate phrase well reflects how those who dealt with St. Martin thought of him. In the 1830s there were no concerned thoughts about the psychological impact of a permanent gastric fistula on this Canadian voyageur, no concerns about the mental effects of repeated tampering with his normal process of digestion, nor even any particular concern about the destitute condition of his family. Crooks and Beaumont were practical men in an increasingly practical century. Beaumont's attitude toward St. Martin was probably as good as most. He had no concern about the ethics of his experiments, but no one else did either. He was not an unkind man, but as a physician he was a man of his age. He also had a personal attitude toward money that meant that when Morrison and Crooks suggested to him that St. Martin might be had, with his family, for an advance of $150, but that there was risk involved, the whole plan fell through. St. Martin did not come to St. Louis, and Beaumont devoted an increasing amount of time to his very lucrative practice.

From the time that Beaumont opened his private practice in St. Louis in 1835, his commitment to his military career began to wane. Never before had he practiced medicine in a sickly, booming, southern town, and for a man who liked money as much as Beaumont, the financial returns from his practice came as a wonderful revelation. This income also encouraged him to indulge more generally in land speculation. Correspondence about his investments in land, particularly after the problems created by the depression in 1837, occupied much of the time that he had left after working at his extensive private practice and his military duties.

Given the pace of his existence in St. Louis, there is good reason to doubt Beaumont's commitment to obtaining St. Martin and restarting his experiments. For the rest of his life, he was periodically to renew his efforts to bring the Canadian to St. Louis, but for a man who became quite well off, his reluctance to risk money on the endeavor went beyond even his normal parsimony. If he had been determined to renew his experiments, he had enough money that even a man of his caution could have risked a little. And it was a little. The sums mentioned usually did not exceed $150 to $200.

Beaumont continued desultory efforts to regain St. Martin, partially because he was still attracted by the fame that his first book had brought him,

62. William Morrison to Ramsay Crooks, May 15, 1839, ibid., 831.

and partially because he was anxious to keep others from sharing in the glory of his experiments. Finally, more than a decade later, when the elation brought on by the success of his practice in St. Louis wore off a little and when he began to feel that his life was slipping away, he became more genuinely interested in regaining St. Martin. He then had the hope of restoring some of his earlier enthusiasm and regaining some of the recognition he had received from his original series of experiments. For the time being, however, Beaumont was happy to be in St. Louis with a flourishing practice. He had no intention of resigning from his military position, because he liked the pay and he was not finding the duties particularly onerous. He thought he had enough seniority to stay where he was, and he had grown used to a service that met his desires. When that situation changed, Beaumont was to react with anger, but it was not to deflect him from pursuing his career in St. Louis.

The End of an Army Career

IN THE SPRING AND summer of 1837, Beaumont, like many others, suddenly realized that the boom conditions had collapsed. The financial panic that had begun in the East reached St. Louis by late spring, and it was to be more than five years before the West had a full recovery.[1] This made it more difficult to collect payment for medical services and threw the land market into considerable confusion, but Beaumont managed not only to stay solvent but also to continue his rise to greater prosperity. It did mean, however, that a good deal of the time that he had left from his private practice and his military duties was devoted to arrangements about his landholdings and the payments related to them.

In June 1837 Beaumont was informed that two one-thousand-dollar notes that he had used in partial payment to Daniel Whitney for property in Green Bay were now in other hands, and he was being asked for payment on the first of them. It had just become due. In these years, payment was often given in the form of staggered notes, payable at future dates, and the receiver often used the notes he received to meet other obligations of his own. While extremely careful with his money, Beaumont was usually meticulous in meeting his formal commitments. In this case, however, the note that was due went unpaid.[2]

1. Adler, *Yankee Merchants,* 33–35; Van Ravenswaay, *St. Louis,* 312–14; Smith, *James Duane Doty,* 209–10.
2. S. W. Beall to Beaumont, June 22, 1837, BC, WU.

In February 1838 the holder, S. W. Beall, wrote to him to say that he had "been mortified" not to have received any reply to two letters asking for payment, but said that he assumed because of Beaumont's "known character for correctness" that they had never reached him. The note that had been due for payment in the previous June had been transferred yet again, and was now in the hands of Beaumont's old friend Dr. Lyman Foot at Fort Winnebago. That Foot had accepted it in payment from Beall is an indication that Beaumont's reputation in such matters was good, for Foot knew Beaumont well.[3]

Beaumont told Beall that he was "equally mortified," and had a long explanation of why the note had not been paid. In essence, he claimed that he had made arrangements to pay the note at Green Bay at the appropriate time, but that the agent he sent to pay had not known where Beall had deposited the note for payment. There was no proper explanation of why this had not been straightened out after the return of Beaumont's agent to St. Louis, or why Beall's second letter had been ignored. Beaumont said he was making immediate arrangements to pay Dr. Foot, and he expressed the hope that Beall's belief in his ability to meet all his obligations promptly had not been weakened. Beall accepted the explanation, apologized to Beaumont, and reminded Beaumont that the second note was due in two months.[4]

Although Beaumont may have had temporary problems in raising funds, he was still financially sound, and much better off than a host of others who had speculated in the booming 1830s. If he did, as seems likely, intentionally defer paying his obligation to Beall, this in all likelihood stemmed from a similar problem he was experiencing in collecting money due to him. He had probably expected to pay the first Whitney note in part with money due to him from the land at Prairie du Chien that he had sold at a handsome paper profit in 1835. The purchaser, Henry Hamilton, speculated extensively in western land, but because of the depression he could not meet his obligations. Hamilton had been a friend of the Beaumonts, and Beaumont agreed to defer payments. He had no real choice. Correspondence on the matter passed back and forth for much of the next decade. Ultimately, in 1847, Hamilton simply transferred the property back to Beaumont, and forfeited the money already paid.[5]

3. S. W. Beall to Beaumont, February 13, 1838, BC, WU.

4. Beaumont to S. W. Beall, March 2, 1838, S. W. Beall to Beaumont, April 8, 1838, BC, WU.

5. These matters produced an extensive correspondence, including Beaumont to Henry Hamilton, August 12, 1837, January 9 and April 29, 1838, May 4, 1841, June

For the rest of his life, Beaumont employed agents to handle his landholdings and engaged in an extensive correspondence with them as well as with actual purchasers and sellers. His closest relationship on these matters was with Hercules Dousman of Prairie du Chien. Dousman, like most others, found himself severely pressed at this time, and in the fall of 1837 he was extremely pleased that Beaumont could oblige him in paying a note for eight hundred dollars that had become due. In the spring of 1838 he told Beaumont that he was "as poor as a *Church rat* as far as Rhino is concerned." The scarcity of money, he wrote, had stopped all speculation and improvements. Dousman was trying to collect rent for Beaumont on the property he still owned at Prairie du Chien, but the tenant was having difficulty making payments. Dousman offered to sue him if Beaumont wanted to, but said it would probably be little use.[6]

Beaumont weathered the financial storm. Although his hopes in Prairie du Chien were never realized, he continued to have solid investments in Green Bay, held on to other property throughout the region, and eventually made excellent investments in land in the St. Louis area. In an age of major land speculation, Beaumont's efforts were modest, but ultimately they were successful. In dealing in property, as in his other affairs, Beaumont was cautious and usually meticulous, and in these years of depression he had the great advantage of his successful practice. Payment was often slower, but the residents of St. Louis felt in desperate need of physicians. For most, it was a bill they paid when they could because they wanted to be able to get a physician when they needed one. In the late 1830s, the West was depressed, but in a time of depression, Beaumont's often excessive financial caution was an advantage, and he continued to prosper.

Since coming to St. Louis, Beaumont had been looking for suitable housing for his family, and in the winter of 1837–1838 he found it in a building owned by a prominent and aging St. Louis resident, William Clark. Clark had managed Indian affairs out of St. Louis, and in a building next to his home at the corner of Main and Vine Streets had a large council chamber as

30, 1842, August 31, 1847; Hamilton to Beaumont, May 20, 1839, February 24 and June 2, 1841, June 4, 1842, July 30 and September 11, 1847; Robert McPherson to Beaumont, April 14, 1839; Beaumont to McPherson, April 29, 1839; Beaumont to Hercules Dousman, September 26, 1847, BC, WU.

6. Hercules Dousman to Beaumont, September 6, 1837, Dousman to Beaumont, May 26, 1838 (quotation), May 22, 1839, Beaumont's account with Dousman, November 1838, BC, WU.

well as offices. The building was remodeled; the first floor into offices, the
second into apartments. The Beaumonts moved in, and for the time being
took their meals with Clark. When Clark moved out to live with his son in
February 1838, Beaumont rented the part of the house that he had occupied.[7]

In the following year, the Beaumont home became the center of a convivial
and distinguished circle. Their old friend Captain Ethan Allen Hitchcock had
been stationed in St. Louis since the previous year. He was a constant visitor,
and for a time in 1838 moved into the old Clark building. Hitchcock brought
a love of music and philosophical discussion to the Beaumont home, and
in the following years was treated as one of the family. Writing in February
1839 from Washington, D.C., Hitchcock commented in a note to Beaumont's
daughter Sarah that her letter had made him quite homesick, and that he
would not have slept "but for having written to the friends I most love
on earth."[8]

Having been brought up in the conviviality of her father's inn at Plattsburgh, Deborah Beaumont had always been happy to open her home to
young officers and a variety of other visitors. Soon after they moved into
the old Clark place, the family developed what became, at least by letter, a
lifelong friendship with young Robert E. Lee and his family. Lee at this time
was still a lieutenant—he was promoted to captain later in the year—and had
been sent to St. Louis in 1837 to improve the harbor. Because of changes in
the course of the Mississippi, there was a buildup of sandbars in the river.
At certain times it was difficult and even dangerous for boats to tie up at
St. Louis. As St. Louis had been made a port of entry, Congress in its 1836–
1837 session voted money to improve the situation, and St. Louis itself added
additional funds.[9]

In 1838 Lee decided to bring his family to St. Louis. They took rooms
with the Beaumonts in the old Clark building, and Mrs. Beaumont provided
their meals for them. They became great friends. Lee later had very happy
memories of his friendship with William Beaumont. His wife, Mary, who was
the daughter of Martha Washington's grandson, became a very close friend
to Deborah Beaumont and to her sixteen-year-old daughter Sarah. When she

7. Letter of James Kennerly, February 22, 1838, James Kennerly Papers, MHS; Van
Ravenswaay, *St. Louis,* 318–20; Pitcock, "The Career of William Beaumont," 117–18.
8. Ethan Hitchcock to Beaumont, February 1839, BC, WU.
9. See introduction to "Letters of Robert E. Lee to Henry Kayser," 1–3; Stella Drumm,
"Robert E. Lee and the Improvement of the Mississippi River," 157–71; Primm, *Lion of
the Valley,* 155–57; Douglas S. Freeman, *R. E. Lee: A Biography,* vol. 1, 138–48.

returned to Arlington in 1839, she sent a gift to Debby with the injunction that she was to wear it at "her *musical soirees*." She was still writing to Sarah Beaumont as late as 1870, when the happy days in St. Louis must have seemed an eternity away to the Lees. Lieutenant Lee's great fame was in the future, but with Hitchcock and Lee as close friends Beaumont could well feel he had come a long way since his days as a schoolteacher in Champlain, New York.[10]

In this last part of his life, as his children grew up, Beaumont inevitably found himself more often called upon to deal with their futures. He was very concerned about their education. Sarah had long been fascinated by music, and at sixteen was also studying French and German. His daughter Lucretia, eleven in 1838, was prone to illness, and temporarily lost her hair at this time after a bout of sickness. His son Israel (usually known as "Bud") was nine, and, like Sarah, was learning music and German. He became quite proficient in the latter, but Sarah was the musician in the family. As she grew up, Major Hitchcock was frequently to be found playing the flute to her piano accompaniment. Beaumont's enjoyment of this was limited by his increasing deafness. It was later remembered that, as his deafness became worse, he grasped the piano with his teeth to have a sense of his daughter's playing.[11]

As she matured, Sarah became somewhat of a problem for Beaumont. She was attractive, got on well with the men who came into the house, and from the age of fifteen began to receive proposals of marriage, usually from younger friends of her father, though it also became quite obvious that Captain Hitchcock, who was more than twenty years older than Sarah, was also smitten. In December 1837, Beaumont was taken aback when his old friend J. Henry Freligh left letters proposing marriage to Sarah. He was relieved that Freligh had approached him rather than Sarah, and tried to put him off. He said that his daughter needed more time, so that eventually she should make her own choice, "free from every passionate impulse or fashionable feeling of Romance & novelty."[12]

This proposal, and its rejection by Beaumont, did nothing to hurt the relations between the two men. Beaumont later endorsed a note for five hundred dollars for Freligh. For Beaumont, this indicated a considerable degree of trust and friendship. Freligh belonged to a Plattsburgh family that

10. Mary Lee to Sarah Beaumont, [1839], September 23, 1870, Robert E. Lee and Mary R. Lee Letters, Bancroft Library, University of California–Berkeley.

11. See ibid., May 31, [1839], December 17, 1839, November 5, 1840; Myer, *Beaumont*, 268.

12. Beaumont to J. Henry Freligh, December 26, 1837, BC, WU.

Beaumont had lodged with in his War of 1812 days, and a Freligh had written to tell the Beaumont family and Beaumont himself of his brother Samuel's death.[13]

A year later Beaumont received another proposal for his daughter Sarah, this time from the old family friend Captain Joseph LaMotte, now serving in Florida. A letter of proposal to Sarah was enclosed in a letter to Beaumont. LaMotte told him to dispose of it as he thought best. Beaumont did not tell Sarah of the proposal, and asked LaMotte if he did not think he was taking too great a risk. Referring to his daughter as a "child," Beaumont wrote that she was young, with her character and disposition perhaps not yet sufficiently developed for judgment. In several months, because he was not entirely clear whether or not Beaumont had handed his proposal to Sarah, LaMotte sent another letter through Beaumont. This time Beaumont simply let six months pass by without answering.[14]

St. Louis continued to be an ideal location for a doctor whose name was known. The dramatic population growth only served to increase the unhealthiness for which the city was renowned, and the city authorities had done little to ease problems connected with public health. A summer visitor in 1838 was appalled at the heat and the dirt. "The lower part of the town is badly drained, and very filthy," he wrote, and he found flies everywhere. A German immigrant who first came to St. Louis in the hot summer months wrote of "sickness, death, and burial" as the constant themes of conversation. The town was more livable in the fall, but its reputation for unhealthiness was justified.[15] Within two or three years of arriving in St. Louis, the expansion of Beaumont's private practice was only limited by the time he could devote to it. His army duties were now only a minor part of his total responsibilities.

Beaumont had never lacked confidence, but his feelings of self-worth were enhanced in these years by not only his private success and the financial rewards it was bringing but also the realization that his research and his book had given him an international reputation. In 1838 the famous British physiologist, Andrew Combe, brought out a British edition of the book. Combe had commented very favorably on Beaumont's work in his own book on the

13. John G. Freligh to Samuel Beaumont Sr., December 10, 1813, BP, YU; J. Henry Freligh to Beaumont, July 11, 1839, January 27, 1840, BC, WU.

14. Joseph LaMotte to Beaumont, December 18, 1838, May 13 and November 11, 1839, Beaumont to LaMotte, February 21 and December 8, 1839, BC, WU.

15. Frederick Marryat, *Diary in America*, 253–57. The German immigrant is quoted in William E. Lass, "Tourists' Impressions of St. Louis, 1766–1859," 10.

physiology of digestion, and in writing to Beaumont told him that he held him in "high estimation."[16]

The Combe edition was the type of recognition that Beaumont had so anxiously sought and hoped for. In his preface, Combe wrote that he was reprinting Beaumont's work because of a "strong sense of its inherent importance." It was valuable, he wrote, not only for the opportunities for observation that Beaumont enjoyed but also because of "the candid and truth seeking spirit in which all his inquiries seem to have been conducted." Combe said of Beaumont that it would be "difficult to point out any observer who excels him in devotion to truth, and freedom from the trammels of theory or prejudice." Although he also stated that Beaumont did not conduct his researches with the systematic approach that might have been adopted by one of the "disciplined physiologists" of Europe, he softened even that criticism by arguing that this was more than made up for by "the implicit reliance which one feels can be placed on the accuracy and candour of his statements." He stated that Beaumont presented his conclusions with a "modesty and fairness" that few in his circumstances could have had.[17]

Combe agreed with others that Beaumont had made no original discoveries, and said that his lack of writing experience had prevented him from making the most of his materials, but he insisted that Beaumont had done what was equally important—he had separated truth from the numerous errors with which it was entangled. Even in commenting on the fact that very few copies of Beaumont's book had reached Great Britain, Combe testified to its influence. He wrote that "everywhere both in British and foreign books, we meet with reference to it."[18] This was the type of recognition that kept alive Beaumont's interest in the possibility of additional work with St. Martin, but he could never bring himself to set aside either the time or the money to make it possible.

To meet all the demands on his time was becoming an increasing problem for Beaumont. His army duties had to be fitted into an increasingly complex schedule. These duties were not particularly onerous, but they took time he could ill afford. He was still involved in the medical treatment of army officers

16. Andrew Combe to Beaumont, May 1, 1838, William Combe to Beaumont, March 18, 1839, Beaumont to William Combe, April 18, 1839, BC, WU; Myer, *Beaumont,* 246; Poynter, "Reception of Beaumont's Discovery in England," 511–12.

17. Beaumont, *Experiments and Observations,* reprinted with notes by Andrew Combe, v–vii.

18. Ibid., vii–xiii.

and their families in St. Louis, the examining of recruits, the purchasing of medical supplies for the western area, and the filing of regular reports on all of these activities, together with the other reports required by the army on a regular basis.

Beaumont very much needed a partner for his private practice, and he regularly received offers from doctors settling in St. Louis, but he was still very reluctant to share his practice. He wanted complete control of his own affairs, and he did not want to divide his profits. In reply to an offer of partnership from Dr. James Sykes in September 1837, he stated, "I am, & ever have been averse to professional copartnerships." But in the early months of 1839 Beaumont, almost overwhelmed by his hectic life in St. Louis, decided to take Dr. Sykes as a partner. In the same month he turned down two other offers of partnerships.[19] The Sykes partnership was to end, like his other medical partnerships, in acrimony, but in this case the partnership also began in controversy.

On March 19, 1839, an advertisement in the *Missouri Republican* announced that Drs. Beaumont and Sykes had formed a partnership, and that they would engage in all branches of "physic and surgery." It also asserted that Dr. Sykes, "having had much experience and success in ophthalmic surgery, will be able to afford effectual relief in most cases of the eye." Such advertisements often appeared in the newspapers in these years, but this one drove deep rifts into the St. Louis medical community.[20]

In the 1830s and 1840s, physicians in communities throughout the United States began to make strong attempts to enhance their prestige and exercise some control over the practice of medicine through formal organizations. Formal attempts in St. Louis began in the mid-1830s. The "regular" physicians made determined efforts to resist the growth of what they considered to be unorthodox medicine. Various forms of botanical medicine had long flourished on a popular level, and under the system of Thomsonianism made great inroads in these years. Homeopathic medicine did not reach St. Louis

19. Beaumont to James Sykes, September 25, 1837 (quotation), Dr. Wills de Hass to Beaumont, March 15, 1839, J. B. McDowell to Beaumont, March 13, 1839, BC, WU.

20. *Missouri Republican,* March 19, 1839. The fullest published account of this affair is Cynthia De Haven Pitcock, "Doctors in Controversy: An Ethical Dispute between Joseph Nash McDowell and William Beaumont." The basic source is the Minutes of the Medical Society of Missouri at St. Louis, in the library of the St. Louis Metropolitan Medical Society, St. Louis, Missouri. My account differs in a number of details from that of Dr. Pitcock.

in any formal sense until the 1840s, but many of the physicians who came to the town had no regular credentials. Of the 146 physicians in St. Louis in 1845, about one-third, including Beaumont himself, did not have medical school diplomas.[21]

The first formal St. Louis Medical Society was organized in 1835–1836. In January 1837 the society was incorporated by the Missouri legislature as the Medical Society of the State of Missouri. In reality, it functioned as the Medical Society of St. Louis, and a regular state medical society did not begin to function until the 1850s. Beaumont was active in the early years of the society, very briefly served as vice president (before resigning), and became chairman of the society's membership committee. This was a sensitive position; resentments were inevitable when practicing physicians were denied admission. Also, Beaumont himself, though he had achieved considerable fame from his research and book, had limited formal credentials. He had attended no medical school, had been certified by a medical society in Vermont, and had been given an honorary degree by the Columbian College of Washington, D.C. Beaumont, however, had very firm views on who was, and who was not, competent, and he had never been afraid to act on his conclusions.[22]

It seems extremely likely that Beaumont's usual outspokenness had already brought him enemies among the St. Louis physicians, and some of them decided to attack as inappropriate the advertisement that Beaumont and Sykes had placed in the *Missouri Republican*. Such advertisements were common, but the society was trying to regulate them. One of the society's bylaws stated that no member would announce by publication in a newspaper "his pretensions to superior qualifications." The assertion in the advertisement regarding Sykes's success in ophthalmic surgery appeared to violate that rule.

A committee was appointed to consider the appropriateness of the Beaumont-Sykes advertisement, and at a meeting in April 1839 Dr. Franklin Knox reported that the advertisement violated the bylaws of the society. A member

21. Kett, *Formation of the American Medical Profession*, 97–142; Rothstein, *American Physicians*, 125–74; M. A. Goldstein, ed., *One Hundred Years of Medicine and Surgery in St. Louis*, 133–35; Cassedy, *Medicine and American Growth*, 232–33n (St. Louis figures).

22. Minutes of the Medical Society; Pitcock, "Doctors in Controversy," 336–39; J. Thomas Scharf, *History of St. Louis City and County*, vol. 2, 1542; Goodwin, *History of Medicine in Missouri*, 123; Goldstein, ed., *One Hundred Years*, 127–28; Myer, *Beaumont*, 272–74.

commented that formal acceptance of the report would virtually expel Beaumont and Sykes, who were not present, from the society. A debate followed, and the report was temporarily tabled, but it was stated that Beaumont and Sykes were to be informed that the committee had concluded that their advertisement was an infraction of the rules.[23]

At the May meeting, a heated discussion took place. Both Beaumont and Sykes vigorously defended their advertisement; Beaumont commented that he was unaccustomed to defending himself "against charges of unprofessional conduct," and Sykes spoke so heatedly that he was declared out of order. Dr. Franklin Knox, who had led the attack on the partners, had to defend himself, because Beaumont counterattacked by asserting that it was not their newspaper advertisement but one placed by Knox that violated the laws of the society. The meeting ended with a motion that Beaumont and Sykes "be respectfully requested" to withdraw their advertisement.[24]

Even after the May meeting, the whole affair became still more complicated, and still further divided the St. Louis medical establishment. On the day after the initial discussion of the committee report on the Beaumont and Sykes advertisement, the recording secretary, Dr. Jonathan B. McDowell, had talked to Beaumont and Sykes and shown them his rough minutes of the meeting. He told them that Drs. Stephen Adreon and E. Y. Watson had wanted to expel them, and that he (McDowell) had helped to prevent this. Adreon and Watson denied this report, and Beaumont and Sykes insisted that the five of them should meet to resolve the discrepancies. They met, but McDowell, Adreon, and Watson could not agree on what their original stances had been, and the whole matter again came before the society in June and July. McDowell got the worst of it. When, at the July meeting, the society resolved that the conduct of Dr. McDowell "has been highly reprehensible" and that Beaumont and Sykes had not been guilty of any "dishonourable conduct" toward McDowell, he resigned and left the meeting.[25]

The regular St. Louis physicians were still divided from the irregulars, but they were also bitterly divided among themselves. This situation persisted throughout the 1840s, and Beaumont continued to be at the heart of it.

Deeply immersed in the St. Louis scene, with a flourishing private practice and international respect, many men would have taken steps to resign from the army medical service, but Beaumont was not only a man of great energy

23. Minutes of the Medical Society.
24. Ibid.
25. Ibid.; Nelson, *Beaumont*, 260, 264, 362.

but also a man who craved financial security at least as much as he desired status. Temporarily, his situation did not require any decision on his part because of the absence of the new Surgeon General Thomas Lawson, but this situation changed in 1838 after Lawson had established himself in his Washington office.

In his early experience, and in his quickness to take offense, Lawson was not unlike Beaumont himself. Nothing is known about his medical education. It must have been extremely limited, as he joined the navy as a surgeon's mate at the age of nineteen. He had transferred to the army before the War of 1812, and Beaumont knew him during the war. At that time they apparently got on well, and Lawson gave his support to Beaumont in one of his early feuds. He was retained in the army medical service after the War of 1812, but came to resent what he regarded as prejudicial treatment. Like Beaumont, he spent much of his time in western posts; also like Beaumont, he was very apt to get into bitter disputes; but unlike Beaumont, he felt that Surgeon General Lovell neglected his interests. He wrote to Lovell at great length to protest what he regarded as favoritism to others, and his own neglect. Mary Gillett has described Lawson as a cantankerous, suspicious sort and has also stated that his "talents were small, his sensitivity to criticism and frustration great." Lawson had spent much of his career resenting the way he was treated and protesting bitterly to the surgeon general. When he assumed office, he quarreled with his own subordinates, as he had previously quarreled with the surgeon general.[26]

After Lawson returned to Washington in 1838, Beaumont eventually became disturbed by rumors that Lawson had been questioning his position in St. Louis and was considering transferring him. When Hitchcock, now a major, went to Washington in the winter of 1838–1839, Beaumont asked him to find out if there was any truth to these rumors. Hitchcock consulted with Lee, who was also in Washington, and concluded there was not the slightest indication of Lawson's ordering a change in Beaumont's station.[27]

Reassured by this news, Beaumont wrote a formal letter to the adjutant general requesting a leave of six weeks in May and June to travel to Green Bay "on some important business of a private nature." Beaumont could use the opportunity to discuss his Green Bay investments with his brother-in-law Thomas Green and his friends Daniel Whitney and Morgan Martin, but

26. Gillett, "Thomas Lawson," 15–19, 24 (quotation); Gillett, *Army Medical Department, 1818–1865*, 33, 53–80.
27. Ethan Hitchcock to Beaumont, February 4, 1839, BC, UC.

a visit to Green Bay was also a family affair; his wife and children wanted to see their Green Bay relatives and friends.[28]

In a covering letter to Surgeon General Lawson, Beaumont wrote as he had become accustomed to writing to his old friend Lovell. He said that if the application met Lawson's approval, he would appreciate it if it could be granted as soon as possible. The public interest would not suffer, he wrote, because a citizen surgeon could easily be employed to perform his official duties during his absence. He even suggested that if it were considered expedient to order a tour of inspection of military hospitals in the region, he could make his journey at the public expense. Beaumont had grown used to writing confident letters to the surgeon general, and this was a confident letter.[29]

Lovell would have replied as a friend and supporter, but Lawson simply replied as a superior who wanted to curb such requests. Beaumont had asked Hitchcock to see Lawson to ask about the leave, and Hitchcock's report was that Lawson had said he could go, but that Beaumont would have to pay the expenses. He also said that Lawson had expressed the opinion that Beaumont should not be stationed in St. Louis but at the Jefferson Barracks.[30] The formal reply from Lawson did not mention Jefferson Barracks, but stated that as similar requests from officers having much stronger claims than those of Beaumont had been denied, his request could not be granted. Lawson did, however, state that if Beaumont's private interests required his presence at Green Bay, and Beaumont would pay the costs of employing a physician to fill in for him, he could go, provided he could get the permission of his commanding general.[31]

With his usual willingness to meet a problem head on, Beaumont now wrote a long, complaining letter to Lawson, attempting to convince him that he was wrong. He would probably have had trouble with Lawson even if he had attempted to be diplomatic, but tact was not Beaumont's strong suit. He chose to fire a broadside at the new surgeon general. He said that the conditions attached to granting the leave—that he should pay for a replacement—disturbed him not so much for the money, but for Lawson's

28. Beaumont to the adjutant general, March 11, 1839, WD, AG, IMOF; Thomas Green to Beaumont, April 23, 1839, BC, WU; Mary Lee to Sarah Beaumont, May 31, 1839, Lee Letters.

29. Beaumont to Thomas Lawson, March 11, 1839, WD, AG, IMOF.

30. Ethan Hitchcock to Beaumont, March 27, 1839, BC, UC.

31. Thomas Lawson to Beaumont, March 27, 1839, BC, WU.

apparent view that he was not entitled to such consideration. If the duties of army officers were so demanding that his request for a replacement could not be met, he wrote, then the army needed more medical officers. If Lawson would not reconsider his decision, wrote Beaumont, he might be compelled to pay for a replacement.[32]

These rather naive comments of Beaumont's infuriated Lawson, because the need for more medical officers had indeed become pressing due to the war against the Seminoles in Florida, and Lawson was keen to use every medical officer he could on that service. He had asked for more medical officers, but in 1838 Congress had only approved an additional seven. To meet the pressing demands for medical officers, Lawson was granting leave only for illness in the case of those officers who had been long on active duty.[33]

Beaumont further maddened Lawson, at a time when many medical officers were in the field in Florida, by complaining that he might have to move ten miles outside St. Louis to Jefferson Barracks. St. Louis itself, wrote Beaumont, was far more appropriate for his location than Jefferson Barracks. At the Barracks, he argued, there was only the commanding general and his family, an occasional handful of recruits, and a few old soldiers, with nothing to do but preserve their health. They spent much of their time in St. Louis, where they had Beaumont's advice and treatment. In St. Louis, said Beaumont, there were six or seven army officers and their families, a recruiting rendezvous, the arsenal with thirty men together with women and children, plus various other army officers, supernumeraries, and transients. Along with treating all these, said Beaumont, he had the duty of being medical purveyor for the western division. His official duties in St. Louis, he wrote, "were constant & multifarious, and *ten times* more important" than any possible service at Jefferson Barracks.

The argument that his official duties in St. Louis were constant was hardly likely to carry much weight with a surgeon general who had undoubtedly heard of Beaumont's extensive private practice, but Beaumont compounded his problems by questioning Lawson's motives. He said it was impossible to conceive the necessity or the propriety of ordering him to any other post or station, unless the object was to force him either to make great sacrifices of interest and inclination, or resign from the army. He said that he could not

32. Beaumont to Lawson, April 14, 1839, WD, AG, IMOF.
33. Gillett, *Army Medical Department, 1818–1865*, 74.

seriously anticipate any order to remove from St. Louis, even though some envious or discontented junior would be happy to see him moved.

To add to the irritation of a surgeon general who was very easily irritated, Beaumont made no bones about his regard for his own abilities. "For any professional advantages I may be supposed to enjoy here," he wrote, "I am not indebted to the Government, but to my own character & exertions." Such advantages were not simply incidental to the station, but were "the fruits of toil, I am sure, if not talent." Another appointee to the station, he wrote, might not do as well.[34]

Beaumont had replied not to an order to move, but simply to the denial of his request that he be given a leave for private purposes with an official temporary replacement paid by the government, and to Hitchcock's report that Lawson thought he should be at Jefferson Barracks. He was right in assuming that Lawson believed he had been granted far too many special privileges, and he was certainly writing to a surgeon general who often dealt in a petty and quarrelsome manner with his subordinates, but in this letter Beaumont was simply daring Lawson to act. So far, Lawson, whatever his thoughts, had not been particularly unreasonable, but he now received a letter that he could only interpret as a challenge to his authority.

For the time being, Lawson kept his silence and left Beaumont in doubt as to his intentions. Unsurprisingly, Beaumont did not follow through on his "threat" to request a leave from his commanding general and pay for a replacement himself. But to his old friend Benjamin King he wrote a letter that contradicted some of his statements concerning the constant nature of his official duties that he had made to Lawson. In August, he told King that he was "in full run of successful & lucrative professional practice in this city," and that he was too constantly engaged in his profession to enjoy his friends or the pleasures of domestic life. His official duties, he said, though as important here as at any other station, were only a small part of his labors. He was presumably confident that his friend would not let Lawson know that most of his work was private.

Beaumont had begun to hear rumors that it was not a move to Jefferson Barracks that he had to fear, but an order to report to the scene of action in Florida. He told King that he did not believe this, but it seemed more a hope than a belief, for he added the unlikely statement that he had too much confidence in the judgment of the surgeon general to think that he would

34. Beaumont to Lawson, April 14, 1839, WD, AG, IMOF.

be moved unless there was some far more pressing need. He said that he expected to retain the St. Louis posting as long as the government saw fit to maintain a station there. In sending his respects to the surgeon general, he expressed the hope that Lawson would leave him quietly where he was. He was getting "too old and infirm, or too indolent and selfish," he wrote, to be ordered away while there were so many juniors requiring active field duty to complete their professional qualifications.[35]

This letter to King was a strange mixture. Beaumont admitted that the great part of his time was devoted to his private practice, but insisted that the amount of official work he had to perform was as much as at any other post. He had, of course, not served in the field since the War of 1812. His confidence that he could keep the St. Louis post indefinitely stemmed partially from the way he had become accustomed to support from Lovell, from his seniority, and from his knowledge that some very senior medical officers had been allowed to retain desirable postings indefinitely; the best known being Dr. Thomas G. Mower in New York.

There had long been difficulties and complaints regarding the assignment of stations for surgeons, but it had become usual for those with seniority to establish themselves in desirable posts. In 1833 the secretary of war had stated as policy that surgeons and assistant surgeons should have choice of stations agreeable to time in rank, but that no surgeon or assistant surgeon would be transferred from an assigned post to make way for another.[36]

This policy had not always sat well in this Jacksonian era, when the principle of rotation in office had been introduced into the political arena. In 1835, considerable political pressure had been brought to bear by friends of Assistant Surgeon Alfred W. Elwes in an attempt to replace Mower, who had been stationed in New York for a dozen years. Elwes and his friends argued that Mower had served in a comfortable station while Elwes had spent most of ten years in "sickly stations." On Lovell's recommendation, the secretary of war rejected this request, and the decision was held to even after New York politicians petitioned the president. It had been emphasized by Lovell that Mower was the second-ranked surgeon, while Elwes was the thirteenth-ranked assistant surgeon.[37]

35. Beaumont to Benjamin King, August 15, 1839, BC, WU.
36. Lovell to Beaumont, October 18, 1833, BC, WU.
37. See Alfred W. Elwes to the secretary of war, January 15, 1835, (with notations by Joseph Lovell), John McKean to the secretary of war, January 20, 1835, secretary of war to John McKean, January 31, 1835, to A. W. Elwes, February 4, 1835, to Winfield

Given his long service and the army attitude to seniority, Beaumont could well have thought that he was to be in St. Louis indefinitely. What he had not counted on was the death of Lovell, the peculiar situation created by the Seminole War, and the appointment of a resentful new surgeon general. Beaumont had challenged Lawson at a time when Lawson could justify moving an experienced surgeon to Florida.

In October, Beaumont's worst fears came true. He was ordered to Fort Brooke, Florida, as part of a medical board to examine surgeons and assistant surgeons. When that duty was completed, he was to report to the commanding general in Florida for assignment. Beaumont was determined not to leave St. Louis, and took the position that if the order stood he would resign. This was not as simple as it seemed. As he was now under orders, he could not resign from the army until he had obeyed the order. Beaumont was informed by Lawson that the secretary of war had decided that "you shall obey the order directing you to Florida, before he will take into consideration the tender of your resignation."[38]

Writing from Virginia at this time, Mary Lee revealed how Beaumont's friends viewed this situation. "I hear your father has been ordered to Florida," she wrote his daughter Sarah, "but suppose of course he will not go as his situation in St. Louis renders him very independent of the Army." That, of course, was the very situation that Lawson objected to. Major Hitchcock, who was in Washington, commiserated with Beaumont, and said it was "all wrong, but it appears beyond remedy." The army, he wrote, had driven out "the best surgeon," for false reasons. His view was that the army should encourage its medical officers to obtain a private practice, for experience was everything, and a large private practice conveyed honor on the service.[39]

Throughout November and into December the situation stayed on hold as Beaumont continued to perform his official duties in St. Louis and submitted his regular reports to Washington, but in the latter month Beaumont's worries temporarily increased because he heard rumors that he was to be dismissed from the service for not obeying the order to proceed to Florida. He now

Scott, February 19, 1835, Memorial to the secretary of war, February 12, 1835, Winfield Scott to the secretary of war, February 19, 1835, Joseph Lovell to the secretary of war, February 21, 1835, BC, WU.

38. General Order #48, September 18, 1839, BC, WU; adjutant general to Beaumont, October 25, 1839, Thomas Lawson to Beaumont, October 26, 1839, BC, WU.

39. Mary Lee to Sarah Beaumont, October 28, 1839, Lee Letters; for letter from Hitchcock, see Myer, *Beaumont*, 256.

realized that rather than waiting for the rescinding of the order, his only hope was that he would be allowed to resign rather than be dismissed. After twenty years of service, he told the adjutant general, he should be allowed to resign, and said he could not believe that "such injustice" as dismissal could be contemplated.[40]

In Washington, Captain Lee tried to find out all he could for his friend in St. Louis. He had a long talk with King, and also called on the surgeon general. Lee's opinion was that the latest crisis had arisen because of the determination of the secretary of war not to allow an officer to resign in order to avoid carrying out an order. His conclusion was that he believed Beaumont's resignation would be accepted to avoid having to dismiss him.[41]

Lee was right. Even before Lee had written, a letter was on the way accepting Beaumont's resignation. His long service, his war record, the increasing fame of his book, all undoubtedly played a part in the decision to ignore his refusal to obey an order. On January 20, 1840, he was informed that his resignation had been accepted, to take effect as of December 31, 1839. In replying, Beaumont was still angry. He referred to "the unexpected & ungrateful acceptance of my resignation," which he said was "a most noble recompense magnanimously awarded to an old officer for duties efficiently performed & a life faithfully spent in the Service of his country."[42]

It should have ended there. Beaumont had been allowed to withdraw semigracefully, and he could now devote even more time to his successful private practice, but, as ever, Beaumont was concerned for his reputation and for his income. Immediately after he heard that his resignation had been accepted, he wrote to Senator Lewis Linn of Missouri, asking him to try to prevent any action of the Senate to fill the vacancy he was creating until he had time to petition the president to be restored to it.[43]

Beaumont petitioned President Martin Van Buren to the effect that at the age of fifty-six, and after twenty-four years of service, he had been "unjustly thrust" from the public service. He asked to be restored to his rank and to his St. Louis post, and listed his services—from the War of 1812 to the Black

40. William Lewis to Beaumont, November 2, 1839, Thomas Lawson to Beaumont, November 7 and December 14, 1839, Beaumont to the adjutant general, December 20, 1839, BC, WU.

41. Robert E. Lee to Sarah Beaumont, January 21, 1840, Lee Letters. See also Hitchcock to Beaumont, January 21, 1840, BC, UC.

42. General Order #2, January 20, 1840, Beaumont to the adjutant general, February 20, 1840, BC, WU.

43. Beaumont to L. F. Linn, February 3 and 5, 1840, BC, WU.

Hawk War. He also wrote of his research on St. Martin, stating that one of the reasons he had been assigned to St. Louis early in 1835 had been to carry out further experiments. He claimed that when Surgeon General Lovell and Secretary of War Lewis Cass had assigned him to St. Louis, it was with the express understanding that the posting was to be permanent, in the same manner as other senior medical officers had been allowed permanent posts as a reward for long and faithful service. He cited a list of such officers, including Mower at New York and King in Washington, D.C. Beaumont also claimed that he had to decline the order to perform a service that he could not perform "because of my well-known infirmity and defect." This was a reference to his increasing deafness. It could be pointed out that it had not prevented him from building up an extensive private practice.[44]

Beaumont tried to enlist political support, but it was all to no avail. In a few months, his friends Lee and Hitchcock advised him that any further appeals would be useless. Lee said that as far as he could learn his memorial to the president had never reached the War Department. If the president did send it there, wrote Lee, it would be referred to Surgeon General Lawson for a report, and in Lee's opinion Lawson not only would not recommend reinstatement but he might well oppose it. Lee told Beaumont that he had tried to impress the adjutant general with the great loss the service would sustain by Beaumont's departure, but Lee said he could do no more. He was not even certain that Beaumont's petition had ever been presented to the president. Lee also reported that Hitchcock, after a visit to the surgeon general, was certain that nothing could be done.[45]

Hitchcock confirmed Lee's opinion. Nothing more could be done, he wrote, because "Lawson will have his own way," and the secretary of war would not take time to revise Lawson's opinion. Hitchcock was a very close friend, and could be quite candid. "I think your re-entering the army is next to impossible," he wrote, "& on this account I almost hope you will give up the thought of it."[46]

Yet Beaumont was waging one other last futile struggle with the army. When it was decided to accept Beaumont's resignation, Surgeon Samuel DeCamp, who was stationed at Jefferson Barracks, was ordered to assume

44. Memorial to Martin Van Buren, [c. February 1840]. This is printed in Myer, *Beaumont*, 258–60.
45. Beaumont to Silas Wright, February 1840, BC, WU; Robert E. Lee to Beaumont, May 19, 1840, in Myer, *Beaumont*, 260–61.
46. Hitchcock to Beaumont, May 28, 1840, BC, WU.

Beaumont's duties in St. Louis as well as his own. As he was ten miles away, and as Beaumont was still hoping to be reinstated, Beaumont continued to perform many of his official duties. This went on through the summer of 1840, although Hitchcock warned him in May that there was no chance that he would receive his regular pay for his services. Hitchcock said that he thought Beaumont's only chance for payment was to charge individual officers and their families in his private capacity, and then have the individual officers obtain recompense for him by submitting an official request.[47]

Beaumont in the spring and summer tried to build up support for his case by having officers sign a statement that he had continued to perform his official duties. As early as April 1, 1840, he wrote up a statement claiming that the government owed him $576.86, primarily for his pay in 1840. He also continued to file reports to the Surgeon General's Office. Surgeon General Lawson's position, a sound one, was that Beaumont had ceased to belong to the army medical service on December 31, 1839, and even suggested that if Beaumont claimed that he had been performing Surgeon DeCamp's duties then DeCamp should pay him. This suggestion inspired Beaumont to draw up a position paper, which he may never have sent, referring to Lawson's "narrow mind," vindictiveness, and tyrannical disposition.[48]

Though now making about ten thousand dollars a year from his practice, Beaumont was also engaged in another skirmish with the treasury department regarding a sum of $6.96 which he had been charged for forage for an additional horse he had kept in July 1839. As late as April 1840, Beaumont was still arguing about this $6.96. "I know my rights & privileges," he wrote to the second auditor of the treasury, "& knowing shall endeavor to maintain them." He also stated that he was "the correct keeper" of his own accounts, and *"comptroller* of my own conscience."[49]

Any hopes that Beaumont might have had that he would be paid for his work in 1840 ended in November, when Lawson informed him that his accounts for the first months of the year, submitted in the previous April, had been denied by the secretary of war. As Beaumont had no authority for rendering any official service to anyone after his resignation had been

47. Beaumont to Lawson, April 1, 1840, draft statement regarding Surgeon DeCamp, draft statement to War Department (unsent), Ethan Hitchcock to Beaumont, May 28, 1840, Beaumont to DeCamp, September 10, 1840, BC, WU.

48. Draft memo [1840], Lawson to Beaumont, November 4, 1840, BC, WU.

49. Beaumont to Joseph LaMotte, December 8, 1839, William Lewis to Beaumont, October 9, 1839, Beaumont to the Second Auditor, April 20, 1840, BC, WU.

accepted, he would have to seek compensation from individuals, not from the government. He would be paid only for the period between December 31 and the time that he received notice that his resignation had been accepted.[50]

For many years, Beaumont had served the army well, but encouraged by Lovell, he had become far too confident of receiving special concessions from the surgeon general. Moreover, since 1833 he had given most of his energy to non-army tasks—first in bringing out his book, and then, in St. Louis, in establishing a large, successful practice. He had also become absorbed in the possibilities of making money through investing in land and property. In essence, he had acted as though he were a private individual who also performed some duties for the army.

If Beaumont had been less eager to squeeze every penny that he could find, then he might have realized that the time had come for him to leave the army medical service before Lawson forced his hand. But Beaumont hated to give up a very steady source of income, and he believed that his long service since 1812 entitled him to very special consideration. This belief was undoubtedly increased by Congress's denial of his petition for reimbursement for his research. Beaumont was a hard-working, meticulous surgeon who for years had probably performed his army duties more conscientiously than most surgeons, but in his last years in the service he had become increasingly used to accepting special perquisites as his right. When he ran into an equally opinionated surgeon general of limited vision, he met his match. Lovell would probably have arranged to keep Beaumont in St. Louis indefinitely, and would have been happy that he was doing so well in private practice, because he liked him and because Lovell was a physician with broad interests as well as the surgeon general. Lawson was very much an army man. Given the characters of Beaumont and Lawson, it was not surprising that their encounter should have ended in such bitterness and acrimony.

Now that he was out of the army, Beaumont, of course, had no intention of leaving St. Louis. His objection to Florida had not simply been an objection to an undesirable posting. He had decided to spend the rest of his life in St. Louis. The town had every advantage for him. The year after his resignation became official, Mary Lee commented in a letter to Sarah Beaumont, "I suppose now your Father has resigned you are fixed at St. Louis for life."[51] She was right. Beaumont settled down as a successful private St. Louis physician, still

50. Lawson to Beaumont, November 4, 1840, BC, WU.
51. Mary Lee to Sarah Beaumont, July 6, 1841, Lee Letters.

occasionally hoping that he could resume his research on St. Martin, devoting most of his energies to making money and to his family, but still with a propensity to engage in public quarrels. He showed few signs of mellowing until his last years.

ELEVEN

Private Practice and Controversy

IN THE SPRING OF 1840, when Beaumont was still hoping that somehow he could win back his position in the army medical service and was trying all possible maneuvers to achieve that end, he became involved in a St. Louis case that was to cause him considerable difficulty. On June 1 he was called to give his opinion on a man who had been beaten on the head in a public street. His decision to treat the case with a trephining operation became the focal point of a celebrated St. Louis trial. In this trial Beaumont's professional judgment, and even his work on St. Martin, was questioned in open court and in the public press.

The Darnes-Davis case, in which the owner of the *Missouri Argus,* Andrew Jackson Davis, was attacked on the street by a prominent local politician, William P. Darnes, had its origin in bitter political infighting among the St. Louis Democrats. The St. Louis Democrats were split on the question of whether the problems of the depression should be tackled by the creation of a third national bank. Under its editor, William Gilpin, the *Argus* virulently attacked those Democrats who supported the creation of the bank. Darnes was a leader in the pro-bank group, and received considerable personal abuse in the columns of the *Argus.* Davis and Darnes had once been friends and allies, but now Darnes blamed Davis for the abuse he was suffering from the articles in the newspaper.[1]

---

1. For the Darnes-Davis case, see Thomas S. Nelson, ed., *A Full and Accurate Report of the Trial of William P. Darnes,* and the reports in the *Missouri Republican,* November 6–19, 1840. Also, Cynthia De Haven Pitcock, "The Involvement of William Beaumont, M.D., in a Medical-Legal Controversy: The Darnes-Davis Case, 1840," 31–45.

On June 1, 1840, Darnes met Davis in the street in the center of St. Louis and beat him on the head with an iron cane. Bleeding profusely, Davis was helped into a nearby hotel and seated on a chair. The first doctor to arrive was Dr. Thomas McMartin, who had an office nearby. The bleeding had stopped, but McMartin diagnosed a fractured skull. There were four major injuries: a compound fracture on the forehead, with severe depression; a crack or fissure in close proximity to this; a severe injury to the left temple, described by McMartin as very complicated; and a fracture that McMartin thought was the worst of all, over the left ear, where the bones "were badly shattered." Davis could not see out of one eye. Two other injuries were superficial.[2]

McMartin had Davis moved to a bed. He was conscious and, when asked by McMartin, said that he was comfortable. Beaumont's partner, Dr. James Sykes, had arrived, and he also examined the wounds. He recommended moving him to a hospital, decided that his only hope was the use of the trephine to ease the pressure on the brain, and recommended sending for Dr. Beaumont. McMartin said that this was done immediately, so that if an operation was necessary, no inflammation might arise.[3]

Beaumont arrived quickly, and after his examination the three doctors decided it was necessary to operate "to elevate the depressed portion of the skull." Beaumont operated, and was assisted by Sykes. Beaumont was unsuccessful at his first attempt to raise the depression on the forehead, but he again applied the trephine, raised the depression to remove pieces of the skull and all the bone splinters that he could find. The trephine was then applied to the fracture at the temple. The bone was elevated, and more pieces removed. Although McMartin considered the fracture over the left ear to be the most severe, it was decided not to use the trephine there. Sykes gave the reason that there was not sufficient depression, and that the fracture was "at the very point, where the great artery of the dura mater enters the brain."[4]

Although anesthetics came into use later in the 1840s, this was still in the age of surgery without their aid. There is no indication in the extensive evidence given later that Davis was given opium or anything else to dull his senses. He was conscious during the operation, although McMartin

2. Nelson, ed., *Full and Accurate Report*, 31–35, 32 (quotation); *Missouri Republican*, November 9, 1840.

3. Nelson, ed., *Full and Accurate Report*, 35–39; *Missouri Republican*, November 9, 1840 (quotation).

4. Nelson, ed., *Full and Accurate Report*, 31–39 (quotations, 32, 36); *Missouri Republican*, November 7 and 9, 1840.

stated that he "gave indication of a wandering intellect." When Beaumont was finished, the wounds were dressed, and Davis left in the hands of the nurses.

Davis lingered for a week, being regularly visited by Dr. Sykes. When he developed a fever and some delirium, Sykes took thirty ounces of blood from him. As his condition became worse, eventually bringing on violent spasms and a paralysis of his right side, he was repeatedly bled and purged. He died on June 8, and a postmortem was performed. This was attended by McMartin, Sykes, and Beaumont, along with six other doctors. As might have been expected, it revealed that the damage had been more extensive than appeared on external examination, or even had been revealed by the operation performed by Beaumont.[5]

Because of the prominent position of the participants and the dramatic encounter in the public street, the case attracted great attention in St. Louis. Darnes was indicted, and it was decided to try him in the fall on the charge of manslaughter. The trial opened on November 5 and was fully reported in the St. Louis press. The first two days were devoted to selecting a jury and examining witnesses to the scene, but on the third day, when the medical evidence began, it gradually became apparent that the defense was to be based on the presumption that Davis had died not from the injuries inflicted by the cane but as a result of Beaumont's operating procedures. This line of defense was suggested by the defense examination of the prosecution's witnesses, and became fully apparent when the witnesses for the defense were brought forward.

In the course of leading Dr. McMartin through his evidence, the prosecution had him testify to Beaumont's reputation. McMartin said he had known him for about a year and a half, and had heard of him before that. Beaumont, said McMartin, had the reputation "of being the curer of a very wonderful case"; that of a gunshot wound in the stomach. He said that he did not know any other man in Missouri "who enjoys a higher reputation for surgical talent." On cross-examination, the first attempts were made to cast doubts on this image of Beaumont. McMartin was asked about the operation of trephining. He said it required great care, but that it did not produce inflammation of the brain. Pressed again, he agreed that it was not necessary in the case of simple fractures, and agreed that the great British

5. Nelson, ed., *Full and Accurate Report,* 31–39; *Missouri Republican,* November 9, 1840 (quotation).

surgeon Sir Astley Cooper argued that it was mistakenly used in such cases, because it rendered the fracture compound and had a tendency to produce inflammation of the brain.[6]

The cross-examination of Beaumont's partner, Dr. Sykes, became more pointed. He was asked about the postmortem and the doctors who attended, and was made to respond to suggestions that serious questions had been raised about the nature of the treatment afforded Davis. Sykes had visited Darnes in prison, and told him that the rumors about the treatment to Davis were unfounded. The defense also pressed Sykes about keeping Davis's skull. He said he had not shown it to many persons, but that he had shown it to some physicians "as a fracture of great extent."[7]

As Beaumont could not be found when called to testify, it was agreed that the defense would open its case, and that Beaumont would be examined later. The leading defense counsel, Beverly Allen, immediately introduced the suggestion that the trephining had been a mistake. He stated in his opening speech that it had to be considered whether Davis died from the wounds he received or from the treatment. He said he was prepared to present evidence that a friend of the deceased, knowing that there were unfavorable reports on the treatment afforded Davis, had wanted to have other physicians, "more widely known and more eminent" at the postmortem, and suggested that Beaumont and Sykes had simply brought in young physicians to back up their case. Allen emphasized Sir Astley Cooper's doubts about the use of trephining, which, he said, was one of the most dangerous procedures in surgery.[8]

Allen ended his presentation at the Saturday session of the court. Beaumont was called by the prosecution when the court went back into session on Monday, November 9. Beaumont's deafness had progressed to the point that it was agreed that the questions would be written out, read to the court, and handed to Beaumont for his answers.[9]

Beaumont first testified to what he saw when he was called, and stated that the "nature and extent of injury clearly called for an operation for the relief of the sufferer." He described the operation, stating that the fractures extended

6. Nelson, ed., *Full and Accurate Report*, 31–35; *Missouri Republican*, November 9, 1840 (quotations).

7. Nelson, ed., *Full and Accurate Report*, 37–39; *Missouri Republican*, November 9, 1840 (quotation).

8. Nelson, ed., *Full and Accurate Report*, 40, 41–55; *Missouri Republican*, November 9, 1840 (quotation).

9. Nelson, ed., *Full and Accurate Report*, 55.

in every direction from the forehead, that the membranes were injured, and that bone splinters were driven deep into the brain.[10]

In describing treatment after the operation, Beaumont showed that his approach to medicine had not undergone any fundamental changes in the previous thirty years. He said that his treatment was antiphlogistic, and had been adopted to prevent inflammation—"bleeding, cathartic, cold applications, antimonial treatment." Beaumont also described what was revealed at the postmortem, and stated that the case evinced some of the most extensive fractures to the skull he had ever seen, and that he was surprised that the victim had not been killed on the spot. As might have been expected by anyone who knew Beaumont, he gave his evidence with great confidence. He said there would have been no doubt in the mind of any surgeon of knowledge or experience that an immediate operation was needed. Davis, said Beaumont, could not possibly have survived his injuries without an operation; with it "there was a chance."

Beaumont was cross-examined as to whether there had really been any symptoms of compression, and as to what he thought of Cooper's work. After giving a detailed account of how compression could be diagnosed, and stating that Cooper was a high authority, he stated firmly that when there was an evident compound fracture and depression of the bone, leading to the inference that bone splinters had been driven into the brain, then the operation of trephining was required. It was, he said, one of the clearest indications in surgery; "there are no two indications or opinions about it." He had not the slightest doubt that this case required the use of the trephine as the only possible chance of saving the patient's life. The defense counsel tried to press him on the possibility that he was mistaken in his opinions, and he sensibly answered: "I am not infallible in my opinions, nor in my treatment of patients. I make no claim to infallibility, I have not vanity enough to think or say, that I was never mistaken."[11]

After a brief reexamination by the prosecution, the defense produced its witnesses. When the medical evidence was reached, the bitter divisions that had plagued the St. Louis Medical Society, and St. Louis physicians in general, became fully apparent. The first medical witness for the defense, Dr. Thomas J. White, was a friend and party associate of Darnes. He testified that he would never perform the trephining operation unless there were clear symptoms

10. *Missouri Republican,* November 10, 1840.
11. Nelson, ed., *Full and Accurate Report,* 55–59; *Missouri Republican,* November 10, 1840.

of compression. The operation itself was dangerous, he said, and frequently added to already existing symptoms. He had heard the symptoms in this case described; there was no compression, and he would not have performed the operation. The prosecution managed to get some modification of this testimony in cross-examination, but the attack on Beaumont's judgment was to continue.[12]

The next medical witness for the defense, Dr. William Carr Lane, was also the mayor of the city. He had not heard all the testimony, and said he had only imperfect knowledge of the wound inflicted on Davis, but he, like White, stressed that the operation of trephining was a very dangerous one. His recommendation was to purge and bleed rather than trephine, although he also stated that he had trephined frequently and usually unsuccessfully.[13]

Following Dr. Lane was Franklin Knox, the physician with whom Beaumont had clashed in the Medical Society over the use of advertisements. Knox was happy to question his judgment on the witness stand. He did not think a trephining operation was advisable without symptoms of compression, and quoted an authority to the effect that more lives had been lost by the use of trephining than ever were saved by it. He said that within the last thirty years he had never heard of any "respectable surgeon" using the trephine except in cases of compression.[14]

The second defense attorney, Joseph B. Crockett, continued the attack on Beaumont's judgment in his long address to the jury. He stressed that Drs. Lane, White, and Knox, all physicians of high reputation, believed that Davis might have recovered from his wounds, and that the trephine was a dangerous instrument only to be resorted to in cases of extreme emergency. Crockett argued that the symptoms justifying the use of the trephine were not present in this case. Depression, he argued, could exist without compression. He continued by citing a whole list of authorities to the effect that without clear symptoms of compression the trephine should not be used.[15]

The third of the defense attorneys, Henry S. Geyer, took up the attack on Beaumont. He stated baldly in discussing the medical issues in the case that the question was whether Davis died from his wounds or from "the unskillful

12. Nelson, ed., *Full and Accurate Report,* 75–78; Pitcock, "Involvement of Beaumont," 41.

13. Nelson, ed., *Full and Accurate Report,* 78–80; Pitcock, "Involvement of Beaumont," 42.

14. Nelson, ed., *Full and Accurate Report,* 80; *Missouri Republican,* November 12, 1840 (quotation).

15. Nelson, ed., *Full and Accurate Report,* 87–99.

treatment of his physicians." Sarcastically, he commented that if a patient died by his doctors, it was called a natural death—if by the act of God, it was called unnatural. The trephine was agreed by all experts to be a highly dangerous instrument, only to be resorted to in the gravest cases, not in such cases as that of Davis, where it had been shown that the symptoms of compression had not been present.[16]

Geyer continued with a personal attack on Beaumont, and used his famous experiments on St. Martin as a means of attacking him. Beaumont had resorted to the trephine, he said, in defiance of the best authorities, "and for the purpose of an experiment." Sykes, he said, decided the case required the advice of the most eminent surgeon in the city, but who did he send for? His own partner. When Beaumont came, said Geyer, he trephined not because the symptoms of compression were present, but because he expected them. This was *"another* experiment." He was boring for symptoms, looking for bone splinters. Dr. Beaumont, he said, "proceeded against authority, and trephined without the symptoms—by guess-work."

Geyer now pulled out all the stops in his attempt to defend his client. He asked how many of the patients of Beaumont and Sykes had failed to survive the use of the trephine. He regretted he could not produce the testimony of the dead or the "maimed survivors." He described St. Martin as a man who was "maimed for life—a living monument of the skill of these operators!" At this, the *Missouri Republican* noted that there was a considerable sensation among the spectators. Geyer said that Dr. McMartin had testified he knew of Beaumont because of his book—it was this that was supposed to qualify him to operate on the head. If this book had conferred immortality, said Geyer, then he could scrape together a few facts, write a pamphlet, and achieve the same.

Even for a defense lawyer, this was wild stuff, but it got worse. He said that in this famous case where Beaumont had supposedly exhibited such great ability he did not cure the patient, but simply kept the hole open so he could look into the stomach. "Who has ever heard of this book?" asked Geyer. He then proceeded to read an extract from it about the digestion of various items of food, said it was a good book, useful for satisfying harmless curiosity, and no doubt containing some valuable discoveries—such as, for example, that people generally ate too much—but he questioned how it could be used here as the basis on which to establish medical fame.

16. Ibid., 122–32; *Missouri Republican,* November 16, 1840 (quotation).

Beaumont, said Geyer, was undoubtedly a man of great curiosity. This had led him to keep a man's stomach open to look into it occasionally—"it was upon the same principle of curiosity which *kept* the hole open in the man's *stomach* that he bored a hole in Davis' *head* to see what was going on there!" Geyer went on and on, attacking the way in which the postmortem was conducted, and continually returning to the question—did Davis die of his wounds or from the treatment of his doctors? He also continued to trivialize Beaumont's book. After speaking at length, he suggested adjournment for lunch with the comment that there were symptoms among the jury that reading Beaumont's book had produced its effect on their stomachs, and they were ready to eat.[17]

In his closing remarks, prosecuting attorney Peter Engle did all he could to remove the defense's contention that it was at least as likely that Davis had died from his treatment as from his wounds, and in the course of this attempt gave some solace to Beaumont by vigorously defending his reputation. He said he was amazed "at the attempt to degrade and cast contempt upon a man, who has the professional and social standing of Dr. Beaumont in this community." He particularly objected to the defense counsel's attempt to ridicule Beaumont's book, and argued that notwithstanding the defense counsel's sneers, "that book has won for its author more fame than ever the gentleman has obtained." He said he held in his hand a German and an English edition, that spoke of it "as opening a new era in science."[18]

The defense tactics worked. The defense counsels had known there was a good deal of sympathy for Darnes on the grounds that he was justified in defending his reputation from malicious personal attacks, and the doubts they had cast on the medical treatment allowed some to believe that Darnes had merely beaten Davis, not killed him. Darnes had been charged with manslaughter in the third degree. He was convicted of manslaughter in the fourth degree and fined five hundred dollars. It could be argued that Beaumont had suffered more severely than Darnes.[19]

Soon after the trial, Beaumont received a partial vindication when he was elected president of the St. Louis Medical Society, but it did little to assuage his bitterness. He devoted his inaugural address to an attack on the divisiveness and pettiness of the St. Louis medical profession, and the

---

17. *Missouri Republican,* November 16 (quotations), November 17, 1840.
18. Ibid., November 18, 1840; Nelson, ed., *Full and Accurate Report,* 232–64.
19. Nelson, ed., *Full and Accurate Report,* 269; Pitcock, "Involvement of Beaumont," 44–45.

willingness of physicians to turn on and testify against their colleagues. He said that in recent years, the meetings of the society had produced little else but "strife, jargon and confusion—angry debate, personal invective, abuse & total disregard of the honor, interest or reputation of the Society." He commented on physicians committing "rank perjury" before a court of law to screen a man from punishment. After his term as president, Beaumont took no further part in the work of the society.[20]

For all Beaumont's problems in the Darnes-Davis case, his decision to remain in St. Louis gave him the extensive practice he wanted. St. Louis grew from 16,469 inhabitants in 1840 to 77,860 in 1850. But this was only part of the story, for others poured into the city. St. Louis was a great jumping-off point for emigrants to the vast regions west of the Mississippi, and a commercial center for an entire region. As the city remained unhealthy, Beaumont had all the patients he could possibly handle. He could not have chosen better for his private practice.[21]

Having decided to spend the rest of his life in St. Louis, Beaumont was anxious to find more substantial living quarters for his family. For many years, they had made do with army quarters or temporary accommodations, and they had demands beyond those imposed by two adults and three children. Major Hitchcock continued to live with them when he was in St. Louis, and Deborah Beaumont continued to welcome friends and guests into their home. Letters to or about the Beaumonts often recall with pleasure the convivial atmosphere engendered by the motherly "Aunt Debby." She was a complete nineteenth-century housewife—mentioned as never without her sewing—but she also had a lively interest in plays, novels, and particularly music. And Beaumont himself very much enjoyed his circle of intimate friends, was supportive of them, and was warm and welcoming in his home.[22]

When Lee and his wife returned to the East, they often wrote affectionately of their happy times with the Beaumonts. Ten years later, Mary Lee still remembered her first day in St. Louis, and her loneliness until she met the Beaumonts and was comforted by Debby. Lee remembered Beaumont with affection. Two years after he left, he wrote that he wished he "could see the Dr. coming in again to my room in his shirt sleeves, with a dose of rhubarb

20. Minutes of the Medical Society of Missouri at St. Louis; Inaugural Address, 1841, BC, WU.

21. Primm, *Lion of the Valley*, 165–66; Van Ravenswaay, *St. Louis*, 324–25; Adler, *Yankee Merchants*, 62–95.

22. Mary Lee to Sarah Beaumont, [1839], December 17, 1839, [summer 1840], November 5, 1840, February 1847, Lee Letters.

in one hand & a glass of toddy in the other." It was a scene he was less likely to see in the future, for Beaumont, who had long worried about the deleterious effects of hard liquor, had given it up in these years. Temperance groups flourished in St. Louis in the late 1830s and early 1840s. According to Lee, Beaumont and his friend Dr. King were "discarding *toddies* from their Suppers of Cold pork & Cabbage."[23]

Lee, like other men who visited the Beaumonts, was a little too fond of the teenage Sarah. In this pre-Freudian age he was even able to keep up a correspondence with her that at a later date might have raised a few eyebrows. He usually addressed her as "My beautiful Tasey," with his wife away regretted that he had no pretty girls to make love to, and asked Sarah if she could come to his relief. In one letter, he commented that he had found his young son in a young lady's bed one morning, and that Sarah must have taught him those tricks because it had certainly not been his father. To a friend in St. Louis, Lee acknowledged his "interest in the pretty women." He said age had brought "no diminution" in his interest.[24]

As his army career was coming to an end, Beaumont was negotiating to move his family into a house on the outskirts of St. Louis. From Robert McPherson, a friend and former judge who handled some of his property matters, he arranged to lease, with the prospect of future purchase, the Gamble Place, which was in the country about a mile from the center of St. Louis. It was a large, white frame house, set in about forty acres. This move was made possible by Beaumont's partnership with Dr. James Sykes. Beaumont kept up his normal daytime practice, riding back and forth to his office, but was able to give his night calls to Sykes.[25]

McPherson provided Beaumont with two hundred dollars to make improvements in the house he had leased, and Beaumont put in several hundred dollars of his own. In the next two years, new fences were erected, a water cistern was built, and fruit trees were transplanted. Beaumont was always busy with his practice, but Debby became a very keen gardener.[26]

23. Lee to Sarah Beaumont, May 16 (quotation), November 18, 1842, March 11, 1843 (quotation), Lee Letters; Lee to Henry Kayser, February 17 and June 16, 1840, in "Letters of Robert E. Lee to Henry Kayser," 17; Van Ravenswaay, *St. Louis*, 315–17.
24. Robert E. Lee to Sarah Beaumont, May 16, 1842, March 11, 1843 (quotation), Lee Letters; Lee to Henry Kayser, June 16, 1845, "Letters of Lee to Henry Kayser," 37–38.
25. Beaumont to Ethan Hitchcock, [c. 1840], extracts in Myer, *Beaumont*, 264–65; Goodwin, *History of Medicine in Missouri*, 57.
26. Robert McPherson to Beaumont, November 25, 1839, Beaumont to McPherson, April 23, 1842, BC, WU.

The family moved into the house in the winter of 1839–1840, and writing to Major Hitchcock, Beaumont gave a euphoric account of their new life there. He said that "the family are delighted with their prospects and perfectly happy." He painted an idyllic picture of his return home in the evening, with a family "happy and delighted" to see him; his daughter Cush (Lucretia) hanging around his neck, his son Bud (Israel) around his waist, and the very adult Sarah "gravely" ushering him in to see "Aunt Debby," who was "cheerful and smiling as a basket of roses." Sarah, he wrote, was "perfectly contented and joyful" with her piano, her sewing, her books, and her pony, and the two younger children were rambling and gamboling through fields and bushes "like two young colts let loose from the stalls." The Beaumonts brought in a young woman, Frances Lynde, from Plattsburgh to act as governess and tutor for the two younger children. Also living with them was Sarah's piano teacher, a young German. He taught the children both the piano and German, and, unsurprisingly, fell in love with Sarah.[27]

In reminiscing of this period, a woman who was about Sarah's age remembered a relaxed and even playful Beaumont. When he first came to see her on a medical visit, he pretended to take her for her brother's mother, and referred to "your son, Madame." She enjoyed going to the Beaumonts more than to any other house in St. Louis. She remembered Deborah Beaumont as "a kind and motherly woman, who did everything to make us happy," and saw a side of Beaumont himself that was rarely visible to the outside world. He was "good fun," she remembered, and "Sarah and her father romped together like two children." She also suggested that his deafness was not quite as severe as some believed. Her comment was that "he was quite deaf when he chose to be," and that on the evenings when young men came to serenade, "the music could never be soft enough but the old doctor would be sure to hear it, deaf as he was." He teased the girls about it in the morning.[28]

Beaumont was still optimistic that a way would be found to keep him in the army, and when news came that his resignation had been accepted, his euphoria cooled a little. He asked his friend Hitchcock to use any influence he had to get him reinstated, to get him payment for continuing his official duties into 1840, and, if all else failed, he told him to make "them" give him "some other fat apt"—post office, subtreasury, customs house, or something of the kind. He was not serious about another appointment—this was a letter to

27. Beaumont to Ethan Hitchcock, [1840], extract in Myer, *Beaumont,* 264–65.
28. Memoir of Lucy Crane Wislizenus, Wislizenus Papers, MHS.

a very good friend—but he was serious about regretting the loss of the money that came with an official appointment.

He tried to convince Hitchcock that he was unhappy not so much at leaving the army but at the manner in which it had happened. The whole family, he wrote, was involved, and though pleasantly situated in their new place, "often feel melancholy." The melancholy was probably mostly Beaumont's. Lee came and stayed for a time in 1840, "and was kind and affectionate," but they missed Hitchcock. Hitchcock had almost daily played duets with Sarah, and Beaumont wrote that the piano sounded more like a death dirge with Hitchcock gone. The sentiment probably came from what he felt, not from what he heard.[29]

The idyll at Gamble Place (which was later to become Beaumont Place) lasted for only a little more than a year. The residence in the country had been made possible by the partnership with Dr. Sykes, but by 1841 that partnership was on the rocks and was ending in the acrimony so typical of Beaumont's medical relationships. It is difficult to get at the full truth of the matter, but part of the problem was undoubtedly that Beaumont viewed his partners as assistants and always tried to assure that he would get the lion's share of the receipts from the practice. He did not really like having a partner, but was forced into it by his very success. He wanted to keep accepting patients, and at different times tried partnerships that he thought would enable him to keep increasing his practice while keeping a large part of its proceeds.

The dissolving of the partnership dragged on for years, and finished up in court, because the two partners could not reach agreement on what moneys were owed to each of them. Beaumont's own written account of the terms of the partnership and the dispute presents, as might be expected, a very one-sided view of the events, but is revealing of some of the possible difficulties.

The original agreement had apparently been an informal one. Beaumont said he had decided in March 1839 to "engage a professional assistant." Sykes obviously viewed the informal arrangement as giving him a little more status than that. Beaumont said that the financial arrangement was for him to get all the returns from the obstetric and consultation fees, while the returns from the general practice were to be divided equally between them. He claimed that Sykes had been charging patients without entering the sums in the common books of the partnership. Sykes did not remember the agreement as Beaumont remembered it, and eventually took him to court.

29. Beaumont to Ethan Hitchcock, April 1, 1840, BC, WU.

Whoever was at fault, some of Beaumont's notes on the breakup make it clear that the practice was a very successful one. He stated in one memo that Sykes had received six thousand dollars in cash out of the partnership, and that he had received eight or ten thousand dollars from Beaumont's private funds for the support of himself and his family. This last amount was because the Beaumonts had boarded the Sykes family in the old Clark house in St. Louis in the first part of their partnership, but the amount seems a great exaggeration. As late as 1846 the two men were still bickering about the financial details of the breakup. Beaumont told his cousin Samuel that he had lost fifteen to twenty thousand dollars to the "infamous villain" Sykes as a result of the Sykes affair, but this again was undoubtedly an exaggeration.[30]

The Lees, who had known Sykes as well as Beaumont, blamed Sykes. Lee asked if Sykes was mad or worse, and his wife said Sykes must be a strange man to accuse Beaumont of wrongdoing, but the Lees had known Beaumont in his private more than in his public capacity, and he was a very different man at home and in public. This concerned money, and Beaumont had great difficulty in seeing another's point of view when money was involved.[31]

The public announcement that the Beaumont-Sykes partnership was at an end was given in the *Missouri Republican* in April 1841. It simply announced that they were dissolving their partnership and would now maintain separate offices, but it also stated that Beaumont was moving back into town. A resident commented that Beaumont would sleep in his office, while his family would move into smaller quarters on the edge of town. Without Sykes to handle his night calls, Beaumont could no longer live at such a distance from the center of town. Beaumont told McPherson that he had been compelled to make this move because of the "constant calls" of his professional duties.[32]

Beaumont wisely held onto the house and land he and his family had so much enjoyed. At first, he deferred a decision on buying it, but in August 1842 he agreed to pay McPherson a total of $14,414 for the property. This was to be paid in six promissory notes—of somewhat varying amounts—that fell

30. Memo regarding James Sykes, [1841], Reasons for dissolving partnership with James Sykes, [1841], copy of discharge of sureties, April 3, 1846, BC, WU; Beaumont to Samuel Beaumont, August 12, 1844, BC, UC.

31. Robert E. Lee to Sarah Beaumont, March 11, 1843, Mary Lee to Sarah Beaumont, May 18, 1843, Lee Letters.

32. *Missouri Republican,* April 1, 1842; William Carr Lane to Mary E. Lane, September 26, 1842, Lane Collection, MHS; Beaumont to Robert McPherson, April 23, 1842, BC, WU.

due each year from July 1, 1843, to July 1, 1848. One reason that Beaumont deferred buying the property was a problem with the title to the whole area on which his house was situated. There was a claim to the area based on an old Spanish land grant, and the case was periodically in the courts in the 1840s. In 1846 Beaumont used the reappearance of the Spanish claim as a reason for suggesting to McPherson that his annual payments might better be suspended until it was all cleared up. McPherson was an agreeable man and a good friend of the Beaumonts, and temporarily allowed Beaumont to defer his payments. Ultimately, Beaumont became financially involved in the settlement of the disputed title. In 1851 he paid almost twenty-five hundred dollars (one thousand dollars in cash, the rest in promissory notes) as his share in paying off those who had held the Spanish claims.[33]

Having returned to the center of the city, Beaumont maintained his office in the basement at the corner of Fourth and Walnut. He held office hours from 7 to 9 A.M., and from 3 to 5 P.M. The unfortunate publicity of the Darnes-Davis case had no noticeable effect on Beaumont's practice. He continued to be remarkably busy, prosperous, and well regarded. His income was ample for his needs. In December 1839 he had told Joseph LaMotte that he was pursuing "his own business to the tune of $10,000 a year." This was at a time when St. Louis was in the midst of a depression. Being Beaumont, he would miss his army salary, but he certainly did not need it.[34]

Half a century later, physicians who recalled these years always remembered Beaumont as one of the most prominent St. Louis physicians. Their memories were undoubtedly helped by Beaumont's fame as an author. One physician, who came to St. Louis in 1840, remembered Beaumont as "the leading physician of the city," a man "much beloved by his friends," but hindered in his practice by his deafness. He commented, however, that the people who liked him "employed his services just the same." Beaumont would have been pleased at the comments of Dr. Simon Pollak, who was born in Vienna and arrived in St. Louis a few years later, for he remembered Beaumont as "a thorough gentleman."[35]

33. Indenture between William and Deborah Beaumont and Robert McPherson, August 24, 1842, BC, UC; Beaumont to Robert McPherson, April 6, 1846, April 21 and June 28, 1847, May 1 and 21, 1849, McPherson to Beaumont, May 3, 1846, May 25 and July 12, 1847, June 21, 1848, March 20 and May 8, 1849, settlement in June 1851, BC, WU.
34. *Missouri Republican,* April 1, 1841; Beaumont to Joseph LaMotte, December 8, 1839, BC, WU.
35. Goldstein, ed., *One Hundred Years,* 29, 31, 41, 44.

Beaumont was also well regarded by Dr. William McPheeters, a graduate of the University of Pennsylvania Medical School who for many years was editor of the *St. Louis Medical and Surgical Journal,* although it appears that he viewed Beaumont with a vision partially obscured by the mists of time. McPheeters came to St. Louis in 1841 as a recent graduate. He remembered finding Beaumont "in full and successful practice," noted that he was "popular alike with the public and with the profession," and commented that his surgical skill was often called upon. His stress on Beaumont's boldness and aggressiveness as a surgeon rings true. McPheeters, who had been entertained in Beaumont's home, remembered Beaumont as a friend and patron of younger members of the profession, and somewhat surprisingly as "a modest, retiring man." This last impression may have been gained because increasingly in the last years of his life Beaumont devoted himself exclusively to his practice, his properties, and his family.[36]

The regard in which Beaumont was held was indicated in 1842 when a group of younger St. Louis doctors joined together to provide free outpatient services to the poor. The "dispensary," as they called it, was located in the basement of the Unitarian Church of Beaumont's friend, the Reverend William Eliot. It was initially supported by private contributions, and the city later added a small annual appropriation. The six young physicians who had formed it pledged to give one hour a day to its work. Beaumont himself accepted an appointment as one of the two consulting physicians. The dispensary lasted for seven years, until its functions were taken over by the city and the local medical colleges.[37]

With St. Louis growing rapidly and transients becoming a constant problem, public health was a major concern, and in the year the dispensary was established Beaumont joined with newcomer Dr. Charles Pope to recommend steps to improve conditions. Arguing that there was too much work for any one public health officer, they wrote that what was needed was one physician to attend the city wards in the local hospital (operated by the Sisters of Charity), another to attend the city workhouse and small-pox hospital, and several physicians to vaccinate the poor. They thought that it was not essential to pay the physician who attended the indigent in the general hospital, but there should be pay for attending the smallpox hospital, for "there is risk

36. Ibid., 80–81; Scharf, *History of St. Louis,* vol. 2, 1527–28.
37. Scharf, *History of St. Louis,* vol. 2, 1528, 1531–32, 1549–50; Goldstein, ed., *One Hundred Years,* 87; John B. Johnson to Beaumont, January 12, 1842, Beaumont to Johnson, January 15, 1842, BC, WU.

in his duty." The task of vaccination, they urged, should be given to the physicians at the new dispensary, and twenty-five cents allowed for each vaccination. The payments would then be placed in the dispensary funds, and thus further help the poor.[38]

In 1845 the city council passed an ordinance to provide for the building of a public hospital, and in the summer of 1846 the St. Louis City Hospital opened with a resident physician, four attending physicians serving three-month terms, and four consulting physicians with one-year terms. Beaumont was appointed as one of the consulting physicians for the first year of the hospital's operation. It had nine wards and space for some ninety patients.[39]

Although the surgical experience that Beaumont had gained in the War of 1812 obviously stood him in good stead throughout his career, his lack of formal training gave him an old-fashioned air by midcentury. A physician who settled in St. Louis late in the 1840s commented that when he arrived, Drs. McDowell and Pope were really the only surgeons of note. He remembered Beaumont not as a surgeon, but as a "very distinguished citizen and physician."[40] Beaumont, with his early-nineteenth-century apprenticeship and a continued dependence on early-nineteenth-century techniques and therapies, was becoming somewhat outmoded.

To the end of his life, Beaumont continued to put great faith in purging and bleeding to treat a variety of symptoms. When his daughter and little granddaughter took a trip in the late 1840s, he sent them with a variety of medications and gave his daughter three long pages of instructions on how to treat a variety of conditions. There was a strong emphasis on cathartics and emetics. He ended his instructions with the statement that if there was inflammation of the throat with much swelling of the tonsils, headache, fever, difficulty in swallowing, distress and pain, sleeplessness, hot head and skin, with short breath, she was to "send for a Doctor, Leeches, cups, Calomel, & without delay."[41]

38. Beaumont and Charles Pope to the City Council of St. Louis, St. Louis–History, MHS.

39. Scharf, *History of St. Louis*, vol. 2, 1550; Goldstein, ed., *One Hundred Years*, 156. The reluctance to establish hospitals in the first half of the nineteenth century is discussed in Charles E. Rosenberg, *The Care of Strangers: The Rise of America's Hospital System*, 3–93.

40. Dr. Elisha Gregory, in Goldstein, ed., *One Hundred Years*, 36.

41. Medical Instructions, BC, UC. In a later hand, this is wrongly identified as instructions for Israel Beaumont.

The heroic dosing and bleeding that had formed the basis of Beaumont's treatment were becoming less common than they had been when Beaumont had begun to practice. Yet knowledge was still so limited, and forms of therapy still so varied, that Beaumont's confidence and his unremitting dedication still brought him all the patients he could handle, and the fame he had achieved through his research and book ensured that, with the exception of those physicians with whom he had clashed, he was regarded in high esteem by his colleagues. True specialization was still rare, and it seemed natural in St. Louis to refer a variety of different medical problems to Beaumont for treatment or comment.[42]

In 1842, John Agnew of St. Louis was asked a favor by a friend. The friend had heard that Agnew was going to Philadelphia, and wanted him to take a description of his medical problem to a skillful physician in St. Louis or in the East. He said that when he was a child he had been afflicted with scrofula of the neck. This had disappeared, but about seven years before small tumors had appeared "on the Glands of the neck and in the arm pits." These had become quite hard, and "in case of cold" the tumor appeared in new places and "more Swell'd." For a "perfect cure" for this condition he was prepared to pay one hundred dollars, a large sum in 1842.[43]

Agnew decided he should consult Beaumont, and Beaumont gave his advice. He said that it would be best for the patient to see him personally, but that from the description he had decided that the patient was suffering from a "scrofulous diathesis of congenital & chronic character." For treatment he sent four prescriptions—two of them containing potassium hydroxide—and said that both internal medicine and ointment would be needed. He also told Agnew to take sulphur and rhubarb and other laxatives, and gave recommendations for the patient's diet. He said the patient should eat lightly; lean meats, rice, milk, brown bread, wild game, birds, and tripe, and should avoid oily and greasy foods, gravies, butter, cheese, pastry, hot bread, and sweet drinks. He recommended drinking "small beer," milk and water, and acorn coffee instead of tea and West Indian coffee. He was also to bathe daily in salt and water. In recommending weak beer, Beaumont meant the patient to keep away from stronger beverages.[44]

Beaumont, who had been remarkably optimistic in even the most hopeless cases, had gained a realism stemming from extensive practice, and he did not

42. See Warner, *Therapeutic Perspective,* 95–100.

43. William Howe to John Agnew, [c. 1842], Beaumont to Howe, December 15, 1842, BC, WU.

44. Beaumont to William Howe, December 15, 1842, BC, WU.

always advocate vigorous intervention. In 1843 he was called to treat a little girl. She had come home from Sunday school feeling sick. Another doctor had immediately diagnosed scarlet fever. She seemed to improve for a time, then worsened. Beaumont was called in, but "as soon as he saw her told them there was no hope." She died within two days.[45]

One aspect of dealing with prominent families in St. Louis that Beaumont was silent on was the medical treatment of their slaves. In 1840 there were more than fifteen hundred slaves in St. Louis, greater than 9 percent of the total population. By 1850 the number had increased to more than twenty-six hundred, but this was now less than 4 percent of the whole. Slavery was to continue to decline in the city in the 1850s, but it was an ever-present aspect of life there, for St. Louis was a considerable slave mart. In one case, Beaumont's certification of the physical condition of a slave was challenged with the comment that one of the men involved in the transaction "had little confidence in Dr. B." Beaumont treated slaves, but his letters do not comment on slavery as an institution. Having determined to spend the rest of his life in St. Louis, he might well have decided to avoid a highly volatile subject. Even his friend William Eliot, who opposed slavery, was very discreet about his opposition. The subject was a very delicate one for a New Englander bent on establishing an extensive practice in a slave state.[46]

For a time shortly after Beaumont left the army, it seemed possible that he would again achieve his dream of visiting Europe with St. Martin, and having someone else pay for it. In August 1840 Benjamin Silliman sent him a letter he had received from England regarding the possibility of Beaumont taking St. Martin there. It had been suggested that a public subscription could be raised to support this. Silliman, who had believed Beaumont was still in the army, had first suggested to the secretary of war that Beaumont should be given leave to cross the Atlantic with St. Martin, but on learning that Beaumont had left the army suggested that he could ask for five hundred or even one thousand pounds from the English for going there.[47] Inspired by this possibility, and perhaps by receiving notice that he had been elected a corresponding member of the National Institution for the Promotion of

45. See Ann E. Lane to Mary E. Lane, January 30, 1843, William C. Lane to Mary E. Lane, February 22, 1843, Lane Collection.

46. Henry L. Patterson to James H. Lucas, November 17, 1844, Lucas Collection, MHS; report of Post Mortem, October 10, 1840, BC, WU; Nelson, Beaumont, 309, 316; Van Ravenswaay, St. Louis, 394, 401; Hunter, "Slavery in St. Louis," 233–65; Primm, Lion of the Valley, 186–87; Eliot, William Greenleaf Eliot, 126.

47. R. D. Thompson to Benjamin Silliman, June 8, 1840, Silliman to Beaumont, August 5, 1840, BC, WU.

Science that had been established in Washington, D.C., Beaumont again wrote to his contact in Canada, William Morrison. He told Morrison that he was ready to make another attempt to get St. Martin, that he wanted him without his family, and that he wanted to take him to Europe. Morrison was to find out if St. Martin would come in the fall of 1840 for two or three years, and if it was safe to advance him money to bring him to St. Louis. As ever, Beaumont had mixed motives. He would have liked to continue his work on St. Martin if he could get support for it, but he was also concerned that if he did not take St. Martin to England, arrangements would be made for St. Martin to go without him. Once again, nothing came of Beaumont's inquiry, or of the English suggestions, but more than a year later Beaumont again wrote to Morrison when he heard a rumor that St. Martin had gone to England and was in the hands of the London professors. The report was untrue, but in 1843 Beaumont heard from St. Martin himself. It led nowhere. Beaumont still wanted St. Martin without his family, and still feared advancing any money.[48]

The breakup of Beaumont's partnership with Dr. Sykes had disrupted both his practice and his home life. He still had more work than he could handle, and still needed a partner, but he did not want to give up any large part of the financial rewards of his practice. His solution was to bring in someone he thought he could control, and to bring him in under very specific terms. For this, he chose George Johnson, a young man who felt very beholden to him.

Johnson had been hospital steward at the arsenal when Beaumont had first come to St. Louis in 1835. The son of a physician, he had become a steward with the specific idea of receiving medical training from Beaumont's predecessor. Beaumont had been urged by various Washingtonians, including the commander in chief of the army, to give his help to Johnson. He was recommended as "a most excellent" young man of large family and small income. He read medicine with Beaumont for three years before, in 1839, he entered the medical school of the University of Pennsylvania.[49]

After arriving in Philadelphia, Johnson wrote to tell Beaumont that in one of the lectures he had attended his professor of physiology had often quoted Beaumont, and had complimented him, although he had also suggested that

48. Francis Markoe to Beaumont, August 22, 1840, Beaumont to Markoe, September 5, 1840, Beaumont to William Morrison, September 5, 1840, February 1842, George Johnson to Beaumont, November 30, 1840, St. Martin to Beaumont, May 24, 1843, BC, WU.

49. J. K. Hook to Beaumont, January 27, 1835; Beaumont, letter of recommendation for George Johnson, September 24, 1839; Beaumont, memo regarding Johnson, March 1849, BC, WU; Scharf, *History of St. Louis,* vol. 2, 1530–31.

Beaumont had been remiss in not going to Europe to have the chyme and gastric juice analyzed by organic chemists there. Johnson had gone to the professor after the lecture to tell him of Beaumont's efforts to obtain an analysis from Silliman and Dunglison. To this, the professor said that there were no organic chemists in the United States, but in his next lecture he apologized for his criticism of Beaumont. Johnson also warned his mentor that he had heard that efforts were being made to get St. Martin to go to London.[50]

When Johnson again wrote to Beaumont in November 1840 to warn him that the Medical Society of London was raising money for the purpose of bringing St. Martin to England, he also wrote warmly of Beaumont's "parental" interest in him. He said he hoped to graduate in the spring, and intended to return to St. Louis, for he feared he would not be admitted into the army medical service.[51]

Beaumont decided that Johnson would be an ideal young man to bring into his practice, and wrote to suggest this. Johnson made the right response, writing how much he was indebted to his "dear, generous friend," who had taken a poor, friendless boy by the hand. The financial arrangements reflected this relationship. Much later, when the relationship had collapsed, Beaumont wrote that Johnson was engaged as "a salaried assistant," to take charge of his office and books and to participate in the practice. Beaumont gave Johnson one thousand dollars a year, together with his board and lodging. After the breakup, Beaumont wrote that he had considered their professional association "in a similar relationship to that of a Merchant to his principal Clerk or Bookkeeper." Johnson was a graduate of the University of Pennsylvania medical school, and grateful as he was to Beaumont, he must have been remarkably acquiescent if he viewed the relationship in this light.[52]

Reminiscing at the end of the century, a physician who had known both Beaumont and Johnson said that Johnson was, or at least became, "a polished gentleman and a brilliant, learned physician." He was, however, "remarkably small," and "barely escaped being a dwarf." On account of this, "and other peculiarities," he was known as "Monkey" Johnson. Beginning in the summer of 1841, Beaumont and Johnson settled into their professional relationship. It

50. George Johnson to Beaumont, January 13 and November 30, 1840, William Gibson to Beaumont, October 26, 1839, BC, WU.
51. George Johnson to Beaumont, November 30, 1840, BC, WU.
52. George Johnson to Beaumont, May 27, 1841, Beaumont, memo regarding Johnson, March 1849, BC, WU.

was to continue without overt difficulties for several years, and by the winter of 1842–1843 Beaumont was able to return with his family to Gamble Place. As Dr. Johnson would now be needed in town to answer night and emergency calls, he moved into a hotel, and Beaumont increased his stipend by two hundred dollars to a less than munificent total of twelve hundred dollars.[53]

In the following years there were signs that Beaumont was at last coming to accept that he had achieved the status and financial ease he had sought since leaving Lebanon as a young man. Writing to his cousin Samuel in 1844, he said that his family was enjoying health, happiness, and abundance, and that "Aunt Debby is em-bon-point, fair, florid, & vivacious as ever." Debby was reveling in her "country" house and its large garden. It was typical of how she was viewed that an old friend, writing from Italy to introduce a physician to Beaumont, sent his "best love" to his "second mother," Mrs. Beaumont.[54]

In a mellow mood in 1846, Beaumont commented to an old friend that having climbed the hill of life, he and his wife were now in its ebbing wane, "satisfied with our selves, our children & friends, caring little for the formalities, follies, & fashions of the present age–the hustling turmoil, vain Shows, pride & pageantry of modern Society." He said they were "cheerfully submissive" to fate, and "ready hand in hand to go & sleep together while we can."

Like his wife, Beaumont's children were generally a comfort rather than a trial. In March 1844, his much-wooed and much-admired daughter Sarah married a young officer, Lieutenant Douglas Irwin.[55] For a time she went with him to the Texas border in Louisiana, but returned as tensions in that area increased. In her absence, Beaumont found consolation in his younger daughter Lucretia. He described her, at the age of seventeen, as "a perfect example of female beauty."

Beaumont's son Israel gave him a touch more anxiety than his girls. At almost fifteen, he was described by Beaumont as a large and overgrown boy, not very forward in his education. To remedy the latter, Beaumont sent him to a school run by a cousin, Beaumont Parks, in Springfield, Illinois. In dealing with his son and his problems of adolescence, Beaumont showed none of

53. Dr. Elisha Gregory, in Goldstein, ed., *One Hundred Years,* 3738; Beaumont, memo regarding George Johnson, March 1849, BC, WU.

54. Beaumont to Samuel Beaumont, August 11, 1844, BC, UC; Captain Gardenier to Beaumont, November 23, 1845, BC, WU.

55. Beaumont to John McCall, April 19, 1846, BC, WU; *Index of St. Louis Marriages, 1804–1876,* vol. 1; Ann E. Lane to Sarah Glasgow, March 2, 1844, and note, Lane Collection.

the impatience he often had in dealing with his colleagues and others in the world outside his family.[56]

With this new contentment, Beaumont was easily able to weather another of the professional and personal disputes to which the St. Louis medical profession was so prone. It left Beaumont comparatively unscathed, although it split the St. Louis physicians even more noisily than the Darnes/Davis affair. The case had begun in 1840. Dr. Stephen Adreon was called in to see Mary Dugan, a St. Louis woman about fifty-five years old, living in a state of "extreme destitution."[57]

Adreon found her vomiting constantly, and complaining of a violent pain in her abdomen and "continued pain in the back and loins." Her abdomen was tense and distended, she was constipated, and she had a weak pulse. Dr. Adreon asked her if she had any evidence of a hernia, which she denied, but he apparently did not conduct a detailed examination. His initial treatment was large doses of calomel and opium, "frequently repeated," and he also made use of mustard plasters. In about a week, she seemed much improved, but now for the first time she asked Adreon to look at "a small tumor" in her groin. She said she had been reluctant to show this, because some of her neighbors had said it was venereal.[58]

Dugan's problem was in the right inguinal region, and Adreon diagnosed an enlarged lymph node. The patient said that it had first appeared seven years before. Adreon, thinking "it mght [sic] possibly be in some way connected" with her recent symptoms, called in Drs. Beaumont and Sykes for consultation. They agreed that there was an enlarged inguinal gland. Within a week after his initial visit, Adreon discharged his patient as "cured." Five days later she again sent for Adreon. She had suffered violent pain in the right inguinal region for two days, and "a large abscess had gathered there." For a week, Adreon used poultices and "an occasional cathartic," and then punctured the abscess; some faecal matter passed through openings in the groin. In a few days the abscess ulcerated, and Adreon did not declare his patient healed for over two months. The destitute Mrs. Dugan did not lack

56. Beaumont to Samuel Beaumont, August 12, 1844, genealogical material, BC, UC.

57. Thomas Reyburn, "Extracts from a Paper on Tuphlo-Enteritis, Read before the Medical Society of St. Louis, March, 1843," 77. There is a discussion of the case in Pitcock, "The Career of William Beaumont," 144–50, also Nelson, *Beaumont,* 267–71; Goodwin, *History of Medicine in Missouri,* 58–59; Goldstein, ed., *One Hundred Years,* 44–45; Beaumont to Thomas Reyburn, August 10, 1846, Reyburn to Beaumont, July 21 and August 1, 1846, BC, WU.

58. Reyburn, "Extracts from a Paper," 77–78.

for medical advice in this period, as Dr. Adreon called in several other doctors in addition to Beaumont and Sykes.

Dr. Thomas Reyburn, who first saw the patient in mid-June, found a small opening in the groin where Dr. Adreon had punctured the abscess, and a "thin faecal discharge." Reyburn's conclusion was that this was a case of "tuphlo-enteritis," or "inflammation and perforative ulceration of the caecum and appendix vermiformis." He also assumed that because of the thinness of the faecal matter the perforation was of the appendix, not the caecum proper.[59]

The controversy that increased the gulf in the already divided St. Louis medical profession, and eventually again took Beaumont into court, arose because in late April, a few days after Dr. Adreon had punctured the abscess, Mary Dugan's minister (who was also a physician) called in two other doctors—Franklin Knox and Thomas White. White later claimed that they visited Dr. Adreon's patient without his permission because her minister reported that Dr. Adreon was neglecting the patient, and asked them in writing to attend. White, like Knox, had clashed bitterly with Beaumont and his friends, and had been particularly embittered since being denied admission to the Medical Society in 1839. Later, in 1846, he claimed that he had been insulted and injured by "reckless enemies" for fourteen years.[60]

From the detailed report of Mary Dugan's minister/physician, and from his own examination, White concluded that Adreon had unknowingly operated on a strangulated hernia, and had cut into the intestines. White had other physicians examine Dugan and confirm his findings, but as soon as Dr. Adreon returned to his patient, Dr. White and his friends kept away. White later claimed that the discharge of faecal matter from the groin was continuous from the time that Adreon operated, and that because of this, Adreon persuaded Dugan to leave the city, which she did in July 1840.[61]

Early in 1844, Dugan returned, and brought suit against Dr. Adreon for malpractice. Such suits, which had been rare in the first half-century of medicine in the new nation, were being brought with increasing frequency in the 1840s as patients became far more willing to challenge the judgment of their physicians. Adreon assumed that she had been persuaded to return and sue by the White-Knox faction of St. Louis physicians, and he asked

59. Reyburn, "Extracts from a Paper," 74, 79–81.
60. T. J. White, "Remarks of T. J. White, M.D.," 52–56.
61. Ibid., 55–58.

Beaumont to appear for the defense. Beaumont's opinion was that Adreon's treatment was skillful and correct.[62]

In the fall of 1844 Beaumont received an unpleasant surprise when the sheriff served him papers that indicated he was to be sued along with Dr. Adreon, and that the plaintiff was asking ten thousand dollars in damages. Beaumont's opinion was that he was named as codefendant in the suit to prevent him giving evidence for the defense. Dugan's lawyers tried to prove that Dr. Adreon had misdiagnosed the case, which was in reality a hernia, and that in cutting into the abscess he had punctured part of the intestine. The case went much better for Beaumont than that of Darnes/Davis.

Once again, the St. Louis physicians argued with each other in open court, and desperately tried to enlist support for their clashing positions. Dr. Simon Pollak, who was a newcomer to St. Louis at that time, later recalled that Dr. White took him to see Dugan to try to enlist his support for his diagnosis, and that on the next day a physician friend of Beaumont's did the same thing. Pollak said all newcomers were importuned by the opposing sides.[63] The trial was bitterly fought for nearly a week, with Dugan's lawyers continuing to claim that Adreon and Beaumont had failed to spot a hernia. The defense claimed that Dugan's condition was tuphlo-enteritis, not a hernia. Happily for Beaumont and his friend Adreon, the jury's verdict was for the defendants.

For the St. Louis medical profession, the trial was only the beginning, for the two sides next argued their case at great length in pamphlets and in the *St. Louis Medical and Surgical Journal.* In February 1848 the case again attracted controversy when Mary Dugan died. Dr. White had secured her permission to perform an autopsy, and it was performed by Dr. Charles Pope. Ten physicians were present, but none of them were from the Adreon-Beaumont side of the argument. A small hernia was found, and the newspapers declared that Dr. White had been correct in his diagnosis, but by that time it was so obvious the St. Louis physicians were polarized that this caused no particular anguish to Beaumont. The saddest feature of the case was that a sad, indigent patient had become a battleground for the St. Louis medical profession.

Such public disputes among the most established physicians in St. Louis, and the difficulty of successfully diagnosing and curing illnesses, helped

---

62. See Kenneth Allen De Ville, *Medical Malpractice in Nineteenth-Century America: Origins and Legacy;* Beaumont to Thomas Reyburn, August 10, 1846, BC, WU.
63. Dr. Simon Pollak, in Goldstein, ed., *One Hundred Years,* 44–45.

encourage the growth of the numerous alternative medical systems that the regular medical practitioners wished to eliminate. Beaumont was a staunch defender of regular medicine to the end of his life. When in 1850 his old and close friend, J. H. Freligh, called in a homeopath because he was desperate for a cure for his sick child, Beaumont wrote a brief note, stating that he felt no appreciable offense at the course Freligh had taken, but that he would now cease his own professional attendance on the child. He said that he could not associate his professional character with *"Homeopathy, Quackery, Humbuggery."*[64]

But for all his strong opinions, Beaumont in the last years of his life shunned professional organizations, and confined his professional attentions to his practice. This probably stemmed from not only his disgust with the contentious St. Louis profession but also his increasing deafness. After withdrawing from the St. Louis Medical Society, Beaumont also turned down an opportunity to participate in the inaugural meeting of what was to become the American Medical Association. In 1846 an old friend, Dr. John McCall, whom he had known in the War of 1812, asked him if he could come to a national medical convention that would meet in May. Beaumont declined, commenting that fifteen or twenty physicians had been elected to represent St. Louis and that this would be more than enough. Out here in the Far West, he wrote, they had M.D.s and professors "of every grade and character, from the truly meritorious, accomplished, and skilful surgeons and Physicians to the veryest charlatan and ignorant asses in Christendom." He thought those sent from St. Louis would give him a sample of the range in the city—"the honorable high-minded and nobly aspiring young minds, radiant with vanity, but not deficient in sound sense and professional skill and acquirements; the invidious, jealous and obsolescent minds; the egregiously egotistical and ignorant blockheads and dunces; some mean and vindictive, and others on a descending scale even down to the very bottom of baseness and rascality." Beaumont may have been a little mellower in his last years, but he had not lost his touch for invective. The convention met in New York and arranged for the establishment of a national medical society at Philadelphia in the following year, but Beaumont was not there.[65]

---

64. Beaumont to J. H. Freligh, January 26, 1849, BC, WU.
65. Beaumont to John McCall, April 19, 1846, BC, WU; Myer, *Beaumont*, 279; Rothstein, *American Physicians*, 114–15; *St. Louis Medical and Surgical Journal* 4 (1846): 263–65.

It is as well that Beaumont could relax at home, for he would have found it hard to throw himself into his practice or his research with such dedication, or to attack his enemies with such conviction, if the tumult he often brought upon himself abroad had also existed close to him.

TWELVE

The Last Years

IN ST. LOUIS, BEAUMONT was known in the 1840s as a prominent local physician who had written a book about the stomach; in the East and in Europe, Beaumont was becoming increasingly famous for his research on human digestion. This was brought home to him quite forcefully in the winter of 1845–1846 by the letters he received from an old acquaintance, Dr. John McCall. This renewed contact with a world removed from brash St. Louis and the infighting of its medical profession revived in Beaumont the hope of renewing his experiments on St. Martin and once again receiving national and international acclaim.

Beaumont's interest was probably first sparked in the fall of 1845 when he was given a chance to reflect on his own mortality. McCall wrote to him to point out that in Andrew Combe's fifth edition of his book on physiology and digestion, there was a reference to the "late" Dr. Beaumont. McCall asked Beaumont to let him know that he was alive, so that he could tell Combe. This letter sparked a correspondence that reminded Beaumont of the larger world of scientific research. McCall later reported how happy Combe was to find out that Beaumont was still alive, and in due course Combe sent Beaumont a copy of his latest edition. When McCall pressed Beaumont, without success, to attend the national medical convention in New York, he mentioned in passing that Beaumont had already "immortalized" himself. After a decade of local disputes, and hearing his work ridiculed in court, this was very pleasant reading for Beaumont.[1]

---

1. John McCall to Beaumont, September 28, 1845, March 21, July 22, July 28, 1846, June 8, 1847, Beaumont to McCall, February 1 and April 19, 1846, William Combe to McCall, July 27, 1846, BC, WU.

Beaumont's interest in the possibility of renewing his research on St. Martin was also stirred early in 1846 when the publisher Chauncey Goodrich of Burlington, Vermont, wrote to Beaumont to suggest a second edition of his *Experiments*. He suggested arrangements by which the publisher would bear the cost and pay Beaumont by giving him some of each thousand copies printed. Busy with his practice, and confident that his cousin Sam knew a lot more about publishing than he did, he referred Goodrich to his cousin to work out the details of the arrangements.

Sam not only settled on the details of how Beaumont would be paid but also went ahead with the publication of the book. Sam had found the publisher difficult to deal with, but they finally agreed that Beaumont would receive two hundred copies of the fifteen hundred books that would be printed. Sam told Beaumont that he thought it was not enough, but that it was all the publisher would agree to. The publisher had guaranteed not to sell in Missouri, or in states to its south and west, but Sam commented that was "all gammon." When the book was thrown into the market, Sam wrote, the publisher would not be able to control the direction in which the books went. Sam gave various reasons for agreeing to terms that he said he did not like: the copyright would expire in one year, and then the publisher could republish it without consulting Beaumont; it would be "mortifying" for Beaumont not to have his work republished; the work would now be published more handsomely than in the first edition; and republication would provide the opportunity to make thorough corrections. Sam reminded his cousin that the work had originally been put out in a great hurry, and said that in looking through it he had been "perfectly astonished" at the errors that occurred on nearly every page. By "errors," Sam meant both typos and infelicities and obscurities of expression. He told Beaumont that in the first 140 pages, he had made nearly three hundred corrections. He emphasized that he had not changed the sense. Essentially, he was not compiling a list of errata but copyediting the text of the first edition.[2]

Sam took full responsibility for the second edition, including writing a preface. In this, he used quotes from European writers in praise of the work. He told Beaumont that from "delicacy," he had written this as if it was by the publisher. That Sam negotiated with the publisher, and made all necessary changes without consulting his cousin, was undoubtedly why, when the second edition finally appeared, it had "corrected by S. Beaumont, M.D.," on the title page. This was true, but it gave an impression that Sam had not

2. See Myer, *Beaumont*, 287–88.

intended; he was a modest man who had no desire to steal any of his cousin's thunder. He told Beaumont that he had tried to have the attribution removed, but was too late.[3]

When Beaumont agreed to the terms his cousin had obtained, he made the uncharacteristic comment, "I care little about the pecuniary profits." Probably what this meant was that in 1846, unlike the first time his book was published, he knew there was little or no money to be made from a scholarly publication, even if it did deal with questions of human digestion. He was content to have his work again brought before the public, and later told Sam that he could keep 150 of the 200 copies that were coming from Goodrich.

In writing to Beaumont about the second edition, Sam had also broached the subject of once again coming to St. Louis and joining his cousin's practice. Beaumont now had an assistant, and he had no desire to lessen his own income by taking on a second assistant. Instead of accepting Sam's offer, he suggested that Sam should go it alone in St. Louis. Beaumont said his own practice was more than he could attend to, even with Dr. Johnson as an assistant: "I decline more practice daily than half the Doctors in the city get in a month." He reminded Sam that when he had been here before he had thought there was too much competition for him ever to think of succeeding in a practice of his own. Now, wrote Beaumont, there was ten times as much competition, but he was succeeding and prospering. He was now, he said, at more than sixty years of age, "in the grand climacteric of life." If Sam came, said Beaumont, he would have to come with a different feeling than on the previous visit. He would have to come with a determination to follow in his cousin's wake and "stem the current" that Beaumont would break for him, for he did not have this much competition in Plattsburgh.[4]

In describing his own success in what he depicted as the cutthroat competition of St. Louis, he frightened his cousin off. Sam was thinking of regular income under Beaumont's patronage and leadership, not of giving up his steady Plattsburgh practice on the gamble of making a big success in St. Louis.[5] He decided to stay in Plattsburgh.

Busy practice or not, the correspondence with McCall and the plans for the second edition of his book had revived Beaumont's interest in the possibility of research on St. Martin. Early in 1846 Beaumont wrote to William Morrison

---

3. Ibid., 288; Beaumont, *Physiology of Digestion*, corrected by Samuel Beaumont.
4. Beaumont to Samuel Beaumont, April 4, 1846, BC, WU.
5. Samuel Beaumont to Beaumont, April 24, 1846, BC, UC.

and mentioned that within the last two or three years, St. Martin had written and expressed a wish to return to him. To make any arrangements presented problems, Beaumont wrote, because Ramsay Crooks had reported that St. Martin had become "an abandoned drunkard," and could not be trusted with an advance. Beaumont thought that the only solution was for someone to bring him. Morrison was asked to find out about St. Martin's condition, and whether he was prepared to come, either on the terms of the 1834 contract or on some better arrangement. Although Beaumont now softened his stance regarding St. Martin's family, again he suggested arrangements that made Morrison's task extremely difficult. He said that if St. Martin could find the means to come, with or without his family, he would pay him what was necessary and reasonable when he reached St. Louis.[6] Beaumont was still hoping to get St. Martin to come to St. Louis without advancing any money.

Although this suggestion did not seem to offer much chance for success, Beaumont immediately wrote to McCall to tell him that he intended to renew his experiments on St. Martin in the coming year. For a time this seemed possible. The ever-patient Morrison gave Beaumont an optimistic report. Although not a teetotaler, St. Martin was now more moderate in his drinking, and, even better news for Beaumont, Morrison said St. Martin had refused to see other medical men on the grounds that he was bound to Beaumont. Morrison thought St. Martin could be sent quickly via New York, and that he did not appear to care whether or not his family went with him. Morrison still thought it would be risky to send money in advance–he might use it on drink, but perhaps somebody could be sent to get him; one hundred dollars would take St. Martin and his family to St. Louis, or fifty dollars would take him there alone, with fifty dollars to be paid to his wife when he reached St. Louis.[7]

Beaumont now made his most determined attempt to obtain St. Martin since his former patient had returned to Canada in 1834. First, he tried to persuade a stranger in Champlain, New York, who was supposed to be coming west, to bring St. Martin with him, but in typical Beaumont fashion, he said he would reimburse him for this when they reached St. Louis. This did not work out, and Beaumont decided that he would send his son Israel for him.[8]

6. Beaumont to William Morrison, April 24, 1846, BC, WU.

7. Beaumont to John McCall, February 1, 1846, William Morrison to Beaumont, February 20, 1846, BC, WU.

8. Beaumont to Ashley Vantine, March 25, 1846, Ashley Vantine to Beaumont, April 17, 1846, Beaumont to William Morrison, March 28, 1846, Beaumont to St. Martin, March 28, 1846, BC, WU.

But Beaumont then had another and cheaper idea. These arrangements were being made in the months when his cousin Sam was still considering settling in St. Louis. If Sam came to St. Louis, he could bring St. Martin with him. He told Sam to go to Canada, and in a burst of euphoria, which was soon to evaporate, he said that if St. Martin would not come without his family then Sam should bring them all–"I must have him Dead or alive." In this case, dealing with someone he knew and could trust, Beaumont was even willing to spend money in advance. He told Sam he was sending him a bill of exchange for two hundred dollars.[9]

A major problem with all this was that when Beaumont wrote to Sam and said that, *if necessary,* he could bring St. Martin with his family, he believed from what Morrison had said that St. Martin was prepared to come without them. He soon heard that this was not the case. With this news, Beaumont's euphoria evaporated, and once again he lost his chance to get St. Martin by deciding that he wanted him, if at all possible, *"without* his family." He had now heard that Sam had decided not to come to St. Louis, so he renewed his plan to send his son, Israel, to try to bring St. Martin to St. Louis.[10]

To prepare the way for Israel, Beaumont wrote to St. Martin and reminded him that his wife had been discontented at Prairie du Chien in 1832. He said that if St. Martin came alone he was willing to help St. Martin send money to his family in Canada, but that if he brought his family to St. Louis he was not to expect any support for them in addition to his own salary. He said that when his son Israel came to bring him, he would leave forty or fifty dollars for the family to tide them over until St. Martin could send money from St. Louis. Beaumont also emphasized to Morrison that if St. Martin insisted on coming with his family, he would have to come with them at his own expense.[11]

For Israel, who was only sixteen, the task of going for St. Martin was a considerable responsibility, and Beaumont arranged for their good friend Major Hitchcock to accompany him for a large part of the journey, and for Sam to go with him from Plattsburgh to make the actual arrangements for St. Martin. In asking Sam to do this, he also asked him to be "kind to the Boy." Hitchcock was available because he had returned from Texas with what

9. Beaumont to Samuel Beaumont, April 4, 1846, BC, WU.
10. William Morrison to Beaumont, April 26, 1846, St. Martin to Beaumont, April 25, 1846, Beaumont to Samuel Beaumont, May 29, 1846, BC, WU.
11. Beaumont to St. Martin, to William Morrison, May 29, 1846, BC, WU.

appeared to be a very persistent case of dysentery, and was traveling to the East to seek additional medical advice.[12]

Before Israel left with Hitchcock in July, Beaumont wrote him a revealing letter of instructions. He told him this excursion was not only for pleasure and amusement, but also for the improvement of his mind and manners, to acquire "a knowledge and right understanding of men," and to witness the ways of the world. He was to lean on Hitchcock, a man "of worth and wisdom," for advice. He was to be wary of forming new and strange acquaintances, affable to all, but intimate with none. He was to be suspicious of everybody, discreet and prudent in everything, and was to be constantly on his guard "against impostors, humbugs, pickpockets, dandies, knaves and fools, the wickedness of men and the wyles of women." He was also to take special care of his health, and to avoid unnecessary exposures, errors in diet, "vicious indulgences and immoral associations of every kind."

If St. Martin was prepared to come without his family, then Sam was to make the detailed arrangements, but it was up to Israel to ensure that St. Martin did not receive more money than was indispensably necessary for him to come to St. Louis. In traveling home, Israel was to take St. Martin in charge as a private servant. He was to keep him in his place, strictly control his time and services, allow no undue familiarity, and not allow him to take the slightest advantage of his youth and inexperience. If St. Martin became obstinate or refractory, then Israel was to stop paying for his travel, discharge him at once, let him work his passage either forward to St. Louis or back to Canada, and proceed without him. To facilitate this, he was to have some agreement drawn up at Plattsburgh to the effect that he could discharge St. Martin, even while en route, without giving him "anything to help himself with." Once again, Beaumont was prepared to take no risks in his efforts to obtain St. Martin for further research. In a letter of introduction for Israel and Sam to William Morrison, he again emphasized that he did not want St. Martin's family; forty or fifty dollars was to be provided for them until St. Martin reached St. Louis.[13]

Early in July, as Beaumont was about to send Israel on his way, St. Martin was dictating a letter in Lower Canada. He told Beaumont that his wife

12. Beaumont to Samuel Beaumont, July 7, 1846, BC, WU; Myer, *Beaumont*, 283; Hitchcock, *Fifty Years in Camp and Field*, 224–27.
13. Beaumont to Israel Beaumont, [July 1846], BC, WU. Most of this letter is reprinted in Myer, *Beaumont*, 285; Beaumont to William Morrison, July 7, 1846, BC, WU.

would not hear of him going without her, and that money alone was of no object to him. Perhaps realizing that his unwillingness to go alone would mean he would not go at all, he said that his wife wanted the money owed to her for washing dresses, shirts, and the like at Prairie du Chien (more than fifteen years earlier). They needed it, he said, because they were poor. But he also made a last effort to sway Beaumont, saying that he was at his service if Beaumont wanted to come to Canada to experiment on his stomach. Also, he said several men in Montreal had asked him to come to them, but he had deferred answering because he preferred going to Beaumont. If he did not hear from Beaumont, however, he intended to spend the next year in Montreal.[14] If Beaumont had been prepared to make arrangements for St. Martin to bring his family to St. Louis, he could have renewed his experiments.

Israel's journey was in vain. After leaving Major Hitchcock in New England, he traveled to Lower Canada with Samuel Beaumont and talked to St. Martin both on his farm near Berthier, and for two hours in Berthier itself. St. Martin was adamant that he would not come to St. Louis without his family, but said that if he was advanced enough out of his wages to pay their expenses he would bring them himself. Israel told him that his father would not agree to this, and Israel and Sam returned without him to Plattsburgh.[15]

Beaumont must have been pleased at Sam's comment that Israel was "a fine manly fellow having the appearance and manner of a much older person," but less so at Sam's suggestion that he should bend his uncompromising stance toward St. Martin. Like Israel, Sam said he was convinced that St. Martin would not come to St. Louis without his family, conceded that Beaumont knew him better than he did, but asked whether there would be any great risk in advancing St. Martin money to bring his family, particularly as he would have the amount deducted from his wages. He raised the key question when he asked his cousin to think whether he considered the object of sufficient importance to risk the money to transport St. Martin and his family to St. Louis. If so, then Sam would do all he could to help.[16]

Beaumont could certainly have afforded the comparatively small amounts of money needed to bring St. Martin and his family to St. Louis, and would have had no difficulty in meeting the requests that would have undoubtedly

14. St. Martin to Beaumont, July 6, 1846, BC, WU.
15. Israel Beaumont to Beaumont, August 1846, William Morrison to Beaumont, August 1846, BC, WU.
16. Samuel Beaumont to Beaumont, August 1846, BC, WU.

come from time to time for small sums beyond the salary paid to St. Martin. But Beaumont had never been so caught up in research that he allowed it to interfere with his main objective of carving out a successful career and making money. This being the case, his desire to avoid spending more than was absolutely necessary prevailed in dealing with St. Martin as it prevailed in the rest of his life. He had sent his son not to make sure that he got St. Martin, but to make sure that he did not waste any money by making travel advances that St. Martin would spend without traveling to St. Louis.

Beaumont would have liked the recognition that would have come from renewing his experiments on St. Martin, and if someone would have paid for it would probably have taken him to Europe to demonstrate his experiments to European doctors. But even if St. Martin had come to St. Louis, Beaumont would in all likelihood have only carried out further experiments in the time he could have squeezed out of his hectic daily practice. It appears extremely unlikely that these experiments would have added anything substantial to what he had already achieved.

Even without St. Martin, Beaumont's life in St. Louis was disrupted in the spring and summer of 1846. The tension on the United States–Mexican border in Texas had erupted into war, and Beaumont's family, friends, and colleagues were involved. Both his son-in-law Lieutenant Douglas Irwin and Major Hitchcock were serving in Texas in the crisis months of early 1846. His daughter Sarah was at home with her own baby daughter, Lucretia ("Lilly"), born in the previous year. Hitchcock, who had been sick for a year, returned to live with the Beaumonts in May, and after going east with Israel, returned in the fall and lived with the Beaumonts again before rejoining the army that was now in Mexico. "If I were to thank God for anything," he wrote in his diary on leaving, "it would be for the friendship of this family, and for its unlimited kindness and confidence."[17]

The news of war undoubtedly stirred in Beaumont memories of his own war service more than thirty years before, and it was at this time that he attempted to secure a cadetship for his son Israel at West Point. In trying to secure political support for this, he stressed his own adherence to the principles of the Democratic party, which was then in power.[18] Israel did not enter the army. Instead, he went for additional education to a school in

17. Hitchcock, *Fifty Years in Camp and Field,* 228.
18. George L. Welcker to Beaumont, October 25, 1846, Joseph G. Totten to Thomas H. Benton, November 17, 1846, BC, WU; Beaumont to Benton, n.d. [1846], Beaumont to William Marcy, n.d. [1846], BC, UC.

Hermann, Missouri. There he received regular but not harsh advice from his father, who praised him for the improving style and language of his letters while urging him to spend his time preparing himself for future usefulness, moral distinction, and gentlemanly eminence. He had Israel keep a careful quarterly account of his expenditures, and when the first accounting came in, he approved it as "being very reasonable & necessary." Fortunately for his family, Beaumont showed his usual parsimony only in dealing with the outside world.[19]

In October, before Major Hitchcock left for Mexico, shattering news reached the Beaumont household. Sarah's husband had been killed in the attack on Monterey. In the following month, writing to his friend the Reverend William Eliot, Beaumont said that Sarah was almost frantic with shock. Her sister Lucretia told a family friend that Sarah was bearing up for the sake of her baby, and in the following year Beaumont arranged for the two young women, with the baby and their brother, to travel east to the Atlantic coast. While there, they paid a short visit to Mary Lee at Arlington.[20]

Within a few months, Sarah's baby daughter had helped dispel a little of the gloom from the Beaumont home. Beaumont wrote to Hitchcock that "Lilly is the delight & happiness of us all, a perfect little chatterbox." The death of Sarah's husband had made Hitchcock seem vulnerable, and just before he left for the front Beaumont commented that "we dread to have him go."[21]

Hitchcock kept his library at the Beaumonts. By the early 1850s it consisted of more than two thousand volumes, many of them on philosophical subjects. Even in time of war, Hitchcock continued to be a very unusual soldier. Beaumont told him in February 1847 that he was fast becoming a convert to his views "of the unrighteousness & absurdity of the present war & manner of conducting it."[22]

In the summer of 1846 the war for a time impinged on Beaumont's practice. In May his assistant volunteered for the Mexican campaign. Fortunately for Beaumont, Johnson was only gone for four months, and in September he returned to his former position. Even with Dr. Johnson in St. Louis, Beaumont

19. Beaumont to Israel Beaumont, January 27, 1848, BC, WU.

20. Hitchcock, *Fifty Years in Camp and Field,* 227; Beaumont to William Eliot, November 4, 1846, BC, WU; Lucretia Beaumont to Mrs. Whitney, November 26, 1846, BC, UC; Mary Lee to Sarah Beaumont, June 6 and July 10, [1847], Lee Letters.

21. Beaumont to Ethan Hitchcock, [February, 1847], Beaumont to William Eliot, November 4, 1846, BC, WU.

22. Beaumont to Ethan Hitchcock, [February 1847], BC, WU; Hitchcock, *Fifty Years in Camp and Field,* 385.

found the demands of his extensive practice taxed him to the limit. Writing to a friend in Green Bay, his daughter Lucretia commented in November 1846 that her father was "as busy as usual, going all day, comes home tire[d] and lays down and goes to sleep as you used to see him last summer."[23]

Beaumont's relationship with Johnson had lasted a lot longer than that with Dr. Sykes, presumably because Johnson owed a great deal to him, had been his pupil, and began their relationship with a great admiration for his old mentor. But by the fall of 1847 the relationship had collapsed. Johnson had been with Beaumont since 1841. His initial one thousand dollars a year had been raised to twelve hundred dollars when the Beaumonts moved to their country house and Johnson had to find his own accommodations. As well as working in the practice, Johnson did much of the bookkeeping. He kept his own accounts in Beaumont's books, and paid himself out of his collections. The relationship was a trusting one on both sides, but as Johnson became more experienced, the financial arrangements were all to Beaumont's advantage. Even in the late 1830s, with St. Louis still in depression, Beaumont had said he was making ten thousand a year, and that had undoubtedly increased.[24]

In November 1847, Johnson stopped entering his accounts in Beaumont's books and made no returns to Beaumont regarding the money he had collected. It appears that at that time Johnson simply opened his own practice with some of the patients that Beaumont considered to be his. Johnson had clearly developed his own relationship with particular patients, and it seems likely that one reason he had stayed so long was that even before November 1847 he had probably received more than the twelve hundred dollars to which Beaumont thought he was entitled. When the two men tried formally to end their relationship early in 1849 and settle the financial details, Beaumont stressed that they had not been partners. Johnson, he insisted, had worked for him as his assistant, principal clerk, or bookkeeper.[25]

In March 1849, at the time of the settlement, Beaumont pressed Johnson to reveal the private accounts he had kept for some time past. Between them, Beaumont and Johnson had been treating literally hundreds of patients, and detailed lists of amounts due ranged from seventy-five cents to more than

23. Beaumont, memo regarding George Johnson, March 1849, BC, WU; Lucretia Beaumont to Mrs. Whitney, November 26, 1846, BC, UC.

24. Beaumont, memo regarding George Johnson, March 1849, Beaumont to Joseph LaMotte, December 8, 1839, BC, WU.

25. Beaumont, memo regarding George Johnson, March 1849, BC, WU.

thirty dollars. Beaumont, as usual, thought he had been treated badly, and dragged his feet on a final settlement. He maintained that they could settle it between themselves if Johnson would show him his private books.[26]

At first, the two men decided they would settle their affairs by appointing referees. There was confusion in naming them, for they were making the arrangements not in person but by brief notes to each other, but they finally left it to two men (one of them Beaumont's old friend Kingsbury). It was understood that if they could not agree, they would name a third as umpire. This did not work because Beaumont's representative, Kingsbury, presumably at Beaumont's direction, would not agree on the appointment of an umpire.[27]

Johnson now proposed that Beaumont accept one of two solutions. Either Johnson would take fifteen hundred dollars in full payment of all the services he had rendered to Beaumont's patients, or he offered to enter into written articles naming impartial referees who would then choose an umpire. The three would decide the whole matter within twenty days. Johnson asked for an answer within twenty four hours but two days later he had not heard, and sent another note, hand-delivered, to Beaumont. This produced results.[28]

Beaumont agreed to give Johnson the fifteen hundred dollars, payable in three notes over the next eighteen months. For this Johnson assigned to Beaumont the right to collect all medical claims or accounts for medical services rendered to Beaumont's patients up to January 1, 1848, except for some 150 accounts that Johnson retained for his own benefit. These last patients owed more than the fifteen hundred dollars. Clearly this was a very prosperous practice. It seems likely that Johnson, who for some time had probably been practicing on his own account as well as receiving his twelve hundred dollars from Beaumont, decided in November 1847 that he had enough patients to go it alone. The situation had arisen because Beaumont took on more patients than he could take care of, but did not want to take a formal partner to share in the costs and the profits of the practice.[29]

Beaumont never forgot what he considered an injury, and in November 1849 he billed Johnson for the use of rooms for himself and his brother from November 1847 to March 1849; that was from the time, Beaumont wrote,

26. Accounting of partnership [sic] with George Johnson, 1844–1849, Beaumont to Johnson, March 15, 1849, BC, WU.

27. George Johnson to Beaumont, March 14, 15, 16, and 20, 1849, Beaumont to Johnson, March 16 and 17, 1849, BC, WU.

28. George Johnson to Beaumont, March 22 and 24, 1849, BC, WU.

29. Accounting of partnership with George Johnson, 1844–1849, BC, WU.

that Johnson took control of the business of Beaumont's office, "irrespective of my interest, convenience, or approbation." He charged eighty dollars–for sixteen months at five dollars per month, saying it was necessary because in November 1847 Johnson had severed himself from Beaumont's employment, and had converted his business to his own use and benefit.[30]

The break with Dr. Johnson meant that Beaumont once again had to leave what had now become Beaumont Place, with its large garden, and move back into the center of the city. Money was no problem, and in 1849 he was able to buy a more convenient house for $10,875, payable in three promissory notes. He retained his house with its ample land on the outskirts of town, for it was an area that was rapidly becoming more generally developed.[31]

Beaumont moved back into the city at a dangerous time, for in 1849 St. Louis was beset by a severe epidemic of cholera. It was a year of calamity for the city. In the middle of May a fire that had begun on a ship at the docks spread through numerous other vessels and onto the land. By the time it was out it had destroyed more than fourteen blocks. The fire was destructive to property, but it was cholera that overwhelmed the medical profession and kept Beaumont working day and night.[32]

Cholera was epidemic in the United States in 1849, and was already spreading in late 1848. In all American cities, there was a tendency of the newspapers and journals to try to play down the first appearances of epidemic diseases, and St. Louis was no exception. Newspapers did not want to scare away visitors and business, and did not want to alarm the local populations. St. Louis was particularly sensitive to the notion of major epidemics, because the local press and journals often tried to counter the prevailing view that St. Louis was a town of great unhealthiness.[33]

The first cases of cholera appeared in St. Louis in January. It was later suggested that the disease had been brought upriver from New Orleans by infected German immigrants. In January 1849 the *St. Louis Medical and Surgical Journal* reported optimistically that the disease appeared to be diminishing in severity in New Orleans, and there had been little of it in St. Louis; only a few "bad cases." The cause of cholera was then unknown, and the editor of the *Journal* pointed out that there had been a great prevalence of

---

30. Beaumont to George Johnson, November 1, 1849, BC, WU.
31. Record of indebtedness to George Clark, August 1, 1849, BC, UC.
32. Van Ravenswaay, *St. Louis*, 385–88; Patrick E. McClear, "The St. Louis Cholera Epidemic," 171–81.
33. Rosenberg, *Cholera Years*, 101–22.

diarrhea and asked whether this was cholera. His answer was yes, that this diarrhea differed only in degree from the fully developed form of the disease. "There appears to be not the slightest evidence," he wrote, "that cholera is a specific disease, or that it is contagious." Others disagreed with him, and there was a continuing argument about whether or not cholera was contagious.[34]

The bacterium that causes cholera was not identified until the 1880s. When ingested, it brought about an acute disease, marked by diarrhea, cramps, and vomiting, with a very high death rate; death often occurred with great rapidity after the symptoms appeared. About half of those contracting the disease died. Writing of the 1849 epidemic in St. Louis, local physician William McPheeters commented that nearly all the worst cases died. With its overcrowding and its lack of any sewer system, St. Louis was an ideal breeding ground for a disease that was spread by water contaminated by human waste. It could also be passed along on unwashed hands or on raw fruit and vegetables. As many suspected that epidemic diseases were caused by unhealthy miasmas in the air, the onset of epidemics in American cities was followed by the cleaning of the streets, and often by the burning of barrels of tar to "purify" the air. McPheeters stated that in January 1849 the unknown "morbid agent" causing cholera already existed in the atmosphere, and that in the first case he knew of local origin, sauerkraut "acted as an exciting cause." A local physician later remembered that all green vegetables, such as cucumbers and cabbages, were excluded from the diet.[35]

By March, the *St. Louis Medical and Surgical Journal* was prepared to admit that for the past two months "the cholera influence has evidently existed in our community." It said that since the first of January, sixty-seven deaths had been reported as being from cholera, but that at least half of these were of individuals who contracted the disease in New Orleans or on their way to St. Louis. The editors suggested that it was necessary that there should be strict adherence to sanitary and hygienic rules.[36]

The disease spread only slowly in the first months of the year, but in March and April there were about two hundred cases. In the next three months

34. *St. Louis Medical and Surgical Journal* 6 (1849): 333; Scharf, *History of St. Louis*, vol. 2, 173; Primm, *Lion of the Valley*, 162; William B. McPheeters, "History of the Epidemic Cholera in St. Louis in 1849," 111.

35. Rosenberg, *Cholera Years*, 1–4; Duffy, *From Humors to Medical Science*, 76–77; Erwin H. Ackerknecht, *History and Geography of the Most Important Diseases*, 23; McPheeters, "History of the Epidemic Cholera," 98–99; Reminiscences of Dr. Elisha H. Gregory, in Goldstein, ed., *One Hundred Years*, 37.

36. *St. Louis Medical and Surgical Journal* 6 (1849): 430–31.

there was a dramatic increase—more than five hundred cases in May, about eighteen hundred in June, and about nineteen hundred in July. By August, the worst was over. There were only about sixty cases in that month, and only thirteen were reported in September. In St. Louis in 1849, there were 4,557 deaths reported from cholera out of a total number of deaths of 8,603. In the previous year, the total number of deaths in St. Louis, from all causes, had only been 2,589.[37]

In late June, with numerous deaths occurring daily, the city council appointed a twelve-man committee to adopt measures to deal with the emergency. They directed the cleaning of the streets, set up emergency hospitals in the schools, and had barrels of tar and sulfur burnt "to dissipate the foul air which has been the cause of such mortality." Special block inspectors were responsible for seeing that all filth was removed from the houses and streets. The sale of vegetables within the city limits was forbidden. A quarantine station was established at Duncan's Island, and a steamer tied up there for that purpose. The object was to examine the passengers on all the steamboats coming from the south. By the time the quarantine was lifted in August, some seventeen hundred individuals had been detained. While the authorities tried to deal with the crisis, thousands fled the city.[38]

A fellow physician later commented that during this cholera epidemic, Beaumont stood at his post, "and with the zeal, courage, and ardor of his early days, devoted himself, day and night to the duties of his calling." Although Beaumont had treated the Sublettes since soon after he had arrived in St. Louis, one of the family mentioned that she could not get him to come to see her daughter, who soon died of cholera. She told her husband that it was almost impossible to get a doctor, "as they, are going all the time." In spite of this, his initial reaction seemed remarkably calm. Major Hitchcock was again at the Beaumonts, and commented in his diary at the end of June that the family were "not particularly alarmed about the cholera, which now rages in the city, carrying off more than 100 inhabitants daily." He said he had been sick during the evening, and had just taken some "cholera drops."[39]

37. McPheeters, "History of the Epidemic Cholera," 100–105; *St. Louis Medical and Surgical Journal* 11 (1853): 225.

38. Van Ravenswaay, *St. Louis*, 388–91, 389 (quotation); Primm, *Lion of the Valley*, 162; Hitchcock, *Fifty Years in Camp and Field*, 335; Scharf, *History of St. Louis*, vol. 2, 1575–79; Patrick E. McLear, "The St. Louis Cholera Epidemic of 1849," 177.

39. Thomas Reyburn, "Memoir of Beaumont," clipping, BC, WU; Frances Sublette to Solomon P. Sublette, May 13, 1849, Sublette Papers; Hitchcock, *Fifty Years in Camp and Field*, 355.

Beaumont, like most other practitioners, tried various treatments for cholera. Amongst other remedies, he advocated forty to sixty drops of a mixture of ammoniated tincture of valerian, opium, camphor, sulphuric ether, and peppermint, with hot friction to the stomach and the extremities. Within a few hours, if his initial treatment did not produce any results, he also used calomel, and if there was congestion, he cupped the patient on the chest, abdomen, and the spinal column. Cupping involved drawing blood by making cuts and creating a partial vacuum by applying a cupping glass. He said that if he was called before congestion was complete, he bled the patient freely. In the course of the summer of 1849, he apparently developed more respect for the disease than he had at the end of June, because he later said that when the patient had reached the stage of collapse, all medical efforts seemed "worse than useless." To a friend he wrote: "May God avert the fell disease from your community, and spare you all individually and professionally from the agonizing pain, distress, and consternation of its visitation."[40]

The great difficulty physicians had in treating cholera was shown by the range of treatments. McPheeters said that one of the first remedies he used was twenty grains of calomel, twenty grains of capsicum (dried cayenne pepper), and ten grains of camphor, but he admitted that this turned out to be harmful. He described a whole list of treatments used either by himself or others: quinine, in large and small doses; opium; morphia; calomel, which he said was regarded by many as the basic treatment; free bleeding; cupping; warm baths; cold douses; mustard plasters; friction with capsicum, dry mustard, and salt; hot bricks; blankets rung out in hot water; and chloroform, both inhaled and taken internally. Bleeding, which was still common in St. Louis, was often used to treat the disease.[41]

The treatments that McPheeters decided were the most beneficial were in reality no better than the others. In the early stages of the disease, when the patient was vomiting, he gave an emetic of salt and mustard, followed by a single dose of twenty grains of calomel. This was followed every fifteen, thirty, or sixty minutes with a powder consisting of five grains each of musk, calomel, and tannin, and four grains of camphor. He also gave injections of lead acetate and laudanum, and made use of "a large blister over the

40. Beaumont, letter on treatment of cholera, [1849], BC, WU; extract in Myer, *Beaumont*, 293–94; see also Irwin H. Pizer and Harriet Steurnagel, "Medical Journals in St. Louis before 1900," 228–29.

41. Rosenberg, *Cholera Years*, 60–67, 150–51; Reminiscences of Dr. Elisha H. Gregory, in Goldstein, ed., *One Hundred Years*, 39; McPheeters, "History of the Epidemic Cholera," 113–15.

abdomen." If the patient showed a tendency to sink, he also gave ten grains of ammonium carbonate in solution every fifteen or thirty minutes.[42]

Beaumont and his family came through the cholera epidemic unscathed, but early in the following year they had to live through another tragedy. This time it had a more direct impact on Beaumont himself. His youngest daughter, Lucretia, whose health had always caused worry, in 1849 had married Herman Canfield, a local artist. She quickly became pregnant and had a child in December 1849, but never recovered from the birth. Early in the new year she died, and her baby did not long survive her.[43] This was a severe blow to Beaumont. It aged him, and made him more concerned about his two surviving children.

In the same month that Lucretia died, Beaumont wrote Israel a long letter of advice. "Discard the bewitching visions & flickering thoughts of passionate love, and Hymenial bliss, during your professional pupilage, *at least,*" he told him. "Relinquish all undue pretensions to *Gallantry,* and obsequious attention to the *Girls, Graces,* or the muses." He wanted him to devote himself to his books, business, and professional studies until he was twenty-five or thirty or more, and "make a *useful* man—dutiful Son, and happy Parents."[44] The idea of usefulness, of steady achievement resulting from continual application, much appealed to Beaumont.

Beaumont gradually gave his son more responsibility in taking care of the family investments in property. Also, Beaumont himself, while not lessening his practice, in his last years devoted a good deal of his time to correspondence concerning his property holdings in Green Bay and Prairie du Chien. He was thinking of the possibility of spending money to improve his Green Bay property, and since moving into the center of St. Louis had decided to take advantage of the city by laying out his property on the outskirts into separate lots. A new county road was being built out from the city through the edge of his property, and his land was in the middle of a booming area. The Green Bay improvements had to wait, but in the following years the subdividing of what became known as the "Beaumont Addition" in St. Louis went on quite rapidly to provide a very useful nest egg for his heirs.[45]

42. McPheeters, "History of the Epidemic Cholera," 115.

43. *Index of St. Louis Marriages, 1804–1876,* vol. 1; Nelson, *Beaumont,* 295; genealogical material, BC, UC.

44. Beaumont to Israel Beaumont, January 26, 1850, BC, UC.

45. Ibid., and Beaumont to Israel Beaumont, September 8 and November 6, 1850, Sale of property in Beaumont Addition, April 15, 1852, Plat of Beaumont Addition, and sale by auction of twenty-two lots, September 26, 1853, BC, UC; Nelson, *Beaumont,* 272–83.

While pressing his son to work hard for success, Beaumont kept up a warm relationship with him. Writing to him on Christmas Eve, 1850, with details of how to deal with an offer to lease some of his land in Green Bay, he asked him to enjoy the next day "right merrily and morally" with all the Beaumont relations and friends at the Bay, and finished his letter, in the early hours, with a Christmas poem. He imagined everyone awake at 6 A.M., *"kissing* for *old Nick's* sake," and breakfasting on molasses, buckwheat cakes, oyster soup, venison, chicken, hot rolls, and butter. Apparently Beaumont's concern about diet did not extend to Christmas. The Beaumonts enjoyed their Christmas and New Year celebrations, and apparently had even adopted the new fashion of having a Christmas tree. When Mary Lee wrote from Arlington on New Year's Day in 1848 she mentioned she had never seen a Christmas tree, but supposed that Sarah's German friends could arrange one for her in true style.[46]

Greater wealth, and a degree of mellowness, did not transform Beaumont's essential nature. When in the fall of 1850 he heard that Congress had passed an act granting land bounties to those who had served from 1812 to 1848, he quickly put in his application for land warrants of 160 acres for himself and his wife, asking Hitchcock, now a colonel, to deliver them in person. The military reserve at Green Bay was being opened for sale, and Beaumont told his son to locate the two quarter sections on the best locations he could find there or anywhere else in the state. "I will suggest you go, select the best site you can, *Squat,* Stick your Stakes, build a hut . . . or chicken coop, for Preemption Sake, till you reserve the warrants to cover the same or more."[47]

But feeling his years, Beaumont began to place more trust and reliance on his son, and in June 1851 formally entrusted him with the task of managing and disposing of his property at Green Bay, as well as other parcels of land in Fond du Lac and at Prairie du Bay on the Wisconsin River. In the fall of that year, he also sent him to Prairie du Chien to deal with problems that had arisen regarding his holdings in the western parts of the state.[48]

46. Beaumont to Israel Beaumont, Christmas Eve, [1850], BC, UC. This is printed in Arno B. Luckhardt, ed., "Three Doctor William Beaumont Letters," 127; Mary Lee to Sarah Beaumont, January 1, 1848, Lee Letters.

47. Deposition to the Judge of the Probate Court, October 28, 1850, BC, WU; Beaumont to Israel Beaumont, March 4, 1851, BC, UC.

48. Memo of property entrusted to Israel Beaumont, June 1851; Beaumont to Israel Beaumont, September 27, 1851, May 28, 1852, Hercules Dousman to Israel Beaumont, February 10, 1852, Israel Beaumont to Beaumont, March 3, 1852, Beaumont Papers, SHSW; Albert E. Ellis to Beaumont, May 5, 1852, BC, WU.

In May 1852 Beaumont was supposed to meet Israel in Prairie du Chien so that they could jointly deal with problems regarding the properties, but he was too busy to leave St. Louis, and asked Israel to do the best he could with the advice of his old friend Hercules Dousman. A month later he was still hoping to pay "a flying visit," but was thwarted by "the rascally Bellyaches & Baby cases of the season." He told Dousman that he could not escape from his professional duties "without doing violence to the feelings" of his patients, particularly the females. He asked Dousman to help Israel all he could, because he was "young and not much used to such business."[49]

Even now, at the end of his life, and showing not the slightest inclination to rest from his professional responsibilities, Beaumont's thoughts sometimes returned to the possibility of securing St. Martin for further research. The usual stimulus to action was some form of outside recognition or contact that reminded him of how St. Martin had brought him to the attention of a larger world. It happened again in early 1850. Beaumont received a letter from Dr. W. G. Edwards in Paris. Edwards was writing on behalf of a famous French physiologist, M. Claude Bernard. He stated that Beaumont's book had begun a new era in the study of the stomach, and that Bernard, among others, was constantly repeating his experiments upon animals. Bernard wanted to know what had become of St. Martin.[50]

Beaumont replied that St. Martin was living, in robust health, still with a stomach opening, and that he was "a reckless reprobate—faithless & intractable." But he also said that in the last few days, for the fourth or fifth time, he had begun an effort to get him back again. In reality, Beaumont wrote to William Morrison on the same day that he wrote to Edwards, asking whether St. Martin might be disposed to come to St. Louis with or without his family.[51]

Morrison replied that St. Martin would come in July, but only with his family, which consisted of his wife and four children. St. Martin wanted to settle his affairs, as he expected to stay in the United States when Beaumont finished with him. He wanted $250 for a year plus board, and he would need $150 in advance for clothes and the passage. This would be deducted from the $250. Morrison said there was no danger in advancing money, as St.

49. Beaumont to Israel Beaumont, May 28, 1852, Beaumont Collection, SHSW; Beaumont to Hercules Dousman, July 8, 1852, Hercules Dousman Papers, SHSW.

50. W. G. Edwards to Beaumont, [December 26, 1850], in Myer, *Beaumont*, 289.

51. Beaumont to W. G. Edwards, January 31, 1850, Beaumont to William Morrison, January 31, 1850, BC, WU.

Martin was now a teetotaler. Beaumont, perhaps realizing that this was his last chance, showed a major change of heart. He agreed to the proposal, even offering to add $50 and make it $300 a year, as long as he was exempted from boarding, supporting, or employing St. Martin's wife and children. He said that he would, however, supply them with a house and lot to live in. He thought it might be best for St. Martin to come in September, when St. Louis would be healthier and Beaumont less busy.[52]

The negotiations began well, but gradually fell apart. It took Beaumont until August to send a one-hundred-dollar advance to Morrison in the form of a bill of exchange. St. Martin was to sign a receipt for it, was to agree to be bound for two years (not one), and promise to refund the one hundred dollars if he did not come. By the time the money got there, St. Martin had gone into the United States for the hay-making season. In late September, Morrison reported that he had still not returned, and then there was silence from Canada. At the end of December, Beaumont wrote to tell Morrison he had heard nothing, and St. Martin had not arrived. This was awkward as Beaumont had been so confident that he had agreed to give a course of lectures at the medical college, and a "resume" of his physiological experiments.[53]

In January 1851 Morrison reported that when St. Martin had returned from the United States he had intended to leave for St. Louis but fell sick. Morrison said his "constitution appears to be ruined," doubted he would ever be well enough to go, and returned the one hundred dollars. Even now the negotiations dragged on, unsuccessfully, for nearly two more years. Beaumont tried luring St. Martin by saying that when St. Martin was in the United States he would help him file for 160 acres on the basis of his army service from 1832 to 1834, but when he heard again that St. Martin was willing to come, he told Morrison he would send no more advances. It was up to St. Martin to come, pay his own way, and be reimbursed. In October 1851, Beaumont relented on this and said he was prepared to send money, but by the time correspondence was exchanged it was too late in the season to come.[54]

52. William Morrison to Beaumont, February 23, 1850, Beaumont to Morrison, May 4, 1850, Beaumont to St. Martin, May 4, 1850, BC, WU.

53. William Morrison to Beaumont, June 24 and September 28, 1850, Beaumont to Morrison, August 4, October 4, and December 30, 1850, Receipt and agreement for St. Martin to sign, August 5, 1850, Beaumont to St. Martin, August 5, 1850, BC, WU.

54. William Morrison to Beaumont, January 21, May 9, October 6, October 30, and December 28, 1851; Beaumont to Morrison, February 16, July 15, October 22, and November 12, 1851, Beaumont to St. Martin, February 16 and July 15, 1851, BC, WU.

Negotiations began again in the spring of 1852. Again, Morrison's news was that St. Martin was prepared to come, but he needed $150 in advance. Beaumont again did not send the money, later telling Morrison that he had planned to come to get him but was too busy. Finally, in October 1852, Beaumont sent one hundred dollars (not $150), with a proposal that St. Martin should come *alone* in the spring of 1853 and that Beaumont would give him three hundred dollars for himself and two hundred dollars to support his family in Canada.[55]

In the fall of 1852 Beaumont became a touch irrational on this subject. He had repeatedly said that he had to secure St. Martin again, and he had repeatedly balked at advancing enough money at the right time, but now, in writing to his cousin Sam, he put all the blame on St. Martin. He told Sam that St. Martin's object seemed only to get heavy advances and then cause disappointment, or to impose himself and his whole family on Beaumont to support them for life. "I have evaded his designs so far," wrote Beaumont, but now he wanted him "at all hazards." He now felt his mortality, and there are indications in his letter that he actually realized that all the blame was not St. Martin's. "I must retrieve my past ignorance, imbecility & professional remissness of a quarter century, or more," he wrote, by intense application to the subject "before I die." He wanted Sam to come to St. Louis and help him on a new edition of his book. He said the professors at the medical school had offered to take up the experiments under their auspices.

Ultimately, the letter to Sam could not disguise what had been the great stumbling block in Beaumont renewing his experiments on St. Martin. He wanted his practice, more particularly the profits of his practice, more than he wanted to conduct research on St. Martin. This was at the heart of his cry about his own "ignorance, imbecility & professional remisness." In urging Sam to think of coming to St. Louis, he noted that there was "an immense professional practice in this City," and admitted that the whole thing was becoming a little too much for him. "I get tired of it, and have been trying hard to withdraw from it altogether," he wrote, "but the more I try the tighter I seem to be held to it by the people." His domestic affairs, he wrote, were "easy, peaceable & pleasant," his family was enjoying "health, happiness, and abundance," but Beaumont could not relax. "I am actually persecuted, worried & almost worn out with valetudinarian importunities, & Hypocondrial

---

55. Beaumont to William Morrison, February 7, October 10, and October 15, 1852, Morrison to Beaumont, May 4, 1852, St. Martin to Beaumont, May 15 and September 25, 1852, Beaumont to St. Martin, October 15, 1852, BC, WU.

groans, repinings & lamentations—amen." Beaumont was driven, not by an all-powerful desire to cure, although certainly he was a dedicated physician who did the best he could by his patients, but by an all-powerful desire to make money.[56]

Beaumont never saw St. Martin again. In October 1852, at the same time that he bared his heart to his cousin, he sent a check for one hundred dollars to Morrison, which he said was "a Sort of Secret Service Money" to get St. Martin to come without his family. He told Morrison to let St. Martin feel that anything he advanced was a loan, but if he would not come alone, Morrison was to advance him no money. St. Martin certainly had his faults and was not easy to deal with, but the main difficulty was Beaumont's fear that he would lose any money he advanced, and that if St. Martin came with his family he would be stuck with their permanent support.[57]

In the winter of 1852–1853, Beaumont continued the schedule that was becoming an increasing burden, but in March he slipped on a step while leaving a patient's home. He hit his head, and wandered around in a dazed condition until taken home by a friend. At first he seemed to have recovered, but a fellow physician stated in a memoir of Beaumont that within a few weeks he began to suffer from a "carbuncle" at the back of his neck. He was ill for five weeks. A severe fever set in, and he suffered a great deal.[58] Trephining was not resorted to, but whether this was Beaumont's decision is unknown.

The Reverend William Eliot was with him a good deal near the end, and noted in his diary that Beaumont bore his terrible sufferings "with the most manly fortitude." Near death, Beaumont asked Eliot to place his name on the church record, and took communion. Eliot helped him make a will, and became his executor. Making the will was difficult, as Beaumont was now very deaf. He died on the night of April 25, 1853, and was buried in Bellefontaine Cemetery. He had bought a plot there in 1850.[59]

Beaumont's will, and the inventory of his estate, testified to the financial success he had sought with such determination. He had valuable property holdings in St. Louis, as well as scattered holdings in Wisconsin; the most

56. Beaumont to Samuel Beaumont, October 20, 1852, BC, WU.
57. Beaumont to William Morrison, October 1852, BC, WU.
58. Thomas Reyburn, "Memoir of Beaumont," clipping, BC, WU; Nelson, *Beaumont,* 320–22.
59. Extract from diary of William Eliot, BC, WU; purchase note of cemetery plot, October 30, 1850, BC, UC.

important of these were in Green Bay. His financial and property dealings had become more extensive in the last years of his life. At his death, he had $12,500 owed to him in the form of notes, payable with interest over the next six years. He also had more than $2,000 owed to him by seventy-six patients. His major bequests were to his son Israel, who received half of the Beaumont Addition tract that remained unsold, valued at $70,000; his daughter Sarah received a fifth part of the same unsold part of the tract, valued at $28,000, as well as his house in town and eight shares of stock in the St. Louis Gas Light Company; his nephews Theodore and Platte Greene received $3,000 each; his granddaughter Lucretia, $1,000; his cousin Sam, $1,000; and Thomas Green, his wife's brother, $1,000. Eliot's Unitarian Church of the Messiah received the only money given outside of the family–$1,500.[60]

Eliot's eulogy managed to convey not only Beaumont's strengths but also how he made enemies. He talked of his promptness in coming to a decision, and of his firmness in maintaining it, of his boldness, his fertility of resources, his faithfulness, and his nerves of steel. He said that because early in his career he was called often to apparently hopeless cases where none but desperate remedies would prevail, he acquired a vigor and strength in his practice, "sometimes misunderstood by the timid." Beaumont had begun as a "heroic" practitioner, and continued to be so until his death.[61]

Fellow St. Louis physician Thomas Reyburn in his memoir of Beaumont also stressed Beaumont's vigor of mind and firmness of purpose, but also, somewhat surprisingly, said that more than any other man he knew, Beaumont possessed a knowledge ("almost intuitive") of human character. Perhaps this meant that he was rarely, if ever, deceived. He always had a clear vision of human deception and human frailty. Reyburn acknowledged that Beaumont's temperament was "ardent," but stated that in the sick room he was "a model of patience and kindness."[62] In his eulogy, Eliot described Beaumont sitting all night by the bedside of a sick child. That sounds like Beaumont; he liked children. What comes through in all comments on Beaumont's death was his decisiveness, his certainty, and his strength. This also comes through in his letters. Only near the end, in his letter to his cousin Sam, does he reveal self-doubt. For most of his life, he knew what he wanted, pursued it relentlessly, and clashed bitterly with those who resisted him.

60. Copy of Beaumont's will, April 14, 1853, BC, UC.

61. Address of the Reverend William Eliot at Beaumont's funeral service, April 26, 1853, BC, WU.

62. Thomas Reyburn, "Memoir of Beaumont," clipping, BC, WU.

CONCLUSION

WRITING MORE THAN ONE hundred years after the publication of Beaumont's book, an eminent physiologist commented that "one truly does not know gastric physiology and pathology as one should until Beaumont has been read critically and *in toto*." He noted that some of Beaumont's conclusions had been corrected, but marveled at "the high degree of accuracy" of Beaumont's fifty-one inferences, and stated that still more could be learned from a careful reading of all of Beaumont's observations.[1]

From the time that his work appeared, Beaumont's work was accepted as a major contribution to the knowledge of human digestion. Ronald L. Numbers and William J. Orr Jr. have shown that its impact was great both in the United States and in Europe. In the United States, it influenced not only how digestion was viewed but also the whole understanding of dietetics. In Europe, it profoundly influenced the course of research into digestion.[2] Even the work of Réaumur and Spallanzani had not ended fundamental disagreements, but after the publication of Beaumont's book, the chemical nature of the digestive process could no longer be challenged by any serious researcher.

Beaumont had no formal training in research, but he had the good sense to report what he saw without attempting to fit his observations into some all-encompassing theory. His lack of detailed training for research in human digestion in some ways helped him, for such training would probably have made him keener to find particular results from his work. As it was, he carried out most of his reading in depth after he had conducted his most important experiments, and the dispassionate way in which he reached his conclusions was evident in his published work.

1. Andrew C. Ivy, "A Present-Day Appreciation of Beaumont's Experiments on Alexis St. Martin," xviii, xxi.
2. Numbers and Orr, "Beaumont's Reception," 590–612.

In the first part of his life, Beaumont was generally confident that he knew a great deal about medicine and therapeutics, but when he began his observation of St. Martin he realized that he knew very little about physiological research. As a physician and military surgeon, he was often opinionated to the point of arrogance, but he had none of this arrogance when engaged in research. "I had no particular hypothesis to support," he wrote in the preface to his book, "and I have therefore honestly recorded the result of each experiment exactly as it occurred."[3]

Given the particular opportunity presented by the wound to St. Martin, and the way that the nature of the wound shaped Beaumont's research, it is not surprising that he wrote as though chymification in the stomach was in itself the process of digestion, but he recognized that there were factors in the process of digestion that he did not understand. He was convinced from his experiments in vitro that there was an unknown element in the gastric juice, but was frustrated in identifying it by the limitations of chemical analysis in his time. Others after him were able to identify pepsin. Similarly, although he attempted only the crudest of experiments relating to bile and the gastric juice, he recognized that they had a role in the digestive process; he had no means of finding out what that role was.

Beaumont was fortunate that St. Martin was thrust upon him, but it was not luck that enabled him to take maximum advantage of the situation. He was remarkable in that he occupies a lone position of importance in American physiological research in the first half of the nineteenth century. The centenary volume on the history of the American Physiological Society, published in 1987, after noting that there was no continuous tradition of experimental physiology in the United States before the Civil War, states that William Beaumont "was a unique phenomenon."[4]

St. Martin lived until 1880, but was never again the subject of significant research. All the ambitious hopes that St. Martin would be examined by experts in eastern and European cities came to nought. But it was appropriate that research of lasting significance on the Canadian voyageur was carried out not in Philadelphia or Paris, but in the old fur trading post of Prairie du Chien. St. Martin fretted as he underwent experiments, but he might well have fretted more if research on him had been conducted in a completely unfamiliar environment. Having his body invaded for research was stressful

3. Beaumont, *Experiments and Observations,* 6.
4. Brobeck, Reynolds, and Appel, eds., *History of the American Physiological Society,* 12.

to St. Martin, but in spite of their often strained relationship, Beaumont remained the only man who was able to examine and test St. Martin's stomach in systematic fashion. Even after St. Martin's death this did not change. When he died, his family members were so determined to avoid an autopsy that they allowed the body to reach an advanced stage of decomposition before burial, and had it placed deeply in a particularly secure grave.[5]

There were obvious disadvantages to conducting research alone in the old, decrepit log hospital in Prairie du Chien, but Beaumont's position as an army surgeon in a lonely western post held some advantages.[6] His pay was regular, his living provided for, and there were long periods of limited duty. The typical physician with a large practice was too busy meeting the demands of his patients, and earning money, to find time for research. This became Beaumont's problem after he left the army. He was delighted at the rewards of his very successful St. Louis practice, and his desire to pursue these rewards gave him less incentive to seek out St. Martin at any cost. This probably did not lessen Beaumont's ultimate reputation, for he had already carried out the research of which he was capable. His opportunism, combined with a sound instinct for research, combined to give him a permanent place in the history of physiology.

5. Osler, "A Backwood Physiologist," 167–69.

6. Pitcock, "The Career of William Beaumont," 161, and Nelson, *Beaumont*, viii, argue that isolation was probably an advantage to Beaumont.

BIBLIOGRAPHY

THE MOST IMPORTANT COLLECTION of Beaumont papers is in the library of the Washington University School of Medicine, in St. Louis. This collection is available on microfilm. There are additional collections of considerable use in the Medical Library of Yale University and the Joseph Regenstein Library of the University of Chicago. The former is of most use for the first part of Beaumont's life, and the latter for his own family. There is much material relating to Beaumont's military career in the Washington University collection as well as in the National Archives in Washington, D.C. The State Historical Society of Wisconsin has microfilm of materials relating to William Beaumont from the Offices of the Adjutant General, the Quartermaster General, and the Surgeon General. The Health Library of the University of Wisconsin has photocopies of material relating to Beaumont from the Offices of the Adjutant General and the Surgeon General.

Among printed materials, the basic book for any study of Beaumont is Jesse S. Myer's *Life and Letters of Dr. William Beaumont.* Myer was in contact with Beaumont's daughters, and has some information unobtainable elsewhere. Among modern authors, Rodney B. Nelson, in *Beaumont: America's First Physiologist,* has done most to seek out new materials relating both to Beaumont's private and public life. Cynthia DeHaven Pitcock, in her dissertation entitled "The Career of William Beaumont, 1783–1853: Science and the Self-Made Man in America," concentrates primarily on his life as a physician and scientist, in the context of the driving ambitions of a nineteenth-century self-made man.

In the following bibliography, I have not attempted to list all of the extensive secondary work on Beaumont, merely those items that have proved to be of most use for this study.

MANUSCRIPTS

American Fur Company Record Books. Mackinac Island, Mackinac Island
    State Park Commission (microfilm).

Beaumont, William. Collection. School of Medicine Library, Washington University, St. Louis.

Beaumont, William. Papers. Beaumont Medical Club, Medical Library, Yale University.

Beaumont, William. Papers. Joseph Regenstein Library, University of Chicago.

Beaumont, William. Papers. Missouri Historical Society, St. Louis.

Beaumont, William. Papers. State Historical Society of Wisconsin, Madison.

Burnett, Thomas P. Papers. State Historical Society of Wisconsin, Area Research Center, University of Wisconsin–Platteville.

Darby, John F. Papers. Missouri Historical Society.

Dousman, Hercules Louis. Papers. State Historical Society of Wisconsin.

Hitchcock Family. Papers. Missouri Historical Society.

Inventory of estate of William Beaumont. Probate Court, St. Louis.

Kennerly, James. Papers. Missouri Historical Society.

Kingsbury, James W. Collection. Missouri Historical Society.

Lane Collection. Missouri Historical Society.

Lee, Robert E. and Mary R. Letters. Bancroft Library, University of California–Berkeley.

Linn, Lewis F. Papers. Missouri Historical Society.

Lucas Collection. Missouri Historical Society.

Martin, Morgan L. Papers. Neville Public Museum, Green Bay, Wisconsin.

Medical Papers. Missouri Historical Society.

Medical Society of Missouri at St. Louis. Minutes, 1835–1851. St. Louis Metropolitan Medical Society, St. Louis.

Michilimackinac County Commissioners. Minutes, 1821–1859. Mackinac Island State Park Commission (microfilm).

Sublette, William. Papers. Missouri Historical Society.

War Department. RG 92. Records of the Office of the Quartermaster General, National Archives.

War Department. RG 94. Records of the Office of the Adjutant General, National Archives, Washington, D.C.

War Department. RG 112. Records of the Office of the Surgeon General, National Archives.

War Department. RG 159. Records of the Office of the Inspector General, National Archives.

Wislizenus Papers. Missouri Historical Society.

PRINTED PRIMARY SOURCES

American Journal of the Medical Sciences 14 (May 1834): 117–49 (review of
　　Beaumont's book).
American Journal of Science and Arts 26 (July 1834): 193–202 (review of
　　Beaumont's book).
American State Papers, Military Affairs. Vols. 1–7. Washington, D.C.: Gales &
　　Seaton, 1832–1861.
Annan, Gertrude L., ed. "Early Letters of William Beaumont Never before
　　Published." *Bulletin of the New York Academy of Medicine* 10 (1934):
　　656–61.
Atwater, Caleb. *Remarks Made on a Tour to Prairie du Chien: Thence to Wash-
　　ington City in 1829.* Columbus, Ohio: Isaac N. Whiting, 1831. Facsimile
　　reprint, New York: Arno, 1975.
Baird, Elizabeth T. "Reminiscences of Early Days on Mackinac Island." *Col-
　　lections of the State Historical Society of Wisconsin* 14: 17–64. Madison:
　　State Historical Society of Wisconsin, 1898.
——. "Reminiscences of Life in Territorial Wisconsin." *Collections of the State
　　Historical Society of Wisconsin* 15: 205–63. Madison: State Historical
　　Society of Wisconsin, 1900.
[Beaumont, William]. Joseph Lovell. "A Case of Wounded Stomach." *Medical
　　Recorder* 8 (January 1825): 14–19.
Beaumont, William. *Experiments and Observations on the Gastric Juice and
　　the Physiology of Digestion.* Plattsburgh, N.Y.: F. P. Allen, 1833.
——. *Experiments and Observations on the Gastric Juice and the Physiology
　　of Digestion.* Reprinted with notes by Andrew Combe, M.D. Edinburgh:
　　Maclachlan & Stewart, 1838.
——. "Further Experiments on the Case of Alexis St. Martin, Who Was
　　Wounded in the Stomach by a Load of Buckshot, Detailed in the Re-
　　corder for Jan. 1825." *Medical Recorder* 9 (January 1826): 94–97.
——, to Judge DeLord, *North Country Notes.* Plattsburgh, N.Y. No. 65 (May
　　1970): 2–3.
——. *The Physiology of Digestion with Experiments on the Gastric Juice.* 2d ed.
　　Corrected by Samuel Beaumont. Burlington, Vt.: Chauncey Goodrich,
　　1847.
Boston Medical and Surgical Journal 9 (January 15, 1834): 365–68 (review
　　of Beaumont's book).
Brunson, Alfred. "Memoir of Thomas Pendleton Burnett." *Collections of the*

State Historical Society of Wisconsin 2: 233–325. Madison: State Historical Society of Wisconsin, 1903.

Combe, George. *Notes on the United States of North America during a Phrenological Visit in 1838–9–40.* 2 vols. Philadelphia: Carey & Hart, 1841.

Cooke, Philip St. George. *Scenes and Adventures in the Army, or, Romance of Military Life.* Philadelphia: Lindsay & Blakiston, 1857.

"Diseases of the Army." *Medical Repository* n.s. 1 (1813): 412–14.

"Dr. Beaumont." *Boston Medical and Surgical Journal* 10 (April 16, 1834): 163.

Drumm, Stella M., and Isaac H. Lionberger, eds. "Correspondence of Robert Campbell, 1834–1845." *Glimpses of the Past* 7 (1941): 3–65.

Ellis, Albert G. "Fifty-Four Years Recollections of Men and Events in Wisconsin." *Collections of the State Historical Society of Wisconsin* 7: 207–68. Madison: State Historical Society of Wisconsin, 1908.

Fonda, John H. "Reminiscences of Wisconsin." *Collections of the State Historical Society of Wisconsin* 5: 205–84. Madison: State Historical Society of Wisconsin, 1907.

"Fort Howard (1824–1832)." *Green Bay Historical Bulletin* 4 (September–October 1928): 3–29.

Hamilton, Henry E. *Incidents and Events in the Life of Gordon Saltonstall Hubbard.* Chicago: Rand, McNally, 1888.

Hemphill, W. Edwin, ed. *The Papers of John C. Calhoun.* Vol. 3, 1818–1819. Columbia: University of South Carolina Press, 1967.

Hesse, Nicholas. "Nicholas Hesse, German Visitor to Missouri, 1835–1837. Part I." Translated by William G. Bek. *Missouri Historical Review* 41 (October 1946): 19–44.

Hitchcock, Ethan Allen, *Fifty Years in Camp and Field: Diary of Major-General Ethan Allen Hitchcock, U.S.A.* New York: G. P. Putnam's Sons, 1909. Facsimile reprint, edited by W. A. Croffut. Freeport, N.Y.: Books for Libraries, 1971.

Hoffman, Charles F. *A Winter in the West by a New Yorker.* 2 vols. New York: Harper, 1835.

Horner, W. E. "A Military Hospital at Buffalo, New York, in the Year 1814." *Medical Examiner* n.s. 8 (December 1852): 754–74; n.s. 9 (January 1853): 1–13, (February 1853): 74–85.

Huntt, Henry. "An Abstract Account of the Diseases which Prevailed among the Soldiers, Received into the General Hospital, at Burlington, Vermont, during the Summer and Autumn of 1814." *American Medical Recorder* 1 (1818): 176–79.

Janowitz, Henry D. "Newly Discovered Letters Concerning William Beaumont, Alexis St. Martin, and the American Fur Company." *Bulletin of the History of Medicine* 22 (November–December 1948): 822–31.

Kellogg, David S. *Recollections of Clinton County and the Battle of Plattsburgh, 1800–1840: Memoirs of Early Residents from the Notebooks of D. S. Kellogg.* Edited by Allan S. Everest. Plattsburgh, N.Y.: Clinton County Historical Association, 1964.

Kemper, Jackson. "Journal of an Episcopalian Missionary's Tour to Green Bay, 1834." *Collections of the State Historical Society of Wisconsin* 14: 394–449. Madison: State Historical Society of Wisconsin, 1898.

Kennerly, William C. *Persimmon Hill: A Narrative of Old St. Louis and the Far West.* As told to Elizabeth Russell. Norman: University of Oklahoma Press, 1949.

Kinzie, Mrs. John H. *Wau-Bun: The Early Day in the Northwest.* Edited by Louise P. Kellogg. Menasha, Wisc.: Banta, 1930.

Lane, J. E. "An Unpublished Beaumont Letter." *Journal of the American Medical Association* 85 (August 22, 1925): 632–33.

——. "Another Unpublished Beaumont Letter." *Journal of the American Medical Association* 99 (July 2, 1932): 57.

"Letters of Robert E. Lee to Henry Kayser, 1838–1846." *Glimpses of the Past* 3 (1936): 1–43.

Lockwood, James H. "Early Times and Events in Wisconsin." *Collections of the State Historical Society of Wisconsin* 2: 98–196. Madison: State Historical Society of Wisconsin, 1903.

Luckhardt, Arno B., ed. "Three Doctor William Beaumont Letters." *Surgery, Gynecology, and Obstetrics* 66 (January–June 1938): 125–27.

McPheeters, William B. "History of the Epidemic Cholera in St. Louis in 1849." *St. Louis Medical and Surgical Journal* 7 (March 1850): 97–120.

Mann, James. *Medical Sketches of the Campaigns of 1812, 13, 14.* Dedham: H. Mann, 1816.

Marryat, Frederick. *Diary in America.* London: Longman, 1839. Reprint, edited by Jules Zanger. Bloomington: Indiana University Press, 1960.

Martin, Morgan L. "Narrative of Morgan L. Martin." *Collections of the State Historical Society of Wisconsin* 11: 385–415. Madison: State Historical Society of Wisconsin, 1888.

"The Medical Profession in St. Louis." *Boston Medical and Surgical Journal* 33 (September 24, 1845): 166–67.

Mereness, Newton D. *The Mereness Calendar: Federal Documents on the Upper Mississippi Valley, 1780–1890.* 13 vols. Boston: Hall, 1971.

Miller, Genevieve, ed. *Wm. Beaumont's Formative Years: Two Early Notebooks, 1811–1821.* New York: Henry Schuman, 1946.

Missouri Republican (St. Louis).

Morse, Jedidiah. *The American Gazetteer.* Boston: S. Hall, 1797. Facsimile reprint, New York: Arno, 1971.

——. *A Report to the Secretary of War on Indian Affairs.* New Haven, Conn.: S. Converse, 1822. Facsimile reprint, New York: Augustus M. Kelley, 1970.

Nelson, Thomas S., ed. *A Full and Accurate Report of the Trial of William P. Darnes.* 2d ed. Boston: Tuttle, Dennett, & Chisholm, 1841.

"Papers on the Last Winter Epidemic in Different Parts of the United States." *Medical Repository* n.s., 1 (1813), 246–67, 329–44.

Plattsburgh Republican (N.Y.)

Pleadwell, F. L. "William Beaumont and the Navy." *Bulletin of the History of Medicine* 15 (January 1944): 107.

Prucha, Francis Paul, ed. *Army Life on the Western Frontier: Selections from the Official Reports Made between 1826 and 1845 by Colonel George Croghan.* Norman: University of Oklahoma Press, 1958.

Radbill, Samuel X., ed. "The Autobiographical Ana of Robley Dunglison, M.D." *Transactions of the American Philosophical Society* n.s. 53, part 8 (1963): 3–212.

Reyburn, Thomas. "Extracts from a Paper on Tuphlo-Enteritis, Read before the Medical Society of St. Louis, March, 1843." *St. Louis Medical and Surgical Journal* 1 (July 1843): 74–82.

——. "Memoir of the Late Dr. Beaumont." *St. Louis Medical and Surgical Journal* 12 (March 1854): 127–39.

Schoolcraft, Henry R. *Summary Narrative of an Exploratory Expedition to the Sources of the Mississippi River in 1820.* Philadelphia: Lippincott, Grambo, 1855.

"Science of Medicine in Missouri." *Boston Medical and Surgical Journal* 31 (August 25, 1844): 82–83.

"Some Account of the Disease which was Epidemic in Some Parts of New-York and New-England, in the Winter of 1812–13." *New England Journal of Medicine and Surgery* 2 (1813): 241–58.

Stambaugh, Samuel. "Report on the Quality and Condition of Wisconsin Territory, 1831." *Collections of the State Historical Society of Wisconsin* 15: 399–438. Madison: State Historical Society of Wisconsin, 1900.

Statistical Report on the Sickness and Mortality in the Army of the United

States... from January, 1819, to January, 1839. Washington: Gideon, 1840.

White, T. J. "Remarks of T. J. White, M.D." *St. Louis Medical and Surgical Journal.* Supplement (July 1846): 51–74.

BOOKS AND DISSERTATIONS

Ackerknecht, Erwin H. *History and Geography of the Most Important Diseases.* New York: Hafner, 1965.

——. *Therapeutics from the Primitives to the 20th Century.* New York: Hafner, 1973.

Adams, Henry K. *A Centennial History of St. Albans, Vermont.* St. Albans: Wallace Printing, 1889.

Adler, Jerry S. *Yankee Merchants and the Making of the Urban West: The Rise and Fall of Antebellum St. Louis.* Cambridge: Cambridge University Press, 1991.

Armour, David. *At the Crossroads: Michilimackinac during the American Revolution.* Mackinac Island: Mackinac Island State Park Commission, 1978.

Armstrong, Robert G. *Historic Lebanon: Highlights of an Historic Town.* Lebanon, Conn.: First Congregational Church, 1950.

Ashburn, Percy M. *A History of the Medical Department of the United States Army.* Boston: Houghton, Mifflin, 1929.

Barboriak, Peter N. "Reporting to the Surgeon General: The Peacetime Practice of Military Surgeons in Antebellum America, 1818–1861." Ph.D. diss., Duke University, 1987.

Binger, Carl. *Revolutionary Doctor: Benjamin Rush, 1746–1813.* New York: Norton, 1966.

Brobeck, John R., Orr E. Reynolds, and Toby A. Appel, eds. *History of the American Physiological Society: The First Century, 1887–1987.* Bethesda, Md.: The Society, 1987.

Brown, Harvey E. *The Medical Department of the United States Army from 1775 to 1873.* Washington, D.C.: Surgeon General's Office, 1873.

Cassedy, James H. *Medicine and American Growth, 1800–1860.* Madison: University of Wisconsin Press, 1986.

Cassidy, Phoebe A., and Roberta S. Sokol, compilers. *Index to the Wm. Beaumont, M.D. (1785–1853) Manuscript Collection.* Introduction by Estelle Brodman. St. Louis: Washington University School of Medicine, 1968.

De Ville, Kenneth A. *Medical Malpractice in Nineteenth-Century America: Origins and Legacy.* New York: New York University Press, 1990.

Duffy, John. *From Humors to Medical Science: A History of American Medicine.* 2d ed. Urbana: University of Illinois Press, 1992.

Dupree, A. Hunter. *Science in the Federal Government: A History of Policies and Activities to 1940.* Cambridge, Mass.: Harvard University Press, 1957.

Eliot, Charlotte C. *William Greenleaf Eliot: Minister, Educator, Philanthropist.* Boston: Houghton, Mifflin, 1904.

Everest, Allan S. *The War of 1812 in the Champlain Valley.* Syracuse, N.Y.: Syracuse University Press, 1982.

Foster, Michael. *Lectures on the History of Physiology during the Sixteenth, Seventeenth and Eighteenth Centuries.* Cambridge: Cambridge University Press, 1924.

Freeman, Douglas S. *R. E. Lee: A Biography.* 4 vols. New York: Scribner's Sons, 1934–1935.

Gillett, Mary C. *The Army Medical Department, 1775–1818.* Washington, D.C.: Center of Military History, United States Army, 1981.

——. *The Army Medical Department, 1818–1865.* Washington, D.C.: Center of Military History, United States Army, 1987.

Goldstein, M. A., ed. *One Hundred Years of Medicine and Surgery in St. Louis.* St. Louis: St. Louis Star, 1900.

Goodman, Nathan G. *Benjamin Rush: Physician and Citizen, 1746–1813.* Philadelphia: University of Pennsylvania Press, 1934.

Goodwin, Edward J. *A History of Medicine in Missouri.* St. Louis: W. L. Smith, 1905.

Haeger, John D. *John Jacob Astor: Business and Finance in the Early Republic.* Detroit: Wayne State University Press, 1991.

Haller, John S. *American Medicine in Transition, 1840–1910.* Urbana: University of Illinois Press, 1981.

Heitman, Francis B. *Historical Register and Dictionary of the United States Army.* Vol. 1. Washington, D.C.: Government Printing Office, 1903.

History of Clinton and Franklin Counties, New York. Philadelphia: J. W. Lewis, 1880.

Horsman, Reginald. *Josiah Nott of Mobile: Southerner, Physician, and Racial Theorist.* Baton Rouge: Louisiana State University Press, 1987.

——. *The War of 1812.* New York: Alfred A. Knopf, 1969.

Index of St. Louis Marriages, 1804–1876. Vol. 1. St. Louis: St. Louis Genealogical Society, 1973.

Kaufman, Martin. *American Medical Education: The Formative Years, 1765–1910.* Westport, Conn.: Greenwood, 1976.

Kett, Joseph F. *The Formation of the American Medical Profession: The Role of Institutions, 1780–1860.* New Haven: Yale University Press, 1968.

Lavender, David. *The Fist in the Wilderness.* New York: Doubleday, 1964.

Lesch, John E. *Science and Medicine in France: The Emergence of Experimental Physiology, 1790–1855.* Cambridge: Harvard University Press, 1984.

McGregor, Deborah K. *Sexual Surgery and the Origins of Gynecology: J. Marion Sims, His Hospital, and His Patients.* New York: Garland, 1989.

Mahon, John. *The War of 1812.* Gainesville: University of Florida Press, 1972.

Medicine in Colonial Massachusetts, 1620–1820. A Conference Held 25 & 26 May 1978 by the Colonial Society of Massachusetts. Boston: Colonial Society of Massachusetts, 1980.

Miles, Wyndham D. *A History of the National Library of Medicine: The Nation's Treasury of Medical Knowledge.* Bethesda, Md.: U.S. Department of Health and Human Services, 1982.

Milne, George McLean. *Lebanon: Three Centuries in a Connecticut Hilltop Town.* Canaan, N.H.: Phoenix, 1986.

Myer, Jesse S. *Life and Letters of Dr. William Beaumont.* St. Louis: C. V. Mosby, 1912.

Nelson, Rodney B. *Beaumont: America's First Physiologist.* Geneva, Ill.: Grant House, 1990.

Nichols, Roger L. *General Henry Atkinson: A Western Military Career.* Norman: University of Oklahoma Press, 1965.

Nissenbaum, Stephen. *Sex, Diet, and Debility in Jacksonian America: Sylvester Graham and Health Reform.* Westport, Conn.: Greenwood Press, 1980.

Norwood, William F. *Medical Education in the United States before the Civil War.* Philadelphia: University of Pennsylvania Press, 1944.

Numbers, Ronald L., ed. *The Education of American Physicians: Historical Essays.* Berkeley: University of California Press, 1980.

Palmer, Peter S. *History of Plattsburgh, N.Y.* Plattsburgh: n.p., 1877.

Pitcock, Cynthia DeHaven. "The Career of William Beaumont, 1785–1853: Science and the Self-Made Man in America." Ph.D. diss., Memphis State University, 1985.

Platt, Charles. *Platt Genealogy in America from the Arrival of Richard Platt in New Haven, Connecticut, in 1638.* New Hope, Pa.: n.p., 1963.

Primm, James N. *Lion of the Valley: St. Louis, Missouri.* Boulder, Colo.: Pruett, 1981.

Prucha, Francis P. *Broadax and Bayonet: The Role of the United States Army in the Development of the Northwest, 1815–1860*. Madison, Wisc.: State Historical Society, 1953.

——. *The Sword of the Republic: The United States Army on the Frontier, 1783–1846*. New York: Macmillan, 1969.

Riznik, Barnes. *Medicine in New England, 1790–1840*. Sturbridge, Mass.: Old Sturbridge Village, 1965 (pamphlet).

Robbins, Christine C. *David Hosack: Citizen of New York*. Philadelphia: American Philosophical Society, 1964.

Rosen, George. *The Reception of William Beaumont's Discovery in Europe*. New York: Schuman's, 1942.

Rosenberg, Charles E. *The Care of Strangers: The Rise of America's Hospital System*. New York: Basic Books, 1987.

——. *The Cholera Years: The United States in 1832, 1849, and 1866*. Chicago: University of Chicago Press, 1962.

Rothschuh, Karl E. *History of Physiology*. Translated and edited by Guenter B. Risse. Huntington, N.Y.: Robert E. Krieger, 1973.

Rothstein, William G. *American Medical Schools and the Practice of Medicine: A History*. New York: Oxford University Press, 1987.

——. *American Physicians in the Nineteenth Century: From Sect to Science*. Baltimore: Johns Hopkins University Press, 1972.

St. Louis Medical Society: Centennial Volume. St. Louis: St. Louis Medical Society, 1939.

Sargent, Frederick. *Hippocratic Heritage: A History of Ideas about Weather and Human Health*. New York: Pergamon Press, 1982.

Scanlan, Peter L. *Prairie du Chien: French, British, American*. Menasha, Wisc.: Banta, 1937.

Scharf, J. Thomas. *History of St. Louis City and County*. 2 vols. Philadelphia: L. H. Everts, 1883.

Shryock, Richard H. *Medicine and Society in America, 1660–1860*. New York: New York University Press, 1960.

——. *Medicine in America: Historical Essays*. Baltimore: Johns Hopkins University Press, 1966.

Smith, Alice Elizabeth. *James Duane Doty: Frontier Promoter*. Madison, Wisc.: State Historical Society, 1954.

Stevens, Frank E. *The Black Hawk War*. Chicago: Frank E. Stevens, 1903.

Sunder, John E. *Bill Sublette: Mountain Man*. Norman: University of Oklahoma Press, 1959.

Tuttle, Mrs. George Fuller, comp. and ed. *Three Centuries in Champlain Valley:*

A Collection of Historical Facts and Incidents. Plattsburgh, N.Y.: Saranac Chapter, Daughters of the American Revolution, 1909.

Van Ravenswaay, Charles. *St. Louis: An Informal History of the City and its People, 1764–1865.* St. Louis: Missouri Historical Society Press, 1991.

Warner, John Harley. *The Therapeutic Perspective: Medical Practice, Knowledge, and Identity in America, 1820–1885.* Cambridge: Harvard University Press, 1986.

Widder, Keith R. *Dr. William Beaumont: The Mackinac Years.* Mackinac Island: Mackinac Island State Park Commission, 1975.

Wolf, Stewart, and Harold G. Wolff. *Human Gastric Function: An Experimental Study of a Man and His Stomach.* London: Oxford University Press, 1943.

ARTICLES

Alexander, Edward P. "Surgeon Beaumont at Prairie du Chien." *Wisconsin Medical Journal* 44 (October 1945): 1006–9.

Anderson, Fanny J. "Medical Practices in Detroit during the War of 1812." *Bulletin of the History of Medicine* 16 (October 1944): 261–75.

Atwater, Edward C. " 'Squeezing Mother Nature': Experimental Physiology in the United States before 1870." *Bulletin of the History of Medicine* 52 (fall 1978): 313–35.

Ayars, Charles W. "Some Notes on the Medical Service of the Army, 1812–1839." *Military Surgeon* 50 (1922): 505–24.

Bates, Donald G. "The Background to John Young's Thesis on Digestion." *Bulletin of the History of Medicine* 36 (July–August 1962): 341–61.

"The Beaumont Homestead." *Green Bay Historical Bulletin* 8 (July 1932): 1–8.

Bensley, Edward H. "Alexis St. Martin." *Journal of the Michigan State Medical Society* 58 (May 1959): 738–41, 765.

——. "Alexis St. Martin and Dr. Bunting." *Bulletin of the History of Medicine* 44 (March–April 1970): 101–8.

Berman, Alex. "The Heroic Approach in 19th Century Therapeutics." *Bulletin of the American Society of Hospital Pharmacists* 2 (September–October 1954): 321–27.

Brodman, Estelle. "Scientific and Editorial Relationships between Joseph Lovell and William Beaumont." *Bulletin of the History of Medicine* 38 (March–April 1964): 127–32.

Bylebyl, Jerome J. "William Beaumont, Robley Dunglison, and the 'Philadelphia Physiologists.' " *Journal of the History of Medicine and Allied Sciences* 25 (January 1970): 3–21.

Cannon, Walter B., and George Higginson. "The Book of William Beaumont after One Hundred Years." *Bulletin of the New York Academy of Medicine* 9 (1933): 568–84.

Cassedy, James H. "An Early American Hangover: The Medical Profession and Intemperance, 1800–1860." *Bulletin of the History of Medicine* 50 (fall 1976): 405–13.

Drumm, Stella. "Robert E. Lee and the Improvement of the Mississippi River." *Missouri Historical Society Collections* 6 (February 1929): 157–71.

Edgar, James D. "The Army Medical Department in the War of 1812." *Military Surgeon* 60 (1927): 301–13.

Estes, J. Worth. "Therapeutic Practice in Colonial New England." In *Medicine in Colonial Massachusetts, 1620–1820,* 289–383. Boston: Colonial Society of Massachusetts, 1980.

Evans, William L. "The Military History of Green Bay." In *Proceedings of the State Historical Society of Wisconsin, 1899,* 128–46. Madison, Wisc.: Democrat Printing, 1900.

Gillett, Mary C. "Thomas Lawson: Second Surgeon General of the U.S. Army: A Character Sketch." *Prologue: The Journal of the National Archives* 14 (spring 1982): 15–24.

Harstad, Peter T. "Disease and Sickness on the Wisconsin Frontier: Cholera." *Wisconsin Magazine of History* 43 (spring 1960): 203–20.

——. "Disease and Sickness on the Wisconsin Frontier: Smallpox and Other Diseases." *Wisconsin Magazine of History* 43 (summer 1960): 253–63.

——. "Frontier Medicine in the Territory of Wisconsin." In *Wisconsin Medicine: Historical Perspectives,* edited by Ronald L. Numbers and Judith Walzer Leavitt, 13–23. Madison: University of Wisconsin Press, 1981.

——. "Sickness and Disease on the Wisconsin Frontier: Malaria, 1820–1850." *Wisconsin Magazine of History* 43 (autumn 1959): 83–96.

Houghton, Harris A. "The Beaumont–St. Martin Contract and the Descendants of Dr. Beaumont." *Bulletin of the New York Academy of Medicine* 9 (1933): 564–67.

——. "Dr. William Beaumont: His Life and Associates in Plattsburgh, N.Y." *Bulletin of the New York Academy of Medicine* 7 (1931): 287–301.

Hume, Erskine. "The Foundation of American Meteorology by the United States Army Medical Department." *Bulletin of the History of Medicine* 8 (February 1940): 202–38.

Hunter, Lloyd A. "Slavery in St. Louis, 1804–1860." *Bulletin of the Missouri Historical Society* 30 (July 1974): 233–65.

Ivy, Andrew C. "A Present-Day Appreciation of Beaumont's Experiments on

Alexis St. Martin." In *A New Print of Life and Letters of Dr. William Beaumont,* edited by Jesse S. Myer, xvii–xxii. St. Louis: C. V. Mosby, 1939.

Kasich, Antony M. "William Prout and the Discovery of Hydrochloric Acid in the Gastric Juice." *Bulletin of the History of Medicine* 20 (July 1946): 340–58.

Kaufman, Martin. "American Medical Education." In *The Education of American Physicians: Historical Essays,* edited by Ronald L. Numbers, 7–28. Berkeley: University of California Press, 1980.

Kellogg, Louise P. "Old Fort Howard." *Wisconsin Magazine of History* 18 (December 1934): 125–40.

Kisch, Bruno. "Jacob Anton Helm and William Beaumont. With a Translation of the First of Helm's *Zwey Kranken-Geschichten* (1803)." *Journal of the History of Medicine and Allied Sciences* 22 (January 1967): 54–80.

——. "Jacob Helm's Observations and Experiments on Human Digestion." *Journal of the History of Medicine and Allied Sciences* 9 (July 1954): 311–28.

Lass, William E. "Tourists' Impressions of St. Louis, 1766–1859. Part II." *Missouri Historical Review* 53 (October 1958): 10–21.

Luckhardt, Arno B. "The Dr. William Beaumont Collection of the University of Chicago." *Bulletin of the History of Medicine* 7 (May 1939): 535–63.

McLear, Patrick E. "The St. Louis Cholera Epidemic of 1849." *Missouri Historical Review* 63 (January 1969): 171–81.

Marsh, Edwin S. "The United States Army and Its Health, 1819–1829." *Military Surgeon* 108 (1951): 501–13.

Martin, Deborah B. "Doctor William Beaumont: His Life in Mackinac and Wisconsin, 1820–1834." *Wisconsin Magazine of History* 4 (1920–1921): 263–80.

——. "Navarino." *Green Bay Historical Bulletin* 1 (April 1925): 11–20.

——. "Navarino: Its Founder and Early History." *Green Bay Historical Bulletin* 1 (February 15, 1925): 1–5.

Martin, Elizabeth S. "A Short Sketch of the Life of Israel Green, "Bud" Beaumont, Son of Dr. William Beaumont." *Green Bay Historical Bulletin* 8 (July 1932): 9–10.

Miller, Genevieve. Review of *The Reception of William Beaumont's Discovery in Europe,* by George Rosen. In *Bulletin of the History of Medicine* 13 (January 1943): 111–13.

Miller, William S. "William Beaumont, M.D. (1785–1853)." *Annals of Medical History* n.s. 5 (1933): 28–51.

——. "William Beaumont and His Book: Elisha North and His Copy of Beaumont's Book." *Annals of Medical History* n.s. 1 (1929): 155–79.

Mitchell, Elaine A. "International Buying Trip: Fort Garry to St. Louis in 1846." *Minnesota History* 36 (June 1958): 37–53.

Mueller, Richard E. "Jefferson Barracks: The Early Years." *Missouri Historical Review* 67 (October 1972): 7–30.

Musser, Ruth, and John C. Krantz. "The Friendship of General Robert E. Lee and Dr. Wm. Beaumont." *Bulletin of the History of Medicine* 6 (May 1938): 467–76.

Numbers, Ronald L. "William Beaumont and the Ethics of Human Experimentation." *Journal of the History of Biology* 12 (spring 1979): 113–35.

Numbers, Ronald L., and William J. Orr Jr. "William Beaumont's Reception at Home and Abroad." *Isis* 72 (December 1981): 590–612.

Osborn, Chase S. "Beaumont–Citizen." *Physician and Surgeon* 22 (1900): 588–91.

Osler, William. "A Backwood Physiologist." In *An Alabama Student and Other Biographical Essays,* 159–88. London: Oxford University Press, 1909.

Patterson, Robert U. "William Beaumont as an Army Officer." *Bulletin of the New York Academy of Medicine* 9 (1933): 555–64.

Phalen, James M. "Surgeon James Mann's Observations on Battlefield Amputations." *Military Surgeon* 87 (1940): 463–66.

Pitcock, Cynthia De Haven. "Doctors in Controversy: An Ethical Dispute between Joseph Nash McDowell and William Beaumont." *Missouri Historical Review* 60 (April 1966): 336–49.

——. "The Involvement of William Beaumont, M.D., in a Medical-Legal Controversy: The Darnes-Davis Case, 1840." *Missouri Historical Review* 59 (October 1964): 31–45.

Pizer, Irwin H. "Source Materials and the Library: The Dispersion of the Beaumont Papers." *Bulletin of the Medical Library Association* 52 (January 1964): 328–36.

Pizer, Irwin H., and Harriet Steuernagel. "Medical Journals in St. Louis before 1900." *Bulletin of the Missouri Historical Society* 20 (April 1964): 221–51.

Poynter, F. N. L. "New Light on the Reception of William Beaumont's Discovery in England." *Journal of the History of Medicine and Allied Sciences* 13 (July 1958): 406–9.

——. "The Reception of William Beaumont's Discovery in England: Two Additional Early References." *Journal of the History of Medicine and Allied Sciences* 12 (October 1957): 511–12.

Risse, Günter B. "The Brownian System of Medicine: Its Theoretical and Practical Implications." *Clio Medica* 5 (1970): 45–51.

———. "The Quest for Certainty in Medicine: John Brown's System of Medicine in France." *Bulletin of the History of Medicine* 45 (January–February 1971): 1–12.

Rosen, George. "Notes on the Reception and Influence of William Beaumont's Discovery." *Bulletin of the History of Medicine* 13 (May 1943): 631–42.

———. "The Reception of William Beaumont's Discovery: Some Comments on Dr. Poynter's Note." *Journal of the History of Medicine and Allied Sciences* 13 (July 1958): 404–6.

Rosenberg, Charles E. "The Therapeutic Revolution: Medicine, Meaning, and Social Change in Nineteenth-Century America." In *The Therapeutic Revolution: Essays in the Social History of American Medicine,* edited by Morris J. Vogel and Charles E. Rosenberg, 3–25. Philadelphia: University of Pennsylvania Press, 1979.

Savitt, Todd. "The Use of Blacks for Medical Experimentation and Demonstration in the Old South." *Journal of Southern History* 48 (August 1982): 331–48.

Smith, Alice E. "Daniel Whitney: Pioneer Wisconsin Businessman." *Wisconsin Magazine of History* 24 (March 1941): 283–304.

Smith, Arthur H. "William Beaumont (November 21, 1785–April 25, 1853)." *Journal of Nutrition* 44 (May 1951): 3–16.

Smith, Dale C. "The Rise and Fall of Typhomalarial Fever: I. Origins." *Journal of the History of Medicine and Allied Sciences* 37 (April 1982): 182–220.

Steiner, Walter R. "Dr. William Beaumont: An Appreciation." *Science* 70 (November 1, 1929): 413–16.

Sullivan, Robert B. "Sanguine Practices: A Historical and Historiographic Reconsideration of Heroic Therapy in the Age of Rush." *Bulletin of the History of Medicine* 68 (summer 1994): 211–34.

Thwaites, Reuben G. "Rear Admiral Melancton Smith, U.S.N." *Green Bay Historical Bulletin* 1 (August 15, 1925): 1–12.

[———]. "Sketch of Morgan L. Martin." *Collections of the State Historical Society of Wisconsin* 11: 380–84. Madison: State Historical Society of Wisconsin, 1888.

Walder, Arnold I. "A Historical Review of the Nature of the Gastric Fluid." *Surgery* 51 (January–June 1962): 546–53.

Wangensteen, Owen H., Jacqueline Smith, and Sarah D. Wangensteen. "Some Highlights in the History of Amputation Reflecting Lessons in Wound

Healing." *Bulletin of the History of Medicine* 41 (March–April 1967): 97–131.

Webb, Henry W. "The Story of Jefferson Barracks." *New Mexico Historical Review* 21 (July 1946): 185–208.

Welch, Archibald. "A Biographical Sketch of Silas Fuller, M.D." *Boston Medical and Surgical Journal* 38 (March 8, 1848): 109–15.

Whittaker, Alfred H. "Observations of Some Physiologists Who Preceded Beaumont." *Journal of the Michigan State Medical Society* 58 (May 1959): 751–56.

Williams, Helen D. "Social Life in St. Louis from 1840 to 1860." *Missouri Historical Review* 31 (October 1936): 10–24.

Wilson, Leonard G. "Fevers and Science in Early Nineteenth Century Medicine." *Journal of the History of Medicine and Allied Sciences* 33 (1978): 386–407.

Zimmerman, Eduard. "Travel into Missouri in October, 1838." *Missouri Historical Review* 9 (October 1914): 33–43.

INDEX